the Nectar of Devotion

BOOKS BY HIS DIVINE GRACE A. C. BHAKTIVEDANTA SWAMI PRABHUPĀDA

Bhagavad-gītā As It Is
Śrīmad-Bhāgavatam (completed by disciples)
Śrī Caitanya-caritāmṛta
Kṛṣṇa, the Supreme Personality of Godhead
Teachings of Lord Caitanya
The Nectar of Devotion
The Nectar of Instruction
Śrī Īśopaniṣad
Light of the Bhāgavata
Easy Journey to Other Planets
Teachings of Lord Kapila, the Son of Devahūti
Teachings of Queen Kuntī
Message of Godhead
The Science of Self-Realization
The Perfection of Yoga
Beyond Birth and Death
On the Way to Kṛṣṇa
Rāja-vidyā: The King of Knowledge
Elevation to Kṛṣṇa Consciousness
Kṛṣṇa Consciousness: The Matchless Gift
Kṛṣṇa Consciousness: The Topmost Yoga System
Perfect Questions, Perfect Answers
Life Comes from Life
The Nārada-bhakti-sūtra (completed by disciples)
The Mukunda-mālā-stotra (completed by disciples)
Geetār-gān (Bengali)
Vairāgya-vidyā (Bengali)
Buddhi-yoga (Bengali)
Bhakti-ratna-boli (Bengali)
Back to Godhead magazine (founder)

BOOKS COMPILED FROM THE TEACHINGS OF HIS DIVINE GRACE A. C. BHAKTIVEDANTA SWAMI PRABHUPĀDA AFTER HIS LIFETIME

Search for Liberation
A Second Chance
The Journey of Self-Discovery
Civilization and Transcendence
The Laws of Nature
Renunciation Through Wisdom
The Quest for Enlightenment
Dharma, the Way of Transcendence
Spiritual Yoga
Bhakti, the Art of Eternal Love
Beyond Illusion and Doubt
The Hare Kṛṣṇa Challenge

the Nectar of Devotion

THE COMPLETE SCIENCE OF BHAKTI-YOGA

A SUMMARY STUDY OF
ŚRĪLA RŪPA GOSVĀMĪ'S BHAKTI-RASĀMṚTA-SINDHU

BY

HIS DIVINE GRACE
A. C. BHAKTIVEDANTA SWAMI
PRABHUPĀDA

FOUNDER-ĀCĀRYA OF THE
INTERNATIONAL SOCIETY FOR KRISHNA CONSCIOUSNESS

THE BHAKTIVEDANTA BOOK TRUST
LOS ANGELES • STOCKHOLM • MUMBAI • SYDNEY

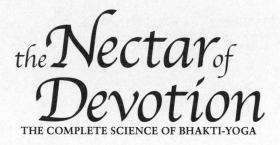

Readers interested in the subject matter of this book
are invited by the International Society
for Krishna Consciousness to correspond with
its Secretary at the following address:

The Bhaktivedanta Book Trust
P.O. Box 341445, Los Angeles, California 90034, USA
Phone: +1-800-927-4152 • Fax: +1-310-837-1056
e-mail: bbt.usa@krishna.com
web: www.krishna.com

The Bhaktivedanta Book Trust
P. O. Box 380, Riverstone, NSW 2765, Australia
Phone: +61-2-96276306 • Fax: +61-2-96276052
e-mail: bbt.wp@krishna.com

Printed in Taiwan

Previous printings: 310,000
Current printing, 2014: 5,000

Library of Congress Cataloging in Publication Data

Bhaktivedanta Swami, A. C. 1896–1977
The nectar of devotion; the complete science of Bhakti Yoga, by A.C. Bhaktivedanta Swami Prabhupāda.
Los Angeles. Bhaktivedanta Book Trust

"A summary study of Śrīla Rūpa Gosvāmī's Bhakti-rasāmṛta-sindhu."

1. Bhakti. I. Rūpagosvāmī, 16th cent. Bhaktirasāmṛtasindhuḥ.
II. Title.

BL1215.B5B45 294.5'4 79-21183
ISBN 0-912776-05-6 MARC

Library of Congress 73 [4]

To the Six Gosvāmīs of Vṛndāvana

nānā-śāstra-vicāraṇaika-nipuṇau sad-dharma-saṁsthāpakau
lokānāṁ hita-kāriṇau tri-bhuvane mānyau śaraṇyākarau
rādhā-kṛṣṇa-padāravinda-bhajanānandena mattālikau
vande rūpa-sanātanau raghu-yugau śrī-jīva-gopālakau

"I offer my respectful obeisances unto the Six Gosvāmīs, namely Śrī Sanātana Gosvāmī, Śrī Rūpa Gosvāmī, Śrī Raghunātha Bhaṭṭa Gosvamī, Śrī Raghunātha dāsa Gosvamī, Śrī Jīva Gosvāmī and Śrī Gopāla Bhaṭṭa Gosvāmī, who are very expert in scrutinizingly studying all the revealed scriptures with the aim of establishing eternal religious principles for the benefit of all human beings. Thus they are honored all over the three worlds, and they are worth taking shelter of because they are absorbed in the mood of the *gopīs* and are engaged in the transcendental loving service of Rādhā and Kṛṣṇa."

Contents

Preface

The Nectar of Devotion is a summary study of *Bhakti-rasāmṛta-sindhu*, which was written in Sanskrit by Śrīla Rūpa Gosvāmī Prabhupāda. He was the chief of the Six Gosvāmīs, who were the direct disciples of Lord Caitanya Mahāprabhu. When he first met Lord Caitanya, Śrīla Rūpa Gosvāmī Prabhupāda was engaged as a minister in the Muhammadan government of Bengal. He and his brother Sanātana were then named Dabira Khāsa and Sākara Mallika respectively, and they held responsible posts as ministers of Nawab Hussain Shah. At that time, five hundred years ago, the Hindu society was very rigid, and if a member of the *brāhmaṇa* caste accepted the service of a Muhammadan ruler he was at once rejected from *brāhmaṇa* society. That was the position of the two brothers, Dabira Khāsa and Sākara Mallika. They belonged to the highly situated *sārasvata-brāhmaṇa* community, but they were ostracized due to their acceptance of ministerial posts in the government of Hussain Shah. It is the grace of Lord Caitanya that He accepted these two exalted personalities as His disciples and raised them to the position of *gosvāmīs,* the highest position of brahminical culture. Similarly, Lord Caitanya accepted Haridāsa Ṭhākura as His disciple, although Haridāsa happened to be born of a Muhammadan family, and Lord Caitanya later on made him the *ācārya* of the chanting of the holy name of the Lord: Hare Kṛṣṇa, Hare Kṛṣṇa, Kṛṣṇa Kṛṣṇa, Hare Hare/ Hare Rāma, Hare Rāma, Rāma Rāma, Hare Hare.

Lord Caitanya's principle is universal. Anyone who knows the science of Kṛṣṇa and is engaged in the service of the Lord is accepted as being in a higher position than a person born in the family of a *brāhmaṇa.* That is the original principle accepted by all Vedic literatures, especially by *Bhagavad-gītā* and *Śrīmad-Bhāgavatam.* The principle of Lord Caitanya's movement in educating and elevating everyone to the exalted post of a *gosvāmī* is taught in *The Nectar of Devotion.*

Lord Caitanya met the two brothers Dabira Khāsa and Sākara Mallika in a village known as Rāmakeli, in the district of Maldah, and after that meeting the brothers decided to retire from government service and join Lord Caitanya. Dabira Khāsa, who was later to become Rūpa Gosvāmī, retired from his post and collected all the money he had accumulated during his service. It is described in the *Caitanya-caritāmṛta* that his accumulated savings in gold coins equaled millions of dollars and filled a large boat. He divided the money in a very exemplary manner, which should be followed by devotees in particular and by humanity in general. Fifty percent of his accumulated wealth was distributed to the Kṛṣṇa conscious persons, namely the *brāhmaṇas* and the Vaiṣṇavas; twenty-five percent was distributed to relatives; and twenty-five percent was kept against emergency expenditures and personal difficulties. Later on, when Sākara Mallika also proposed to retire, the Nawab was very much agitated and put him into jail. But Sākara Mallika, who was later to become Śrīla Sanātana Gosvāmī, took advantage of his brother's personal money, which had been deposited with a village banker, and escaped from the prison of Hussain Shah. In this way both brothers joined Lord Caitanya Mahāprabhu.

Rūpa Gosvāmī first met Lord Caitanya at Prayāga (Allahabad, India), and on the Daśāśvamedha bathing *ghāṭa* of that holy city the Lord instructed him continually for ten days. The Lord particularly instructed Rūpa Gosvāmī on the science of Kṛṣṇa consciousness. These teachings of Lord Caitanya to Śrīla Rūpa Gosvāmī Prabhupāda are narrated in our book *Teachings of Lord Caitanya.*

Later, Śrīla Rūpa Gosvāmī Prabhupāda elaborated the teachings of the Lord with profound knowledge of revealed scriptures and authoritative references from various Vedic literatures. Śrīla Śrīnivāsa Ācārya describes in his prayers to the Six Gosvāmīs that they were all highly learned scholars, not only in Sanskrit but also in foreign languages such as Persian and Arabic. They very scrutinizingly studied all the Vedic scriptures in order to establish the cult of Caitanya Mahāprabhu on the authorized principles of Vedic knowledge. The present Kṛṣṇa consciousness movement is also based on the authority of Śrīla Rūpa Gosvāmī Prabhupāda. We are therefore generally known as *rūpānugas,* or followers in the footsteps of Śrīla Rūpa Gosvāmī Prabhupāda. It is only for our guidance that Śrīla Rūpa Gosvāmī prepared his book *Bhakti-rasāmṛta-sindhu,* which is now presented in the form of *The Nectar of Devotion.* Persons engaged in the Kṛṣṇa consciousness movement may take advantage of this great literature and be very solidly situated in Kṛṣṇa consciousness.

Bhakti means "devotional service." Every service has some attractive feature which drives the servitor progressively on and on. Every one of us within this world is perpetually engaged in some sort of service, and the impetus for such service is the pleasure we derive from it. Driven by affection for his wife and children, a family man works day and night. A philanthropist works in the same way for love of the greater family, and a nationalist for the cause of his country and countrymen. That force which drives the philanthropist, the householder and the nationalist is called *rasa,* or a kind of mellow (relationship) whose taste is very sweet. *Bhakti-rasa* is a mellow different from the ordinary *rasa* enjoyed by mundane workers. Mundane workers labor very hard day and night in order to relish a certain kind of *rasa* which is understood as sense gratification. The relish or taste of the mundane *rasa* does not long endure, and therefore mundane workers are always apt to change their position of enjoyment. A businessman is not satisfied by working the whole week; therefore, wanting a change for the weekend, he goes to a place where he tries to forget his business activities. Then, after the weekend is spent in forgetfulness, he again changes his position and resumes his actual business activities. Material engagement means accepting a particular status for some time and then changing it. This position of changing back and forth is technically known as *bhoga-tyāga,* which means a position of alternating sense enjoyment and renunciation. A living entity cannot steadily remain either in sense enjoyment or in renunciation. Change is going on perpetually, and we cannot be happy in either state, because of our eternal constitutional position. Sense gratification does not endure for long, and it is therefore called *capala-sukha,* or flickering happiness. For example, an ordinary family man who works very hard day and night and is successful in giving comforts to the members of his family thereby relishes a kind of mellow, but his whole advancement of material happiness immediately terminates along with his body as soon as his life is over. Death is therefore taken as the representative of God for the atheistic class of men. The devotee realizes the presence of God by devotional service, whereas the atheist realizes the presence of God in the shape of death. At death everything is finished, and one has to begin a new chapter of life in a new situation, perhaps higher or lower than the last one. In any field of activity—political, social, national or international—the result of our actions will be finished with the end of life. That is sure.

Bhakti-rasa, however, the mellow relished in the transcendental loving service of the Lord, does not finish with the end of life. It continues perpetually and is therefore called *amṛta,* that which does not die but exists eternally. This is confirmed in all Vedic literatures. *Bhagavad-gītā* says that a little advancement in *bhakti-rasa* can save the devotee from the greatest danger—that of missing the opportunity for human life. The *rasas* derived from our feelings in social life, in family life or in the greater family life of altruism, philanthropy, nationalism, socialism, communism, etc., do not guarantee that one's next life will be as a human being. We prepare our next life by our actual activities in the present life. A living entity is offered a particular type of body as a result of his action in the present body. These activities are taken into account by a superior authority known as *daiva,* or the authority of God. This *daiva* is explained in *Bhagavad-gītā* as the prime cause of everything, and in *Śrīmad-Bhāgavatam* it is stated that a man takes his next body by *daiva-netreṇa,* which means by the supervision of the authority of the Supreme. In an ordinary sense, *daiva* is explained as "destiny." *Daiva* supervision gives us a body selected from 8,400,000 forms; the choice does not depend on our selection, but is awarded to us according to our destiny. If our body at present is engaged in the activities of Kṛṣṇa consciousness, then it is guaranteed that we will have at least a human body in our next life. A human being engaged in Kṛṣṇa consciousness, even if unable to complete the course of *bhakti-yoga,* takes birth in the higher divisions of human society so that he can automatically further his advancement in Kṛṣṇa consciousness. Therefore, all bona fide activities in Kṛṣṇa consciousness are *amṛta,* or permanent. This is the subject matter of *The Nectar of Devotion.*

This eternal engagement in *bhakti-rasa* can be understood by a serious student upon studying *The Nectar of Devotion*. Adoption of *bhakti-rasa,* or Kṛṣṇa consciousness, will immediately bring one to an auspicious life free from anxieties and will bless one with transcendental existence, thus minimizing the value of liberation. *Bhakti-rasa* itself is sufficient to produce a feeling of liberation, because it attracts the attention of the Supreme Lord, Kṛṣṇa. Generally, neophyte devotees are anxious to see Kṛṣṇa, or God, but God cannot be seen or known by our present materially blunt senses. The process of devotional service as it is recommended in *The Nectar of Devotion* will gradually elevate one from the material condition of life to the spiritual status, wherein the devotee becomes purified of all designations. The senses can then become uncontaminated, being constantly in touch with *bhakti-rasa.* When the purified senses are employed in the service of the Lord, one becomes situated in *bhakti-rasa* life, and any action performed for the satisfaction of Kṛṣṇa in this transcendental *bhakti-rasa* stage of life can be relished perpetually. When one is thus engaged in devotional service, all varieties of *rasas,* or mellows, turn into eternity. In the beginning one is trained according to the principles of regulation under the guidance of the *ācārya,* or spiritual master, and gradually, when one is elevated, devotional service becomes automatic and spontaneous eagerness to serve Kṛṣṇa. There are twelve kinds of *rasas,* as will be explained in this book, and by renovating our relationship with Kṛṣṇa in five primary *rasas* we can live eternally in full knowledge and bliss.

The basic principle of the living condition is that we have a general propensity to love someone. No one can live without loving someone else. This propensity is present in every living being. Even an animal like a tiger has this loving propensity at least in a dormant stage, and it is certainly present in the human beings. The missing point, however, is where to repose our love so that everyone can become happy. At the present moment the human society teaches one to love his country or family or his personal self, but there is no information where to repose the loving propensity so that everyone can become happy. That missing point is Kṛṣṇa, and *The Nectar of Devotion* teaches us how to stimulate our original love for Kṛṣṇa and how to be situated in that position where we can enjoy our blissful life.

In the primary stage a child loves his parents, then his brothers and sisters, and as he daily grows up he begins to love his family, society, community, country, nation, or even the whole human society. But the loving propensity is not satisfied even by loving all human society; that loving propensity remains imperfectly fulfilled until we know who is the supreme beloved. Our love can be fully satisfied only when it is reposed in Kṛṣṇa. This theme is the sum and substance of *The Nectar of Devotion,* which teaches us how to love Kṛṣṇa in five different transcendental mellows.

Our loving propensity expands just as a vibration of light or air expands, but we do not know where it ends. *The Nectar of Devotion* teaches us the science of loving every one of the living entities perfectly by the easy method of loving Kṛṣṇa. We have failed to create peace and harmony in human society, even by such great attempts as the United Nations, because we do not know the right method. The method is very simple, but one has to understand it with a cool head. *The Nectar of Devotion* teaches all men how to perform the simple and natural method of loving Kṛṣṇa, the Supreme Personality of Godhead. If we learn how to love Kṛṣṇa, then it is very easy to immediately and simultaneously love every living being. It is like pouring water on the root of a tree or supplying food to one's stomach. The method of pouring water on the root of a tree or supplying foodstuffs to the stomach is universally scientific and practical, as every one of us has experienced. Everyone knows well that when we eat something, or in other words, when we put foodstuffs in the stomach, the energy created by such action is immediately distributed throughout the whole body. Similarly, when we pour water on the root, the energy thus created is immediately distributed throughout the entirety of even the largest tree. It is not possible to water the tree part by part, nor is it possible to feed the different parts of the body separately. *The Nectar of Devotion* will teach us how to turn the one switch that will immediately brighten everything, everywhere. One who does not know this method is missing the point of life.

As far as material necessities are concerned, the human civilization at the present moment is very much advanced in living comfortably, but still we are not happy, because we are missing the point. The material comforts of life alone are not sufficient to make us happy. The vivid example is America: the richest nation of the world, having all facilities for material comfort, is producing a class of men completely confused and frustrated in life. I am appealing herewith to such confused men to learn the art of devotional service as directed in *The Nectar of Devotion,* and I am sure that the fire of material existence burning within their hearts will be immediately extinguished. The root cause of our dissatisfaction is that our dormant loving propensity has not been fulfilled despite our great advancement in the materialistic way of life. *The Nectar of Devotion* will give us practical hints how we can live in this material world perfectly engaged in devotional service and thus fulfill all our desires in this life and the next. *The Nectar of Devotion* is not presented to condemn any way of materialistic life, but the attempt is to give information to religionists, philosophers and people in general how to love Kṛṣṇa. One may live without material discomfiture, but at the same time he should learn the art of loving Kṛṣṇa. At the present moment we are inventing so many ways to utilize our propensity to love, but factually we are missing the real point: Kṛṣṇa. We are watering all parts of the tree, but missing the tree's root. We are trying to keep our body fit by all means, but we are neglecting to supply foodstuffs to the stomach. Missing Kṛṣṇa means missing one's self also. Real self-realization and realization of Kṛṣṇa go together simultaneously. For example, seeing oneself in the morning means seeing the sunrise also; without seeing the sunshine no one can see himself. Similarly, unless one has realized Kṛṣṇa there is no question of self-realization.

The Nectar of Devotion is specifically presented for persons who are now engaged in the Kṛṣṇa consciousness movement. I beg to offer my sincere thanks to all my friends and disciples who are helping me to push forward the Kṛṣṇa consciousness movement in the Western countries, and I beg to acknowledge, with thanks, the contribution made by my beloved disciple Śrīmān Jayānanda Brahmacārī. My thanks are due as well to the directors of ISKCON Press, who have taken so much care in publishing this great literature. Hare Kṛṣṇa.

A.C. Bhaktivedanta Swami

April 13, 1970
ISKCON Headquarters
3764 Watseka Ave.
Los Angeles, California

Introduction

Invoking auspiciousness: Lord Śrī Kṛṣṇa is the Supreme Personality of Godhead, the cause of all causes, the reservoir of all *rasas,* or relationships, which are called neutrality (passive adoration), servitorship, friendship, parenthood, conjugal love, comedy, compassion, fear, chivalry, ghastliness, wonder and devastation. He is the supreme attractive form, and by His universal and transcendental attractive features He has captivated all the *gopīs,* headed by Tārakā, Pālikā, Śyāmā, Lalitā, and ultimately Śrīmatī Rādhārāṇī. Let His Lordship's grace be on us so that there may not be any hindrance in the execution of this duty of writing *The Nectar of Devotion,* impelled by His Divine Grace Śrī Śrīmad Bhaktisiddhānta Sarasvatī Gosvāmī Prabhupāda.

Let me offer my respectful obeisances unto the lotus feet of Śrīla Rūpa Gosvāmī Prabhupāda and of Śrīla Bhaktisiddhānta Sarasvatī Gosvāmī Prabhupāda, by whose inspiration I have been engaged in the matter of compiling this summary study of *Bhakti-rasāmṛta-sindhu.* This is the sublime science of devotional service as propounded by Śrī Caitanya Mahāprabhu, who appeared five hundred years ago in West Bengal, India, to propagate the movement of Kṛṣṇa consciousness.

Śrīla Rūpa Gosvāmī begins his great book by offering his respectful obeisances unto Śrī Sanātana Gosvāmī, who is his elder brother and spiritual master, and he prays that *Bhakti-rasāmṛta-sindhu* may be very pleasing to him. He further prays that by residing in that ocean of nectar, Śrī Sanātana Gosvāmī may always feel transcendental pleasure in the service of Rādhā and Kṛṣṇa.

Let us offer our respectful obeisances to all the great devotees and *ācāryas* (holy teachers), who are compared to sharks in the great ocean of nectar and who do not care for the various rivers of liberation. Impersonalists are very fond of merging into the Supreme, like rivers that come down and merge into the ocean. The ocean can be compared to liberation, and the rivers to all the different paths of liberation. The impersonalists are dwelling in the river water, which eventually comes to mix with the ocean. They have no information, however, that within the ocean, as within the river, there are innumerable aquatic living entities. The sharks who dwell in the ocean do not care for the rivers which are gliding down into it. The devotees eternally live in the ocean of devotional service, and they do not care for the rivers. In other words, those who are pure devotees always remain in the ocean of transcendental loving service to the Lord and have no business with the other processes, which are compared to the rivers that only gradually come to the ocean.

Śrīla Rūpa Gosvāmī prays to his spiritual master, Śrīla Sanātana Gosvāmī, for the protection of *Bhakti-rasāmṛta-sindhu*—"The Ocean of the Pure Nectar of Devotional Service"—from the argumentative logicians who unnecessarily meddle in the science of service to the Lord. He compares their arguments and logic to volcanic eruptions in the midst of the ocean. In the midst of the ocean, volcanic eruptions can do very little harm, and similarly, those who are against devotional service to the Lord and who put forward many philosophical theses about the ultimate transcendental realization cannot disturb this great ocean of devotional service.

The author of *Bhakti-rasāmṛta-sindhu,* Śrīla Rūpa Gosvāmī, very humbly submits that he is just trying to spread Kṛṣṇa consciousness all over the world, although he humbly thinks himself unfit for this work. That should be the attitude of all preachers of the Kṛṣṇa consciousness movement, following in the footsteps of Śrīla Rūpa Gosvāmī. We should never think of ourselves as great preachers, but should always consider that we are simply instrumental to the previous *ācāryas,* and simply by following in their footsteps we may be able to do something for the benefit of suffering humanity.

Bhakti-rasāmṛta-sindhu is divided into four parts, just as the ocean is sometimes divided into four parts, and there are different sections within each of these four divisions. Originally, in *Bhakti-rasāmṛta-sindhu,* the ocean is divided like the watery ocean into east, south, west and north, while the subsections within these different divisions are called waves. As in the ocean there are always different waves, either on the eastern side, the southern side, the western side or the northern side, *Bhakti-rasāmṛta-sindhu* similarly has different waves. In the first part there are four waves, the first being a general description of devotional service. The second concerns the regulative principles for executing devotional service, and the third wave, devotional service in ecstasy. In the fourth is the ultimate goal, love of God. These will be explicitly described along with their different symptoms.

The authorized descriptions of *bhakti,* or devotional service, following in the footsteps of previous *ācāryas,* can be summarized in the following statement by Śrīla Rūpa Gosvāmī: "first-class devotional service is known by one's tendency to be fully engaged in Kṛṣṇa consciousness, serving the Lord favorably." The purport is that one may also be in Kṛṣṇa consciousness unfavorably, but that cannot be counted as pure devotional service. Pure devotional service should be free from the desire for any material benefit or for sense gratification, as these desires are cultivated through fruitive activities and philosophical speculation. Generally, people are engaged in different activities to get some material profit, while most philosophers are engaged in proposing transcendental realization through volumes of word jugglery and speculation. Pure devotional service must always be free from such fruitive activities and philosophical speculations. One has to learn Kṛṣṇa consciousness, or pure devotional service, from the authorities by spontaneous loving service.

This devotional service is a sort of cultivation. It is not simply inaction for people who like to be inactive or devote their time to silent meditation. There are many different methods for people who want this, but cultivation of Kṛṣṇa consciousness is different. The particular word used by Śrīla Rūpa Gosvāmī in this connection is *anuśīlana,* or cultivation by following the predecessor teachers (*ācāryas*). As soon as we say "cultivation," we must refer to activity. Without activity, consciousness alone cannot help us. All activities may be divided into two classes: one class may be for achieving a certain goal, and the other may be for avoiding some unfavorable circumstance. In Sanskrit, these activities are called *pravṛtti* and *nivṛtti*—positive and negative action. There are many examples of negative action. For instance, a diseased person has to be cautious and take medicine in order to avoid some unfavorable illness.

Those who are cultivating spiritual life and executing devotional service are always engaged in activity. Such activity can be performed with the body or with the mind. Thinking, feeling and willing are all activities of the mind, and when we will to do something, the activity comes to be manifest by the gross bodily senses. Thus, in our mental activities we should always try to think of Kṛṣṇa and try to plan how to please Him, following in the footsteps of the great *ācāryas* and the personal spiritual master. There are activities of the body, activities of the mind and activities of speech. A Kṛṣṇa conscious person engages his words in preaching the glories of the Lord. This is called *kīrtana*. And by his mind a Kṛṣṇa conscious person always thinks of the activities of the Lord—as He is speaking on the Battlefield of Kurukṣetra or engaging in His various pastimes in Vṛndāvana with His devotees. In this way one can always think of the activities and pastimes of the Lord. This is the mental culture of Kṛṣṇa consciousness.

Similarly, we can offer many services with our bodily activities. But all such activities must be in relationship with Kṛṣṇa. This relationship is established by connecting oneself with the bona fide spiritual master, who is the direct representative of Kṛṣṇa in disciplic succession. Therefore, the execution of Kṛṣṇa conscious activities with the body should be directed by the spiritual master and then performed with faith. The connection with the spiritual master is called initiation. From the date of initiation by the spiritual master, the connection between Kṛṣṇa and a person cultivating Kṛṣṇa consciousness is established. Without initiation by a bona fide spiritual master, the actual connection with Kṛṣṇa consciousness is never performed.

This cultivation of Kṛṣṇa consciousness is not material. The Lord has three general energies—namely the external energy, the internal energy and the marginal energy. The living entities are called marginal energy, and the material cosmic manifestation is the action of the external, or material, energy. Then there is the spiritual world, which is a manifestation of the internal energy. The living entities, who are called marginal energy, perform material activities when acting under the inferior, external energy. And when they engage in activities under the internal, spiritual energy, their activities are called Kṛṣṇa conscious. This means that those who are great souls or great devotees do not act under the spell of material energy, but act instead under the protection of the spiritual energy. Any activities done in devotional service, or in Kṛṣṇa consciousness, are directly under the control of spiritual energy. In other words, energy is a sort of strength, and this strength can be spiritualized by the mercy of both the bona fide spiritual master and Kṛṣṇa.

In the *Caitanya-caritāmṛta,* by Kṛṣṇadāsa Kavirāja Gosvāmī, Lord Caitanya states that it is a fortunate person who comes in contact with a bona fide spiritual master by the grace of Kṛṣṇa. One who is serious about spiritual life is given by Kṛṣṇa the intelligence to come in contact with a bona fide spiritual master, and then by the grace of the spiritual master one becomes advanced in Kṛṣṇa consciousness. In this way the whole jurisdiction of Kṛṣṇa consciousness is directly under the spiritual energy—Kṛṣṇa and the spiritual master. This has nothing to do with the material world. When we speak of "Kṛṣṇa" we refer to the Supreme Personality of Godhead, along with His many expansions. He is expanded by His plenary parts and parcels, His differentiated parts and parcels and His different energies. "Kṛṣṇa," in other words, means everything and includes everything. Generally, however, we should understand "Kṛṣṇa" to mean Kṛṣṇa and His personal expansions. Kṛṣṇa expands Himself as Baladeva, Saṅkarṣaṇa, Vāsudeva, Aniruddha, Pradyumna, Rāma, Nṛsiṁha and Varāha, as well as many other incarnations and innumerable Viṣṇu expansions. These are described in the *Śrīmad-Bhāgavatam* to be as numerous as the uncountable waves. So Kṛṣṇa includes all such expansions, as well as His pure devotees. In the *Brahma-saṁhitā* it is stated that Kṛṣṇa's expansions are all complete in eternity, blissfulness and cognizance.

Devotional service means to prosecute Kṛṣṇa conscious activities which are favorable to the transcendental pleasure of the Supreme Lord, Kṛṣṇa, and any activities which are not favorable to the transcendental favor of the Lord cannot be accepted as devotional service. For example, great demons like Rāvaṇa, Kaṁsa and Hiraṇyakaśipu were always thinking of Kṛṣṇa, but they were thinking of Him as their enemy. This sort of thinking cannot be accepted as *bhakti,* or Kṛṣṇa consciousness.

The impersonalists sometimes misunderstand devotional service in such a way that they divide Kṛṣṇa from His paraphernalia and pastimes. For example, the *Bhagavad-gītā* is spoken on the Battlefield of Kurukṣetra, and the impersonalists say that although Kṛṣṇa is of interest, the Battlefield of Kurukṣetra isn't. The devotees, however, also know that the Battlefield of Kurukṣetra by itself has nothing to do with their business, but in addition they know that "Kṛṣṇa" does not mean just Kṛṣṇa alone. He is always with His associates and paraphernalia. For instance, if someone says, "Give something to eat to the man with the weapons," the eating process is done by the man and not by the weapons. Similarly, in Kṛṣṇa consciousness, a devotee may be interested in the paraphernalia and locations—such as the Battlefield of Kurukṣetra—which are associated with Kṛṣṇa, but he is not concerned with simply any battlefield. He is concerned with Kṛṣṇa—His speech, His instructions, etc. It is because Kṛṣṇa is there that the battlefield is so important.

This is the summary understanding of what Kṛṣṇa consciousness is. Without this understanding one is sure to misunderstand why the devotees are interested in the Battlefield of Kurukṣetra. One who is interested in Kṛṣṇa becomes interested in His different pastimes and activities.

The definition of a pure devotee, as given by Rūpa Gosvāmī in *Bhakti-rasāmṛta-sindhu,* can be summarized thus: his service is favorable and is always in relation to Kṛṣṇa. In order to keep the purity of such Kṛṣṇa conscious activities, one must be freed from all material desires and philosophical speculation. Any desire except for the service of the Lord is called material desire. And "philosophical speculation" refers to the sort of speculation which ultimately arrives at a conclusion of voidism or impersonalism. This conclusion is useless for a Kṛṣṇa conscious person. Only rarely by philosophical speculation can one reach the conclusion of worshiping Vāsudeva, Kṛṣṇa. This is confirmed in the *Bhagavad-gītā* itself. The ultimate end of philosophical speculation, then, must be Kṛṣṇa, with the understanding that Kṛṣṇa is everything, the cause of all causes, and that one should therefore surrender unto Him. If this ultimate goal is reached, then philosophical advancement is favorable, but if the conclusion of philosophical speculation is voidism or impersonalism, that is not *bhakti.*

Karma, or fruitive activities, are sometimes understood to be ritualistic activities. There are many persons who are very much attracted by the ritualistic activities described in the *Vedas.* But if one becomes attracted simply to ritualistic activities without understanding Kṛṣṇa, his activities are unfavorable to Kṛṣṇa consciousness. Actually, Kṛṣṇa consciousness can be based simply on hearing, chanting, remembering, etc. Described in the *Śrīmad-Bhāgavatam* are nine different processes, besides which everything done is unfavorable to Kṛṣṇa consciousness. Thus, one should always be guarding against falldowns.

Śrīla Rūpa Gosvāmī has also mentioned in this definition of *bhakti* the word *jñāna-karmādi.* This *karmādi* (fruitive work) consists of activities which are unable to help one attain to pure devotional service. Many forms of so-called renunciation are also not favorable to Kṛṣṇa conscious devotional service.

Śrīla Rūpa Gosvāmī has also quoted a definition from the *Nārada-pañcarātra,* as follows: "One should be free from all material designations and, by Kṛṣṇa consciousness, must be cleansed of all material contamination. He should be restored to his pure identity, in which he engages his senses in the service of the proprietor of the senses." So when our senses are engaged for the actual proprietor of the senses, that is called devotional service. In our conditional state, our senses are engaged in serving these bodily demands. When the same senses are engaged in executing the order of Kṛṣṇa, our activities are called *bhakti.*

As long as one identifies himself as belonging to a certain family, a certain society or a certain person, he is said to be covered with designations. When one is fully aware that he does not belong to any family, society or country, but is eternally related to Kṛṣṇa, he then realizes that his energy should be employed not in the interests of so-called family, society or country, but in the interests of Kṛṣṇa. This is purity of purpose and the platform of pure devotional service in Kṛṣṇa consciousness.

PART ONE

1

Characteristics of Pure Devotional Service

In *Śrīmad-Bhāgavatam,* Third Canto, Twenty-ninth Chapter, verses 12 and 13, Śrīla Kapiladeva, while instructing His mother, has given the following characteristics of pure devotional service: "My dear mother, those who are My pure devotees, and who have no desire for material benefit or philosophical speculation, have their minds so much engaged in My service that they are never interested in asking Me for anything—except to be engaged in that service. They do not even beg to live in My abode with Me."

There are five kinds of liberation, namely to become one with the Lord, to live with the Supreme Lord on the same planet, to have the same features as the Lord, to enjoy the same opulences as the Lord and to live as a companion of the Lord. A devotee, what to speak of rejecting material sense gratification, does not even want any of the five kinds of liberation. He is satisfied simply by discharging loving service to the Lord. That is the characteristic of pure devotion.

In the above statement by Kapiladeva from *Śrīmad-Bhāgavatam,* the actual position of a pure devotee is described, and the primary characteristics of devotional service are also defined. Further characteristics of devotional service are described by Rūpa Gosvāmī with evidences from different scriptures. He states that there are six characteristics of pure devotional service, which are as follows:

(1) Pure devotional service brings immediate relief from all kinds of material distress.

(2) Pure devotional service is the beginning of all auspiciousness.

(3) Pure devotional service automatically puts one in transcendental pleasure.

(4) Pure devotional service is rarely achieved.

(5) Those in pure devotional service deride even the conception of liberation.

(6) Pure devotional service is the only means to attract Kṛṣṇa.

Kṛṣṇa is all-attractive, but pure devotional service attracts even Him. This means that pure devotional service is even transcendentally stronger than Kṛṣṇa Himself, because it is Kṛṣṇa's internal potency.

Relief from Material Distress

In *Bhagavad-gītā,* the Lord says that one should surrender unto Him, giving up all other engagements. The Lord also gives His word there that He will protect surrendered souls from the reactions of all sinful activities. Śrīla Rūpa Gosvāmī says that the distresses from sinful activities are due both to the sins themselves and to sins committed in our past lives. Generally, one commits sinful activities due to ignorance. But ignorance is no excuse for evading the reaction—sinful activities. Sinful activities are of two kinds: those which are mature and those which are not mature. The sinful activities for which we are suffering at the present moment are called mature. The many sinful activities stored within us for which we have not yet suffered are considered immature. For example, a man may have committed criminal acts, but not yet been arrested for them. Now, as soon as he is detected, arrest is awaiting him. Similarly, for some of our sinful activities we are awaiting distresses in the future, and for others, which are mature, we are suffering at the present moment.

In this way there is a chain of sinful activities and their concomitant distresses, and the conditioned soul is suffering life after life due to these sins. He is suffering in the present life the results of sinful activities from his past life, and he is meanwhile creating further sufferings for his future life. Mature sinful activities are exhibited if one is suffering from some chronic disease, if one is suffering from some legal implication, if one is born in a low and degraded family or if one is uneducated or very ugly.

There are many results of past sinful activities for which we are suffering at the present moment, and we may be suffering in the future due to our present sinful activities. But all of these reactions to sinful deeds can immediately be stopped if we take to Kṛṣṇa consciousness. As evidence for this, Rūpa Gosvāmī quotes from *Śrīmad-Bhāgavatam,* Eleventh Canto, Fourteenth Chapter, verse 19. This verse is in connection with Lord Kṛṣṇa's instruction to Uddhava, where He says, "My dear Uddhava, devotional service unto Me is just like a blazing fire which can burn into ashes unlimited fuel supplied to it." The purport is that as the blazing fire can burn any amount of fuel to ashes, so devotional service to the Lord in Kṛṣṇa consciousness can burn up all the fuel of sinful activities. For example, in the *Gītā* Arjuna thought that fighting was a sinful activity, but Kṛṣṇa engaged him on the battlefield under His order, and so the fighting became devotional service. Therefore, Arjuna was not subjected to any sinful reaction.

Śrīla Rūpa Gosvāmī quotes another verse from the Third Canto of *Śrīmad-Bhāgavatam,* Thirty-third Chapter, verse 6, in which Devahūti addresses her son, Kapiladeva, and says, "My dear Lord, there are nine different kinds of devotional service, beginning from hearing and chanting. Anyone who hears about Your pastimes, who chants about Your glories, who offers You obeisances, who thinks of You and, in this way, executes any of the nine kinds of devotional service—even if he is born in a family of dog-eaters [the lowest grade of mankind]—becomes immediately qualified to perform sacrifices." As such, how is it possible that anyone actually engaged in devotional service in full Kṛṣṇa consciousness has not become purified? It is not possible. One who is engaged in Kṛṣṇa consciousness and devotional service has without doubt become freed from all contaminations of material sinful activities. Devotional service therefore has the power to actually nullify all kinds of reactions to sinful deeds. A devotee is nevertheless always alert not to commit any sinful activities; this is his specific qualification as a devotee. Thus *Śrīmad-Bhāgavatam* states that by performing devotional service a person who was born even in a family of dog-eaters may become eligible to take part in the performance of the ritualistic ceremonies recommended in the *Vedas.* It is implicit in this statement that a person born into a family of dog-eaters is generally not fit for performing *yajña,* or sacrifice. The priestly caste in charge of performing these ritualistic ceremonies recommended in the *Vedas* is called the *brāhmaṇa* order. Unless one is a *brāhmaṇa,* he cannot perform these ceremonies.

A person is born in a *brāhmaṇa* family or in a family of dog-eaters due to his past activities. If a person is born in a family of dog-eaters, it means that his past activities were all sinful. But if even such a person takes to the path of devotional service and begins to chant the holy names of the Lord—Hare Kṛṣṇa, Hare Kṛṣṇa, Kṛṣṇa Kṛṣṇa, Hare Hare/ Hare Rāma, Hare Rāma, Rāma Rāma, Hare Hare—he is at once fit to perform the ritualistic ceremonies. This means that his sinful reactions have immediately become neutralized.

It is stated in the *Padma Purāṇa* that there are four kinds of effects due to sinful activities, which are listed as follows: (1) the effect which is not yet fructified, (2) the effect which is lying as seed, (3) the effect which is already mature and (4) the effect which is almost mature. It is also stated that all these four effects become immediately vanquished for those who surrender unto the Supreme Personality of Godhead, Viṣṇu, and become engaged in His devotional service in full Kṛṣṇa consciousness.

Those effects described as "almost mature" refer to the distress from which one is suffering at present, and the effects "lying as seed" are in the core of the heart, where there is a certain stock of sinful desires which are like seeds. The Sanskrit word *kūṭam* means that they are almost ready to produce the seed, or the effect of the seed. "An immature effect" refers to the case where the seedling has not begun. From this statement of *Padma Purāṇa* it is understood that material contamination is very subtle. Its beginning, its fruition and results, and how one suffers such results in the form of distress, are part of a great chain. When one catches some disease, it is often very difficult to ascertain the cause of the disease, where it originated and how it is maturing. The suffering of a disease, however, does not appear all of a sudden. It actually takes time. And as in the medical field, for precaution's sake, the doctor injects a vaccination to prevent the growing of contamination, the practical injection to stop all the fructifications of the seeds of our sinful activities is simply engagement in Kṛṣṇa consciousness.

In this connection, Śukadeva Gosvāmī speaks in the Sixth Canto of *Śrīmad-Bhāgavatam,* Second Chapter, verse 17, about the story of Ajāmila, who began life as a fine and dutiful *brāhmaṇa* but in his young manhood became wholly corrupted by a prostitute. At the end of his wicked life, just by calling the name "Nārāyaṇa [Kṛṣṇa]," he was saved despite so much sin. Śukadeva points out that austerity, charity and the performance of ritualistic ceremonies for counteracting sinful activities are recommended processes but that by performing them one cannot remove the sinful desire-seed from the heart, as was the case with Ajāmila in his youth. This sinful desire-seed can be removed only by achieving Kṛṣṇa consciousness. And this can be accomplished

His Divine Grace A.C. Bhaktivedanta Swami Prabhupāda
Founder-*Ācārya* of the International Society for Krishna Consciousness

Śrīla Bhaktisiddhānta Sarasvatī Gosvāmī Mahārāja
the spiritual master of
His Divine Grace A.C. Bhaktivedanta Swami Prabhupāda
and foremost scholar and devotee in the recent age

Śrīla Gaurakiśora dāsa Bābājī Mahārāja
the spiritual master of
Śrīla Bhaktisiddhānta Sarasvatī Gosvāmī Mahārāja
and intimate student of Śrīla Ṭhākura Bhaktivinoda

Śrīla Ṭhākura Bhaktivinoda
the pioneer of the program to inundate
the entire world with Kṛṣṇa consciousness

Śrīla Rūpa Gosvāmī (*right*), the author of *Bhakti-rasāmṛta-sindhu,* and Śrīla Sanātana Gosvāmi (*left*), his elder brother and spiritual master.

The *bhajana-kuṭira* (place of worship) of Śrīla Rūpa Gosvāmī at the Rādhā-Dāmodara temple, Vṛndāvana, India.

The interior of the *samādhi,* or shrine, of Śrīla Rūpa Gosvāmī. On the altar are his *japa-mālā,* or chanting beads, sanctified by his chanting of the holy names of the Lord.

Śrī Caitanya Mahāprabhu appeared five hundred years ago in West Bengal, India, to propagate the chanting of Hare Kṛṣṇa all over the world. (p. xix)

very easily by chanting the *mahā-mantra,* or Hare Kṛṣṇa *mantra,* as recommended by Śrī Caitanya Mahāprabhu. In other words, unless one adopts the path of devotional service, he cannot be one-hundred-percent clean from all the reactions of sinful activities.

By performing Vedic ritualistic activities, by giving money in charity and by undergoing austerity, one can temporarily become free from the reactions of sinful activities, but at the next moment he must again become engaged in sinful activities. For example, a person suffering from venereal disease on account of excessive indulgence in sex life has to undergo some severe pain in medical treatment, and he is then cured for the time being. But because he has not been able to remove the sex desire from his heart, he must again indulge in the same thing and become a victim of the same disease. So medical treatment may give temporary relief from the distress of such venereal disease, but unless one is trained to understand that sex life is abominable, it is impossible to be saved from such repeated distress. Similarly, the ritualistic performances, charity and austerity which are recommended in the *Vedas* may temporarily stop one from acting in sinful ways, but as long as the heart is not clear, one will have to repeat sinful activities again and again.

Another example given in *Śrīmad-Bhāgavatam* concerns the elephant who enters into a lake and takes a bath very seriously, cleansing his body thoroughly. Then as soon as he comes onto shore he again takes some dust from the earth and throws it over his body. Similarly, a person who is not trained in Kṛṣṇa consciousness cannot become completely free from the desire for sinful activities. Neither the *yoga* process nor philosophical speculations nor fruitive activities can save one from the seeds of sinful desires. Only by being engaged in devotional service can this be done.

There is another evidence in the Fourth Canto of *Śrīmad-Bhāgavatam,* Twenty-second Chapter, verse 39, wherein Sanat-kumāra says, "My dear King, the false ego of a human being is so strong that it keeps him in material existence as if tied up by a strong rope. Only the devotees can cut off the knot of this strong rope very easily, by engaging themselves in Kṛṣṇa consciousness. Others, who are not in Kṛṣṇa consciousness but are trying to become great mystics or great ritual performers, cannot advance like the devotees. Therefore, it is the duty of everyone to engage himself in the activities of Kṛṣṇa consciousness in order to be freed from the tight knot of false ego and engagement in material activities."

This tight knot of false ego is due to ignorance. As long as one is ignorant about his identity, he is sure to act wrongly and thereby become entangled in material contamination. This ignorance of factual knowledge can also be dissipated by Kṛṣṇa consciousness, as is confirmed in the *Padma Purāṇa* as follows: "Pure devotional service in Kṛṣṇa consciousness is the highest enlightenment, and when such enlightenment is there, it is just like a blazing forest fire, killing all the inauspicious snakes of desire." The example is being given in this connection that when there is a forest fire the extensive blazing automatically kills all the snakes in the forest. There are many, many snakes on the ground of the forest, and when a fire takes place, it burns the dried foliage, and the snakes are immediately attacked. Animals who have four legs can flee from the fire or can at least try to flee, but the snakes are immediately killed. Similarly, the blazing fire of Kṛṣṇa consciousness is so strong that the snakes of ignorance are immediately killed.

Kṛṣṇa Consciousness Is All-auspicious

Śrīla Rūpa Gosvāmī has given a definition of auspiciousness. He says that actual auspiciousness means welfare activities for all the people of the world. At the present moment groups of people are engaged in welfare activities in terms of society, community or nation. There is even an attempt in the form of the United Nations for world-help activity. But due to the shortcomings of limited national activities, such a general mass welfare program for the whole world is not practically possible. The Kṛṣṇa consciousness movement, however, is so nice that it can render the highest benefit to the entire human race. Everyone can be attracted by this movement, and everyone can feel the result. Therefore, Rūpa Gosvāmī and other learned scholars agree that a broad propaganda program for the Kṛṣṇa consciousness movement of devotional service all over the world is the highest humanitarian welfare activity.

How the Kṛṣṇa consciousness movement can attract the attention of the whole world and how each and every man can feel pleasure in this Kṛṣṇa consciousness is stated in the *Padma Purāṇa* as follows: "A person who is engaged in devotional service in full Kṛṣṇa consciousness is to be understood to be doing the best service to the whole world and to be pleasing everyone in the world. In addition to human society, he is pleasing even the trees and animals, because they also become attracted by such a movement." A practical example of this was shown by Lord Caitanya when He was traveling through the forests of Jhārikhaṇḍa in central India for spreading His *saṅkīrtana* movement. The tigers, the elephants, the deer and all the other wild animals joined Him and were participating, in their own ways, by dancing and chanting Hare Kṛṣṇa.

Furthermore, a person engaged in Kṛṣṇa consciousness, acting in devotional service, can develop all the good qualities that are generally found in the demigods. It is said by Śukadeva Gosvāmī in the Fifth Canto of *Śrīmad-Bhāgavatam,* Eighteenth Chapter, verse 12, "My dear King, persons who have unflinching faith in Kṛṣṇa and are without any duplicity can develop all the good qualities of the demigods. On account of a devotee's high grade of Kṛṣṇa consciousness, even the demigods like to live with him, and therefore it can be understood that the qualities of the demigods have developed within his body."

On the other hand, a person who is not in Kṛṣṇa consciousness has no good qualities. He may be highly educated from the academic point of view, but in the actual field of his activities he can be seen to be baser than the animals. Even though a person is highly educated academically, if he cannot go beyond the sphere of mental activities then he is sure to perform only material activities and thus remain impure. There are so many persons in the modern world who have been highly educated in the materialistic universities, but it is seen that they cannot take up the movement of Kṛṣṇa consciousness and develop the high qualities of the demigods.

For example, a Kṛṣṇa conscious boy, even if he is not very well educated by the university standard, can immediately give up all illicit sex life, gambling, meat-eating and intoxication, whereas those who are not in Kṛṣṇa consciousness, although very highly educated, are often drunkards, meat-eaters, sexmongers and gamblers. These are practical proofs of how a Kṛṣṇa conscious person becomes highly developed in good qualities, whereas a person who is not in Kṛṣṇa consciousness cannot do so. We experience that even a young boy in Kṛṣṇa consciousness is unattached to cinemas, nightclubs, naked dance shows, restaurants, liquor shops, etc. He becomes completely freed. He saves his valuable time from being extravagantly spent in the way of smoking, drinking, attending the theater and dancing.

One who is not in Kṛṣṇa consciousness usually cannot sit silently even for half an hour. The *yoga* system teaches that if you become silent you will realize that you are God. This system may be all right for materialistic persons, but how long will they be able to keep themselves silent? Artificially, they may sit down for so-called meditation, but immediately after their yogic performance they will engage themselves again in such activities as illicit sex life, gambling, meat-eating and many other nonsensical things. But a Kṛṣṇa conscious person gradually elevates himself without endeavoring for this so-called silent meditation. Simply because he is engaged in Kṛṣṇa consciousness he automatically gives up all this nonsense and develops a high character. One develops the highest character by becoming a pure devotee of Kṛṣṇa. The conclusion is that no one can truly have any good qualities if he is lacking Kṛṣṇa consciousness.

Happiness in Kṛṣṇa Consciousness

Śrīla Rūpa Gosvāmī has analyzed the different sources of happiness. He has divided happiness into three categories, which are (1) happiness derived from material enjoyment, (2) happiness derived by identifying oneself with the Supreme Brahman and (3) happiness derived from Kṛṣṇa consciousness.

In the *tantra-śāstra* Lord Śiva speaks to his wife, Satī, in this way: "My dear wife, a person who has surrendered himself at the lotus feet of Govinda and who has thus developed pure Kṛṣṇa consciousness can be very easily awarded all the perfections desired by the impersonalists; and beyond this, he can enjoy the happiness achieved by the pure devotees."

Happiness derived from pure devotional service is the highest, because it is eternal. The happiness derived from material perfection or understanding oneself to be Brahman is inferior because it is temporary. There is no preventing one's falling down from material happiness, and there is even every chance of falling down from the spiritual happiness derived out of identifying oneself with the impersonal Brahman.

It has been seen that great Māyāvādī (impersonalist) *sannyāsīs*—very highly educated and almost realized souls—may sometimes take to political activities or to social welfare activities. The reason is that they actually do not derive any ultimate transcendental happiness in the impersonal understanding and therefore must come down to the material platform and take to such mundane affairs. There are many instances, especially in India, where these Māyāvādī *sannyāsīs* descend to the material platform again. But a person who is fully in Kṛṣṇa consciousness will never return to any sort of material platform. However alluring and attracting they may be, he always knows that no material welfare activities can compare to the spiritual activity of Kṛṣṇa consciousness.

The mystic perfections achieved by actually successful *yogīs* are eight in number. *Aṇimā-siddhi* refers to the power by which one can become so small that he can enter into a stone. Modern scientific improvements also enable us to enter into stone, because they provide for excavating so many subways, penetrating the hills, etc. So *aṇimā-siddhi,* the mystic perfection of trying to enter into stone, has also been achieved by material science. Similarly, all of the *yoga-siddhis,* or perfections, are material arts. For example, in one *yoga-siddhi* there is development of the power to become so light that one can float in the air or on water. That is also being performed by modern scientists. They are flying in the air, they are floating on the surface of the water, and they are traveling under the water.

After comparing all these mystic *yoga-siddhis* to materialistic perfections, we find that the materialistic scientists try for the same perfections. So actually there is no difference between mystic perfection and materialistic perfection. A German scholar once said that the so-called *yoga* perfections had already been achieved by the modern scientists, and so he was not concerned with them. He intelligently went to India to learn how he could understand his eternal relationship with the Supreme Lord by means of *bhakti-yoga,* devotional service.

Of course, in the categories of mystic perfection there are certain processes which the material scientists have not yet been able to develop. For instance, a mystic *yogī* can enter into the sun planet simply by using the rays of the sunshine. This perfection is called *laghimā*. Similarly, a *yogī* can touch the moon with his finger. Though the modern astronauts go to the moon with the help of spaceships, they undergo many difficulties, whereas a person with mystic perfection can extend his hand and touch the moon with his finger. This *siddhi* is called *prāpti,* or acquisition. With this *prāpti-siddhi,* not only can the perfect mystic *yogī* touch the moon planet, but he can extend his hand anywhere and take whatever he likes. He may be sitting thousands of miles away from a certain place, and if he likes he can take fruit from a garden there. This is *prāpti-siddhi.*

The modern scientists have manufactured nuclear weapons with which they can destroy an insignificant part of this planet, but by the *yoga-siddhi* known as *īśitā* one can create and destroy an entire planet simply at will. Another perfection is called *vaśitā,* and by this perfection one can bring anyone under his control. This is a kind of hypnotism which is almost irresistible. Sometimes it is found that a *yogī* who may have attained a little perfection in this *vaśitā* mystic power comes out among the people and speaks all sorts of nonsense, controls their minds, exploits them, takes their money and then goes away.

There is another mystic perfection, which is known as *prākāmya* (magic). By this *prākāmya* power one can achieve anything he likes. For example, one can make water enter into his eye and then again come out from within the eye. Simply by his will he can perform such wonderful activities.

The highest perfection of mystic power is called *kāmāvasāyitā.* This is also magic, but whereas the *prākāmya* power acts to create wonderful effects within the scope of nature, *kāmāvasāyitā* permits one to contradict nature—in other words, to do the impossible. Of course, one can derive great amounts of temporary happiness by achieving such yogic materialistic perfections.

Foolishly, people who are enamored of the glitter of modern materialistic advancement are thinking that the Kṛṣṇa consciousness movement is for less intelligent men. "I am better off being busy with my material comforts—maintaining a nice apartment, family and sex life." These people do not know that at any moment they can be kicked out of their material situation. Due to ignorance, they do not know that real life is eternal. The temporary comforts of the body are not the goal of life, and it is due only to darkest ignorance that people become enamored of the glittering advancement of material comforts. Śrīla Bhaktivinoda Ṭhākura has therefore said that the advancement of material knowledge renders a person more foolish, because it causes one to forget his real identity by its glitter. This is doom for him, because this human form of life is meant for getting out of material contamination. By the advancement of material knowledge, people are becoming more and more entangled in material existence. They have no hope of being liberated from this catastrophe.

In the *Hari-bhakti-sudhodaya* it is stated that Prahlāda Mahārāja, a great devotee of the Lord, prayed to Nṛsiṁhadeva (the half-lion, half-man incarnation) as follows: "My dear Lord, I repeatedly pray unto Your lotus feet that I may simply be stronger in devotional service. I simply pray that my Kṛṣṇa consciousness may be more strong and steady, because happiness derived out of Kṛṣṇa consciousness and devotional service is so powerful that with it one can have all the other perfections of religiousness, economic development, sense gratification and even the attainment of liberation from material existence."

Actually, a pure devotee does not aspire after any of these perfections, because the happiness derived from devotional service in Kṛṣṇa consciousness is so transcendental and so unlimited that no other happiness can compare to it. It is said that even one drop of happiness in Kṛṣṇa consciousness stands beyond comparison with an ocean of happiness derived from any other activity. Thus, any person who has developed even a little quantity of pure devotional service can very easily kick out all the other kinds of happiness derived from religiousness, economic development, sense gratification and liberation.

There was a great devotee of Lord Caitanya known as Kholāvecā Śrīdhara, who was a very poor man. He was doing a small business selling cups made from the leaves of plantain trees, and his income was almost nothing. Still, he was spending fifty percent of his small income on the worship of the Ganges, and with the other fifty percent he was somehow living. Lord Caitanya once revealed Himself to this confidential devotee, Kholāvecā Śrīdhara, and offered him any opulence he liked. But Śrīdhara informed the Lord that he did not want any material opulence. He was quite happy in his present position and wanted only to gain unflinching faith and devotion unto the lotus feet of Lord Caitanya. That is the position of pure devotees. If they can be engaged twenty-four hours each day in devotional service they do not want anything else, not even the happiness of liberation or of becoming one with the Supreme.

In the *Nārada-pañcarātra* it is also said that any person who has developed even a small amount of devotional service doesn't care a fig for any kind of happiness derived from religiousness, economic development, sense gratification or the five kinds of liberation. Any kind of happiness derived from religiousness, economic development, liberation or sense gratification cannot even dare to enter into the heart of a pure devotee. It is stated that as the personal attendants and maidservants of a queen follow the queen with all respect and obeisances, similarly the joys of religiousness, economic development, sense gratification and liberation follow the devotional service of the Lord. In other words, a pure devotee does not lack any kind of happiness derived from any source. He does not want anything but service to Kṛṣṇa, but even if he should have another desire, the Lord fulfills this without the devotee's asking.

The Rareness of Pure Devotional Service

In the preliminary phase of spiritual life there are different kinds of austerities, penances and similar processes for attaining self-realization. However, even if an executor of these processes is without any material desire, he still cannot achieve devotional service. And aspiring by oneself alone to achieve devotional service is also not very hopeful, because Kṛṣṇa does not agree to award devotional service to merely anyone. Kṛṣṇa can easily offer a person material happiness or even liberation, but He does not agree very easily to award a person engagement in His devotional service. Devotional service can in fact be attained only through the mercy of a pure devotee. In the *Caitanya-caritāmṛta* (*Madhya* 19.151) it is said, "By the mercy of the spiritual master who is a pure devotee and by the mercy of Kṛṣṇa one can achieve the platform of devotional service. There is no other way."

The rarity of devotional service is also confirmed in the *tantra-śāstra,* where Lord Śiva says to Satī, "My dear Satī, if one is a very fine philosopher, analyzing the different processes of knowledge, he can achieve liberation from the material entanglement. By performance of the ritualistic sacrifices recommended in the *Vedas* one can be elevated to the platform of pious activities and thereby enjoy the material comforts of life to the fullest extent. But all such endeavors can hardly offer anyone devotional service to the Lord, not even if one tries for it by such processes for many, many thousands of births."

In *Śrīmad-Bhāgavatam* it is also confirmed by Prahlāda Mahārāja that merely by personal efforts or by the instructions of higher authorities one cannot attain to the stage of devotional service. One must become blessed by the dust of the lotus feet of a pure devotee, who is completely freed from the contamination of material desires.

In the Fifth Canto of *Śrīmad-Bhāgavatam,* Sixth Chapter, verse 18, Śukadeva Gosvāmī also says to Mahārāja Parīkṣit, "My dear King, it is Lord Kṛṣṇa, known as Mukunda, who is the eternal protector of the Pāṇḍavas and the Yadus. He is also your spiritual master and instructor in every respect. He is the only worshipable God for you. He is very dear and affectionate, and He is the director of all your activities, both individual and familial. And what's more, He sometimes carries out your orders as if He were your messenger! My dear King, how very fortunate you are, because for others all these favors given to you by the Supreme Lord would not even be dreamt of." The purport to this verse is that the Lord easily offers liberation, but He rarely agrees to offer a soul devotional service, because by devotional service the Lord Himself becomes purchased by the devotee.

The Happiness of Becoming One with the Supreme

Śrīla Rūpa Gosvāmī says that if *brahmānanda,* or the happiness of becoming one with the Supreme, is multiplied by one trillionfold, it still cannot compare to an atomic fraction of the happiness derived from the ocean of devotional service.

In the *Hari-bhakti-sudhodaya* Prahlāda Mahārāja, while satisfying Lord Nṛsiṁhadeva by his prayers, says, "My dear Lord of the universe, I am feeling transcendental pleasure in Your presence and have become merged in the ocean of happiness. I now consider the happiness of *brahmānanda* to be no more than the water in the impression left by a cow's hoof in the earth, compared to this ocean of bliss." Similarly, it is confirmed in the *Bhāvārtha-dīpikā,* Śrīdhara Svāmī's commentary on the *Śrīmad-Bhāgavatam,* "My dear Lord, some of the fortunate persons who are swimming in the ocean of Your nectar of devotion, and who are relishing the nectar of the narration of Your pastimes, certainly know ecstasies which immediately minimize the value of the happiness derived from religiousness, economic development, sense gratification and liberation. Such a transcendental devotee regards any kind of happiness other than devotional service as no better than straw in the street."

Attracting Kṛṣṇa

Śrīla Rūpa Gosvāmī has stated that devotional service attracts even Kṛṣṇa. Kṛṣṇa attracts everyone, but devotional service attracts Kṛṣṇa. The symbol of devotional service in the highest degree is Rādhārāṇī.

Kṛṣṇa is called Madana-mohana, which means that He is so attractive that He can defeat the attraction of thousands of Cupids. But Rādhārāṇī is still more attractive, for She can even attract Kṛṣṇa. Therefore devotees call Her Madana-mohana-mohinī—the attractor of the attractor of Cupid.

To perform devotional service means to follow in the footsteps of Rādhārāṇī, and devotees in Vṛndāvana put themselves under the care of Rādhārāṇī in order to achieve perfection in their devotional service. In other words, devotional service is not an activity of the material world; it is directly under the control of Rādhārāṇī. In *Bhagavad-gītā* it is confirmed that the *mahātmās,* or great souls, are under the protection of *daivī prakṛti,* the internal energy—Rādhārāṇī. So, being directly under the control of the internal potency of Kṛṣṇa, devotional service attracts even Kṛṣṇa Himself.

This fact is corroborated by Kṛṣṇa in the Eleventh Canto of *Śrīmad-Bhāgavatam,* Fourteenth Chapter, verse 20, where He says, "My dear Uddhava, you may know it from Me that the attraction I feel for devotional service rendered by My devotees is not to be attained even by the performance of mystic *yoga,* philosophical speculation, ritualistic sacrifices, the study of *Vedānta,* the practice of severe austerities or the giving of everything in charity. These are, of course, very nice activities, but they are not as attractive to Me as the transcendental loving service rendered by My devotees."

How Kṛṣṇa becomes attracted by the devotional service of His devotees is described by Nārada in *Śrīmad-Bhāgavatam,* Seventh Canto, Tenth Chapter, verses 48 and 49. There Nārada addresses King Yudhiṣṭhira while the King is appreciating the glories of the character of Prahlāda Mahārāja. A devotee always appreciates the activities of other devotees. Yudhiṣṭhira Mahārāja was appreciating the qualities of Prahlāda, and that is one symptom of a pure devotee. A pure devotee never thinks himself great; he always thinks that other devotees are greater than himself. The King was thinking, "Prahlāda Mahārāja is actually a devotee of the Lord, while I am nothing," and while thinking this he was addressed by Nārada as follows: "My dear King Yudhiṣṭhira, you [the Pāṇḍava brothers] are the only fortunate people in this world. The Supreme Personality of Godhead has appeared on this planet and is presenting Himself to you as an ordinary human being. He is always with you in all circumstances. He is living with you and covering Himself from the eyes of others. Others cannot understand that He is the Supreme Lord, but He is still living with you as your cousin, as your friend and even as your messenger. Therefore you must know that nobody in this world is more fortunate than you."

In *Bhagavad-gītā* when Kṛṣṇa appeared in His universal form Arjuna prayed, "My dear Kṛṣṇa, I thought of You as my cousin-brother, and so I have shown disrespect to You in so many ways, calling You 'Kṛṣṇa' or 'friend.' But You are so great that I could not understand." So that was the position of the Pāṇḍavas; although Kṛṣṇa is the Supreme Personality of Godhead, the greatest among all greats, He remained with those royal brothers, being attracted by their devotion, by their friendship and by their love. That is the proof of how great this process of devotional service is. It can attract even the Supreme Personality of Godhead. God is great, but devotional service is greater than God because it attracts Him. People who are not in devotional service can never understand what great value there is in rendering service to the Lord.

2

The First Stages of Devotion

The three categories of devotional service which Śrīla Rūpa Gosvāmī describes in *Bhakti-rasāmṛta-sindhu* are listed as devotional service in practice, devotional service in ecstasy and devotional service in pure love of Godhead. There are many subheadings in each of these categories. Generally it is understood that in the category of devotional service in practice there are two different qualities, devotional service in ecstasy has four qualities, and devotional service in pure love of Godhead has six qualities. These qualities will be explained by Śrīla Rūpa Gosvāmī later on.

In this connection, Śrīla Rūpa Gosvāmī suggests that the person eligible for Kṛṣṇa consciousness, or devotional service, can be classified by his particular taste. He says that devotional service is a continual process from one's previous life. No one can take to devotional service unless he has had some previous connection with it. For example, suppose in this life I practice devotional service to some extent. Even though it is not one-hundred-percent perfectly performed, whatever I have done will not be lost. In my next life, from the very point where I stop in this life, I shall begin again. In this way there is always a continuity. But even if there is no continuity, if only by chance a person takes interest in a pure devotee's instruction, he can be accepted and can advance in devotional service. Anyway, for persons who have a natural taste for understanding books like *Bhagavad-gītā* and *Śrīmad-Bhāgavatam,* devotional service is easier than for those who are simply accustomed to mental speculation and argumentative processes.

To support this statement there are many authoritative assertions by the learned scholars of bygone ages. According to their general opinion, a person may become governed by certain convictions derived by his own arguments and decisions. Then another person, who may be a greater logician, will nullify these conclusions and establish another thesis. In this way the path of argument will never be safe or conclusive. *Śrīmad-Bhāgavatam* recommends, therefore, that one follow in the footsteps of the authorities.

Here is a general description of devotional service given by Śrī Rūpa Gosvāmī in his *Bhakti-rasāmṛta-sindhu*. Previously, it has been stated that devotional service can be divided into three categories—namely devotional service in practice, devotional service in ecstasy and devotional service in pure love of God. Now Śrī Rūpa Gosvāmī proposes to describe devotional service in practice.

Practice means employing our senses in some particular type of work. Therefore devotional service in practice means utilizing our different sensory organs in service to Kṛṣṇa. Some of the senses are meant for acquiring knowledge, and some are meant for executing the conclusions of our thinking, feeling and willing. So practice means employing both the mind and the senses in practical devotional service. This practice is not for developing something artificial. For example, a child learns or practices to walk. This walking is not unnatural. The walking capacity is there originally in the child, and simply by a little practice he walks very nicely. Similarly, devotional service to the Supreme Lord is the natural instinct of every living entity. Even uncivilized men like the aborigines offer their respectful obeisances to something wonderful exhibited by nature's law, and they appreciate that behind some wonderful exhibition or action there is something supreme. So this consciousness, though lying dormant in those who are materially contaminated, is found in every living entity. And, when purified, this is called Kṛṣṇa consciousness.

There are certain prescribed methods for employing our senses and mind in such a way that our dormant consciousness for loving Kṛṣṇa will be invoked, as much as the child, with a little practice, can begin to walk. One who has no basic walking capacity cannot walk by practice. Similarly, Kṛṣṇa consciousness cannot be aroused simply by practice. Actually there is no such practice. When we wish to develop our innate capacity for devotional service, there are certain processes which, by our accepting and executing them, will cause that dormant capacity to be invoked. Such practice is called *sādhana-bhakti*.

Every living entity under the spell of material energy is held to be in an abnormal condition of madness. In *Śrīmad-Bhāgavatam* it is said, "Generally, the conditioned soul is mad, because he is always engaged in activities which are the causes of bondage and suffering." The spirit soul in his original condition is joyful, blissful, eternal and full of knowledge. Only by his implication in material activities has he become miserable, temporary and full of ignorance. This is due to *vikarma*. *Vikarma* means "actions which should not be done." Therefore, we must practice *sādhana-bhakti*—which means to offer *maṅgala-ārati* (Deity worship) in the morning, to refrain from certain material activities, to offer obeisances to the spiritual master and to follow many other rules and regulations which will be discussed here one after another. These practices will help one become cured of madness. As a man's mental disease is cured by the directions of a psychiatrist, so this *sādhana-bhakti* cures the conditioned soul of his madness under the spell of *māyā*, material illusion.

Nārada Muni mentions this *sādhana-bhakti* in *Śrīmad-Bhāgavatam*, Seventh Canto, First Chapter, verse 32. He says there to King Yudhiṣṭhira, "My dear King, one has to fix his mind on Kṛṣṇa by any means." That is called Kṛṣṇa consciousness. It is the duty of the *ācārya*, the spiritual master, to find the ways and means for his disciple to fix his mind on Kṛṣṇa. That is the beginning of *sādhana-bhakti*.

Śrī Caitanya Mahāprabhu has given us an authorized program for this purpose, centered around the chanting of the Hare Kṛṣṇa *mantra*. This chanting has so much power that it immediately attaches one to Kṛṣṇa. That is the beginning of *sādhana-bhakti*. Somehow or other, one has to fix his mind on Kṛṣṇa. The great saint Ambarīṣa Mahārāja, although a responsible king, fixed his mind on Kṛṣṇa, and similarly anyone who tries to fix his mind in this way will very rapidly make progress in successfully reviving his original Kṛṣṇa consciousness.

Now this *sādhana-bhakti*, or practice of devotional service, may also be divided into two parts. The first part is called service according to regulative principles: one has to follow these different regulative principles by the order of the spiritual master or on the strength of authoritative scriptures, and there can be no question of refusal. That is called *vaidhi*, or regulated. One has to do it without argument. Another part of *sādhana-bhakti* is called *rāgānugā*. *Rāgānugā* refers to the point at which, by following the regulative principles, one becomes a little more attached to Kṛṣṇa and executes devotional service out of natural love. For example, a person engaged in devotional service may be ordered to rise early in the morning and offer *ārati*, which is a form of Deity worship. In the beginning, by the order of his spiritual master, one rises early in the morning and offers *ārati,* but then he develops real attachment. When he gets this attachment, he automatically tries to decorate the Deity and prepare different kinds of dresses and thinks of different plans to execute his devotional service nicely. Although it is within the category of practice, this offering of loving service is spontaneous. So the practice of devotional service, *sādhana-bhakti,* can be divided into two parts—namely, regulative and spontaneous.

Rūpa Gosvāmī defines the first part of devotional practice, or *vaidhi-bhakti,* as follows: "When there is no attachment or no spontaneous loving service to the Lord, and one is engaged in the service of the Lord simply out of obedience to the order of the spiritual master or in pursuance of the scriptures, such obligatory service is called *vaidhi-bhakti.*"

These principles of *vaidhi-bhakti* are also described in *Śrīmad-Bhāgavatam,* Second Canto, First Chapter, verse 5, where Śukadeva Gosvāmī instructs the dying Mahārāja Parīkṣit as to his course of action. Mahārāja Parīkṣit met Śukadeva Gosvāmī just a week before his death, and the King was perplexed as to what should be done before he was to pass on. Many other sages also arrived there, but no one could give him the proper direction. Śukadeva Gosvāmī, however, gave this direction to him as follows: "My dear King, if you want to be fearless in meeting your death next week (for actually everyone is afraid at the point of death), then you must immediately begin the process of hearing and chanting and remembering God." If one can chant and hear Hare Kṛṣṇa and always remember Lord Kṛṣṇa, then he is sure to become fearless of death, which may come at any moment.

In the statements of Śukadeva Gosvāmī it is said that the Supreme Personality of Godhead is Kṛṣṇa. Therefore Śukadeva recommends that one should always hear about Kṛṣṇa. He does not recommend that one hear and chant about the demigods. The Māyāvādīs (impersonalists) say that one may chant any name, either that of Kṛṣṇa or those of the demigods, and the result will be the same. But actually this is not a fact. According to the authorized version of *Śrīmad-Bhāgavatam,* one has to hear and chant about Lord Viṣṇu (Kṛṣṇa) only.

So Śukadeva Gosvāmī has recommended to Parīkṣit Mahārāja that in order to be fearless of death, one has to hear and chant and remember the Supreme Personality of Godhead, Kṛṣṇa, by all means. He also mentions that the Supreme Personality of Godhead is *sarvātmā*. *Sarvātmā* means "the Supersoul of everyone." Kṛṣṇa is also mentioned as *īśvara,* the supreme controller who is situated in everyone's heart. Therefore, if some way or other we become attached to Kṛṣṇa, He will make us free from all danger. In *Bhagavad-gītā* it is said that anyone who becomes a devotee of the Lord is never vanquished. Others, however, are always vanquished. "Vanquished" means that after getting this human form of life, a person does not come out of the entanglement of birth and death and thus misses his golden opportunity. Such a person does not know where he is being thrown by the laws of nature.

Suppose one does not develop Kṛṣṇa consciousness in this human form of life. He will be thrown into the cycle of birth and death, involving 8,400,000 species of life, and his spiritual identity will remain lost. One does not know whether he is going to be a plant, or a beast, or a bird, or something like that, because there are so many species of life. The recommendation of Rūpa Gosvāmī for reviving our original Kṛṣṇa consciousness is that somehow or other we should apply our minds to Kṛṣṇa very seriously and thus also become fearless of death. After death we do not know our destination, because we are completely under the control of the laws of nature. Only Kṛṣṇa, the Supreme Personality of Godhead, is controller over the laws of nature. Therefore, if we take shelter of Kṛṣṇa seriously, there will be no fear of being thrown back into the cycle of so many species of life. A sincere devotee will surely be transferred to the abode of Kṛṣṇa, as affirmed in *Bhagavad-gītā*.

In the *Padma Purāṇa,* also, the same process is advised. There it is said that one should always remember Lord Viṣṇu. This is called *dhyāna,* or meditation—always remembering Kṛṣṇa. It is said that one has to meditate with his mind fixed upon Viṣṇu. *Padma Purāṇa* recommends that one always fix his mind on the form of Viṣṇu by meditation and not forget Him at any moment. And this state of consciousness is called *samādhi,* or trance.

We should always try to mold the activities of our lives in such a way that we will constantly remember Viṣṇu, or Kṛṣṇa. That is Kṛṣṇa consciousness. Whether one concentrates his mind on the four-handed form of Viṣṇu or on the form of two-handed Kṛṣṇa, it is the same. The *Padma Purāṇa* recommends: somehow or other always think of Viṣṇu, without forgetting Him under any circumstances. Actually this is the most basic of all regulative principles. For, when there is an order from a superior about doing something, there is simultaneously a prohibition. When the order is that one should always remember Kṛṣṇa, the prohibition is that one should never forget Him. Within this simple order and prohibition, all regulative principles are found complete.

This regulative principle is applicable to all *varṇas* and *āśramas,* the castes and occupations of life. There are four *varṇas,* namely the *brāhmaṇas* (priests and intellectuals), the *kṣatriyas* (warriors and statesmen), the *vaiśyas* (businessmen and farmers) and the *śūdras* (laborers and servants). There are also four standard *āśramas,* namely *brahmacarya* (student life), *gṛhastha* (householder), *vānaprastha* (retired) and *sannyāsa* (renounced). The regulative principles are not only for the *brahmacārīs* (celibate students) to follow, but are applicable for all. It doesn't matter whether one is a beginner—a *brahmacārī*—or is very advanced—a *sannyāsī.* The principle of remembering the Supreme Personality of Godhead constantly and not forgetting Him at any moment is meant to be followed by everyone without fail.

If this injunction is followed, then all other rules and regulations will automatically fall into line. All other rules and regulations should be treated as assistants or servants to this one basic principle. The injunctions of rules and regulations and the resultant reactions are mentioned in the Eleventh Canto of *Śrīmad-Bhāgavatam,* Fifth Chapter, verses 2 and 3. Camasa Muni, one of the nine sages who came to instruct King Nimi, addressed the King and said, "The four social orders, namely the *brāhmaṇas,* the *kṣatriyas,* the *vaiśyas* and the *śūdras,* have come out of the different parts of the universal form of the Supreme Lord as follows: the *brāhmaṇas* have come out from the head, the *kṣatriyas* have come out from the arms, the *vaiśyas* have come out from the waist, and the *śūdras* have come out from the legs. Similarly, the *sannyāsīs* have come out from the head, the *vānaprasthas* from the arms, the *gṛhasthas* from the waist and the *brahmacārīs* from the legs."

These different orders of society and grades of spiritual advancement are conceived in terms of qualification. It is confirmed in *Bhagavad-gītā* that the four social orders and the four spiritual orders are created by the Lord Himself, in terms of different individual qualities. As the different parts of the body have different types of activities, so the social orders and spiritual orders also have different types of activities in terms of qualification and position. The target of these activities, however, is always the Supreme Personality of Godhead. As confirmed in *Bhagavad-gītā,* "He is the supreme enjoyer." So, whether one is a *brāhmaṇa* or a *śūdra,* one has to satisfy the Supreme Lord by one's activities. This is also confirmed in *Śrīmad-Bhāgavatam* by a verse which reads, "Everyone must be engaged in his particular duty, but the perfection of such work should be tested by how far the Lord is satisfied with such activities." The injunction herein is that one has to act according to his position, and by such activities one must either satisfy the Supreme Personality or else fall down from one's position.

For example a *brāhmaṇa,* who is born out of the head of the Lord, has as his business to preach the transcendental Vedic sounds, or *śabda-brahma*. Because the *brāhmaṇa* is the head, he has to preach the transcendental sound, and he also has to eat on behalf of the Supreme Lord. According to Vedic injunctions, when a *brāhmaṇa* eats it is to be understood that the Personality of Godhead is eating through him. It is not, however, that the *brāhmaṇa* should simply eat on behalf of the Lord and not preach the message of *Bhagavad-gītā* to the world. Actually, one who preaches the message of the *Gītā* is very dear to Kṛṣṇa, as is confirmed in the *Gītā* itself. Such a preacher is factually a *brāhmaṇa,* and thus by feeding him one feeds the Supreme Lord directly.

Similarly, the *kṣatriya* has to protect people from the onslaughts of *māyā*. That is his duty. For example, as soon as Mahārāja Parīkṣit saw that a black man was attempting to kill a cow, he immediately took his sword, wanting to kill the black man, whose name was Kali.* That is a *kṣatriya's* duty. Violence is required in order to give protection. In *Bhagavad-gītā* Lord Kṛṣṇa directly gave His order to Arjuna to commit violence on the Battlefield of Kurukṣetra, just to give protection to the people in general.

The *vaiśyas* are meant for producing agricultural products, trading them and distributing them. And the working class, or *śūdras,* are those who haven't the intelligence of the *brāhmaṇas* or the *kṣatriyas* or the *vaiśyas,* and therefore they are meant to help these higher classes by bodily labor. In this way, there is full cooperation and spiritual

*Not to be confused with Kālī, the demigoddess who is the devastating feature of material nature.

advancement among all the different orders of society. And when there is no such cooperation, the members of society will fall down. That is the present position in the Kali-yuga, this age of quarrel. Nobody is doing his duty, and everyone is simply puffed up by calling himself a *brāhmaṇa* (intellectual) or a *kṣatriya* (soldier or statesman). But actually such people are without status. They are out of touch with the Supreme Personality of Godhead because they are not Kṛṣṇa conscious. Therefore, the Kṛṣṇa consciousness movement is intended to set the whole of human society in proper condition, so that everyone will be happy and take profit from developing Kṛṣṇa consciousness.

Lord Śrī Kṛṣṇa instructed Uddhava that by following the injunctions of the social and spiritual orders of human society, one can satisfy the Supreme Personality of Godhead, and as a result of such satisfaction the whole society gets all the necessities of life amply and without difficulty. This is because, after all, the Supreme Personality of Godhead maintains all other living entities. If the whole society performs its respective duties and remains in Kṛṣṇa consciousness, there is no doubt that all of its members will live very peacefully and happily. Without wanting the necessities of life, the whole world will be turned into Vaikuṇṭha, a spiritual abode. Even without being transferred to the kingdom of God, by following the injunctions of *Śrīmad-Bhāgavatam* and prosecuting the duties of Kṛṣṇa consciousness all human society will be happy in all respects.

There is a similar statement by Śrī Kṛṣṇa Himself to Uddhava, in the Eleventh Canto of *Śrīmad-Bhāgavatam*, Twenty-seventh Chapter, verse 49. The Lord says there, "My dear Uddhava, all persons are engaged in activities, whether those indicated in the revealed scriptures or ordinary worldly activities. If by the result of either of such activities they worship Me in Kṛṣṇa consciousness, then automatically they become very happy within this world, as well as in the next. Of this there is no doubt." We can conclude from this statement by Kṛṣṇa that activities in Kṛṣṇa consciousness will give everyone all perfection in all desires.

Thus the Kṛṣṇa consciousness movement is so nice that there is no need of even designating oneself *brāhmaṇa, kṣatriya, vaiśya, śūdra, brahmacārī, gṛhastha, vānaprastha* or *sannyāsī*. Let everyone be engaged in whatever occupation he now has. Simply let him worship Lord Kṛṣṇa by the result of his activities in Kṛṣṇa consciousness. That will adjust the whole situation, and everyone will be happy and peaceful within this world. In the *Nārada-pañcarātra* the regulative principles of devotional service are described as follows: "Any activities sanctioned in the revealed scriptures and aiming at the satisfaction of the Supreme Personality of Godhead are accepted by saintly teachers as the regulative principles of devotional service. If one regularly executes such service unto the Supreme Personality of Godhead under the direction of a bona fide spiritual master, then gradually he rises to the platform of serving in pure love of God."

3
Eligibility of the Candidate for Accepting Devotional Service

On account of his association with *mahātmās,* or great souls one-hundred-percent in the devotional service of the Lord, one may attain a little bit of attraction for Śrī Kṛṣṇa. But at the same time one may remain very much attached to fruitive activities and material sense enjoyment and not be prepared to undergo the different types of renunciation. Such a person, if he has unflinching attraction to Kṛṣṇa, becomes an eligible candidate for discharging devotional service.

This attraction for Kṛṣṇa consciousness in association with pure devotees is the sign of great fortune. It is confirmed by Lord Caitanya that only the fortunate persons, by the mercy of both a bona fide spiritual master and Kṛṣṇa, will get the seed of devotional service. In this connection, Lord Kṛṣṇa says in *Śrīmad-Bhāgavatam,* Eleventh Canto, Twentieth Chapter, verse 8, "My dear Uddhava, only by exceptional fortune does someone become attracted to Me. And even if one is not completely detached from fruitive activities, or is not completely attached to devotional service, such service is quickly effective."

Devotees may be divided into three classes. The devotee in the first or uppermost class is described as follows. He is very expert in the study of relevant scriptures, and he is also expert in putting forward arguments in terms of those scriptures. He can very nicely present conclusions with perfect discretion and can consider the ways of devotional service in a decisive way. He understands perfectly that the ultimate goal of life is to attain to the transcendental loving service of Kṛṣṇa, and he knows that Kṛṣṇa is the only object of worship and love. This first-class devotee is one who has strictly followed the rules and regulations under the training of a bona fide spiritual master and has sincerely obeyed him in accord with revealed scriptures. Thus, being fully trained to preach and become a spiritual master himself, he is considered first class. The first-class devotee never deviates from the principles of higher authority, and he attains firm faith in the scriptures by understanding with all reason and arguments. When we speak of arguments and reason, it means arguments and reason on the basis of revealed scriptures. The first-class devotee is not interested in dry speculative methods meant for wasting time. In other words, one who has attained a mature determination in the matter of devotional service can be accepted as the first-class devotee.

The second-class devotee has been defined by the following symptoms: he is not very expert in arguing on the strength of revealed scripture, but he has firm faith in the objective. The purport of this description is that the second-class devotee has firm faith in the procedure of devotional service unto Kṛṣṇa, but he may sometimes fail to offer arguments and decisions on the strength of revealed scripture to an opposing party. But at the same time he is still undaunted within himself as to his decision that Kṛṣṇa is the supreme object of worship.

The neophyte or third-class devotee is one whose faith is not strong and who, at the same time, does not recognize the decision of the revealed scripture. The neophyte's faith can be changed by someone else with strong arguments or by an opposite decision. Unlike the second-class devotee, who also cannot put forward arguments and evidences from the scripture, but who still has all faith in the objective, the neophyte has no firm faith in the objective. Thus he is called the neophyte devotee.

Further classification of the neophyte devotee is made in the *Bhagavad-gītā*. It is stated there that four classes of men—namely those who are distressed, those who are in need of money, those who are inquisitive and those who are wise—begin devotional service and come to the Lord for relief in the matter of their respective self-satisfaction. They go into some place of worship and pray to God for mitigation of material distress, or for some economic development, or to satisfy their inquisitiveness. And a wise man who simply realizes the greatness of God is also counted among the neophytes. Such beginners can be elevated to the second-class or first-class platform if they associate with pure devotees.

An example of the neophyte class is Mahārāja Dhruva. He was in need of his father's kingdom and therefore engaged himself in devotional service to the Lord. Then in the end, when he was completely purified, he declined to accept any material benediction from the Lord. Similarly, Gajendra was distressed and prayed to Kṛṣṇa for protection, after which he became a pure devotee. Similarly Sanaka, Sanātana, Sananda and Sanat-kumāra were all in the category of wise, saintly persons, and they were also attracted by devotional service. A similar thing happened to the assemblage in the Naimiṣāraṇya Forest, headed by the sage Śaunaka. They were inquisitive and were always asking Sūta Gosvāmī about Kṛṣṇa. Thus they achieved the association of a pure devotee and became pure devotees themselves. So that is the way of elevating oneself. In whatever condition one may be, if he is fortunate enough to associate with pure devotees, then very quickly he is elevated to the second-class or first-class platform.

These four types of devotees have been described in the Seventh Chapter of *Bhagavad-gītā,* and they have all been accepted as pious. Without becoming pious, no one can come to devotional service. It is explained in *Bhagavad-gītā* that only one who has continually executed pious activities and whose sinful reactions in life have completely stopped can take to Kṛṣṇa consciousness. Others cannot. The neophyte devotees are classified into four groups—the distressed, those in need of money, the inquisitive and the wise—according to their gradations of pious activities. Without pious activities, if a man is in a distressed condition he becomes an agnostic, a communist or something like that. Because he does not firmly believe in God, he thinks that he can adjust his distressed condition by totally disbelieving in Him.

Lord Kṛṣṇa, however, has explained in the *Gītā* that out of these four types of neophytes, the one who is wise is very dear to Him, because a wise man, if he is attached to Kṛṣṇa, is not seeking an exchange of material benefits. A wise man who becomes attached to Kṛṣṇa does not want any return from Him, either in the form of relieving distress or in gaining money. This means that from the very beginning his basic principle of attachment to Kṛṣṇa is, more or less, love. Furthermore, due to his wisdom and study of *śāstras* (scriptures), he can understand also that Kṛṣṇa is the Supreme Personality of Godhead.

It is confirmed in *Bhagavad-gītā* that after many, many births, when one becomes actually wise, he surrenders unto Vāsudeva, knowing perfectly well that Kṛṣṇa (Vāsudeva) is the origin and cause of all causes. Therefore, he sticks to the lotus feet of Kṛṣṇa and gradually develops love for Him. Although such a wise man is very dear to Kṛṣṇa, the others are also accepted as very magnanimous, because even though they are distressed or in need of money, they have come to Kṛṣṇa for satisfaction. Thus they are accepted as liberal, broad-minded *mahātmās*.

Without being elevated to the position of a *jñānī*, or wise man, one cannot stick to the principle of worshiping the Supreme Personality of Godhead. The less intelligent or those whose intelligence has been taken away by the spell of *māyā* are attached to different demigods on account of the influence of the modes of nature. The wise man is he who has thoroughly understood that he is spirit soul and not simply a body. Because he realizes that he is spirit and Kṛṣṇa is the supreme spirit, he knows that his intimate relationship should be with Kṛṣṇa, not with this body. The distressed and the man in want of money are in the material concept of life, because distress and need of money are both in relationship with this body. One who is inquisitive may be a little above the distressed and the man in need of money, but still he is on the material platform. But a wise man who seeks Kṛṣṇa knows perfectly well that he is spirit soul, or Brahman, and that Kṛṣṇa is the supreme spirit soul, or Parabrahman. He knows that the spirit soul, being subordinate and finite, should always dovetail himself with the infinite and supreme soul, Kṛṣṇa. That is the relationship of the wise man with Kṛṣṇa.

It can be concluded that a person who is freed from the bodily concept of life is an eligible candidate for pure devotional service. It is also confirmed in the *Bhagavad-gītā* that after Brahman realization, when one is freed from material anxieties and can see every living entity on an equal level, he is eligible to enter into devotional service.

As stated before, there are three kinds of happiness—material, spiritual and devotional. Devotional service and the happiness due to its execution are not possible as long as one is materially affected. If someone has desire for material enjoyment or for becoming one with the Supreme, these are both considered material concepts. Because the impersonalists cannot appreciate the spiritual happiness of association and the exchange of loving affairs with the Supreme Personality of Godhead, their ultimate goal is to become one with the Lord. This concept is simply an extension of the material idea. In the material world, everyone is trying to be the topmost head man among all his fellow men or neighbors. Either communally, socially or nationally, everyone is competing to be greater than all others, in the material concept of life. This greatness can be extended to the unlimited, so that one actually wants to become one with the greatest of all, the Supreme Lord. This is also a material concept, although maybe a little more advanced.

However, the perfect spiritual concept of life is complete knowledge of one's constitutional position, in which one knows enough to dovetail himself in the transcendental loving service of the Lord. One must know that he is finite and that the Lord is infinite. Thus it is not possible to actually become one with the Lord even if one aspires for this. It is simply not possible. Therefore, anyone who has any desire or aspiration for satisfying his senses by becoming more and more important, either in the material sense or in the spiritual sense, cannot actually relish the really sweet taste of devotional service. Śrīla Rūpa Gosvāmī has therefore compared possessing these *bhukti* (material) and *mukti* (liberation) desires with being influenced by the black art of a witch: in both cases one is in trouble. *Bhukti* means material enjoyment, and *mukti* means to become freed from material anxiety and to become one with the Lord. These desires are compared to being haunted by ghosts and witches, because while these aspirations for material enjoyment or spiritual oneness with the Supreme remain, no one can relish the actual transcendental taste of devotional service.

A pure devotee never cares for liberation. Lord Caitanya Mahāprabhu prayed to Kṛṣṇa, "My dear son of Nanda, I do not want any material happiness in the shape of many followers, nor immense opulence in wealth, nor any beautiful wife, nor do I want cessation from material existence. I may take birth many times, one after another, but what I pray from You is that My devotion unto You may always remain unflinching."

The attention of a pure devotee is so much attracted to glorification of the Lord's pastimes, name, qualities, forms, etc., that the devotee does not care for *mukti*. Śrī Bilvamaṅgala Ṭhākura has said, "If I am engaged in devotional service unto You, my dear Lord, then very easily can I perceive Your presence everywhere. And as far as liberation is concerned, I think liberation stands at my door with folded hands, waiting to serve me." To pure devotees, therefore, liberation and spiritual emancipation are not very important things.

In this connection, in the Third Canto of *Śrīmad-Bhāgavatam*, Chapter Twenty-five, verse 36, Kapiladeva has advised His mother, Devahūti, as follows: "My dear mother, My pure devotees are charmed by seeing My different forms, the beauty of My face, the structure of

My body so enchanting. My laughing, My pastimes and My glance appear to them so beautiful that their minds are always absorbed in thoughts of Me and their lives are dedicated fully unto Me. Although such people do not desire any kind of liberation or any kind of material happiness, still I give them a place among My associates in the supreme abode."

This evidence from *Śrīmad-Bhāgavatam* gives assurance to the pure devotee of being elevated to association with the Supreme Personality of Godhead. Śrīla Rūpa Gosvāmī remarks in this connection that one who is actually attracted by the beauty of the lotus feet of Śrī Kṛṣṇa or His service, and whose heart, by such attraction, is always full with transcendental bliss, will naturally never aspire after the liberation which is so valuable to the impersonalists.

A similar passage is also there in the Third Canto, Fourth Chapter, verse 15, of the same book, wherein Uddhava addresses Lord Kṛṣṇa and says, "My dear Lord, for persons who are engaged in Your transcendental loving service there is nothing worth obtaining from religiousness, economic development, sense gratification or liberation—although happiness from these different sources can be very easily had by them. In spite of such facilities, my dear Lord, I do not aspire to achieve any such results. My only prayer is that I may have unflinching faith and devotion unto Your lotus feet."

A similar passage appears in the Third Canto, Twenty-fifth Chapter, verse 34, wherein Kapiladeva instructs His mother and says, "My dear mother, devotees whose hearts are always filled in the service of My lotus feet and who are prepared to do anything for My satisfaction, especially those fortunate devotees who assemble together to understand My qualities, pastimes and form and thus glorify Me congregationally and derive transcendental pleasure therefrom, never desire to become one with Me. And what to speak of becoming one with Me, if they are offered a post like Mine in My abode, or opulence like Mine, or even personal association with Me with similar bodily features, they refuse to accept, because they are satisfied simply by being engaged in My devotional service."

In *Śrīmad-Bhāgavatam*, Fourth Canto, Ninth Chapter, verse 10, King Dhruva says, "My dear Lord, the transcendental pleasure derived by meditation upon Your lotus feet, which is enjoyed by the pure devotees, cannot be approached by the transcendental pleasure derived by the impersonalists through self-realization. So how can the fruitive workers, who at most can aspire to promotion to the higher heavenly planets, understand You, and how can they be described as enjoying a happiness similar to the devotees' happiness?"

4
Devotional Service Surpasses All Liberation

How much a devotee is seriously attached to the devotional service of the Supreme Personality of Godhead can be understood from the statement of Mahārāja Pṛthu (Ādi-rāja) which is described in *Śrīmad-Bhāgavatam,* Fourth Canto, Twentieth Chapter, verse 24. He prays to the Supreme Personality of Godhead thus: "My dear Lord, if after taking liberation I have no chance of hearing the glories of Your Lordship, glories chanted by pure devotees from the core of their hearts in praise of Your lotus feet, and if I have no chance for this honey of transcendental bliss, then I shall never ask for liberation or this so-called spiritual emancipation. I shall simply always pray unto Your Lordship that You may give me millions of tongues and millions of ears, so that I can constantly chant and hear of Your transcendental glories."

The impersonalists desire to merge into the existence of the Supreme, but without keeping their individuality they have no chance of hearing and chanting the glories of the Supreme Lord. Because they have no idea of the transcendental form of the Supreme Lord, there is no chance of their chanting and hearing of His transcendental activities. In other words, unless one is already beyond liberation, one cannot relish the transcendental glories of the Lord, nor can one understand the transcendental form of the Lord.

A similar statement is found in *Śrīmad-Bhāgavatam,* Fifth Canto, Fourteenth Chapter, verse 44. Śukadeva Gosvāmī addresses Parīkṣit Mahārāja there and says, "The great soul King Bharata was so much attached to the service of the lotus feet of Kṛṣṇa that he very easily gave up his lordship over the earthly planet and his affection for his children, society, friends, royal opulence and beautiful wife. He was so very lucky that the goddess of fortune was pleased to offer him all kinds of material concessions, but he never accepted any of these material opulences."

Śukadeva Gosvāmī praises this behavior of King Bharata very highly. He says, "Any person whose heart is attracted by the transcendental qualities of the Supreme Personality of Godhead, Madhusūdana, does not care even for that liberation which is aspired to by many great sages, what to speak of material opulences."

In the *Bhāgavatam,* Sixth Canto, Eleventh Chapter, verse 25, there is a similar statement by Vṛtrāsura, who addresses the Lord as follows: "My dear Lord, by leaving Your transcendental service I may be promoted to the planet called Dhruvaloka [the polestar], or I may gain lordship over all the planetary systems of the universe. But I do not aspire to this. Nor do I wish the mystic perfections of *yoga* practice, nor do I aspire to spiritual emancipation. All I wish for, my Lord, is Your association and transcendental service eternally."

This statement is confirmed by Lord Śiva in *Śrīmad-Bhāgavatam,* Sixth Canto, Seventeenth Chapter, verse 28, wherein Lord Śiva addresses Satī thus: "My dear Satī, persons who are devoted to Nārāyaṇa [Kṛṣṇa] are not afraid of anything. If they are elevated to the higher planetary systems, or if they get liberation from material contamination, or if they are pushed down to the hellish condition of life—or, in fact, in any situation whatever—they are not afraid of anything. Simply because they have taken shelter of the lotus feet of Nārāyaṇa, for them any position in the material world is as good as another."

There is a similar statement by Indra, the King of heaven, in *Śrīmad-Bhāgavatam,* Sixth Canto, Eighteenth Chapter, verse 74. There Indra addresses mother Diti in this manner: "My dear mother, persons who have given up all kinds of desire and are simply engaged in devotional service to the Lord know what is actually their self-interest. Such persons are actually serving their self-interests and are considered first-class experts in the matter of advancing to the perfectional stage of life."

In the Seventh Canto of the *Bhāgavatam,* Sixth Chapter, verse 25, Mahārāja Prahlāda says, "My dear friends born into atheistic families, if you can please the Supreme Personality of Godhead, Kṛṣṇa, then there is nothing more rare in this world. In other words, if the Supreme Lord Kṛṣṇa is pleased with you, then any desire you may have within the core of your heart can be fulfilled without any doubt. As such, what is the use of elevating yourself by the results of fruitive activities, which are automatically achieved in all events by the modes of material nature? And what is the use for you of spiritual emancipation or liberation from material bondage? If you are always engaged in chanting the glories of the Supreme Lord and always relishing the nectar of the lotus feet of the Lord, then there is no necessity for any of these." By this statement of Prahlāda Mahārāja it is clearly understood that one who takes pleasure in chanting and hearing the transcendental glories of the Lord has already surpassed all kinds of material benedictions, including the results of pious fruitive activities, sacrifices and even liberation from material bondage.

Similarly, in the same Seventh Canto, Eighth Chapter, verse 42, when the demigods are offering prayers to Lord Nṛsiṁha, Indra the King of heaven says, "O supreme one, these demons talk of our share of participation in the performances of ritualistic sacrifices, but simply by Your appearance as Lord Nṛsiṁhadeva You have saved us from terrible fears. Actually, our shares in the sacrificial performances are due to You only, because You are the supreme enjoyer of all sacrifices. You are the Supersoul of every living entity, and therefore You are the actual owner of everything. Long were our hearts always filled with fear of this demon, Hiraṇyakaśipu. But You are so kind toward us that by killing him You have removed that fear from within our hearts and have given us the chance to place Your Lordship within our hearts again. For persons who are engaged in the transcendental loving service of Your Lordship, all the opulences which were taken away from us by the demons are counted as nothing. Devotees do not care even for liberation, what to speak of these material opulences. Actually, we are not enjoyers of the fruits of sacrifices. Our only duty is to always be engaged in Your service, for You are the enjoyer of everything."

The purport of this statement by Indra is that beginning from Brahmā down to the insignificant ant, no living entities are meant for enjoying the material opulences. They are simply meant for offering everything to the supreme proprietor, the Personality of Godhead. By doing so, they automatically enjoy the benefit. The example can be cited again of the different parts of the body collecting foodstuffs and cooking them so that ultimately a meal may be offered to the stomach. After it has gone to the stomach, all the parts of the body equally enjoy the benefit of the meal. So, similarly, everyone's duty is to satisfy the Supreme Lord, and then automatically everyone will become satisfied.

A similar verse is found in the Eighth Canto, Third Chapter, of *Śrīmad-Bhāgavatam,* verse 20. Gajendra says there, "My dear Lord, I have no experience of the transcendental bliss derived from Your devotional service, so therefore I have asked from You some favor. But I know that persons who are pure devotees and have, by serving the lotus feet of great souls, become freed from all material desires, are always merged in the ocean of transcendental bliss and, as such, are always satisfied simply by glorifying Your auspicious characteristics. For them there is nothing else to aspire to or pray for."

In the Ninth Canto of the *Bhāgavatam,* Fourth Chapter, verse 67, the Lord of Vaikuṇṭha replies to Durvāsā Muni thus: "My pure devotees are always satisfied being engaged in devotional service, and therefore they do not aspire even after the five liberated stages, which are (1) to be one with Me, (2) to achieve residence on My planet, (3) to have My opulences, (4) to possess bodily features similar to Mine and (5) to gain personal association with Me. So when they are not interested even in these liberated positions, you can know how little they care for material opulences or material liberation."

There is a similar prayer by the *nāga-patnīs* (wives of the Kāliya serpent), in the Tenth Canto of *Śrīmad-Bhāgavatam,* Sixteenth Chapter, verse 37. The *nāga-patnīs* say there, "Dear Lord, the dust of Your lotus feet is very wonderful. Any person who is fortunate enough to achieve this dust does not care for heavenly planets, lordship over all the planetary systems, the mystic perfections of *yoga,* or even liberation from material existence. In other words, anyone who adores the dust of Your lotus feet does not care a fig for all other perfectional stages."

There is a similar statement in the Tenth Canto, Eighty-seventh Chapter, verse 21, wherein the Śrutis, the *Vedas* personified, pray to the Lord as follows: "Dear Lord, it is very difficult to understand spiritual knowledge. Your appearance here, just as You are, is to explain to us this most difficult subject of knowledge of the spirit. As such, Your devotees who have left their domestic comforts to associate with the liberated *ācāryas* [teachers] are now fully merged in the devotional service of Your Lordship, and thus they do not care for any so-called liberation."

In explaining this verse it should be noted that spiritual knowledge means understanding the self and the Supersoul, or Superself. The individual soul and the Supersoul are qualitatively one, and therefore both of them are known as Brahman, or spirit. But knowledge of Brahman is very difficult to understand. There are so many philosophers engaged in the matter of understanding the soul, but they are unable to make any tangible advancement. It is confirmed in *Bhagavad-gītā* that out of many millions of persons, only one may try to understand what is spiritual knowledge, and out of many such persons who are trying to understand, only one or a few may know what is the Supreme Personality of Godhead. So this verse says that spiritual knowledge is very difficult to achieve, and so in order to make it more easily attainable, the Supreme Lord Himself comes in His original form as Śrī Kṛṣṇa and gives His instruction directly to an associate like Arjuna, just so that the people in general may take advantage of this spiritual knowledge. This verse also explains that liberation means having completely given up all the material comforts of life. Those who are impersonalists are satisfied by simply being liberated from the material circumstances, but those who are devotees can automatically give up material life and also enjoy the transcendental bliss of hearing and chanting the wonderful activities of Lord Kṛṣṇa.

In the Eleventh Canto of *Śrīmad-Bhāgavatam,* Twentieth Chapter, verse 34, Lord Kṛṣṇa says to Uddhava, "My dear Uddhava, the devotees who have completely taken shelter of My service are so steadfast in devotional service that they have no other desire. Even if they are offered the four kinds of spiritual opulences,* they will refuse to accept them. So what to speak of their desiring anything within the material world!" Similarly, Lord Kṛṣṇa says in another passage of the *Bhāgavatam,* Eleventh Canto, Fourteenth Chapter, verse 14, "My dear Uddhava, a person whose consciousness is completely absorbed in My thought and activities does not aspire even to occupy the post of Brahmā, or the post of Indra, or the post of lordship over the planets, or the eight kinds of mystic perfections, or even liberation itself." In the Twelfth Canto of *Śrīmad-Bhāgavatam,* Tenth Chapter, verse 6, Lord Śiva says to Devī, "My dear Devī, this great *brāhmaṇa* sage Mārkaṇḍeya has attained unflinching faith and devotion unto the Supreme Personality of Godhead, and as such he does not aspire after any benedictions, including liberation from the material world."

*The fifth kind of liberation, merging with the Supreme, is not considered an opulence in spiritual variegated existence.

Similarly, there is a statement in *Padma Purāṇa* describing the ritualistic function during the month of Kārttika (October–November). During this month, in Vṛndāvana it is the regulative principle to pray daily to Lord Kṛṣṇa in His Dāmodara form. The Dāmodara form refers to Kṛṣṇa in His childhood when He was tied up with rope by His mother, Yaśodā. *Dāma* means "ropes," and *udara* means "the abdomen." So Mother Yaśodā, being very disturbed by naughty Kṛṣṇa, bound Him round the abdomen with a rope, and thus Kṛṣṇa is named Dāmodara. During the month of Kārttika, Dāmodara is prayed to as follows: "My dear Lord, You are the Lord of all, the giver of all benedictions." There are many demigods, like Lord Brahmā and Lord Śiva, who sometimes offer benedictions to their respective devotees. For example, Rāvaṇa was blessed with many benedictions by Lord Śiva, and Hiraṇyakaśipu was blessed by Lord Brahmā. But even Lord Śiva and Lord Brahmā depend upon the benedictions of Lord Kṛṣṇa, and therefore Kṛṣṇa is addressed as the Lord of all benefactors. As such, Lord Kṛṣṇa can offer His devotees anything they want, but still, the devotee's prayer continues, "I do not ask You for liberation or any material facility up to the point of liberation. What I want as Your favor is that I may always think of Your form in which I see You now, as Dāmodara. You are so beautiful and attractive that my mind does not want anything besides this wonderful form." In this same prayer, there is another passage, in which it is said, "My dear Lord Dāmodara, once when You were playing as a naughty boy in the house of Nanda Mahārāja, You broke the box containing yogurt, and because of that, Mother Yaśodā considered You an offender and tied You with rope to the household grinding mortar. At that time You delivered two sons of Kuvera, Nalakūvara and Maṇigrīva, who were staying there as two *arjuna* trees in the yard of Nanda Mahārāja. My only request is that by Your merciful pastimes You may similarly deliver me."

The story behind this verse is that the two sons of Kuvera (the treasurer of the demigods) were puffed up on account of the opulence of their father, and so once on a heavenly planet they were enjoying themselves in a lake with some naked damsels of heaven. At that time the great saint Nārada Muni was passing on the road and was sorry to see the behavior of the sons of Kuvera. Seeing Nārada passing by, the damsels of heaven covered their bodies with cloth, but the two sons, being drunkards, did not have this decency. Nārada became angry with their behavior and cursed them thus: "You have no sense, so it is better if you become trees instead of the sons of Kuvera." Upon hearing this, the boys came to their senses and begged Nārada to be pardoned for their offenses. Nārada then said, "Yes, you shall become trees, *arjuna* trees, and you will stand in the courtyard of Nanda Mahārāja. But Kṛṣṇa Himself will appear in time as the foster son of Nanda, and He will deliver you." In other words, the curse of Nārada was a benediction to the sons of Kuvera because indirectly it was foretold that they would be able to receive the favor of Lord Kṛṣṇa. After that, Kuvera's two sons stood as two big *arjuna* trees in the courtyard of Nanda Mahārāja until Lord Dāmodara, in order to fulfill the desire of Nārada, dragged the grinding mortar to which He was tied and struck the two trees, violently causing them to fall down. From out of these fallen trees came Nalakūvara and Maṇigrīva, who had by then become great devotees of the Lord.

There is a passage in the *Hayaśīrṣa-pañcarātra* which states, "My dear Lord, O Supreme Personality of Godhead, I do not want any resultant benediction from my religious life, nor do I want any economic development, nor do I want to enjoy sense gratification, nor liberation. I simply pray to be an eternal servant at Your lotus feet. Kindly oblige me and give me this benediction."

In the same *Hayaśīrṣa-pañcarātra,* after Nṛsiṁhadeva wanted to give benedictions to Prahlāda Mahārāja, Prahlāda did not accept any material benediction and simply asked the favor of the Lord to remain His eternal devotee. In this connection, Prahlāda Mahārāja cited the example of Hanumān, the eternal servitor of Lord Rāmacandra, who also set an example by never asking any material favor from the Lord. He always remained engaged in the Lord's service. That is the ideal character of Hanumān, for which he is still worshiped by all devotees. Prahlāda Mahārāja also offered his respectful obeisances unto Hanumān. There is a well-known verse spoken by Hanumān in which he says, "My dear Lord, if You like You can give me salvation from this material existence, or the privilege of merging into Your existence, but I do not wish any of these things. I do not want anything which diminishes my relationship with You as servant to master, even after liberation."

In a similar passage in the *Nārada-pañcarātra* it is stated, "My dear

Lord, I do not wish any perfectional stage by performing the ritualistic religious ceremonies or by economic development or by sense gratification or liberation. I simply pray that You grant me the favor of keeping me under Your lotus feet. I do not wish any kind of liberation such as *sālokya* (to reside on Your planet) or *sārūpya* (to have the same bodily features as You). I simply pray for Your favor that I may be always engaged in Your loving service."

Similarly, in the Sixth Canto, Fourteenth Chapter, verses 4–6, of *Śrīmad-Bhāgavatam,* Mahārāja Parīkṣit inquires from Śukadeva Gosvāmī, "My dear *brāhmaṇa,* I understand that the demon Vṛtrāsura was a greatly sinful person and that his mentality was completely absorbed in the modes of passion and ignorance. How did he develop to such a perfectional stage of devotional service to Nārāyaṇa? I have heard that even great persons who have undergone severe austerities and who are liberated with full knowledge must strive to become devotees of the Lord. It is understood that such persons are very rare and almost never to be seen, so I am astonished that Vṛtrāsura became such a devotee!"

In the above verses, the most important thing to be noted is that there may be many liberated persons who have merged into the existence of the impersonal Brahman, but a devotee of the Supreme Personality of Godhead, Nārāyaṇa, is very, very rare. Even out of millions of liberated persons, only one is fortunate enough to become a devotee.

In *Śrīmad-Bhāgavatam,* First Canto, Eighth Chapter, verse 20, Queen Kuntī is praying to Lord Kṛṣṇa at the time of His departure, "My dear Kṛṣṇa, You are so great that You are inconceivable even to great stalwart scholars and *paramahaṁsas* [fully liberated souls]. So if such great sages, who are transcendental to all the reactions of material existence, are unable to know You, then as far as we are concerned, belonging to the less intelligent woman class, how is it possible for us to know Your glories? How can we understand You?" In this verse, the particular thing to be noted is that the Personality of Godhead is not understood by great liberated persons, but only by devotees such as Queen Kuntī in her humbleness. Although she was a woman and was considered less intelligent than a man, still she realized the glories of Kṛṣṇa. That is the purport of this verse.

Another passage which is very important is in *Śrīmad-Bhāgavatam,* First Canto, Seventh Chapter, verse 10, and is called "the *ātmārāma* verse." In this *ātmārāma* verse it is stated that even those who are completely liberated from material contamination are attracted by the transcendental qualities of Lord Kṛṣṇa.* The purport of this verse is that a liberated soul has absolutely no desire at all for material enjoyment; he is wholly freed from all kinds of material desires, yet still he is irresistibly attracted by the desire to hear and understand the pastimes of the Lord. We may therefore conclude that the glories and pastimes of the Lord are not material. Otherwise, how could the liberated persons known as *ātmārāmas* be attracted by such pastimes? That is the important point in this verse.

From the above statement it is found that a devotee is not after any of the stages of liberation. There are five stages of liberation, already explained as being (1) to become one with the Lord, (2) to live on the same planet as the Lord, (3) to obtain the same bodily features as the Lord, (4) to have the same opulences as the Lord and (5) to have constant association with the Lord. Out of these five liberated stages, the one which is known as *sāyujya,* or to merge into the existence of the Lord, is the last to be accepted by a devotee. The other four liberations, although not desired by devotees, still are not against the devotional ideals. Some of the liberated persons who have achieved these four stages of liberation may also develop affection for Kṛṣṇa and be promoted to the Goloka Vṛndāvana planet in the spiritual sky. In other words, those who are already promoted to the Vaikuṇṭha planets and who possess the four kinds of liberation may also sometimes develop affection for Kṛṣṇa and become promoted to Kṛṣṇaloka.

So those who are in the four liberated states may still be going through different stages of existence. In the beginning they may want the opulences of Kṛṣṇa, but at the mature stage the dormant love for Kṛṣṇa exhibited in Vṛndāvana becomes prominent in their hearts. As such, the pure devotees never accept the liberation of *sāyujya,* to become one with the Supreme, though sometimes they may accept as favorable the other four liberated states.

Out of many kinds of devotees of the Supreme Personality of Godhead, the one who is attracted to the original form of the Lord, Kṛṣṇa in

*This *ātmārāma* verse was nicely explained by Lord Caitanya to Sanātana Gosvāmī and Sārvabhauma Bhaṭṭācārya. There are detailed explanations of this verse in the author's *Śrī Caitanya-caritāmṛta* and *Teachings of Lord Caitanya.*

Vṛndāvana, is considered to be the foremost, first-class devotee. Such a devotee is never attracted by the opulences of Vaikuṇṭha, or even of Dvārakā, the royal city where Kṛṣṇa ruled. The conclusion of Śrī Rūpa Gosvāmī is that the devotees who are attracted by the pastimes of the Lord in Gokula, or Vṛndāvana,* are the topmost devotees.

A devotee who is attached to a particular form of the Lord does not wish to redirect his devotion to other forms. For example, Hanumān, the devotee of Lord Rāmacandra, knew that there is no difference between Lord Rāmacandra and Lord Nārāyaṇa, and yet he still wanted to render service only unto Lord Rāmacandra. That is due to the specific attraction of a particular devotee. There are many, many forms of the Lord, but Kṛṣṇa is still the original form. Though all of the devotees of the different forms of the Lord are in the same category, still it is said that those who are devotees of Lord Kṛṣṇa are the topmost in the list of all devotees.

---

*Vṛndāvana is the transcendental place where Kṛṣṇa enjoys His eternal pastimes as a boy, and it is considered the topmost sphere in all existence. When this Vṛndāvana is exhibited in the material world the place is known as Gokula, and in the spiritual world it is called Goloka, or Goloka Vṛndāvana.

5

The Purity of Devotional Service

All of the previous instructions imparted by Śrīla Rūpa Gosvāmī in his broad statements can be summarized thus: as long as one is materially inclined or desirous of merging into the spiritual effulgence, one cannot enter into the realm of pure devotional service. Next, Rūpa Gosvāmī states that devotional service is transcendental to all material considerations and that it is not limited to any particular country, class, society or circumstance. As stated in *Śrīmad-Bhāgavatam*, devotional service is transcendental and has no cause. Devotional service is executed without any hope for gain, and it cannot be checked by any material circumstances. It is open for all, without any distinction, and it is the constitutional occupation of the living entities.

In the Middle Ages, after the disappearance of Lord Caitanya's great associate Lord Nityānanda, a class of priestly persons claimed to be the descendants of Nityānanda, calling themselves the *gosvāmī* caste. They further claimed that the practice and spreading of devotional service belonged only to their particular class, which was known as Nityānanda-vaṁśa. In this way, they exercised their artificial power for some time, until Śrīla Bhaktisiddhānta Sarasvatī Ṭhākura, the powerful *ācārya* of the Gauḍīya Vaiṣṇava *sampradāya*, completely smashed their idea. There was a great hard struggle for some time, but it has turned out successfully, and it is now correctly and practically established that devotional service is not restricted to a particular class of men. Besides that, anyone who is engaged in devotional service is already at the status of being a high-class *brāhmaṇa*. So Śrīla Bhaktisiddhānta Sarasvatī Ṭhākura's struggle for this movement has come out successful.

It is on the basis of his position that anyone can now become a Gauḍīya Vaiṣṇava, from any part of the world or any part of the universe. Anyone who is a pure Vaiṣṇava is situated transcendentally, and therefore the highest qualification in the material world, namely to be in the mode of goodness, has already been achieved by such a person. Our Kṛṣṇa consciousness movement in the Western world is based on the above-mentioned proposition of Śrīla Bhaktisiddhānta Sarasvatī Gosvāmī Prabhupāda, our spiritual master. On his authority, we are claiming members from all sections of the Western countries. The so-called *brāhmaṇas* claim that one who is not born into a *brāhmaṇa* family cannot receive the sacred thread and cannot become a high-grade Vaiṣṇava. But we do not accept such a theory, because it is not supported by Rūpa Gosvāmī nor by the strength of the various scriptures.

Śrīla Rūpa Gosvāmī specifically mentions herein that every man has the birthright to accept devotional service and to become Kṛṣṇa conscious. He has given many evidences from many scriptures, and he has especially quoted one passage from *Padma Purāṇa,* wherein the sage Vasiṣṭha tells King Dilīpa, "My dear King, everyone has the right to execute devotional service, just as he has the right to take early bath in the month of Māgha [December–January]." There is more evidence in the *Skanda Purāṇa,* in the *Kāśī-khaṇḍa* portion, where it is said, "In the country known as Mayūradhvaja, the lower-caste people, who are considered less than *śūdras,* are also initiated in the Vaiṣṇava cult of devotional service. And when they are properly dressed, with *tilaka* on their bodies and beads in their hands and on their necks, they appear to be coming from Vaikuṇṭha. In fact, they look so very beautiful that immediately they surpass the ordinary *brāhmaṇas.*"

Thus a Vaiṣṇava automatically becomes a *brāhmaṇa.* This idea is also supported by Sanātana Gosvāmī in his book *Hari-bhakti-vilāsa,* which is the Vaiṣṇava guide. Therein he has clearly stated that any person who is properly initiated into the Vaiṣṇava cult certainly becomes a *brāhmaṇa,* as much as the metal known as *kaṁsa* (bell metal) is turned into gold by the mixture of mercury. A bona fide spiritual master, under the guidance of authorities, can turn anyone to the Vaiṣṇava cult so that naturally he may come to the topmost position of a *brāhmaṇa.*

Śrīla Rūpa Gosvāmī warns, however, that if a person is properly initiated by a bona fide spiritual master, he should not think that simply by the acceptance of such initiation his business is then finished. One still has to follow the rules and regulations very carefully. If after accepting the spiritual master and being initiated one does not follow the rules and regulations of devotional service, then he is again fallen. One must be very vigilant to remember that he is the part and parcel of the transcendental body of Kṛṣṇa, and that it is his duty as part and parcel to give service to the whole, or Kṛṣṇa. If we do not render service to Kṛṣṇa then again we fall down. In other words, simply becoming initiated does not elevate one to the position of a high-class *brāhmaṇa*. One also has to discharge the duties and follow the regulative principles very rigidly.

Śrī Rūpa Gosvāmī also says that if one is regularly discharging devotional service, there will be no question of a falldown. But even if circumstantially there is some falldown, the Vaiṣṇava need have nothing to do with the *prāyaścitta,* the ritualistic ceremony for purification. If someone falls down from the principles of devotional service, he need not take to the *prāyaścitta* performances for reformation. He simply has to execute the rules and regulations for discharging devotional service, and this is sufficient for his reinstatement. This is the mystery of the Vaiṣṇava (devotional) cult.

Practically there are three processes for elevating one to the platform of spiritual consciousness. These processes are called *karma, jñāna* and *bhakti*. Ritualistic performances are in the field of *karma*. Speculative processes are in the field of *jñāna*. One who has taken to *bhakti,* the devotional service of the Lord, need have nothing to do with *karma* or *jñāna*. It has been already explained that pure devotional service is without any tinge of *karma* or *jñāna*. *Bhakti* should have no tinge of philosophical speculation or ritualistic performances.

In this connection Śrīla Rūpa Gosvāmī gives evidence from *Śrīmad-Bhāgavatam,* Eleventh Canto, Twenty-first Chapter, verse 2, in which Lord Kṛṣṇa says to Uddhava, "The distinction between qualification and disqualification may be made in this way: persons who are already elevated in discharging devotional service will never again take shelter of the processes of fruitive activity or philosophical speculation. If one sticks to devotional service and is conducted by regulative principles given by the authorities and *ācāryas,* that is the best qualification."

This statement is supported in *Śrīmad-Bhāgavatam,* First Canto, Fifth Chapter, verse 17, wherein Śrī Nārada Muni advises Vyāsadeva thus: "Even if one does not execute his specific occupational duty but immediately takes direct shelter of the lotus feet of Hari [Kṛṣṇa], there will be no fault on his part, and in all circumstances his position is secure. Even if, by some bad association, he falls down while executing devotional service, or if he doesn't finish the complete course of devotional service and dies untimely, still he is not at a loss. A person who is simply discharging his occupational duty in *varṇa* and *āśrama,* however, with no Kṛṣṇa consciousness, practically does not gain the true benefit of human life." The purport is that all conditioned souls who are engaged very frantically in activities for sense gratification, without knowing that this process will never help them get out of material contamination, are awarded only with repeated births and deaths.

In the Fifth Canto of *Śrīmad-Bhāgavatam* it is clearly stated by Ṛṣabhadeva to His sons, "Persons engaged in fruitive activities are repeatedly accepting birth and death, and until they develop a loving feeling for Vāsudeva, there will be no question of getting out from these stringent laws of material nature." As such, any person who is very seriously engaged in his occupational duties in the *varṇas* and *āśramas,* and who does not develop love for the Supreme Personality of Godhead, Vāsudeva, should be understood to be simply spoiling his human form of life.

This is confirmed also in the Eleventh Canto of *Śrīmad-Bhāgavatam,* Eleventh Chapter, verse 32, in which the Lord says to Uddhava, "My dear Uddhava, any person who takes shelter of Me in complete surrender and follows My instructions, giving up all occupational duties, is to be considered the first-class man." In this statement of the Supreme Personality of Godhead, it is understood that people who are generally attracted to philanthropic, ethical, moral, altruistic, political and social welfare activities may be considered nice men only in the calculation of the material world. From *Śrīmad-Bhāgavatam* and other authentic Vedic scriptures we learn further that if a person simply acts in Kṛṣṇa consciousness and discharges devotional service, he is considered to be far, far better situated than all of those persons engaged in philanthropic, ethical, moral, altruistic and social welfare activities.

The same thing is still more emphatically confirmed in *Śrīmad-Bhāgavatam,* Eleventh Canto, Fifth Chapter, verse 41, in which Karabhājana Muni addresses Mahārāja Nimi as follows: "My dear King, if someone gives up his occupational duties as they are prescribed for the different *varṇas* and *āśramas,* but takes complete shelter, surrendering himself unto the lotus feet of the Lord, such a person is no more a debtor, nor has he any obligation to perform the different kinds of activities we render to the great sages, ancestors, living entities and family and society members. Nor has he any need to bother executing the five kinds of *yajñas* [sacrifices] for becoming free from sinful contamination. Simply by discharging devotional service, he is freed from all kinds of obligations." The purport is that as soon as a man takes his birth, he is immediately indebted to so many sources. He is indebted to the great sages because he profits by reading their authoritative scriptures and books. For example, we take advantage of the books written by Vyāsadeva. Vyāsadeva has left for us all the *Vedas*. Before Vyāsadeva's writing, the Vedic literature was simply heard, and the disciples would learn the *mantras* quickly by hearing and not by reading. Later on, Vyāsadeva thought it wise to write down the *Vedas*, because in this age people are short-memoried and unable to remember all the instructions given by the spiritual master. Therefore, he left all the Vedic knowledge in the form of books, such as the *Purāṇas*, *Vedānta*, *Mahābhārata* and *Śrīmad-Bhāgavatam*.

There are many other sages, like Śaṅkarācārya, Gautama Muni and Nārada Muni, to whom we are indebted because we take advantage of their knowledge. Similarly, we are obliged to our forefathers, because we take our birth in a particular family, where we take all advantages and inherit property. Therefore, we are indebted to the forefathers and have to offer them *piṇḍa* (*prasāda*) after they are dead. Similarly, to the people in general we are also indebted, as well as to our relatives, friends and even animals such as cows and dogs who render us so much service.

In this way, we are indebted to the demigods, to the forefathers, to the sages, to the animals and to society in general. It is our duty to repay them all by proper discharge of service. But by the one stroke of devotional service, if someone gives up all obligations and simply surrenders unto the Supreme Personality of Godhead, he is no longer a debtor, nor obliged to any other source of benefit.

In *Bhagavad-gītā* also, the Lord says, "Give up all your occupations and just become surrendered unto Me. I give you assurance that I shall give you protection from all sinful reactions." One may think that because he is surrendering unto the Supreme Personality of Godhead he will not be able to perform all of his other obligations. But the Lord says repeatedly, "Don't hesitate. Don't consider that because you are giving up all other engagements there will be some flaw in your life.

Don't think like that. I will give you all protection." That is the assurance of Lord Kṛṣṇa in *Bhagavad-gītā.*

There is additional evidence in the *Agastya-saṁhitā:* "As the regulative principles of scripture are not required by a liberated person, so the ritualistic principles indicated in the Vedic supplements are also not required for a person duly engaged in the service of Lord Rāmacandra." In other words, the devotees of Lord Rāmacandra, or Kṛṣṇa, are already liberated persons and are not required to follow all the regulative principles mentioned in the ritualistic portions of the Vedic literature.

Similarly, in the Eleventh Canto of *Śrīmad-Bhāgavatam,* Fifth Chapter, verse 42, Karabhājana Muni addresses King Nimi and says, "My dear King, a person who has given up the worship of the demigods and has completely concentrated his energy in the devotional service of the Supreme Personality of Godhead has become very, very dear to the Lord. As such, if by chance or mistake he does something which is forbidden, there is no need for him to perform any purificatory ceremonies. Because the Lord is situated within his heart, He takes compassion for the devotee's accidental mistake and corrects him from within." It is also confirmed in *Bhagavad-gītā* in many places that the Supreme Personality of Godhead, Kṛṣṇa, takes a special interest in His devotees and declares emphatically that nothing can cause His devotees to fall down. He is always protecting them.

6
How to Discharge Devotional Service

Śrīla Rūpa Gosvāmī states that his elder brother (Sanātana Gosvāmī) has compiled *Hari-bhakti-vilāsa* for the guidance of the Vaiṣṇavas and therein has mentioned many rules and regulations to be followed by the Vaiṣṇavas. Some of them are very important and prominent, and Śrīla Rūpa Gosvāmī will now mention these very important items for our benefit. The purport of this statement is that Śrīla Rūpa Gosvāmī proposes to mention only basic principles, not details. For example, a basic principle is that one has to accept a spiritual master. Exactly how one follows the instructions of his spiritual master is considered a detail. For example, if one is following the instruction of his spiritual master and that instruction is different from the instructions of another spiritual master, this is called detailed information. But the basic principle of acceptance of a spiritual master is good everywhere, although the details may be different. Śrīla Rūpa Gosvāmī does not wish to enter into details here, but wants to place before us only the principles.

He mentions the basic principles as follows: (1) accepting the shelter of the lotus feet of a bona fide spiritual master, (2) becoming initiated by the spiritual master and learning how to discharge devotional service from him, (3) obeying the orders of the spiritual master with faith and devotion, (4) following in the footsteps of great *ācāryas* (teachers) under the direction of the spiritual master, (5) inquiring from the spiritual master how to advance in Kṛṣṇa consciousness, (6) being prepared to give up anything material for the satisfaction of the Supreme Personality of Godhead, Śrī Kṛṣṇa (this means that when we are engaged in the devotional service of Kṛṣṇa, we must be prepared to give up something which we may not like to give up, and also we have to accept something which we may not like to accept), (7) residing in a sacred place of pilgrimage like Dvārakā or Vṛndāvana, (8) accepting only what is necessary, or dealing with the material world only as far as necessary, (9) observing the fasting day on Ekādaśī and (10) worshiping sacred trees like the banyan tree.

These ten items are preliminary necessities for beginning the discharge of devotional service in regulative principles. In the beginning, if a neophyte devotee observes the above-mentioned ten principles, surely he will quickly make good advancement in Kṛṣṇa consciousness.

The next set of instructions is listed as follows: (1) One should rigidly give up the company of nondevotees. (2) One should not instruct a person who is not desirous of accepting devotional service. (3) One should not be very enthusiastic about constructing costly temples or monasteries. (4) One should not try to read too many books, nor should one develop the idea of earning his livelihood by lecturing on or professionally reciting *Śrīmad-Bhāgavatam* or *Bhagavad-gītā*. (5) One should not be neglectful in ordinary dealings. (6) One should not be under the spell of lamentation in loss or jubilation in gain. (7) One should not disrespect the demigods. (8) One should not give unnecessary trouble to any living entity. (9) One should carefully avoid the various offenses in chanting the holy name of the Lord or in worshiping the Deity in the temple. (10) One should be very intolerant toward the blasphemy of the Supreme Personality of Godhead, Kṛṣṇa, or His devotees.

Without following the above-mentioned ten principles, one cannot properly elevate himself to the platform of *sādhana-bhakti,* or devotional service in practice. Altogether, Śrīla Rūpa Gosvāmī mentions twenty items, and all of them are very important. Out of the twenty, the first three—namely accepting the shelter of a bona fide spiritual master, taking initiation from him and serving him with respect and reverence—are the most important.

The next important items are as follows: (1) One should decorate the body with *tilaka,* which is the sign of the Vaiṣṇavas. (The idea is that as soon as a person sees these marks on the body of the Vaiṣṇava, he will immediately remember Kṛṣṇa. Lord Caitanya said that a Vaiṣṇava is he who, when seen, reminds one of Kṛṣṇa. Therefore, it is essential that a Vaiṣṇava mark his body with *tilaka* to remind others of Kṛṣṇa.) (2) In marking such *tilaka,* sometimes one may write Hare Kṛṣṇa on the body. (3) One should accept flowers and garlands that have been offered to the Deity and the spiritual master and put them on one's body. (4) One should learn to dance before the Deity. (5) One should learn to bow down immediately upon seeing the Deity or the spiritual master. (6) As soon as one visits a temple of Lord Kṛṣṇa, one must stand up. (7) When the Deity is being borne for a stroll in the street, a devotee should immediately follow the procession. (In this connection it may be noted that in India, especially in Viṣṇu temples, the system is that apart from the big Deity who is permanently situated in the main area of the temple, there is a set of smaller Deities which are taken in procession in the evening. In some temples it is the custom to hold a big procession in the evening with a band playing and a nice big umbrella over the Deities, who sit on decorated thrones on the cart or palanquin, which is carried by devotees. The Deities come out onto the street and travel in the neighborhood while the people of the neighborhood come out to offer *prasāda*. The residents of the neighborhood all follow the procession, so it is a very nice scene. When the Deity is coming out, the servitors in the temple put forward the daily accounts before Them: so much was the collection, so much was the expenditure. The whole idea is that the Deity is considered to be the proprietor of the whole establishment, and all the priests and other people taking care of the temple are considered to be the servants of the Deity. This system is very, very old and is still followed. So, therefore, it is mentioned here that when the Deity is on stroll the people should follow behind.) (8) A devotee must visit a Viṣṇu temple at least once or twice every day, morning and evening. (In Vṛndāvana this system is followed very strictly. All the devotees in town go every morning and evening to visit different temples. Therefore during these times there are considerable crowds all over the city. There are about five thousand temples in Vṛndavana city. Of course it is not possible to visit all the temples, but there are at least one dozen very big and important temples which were started by the Gosvāmīs and which should be visited.) (9) One must circumambulate the temple building at least three times. (In every temple there is an arrangement to go around the temple at least three times. Some devotees go around more than three times—ten times, fifteen times—according to their vows. The Gosvāmīs used to circumambulate Govardhana Hill.) One should also circumambulate the whole Vṛndāvana area. (10) One must worship the Deity in the temple according to the regulative principles. (Offering *ārati* and *prasāda*, decorating the Deity, etc.—these things must be observed regularly.) (11) One must render personal service to the Deities. (12) One must sing. (13) One must perform *saṅkīrtana.* (14) One must chant. (15) One must offer prayers. (16) One must recite notable prayers. (17) One must taste *mahā-prasāda* (food from the very plate offered before the Deities). (18) One must drink *caraṇāmṛta* (water from the bathing of the Deities, which is offered to guests). (19) One must smell the incense and flowers offered to the Deity. (20) One must touch the lotus feet of the Deity. (21) One must see the Deity with great devotion. (22) One must offer *ārati* (*ārātrika*) at different times. (23) One must hear about the Lord and His pastimes from *Śrīmad-Bhāgavatam, Bhagavad-gītā* and similar books. (24) One must pray to the Deity for His mercy. (25) One should remember the Deity. (26) One should meditate upon the Deity. (27) One should render some voluntary service. (28) One should think of the Lord as one's friend. (29) One should offer everything to the Lord. (30) One should offer a favorite article (such as food or a garment). (31) One should take all kinds of risks and perform all endeavors for Kṛṣṇa's benefit. (32) In every condition, one should be a surrendered soul. (33) One should pour water on the *tulasī* tree. (34) One should regularly hear *Śrīmad-Bhāgavatam* and similar literature. (35) One should live in a sacred place like Mathurā, Vṛndāvana or Dvārakā. (36) One should offer service to Vaiṣṇavas (devotees). (37) One should arrange one's devotional service according to one's means. (38) In the month of Kārttika (October and November), one should make arrangements for special services. (39) During Janmāṣṭamī (the time of Kṛṣṇa's appearance in this world) one should observe a special service. (40) One should do whatever is done with great care and devotion for the Deity. (41) One should relish the pleasure of *Bhāgavatam* reading among devotees and not among outsiders. (42) One should associate with devotees who are considered more advanced. (43) One should chant the holy name of the Lord. (44) One should live in the jurisdiction of Mathurā.

Now, the total regulative principles come to an aggregate of sixty-four items. As we have mentioned, the first are the primary ten regulative principles. Then come the secondary ten regulative principles, and added to these are forty-four other activities. So all together there are sixty-four items for discharging the regulative practice of devotional service. Out of these sixty-four items, five items—namely worshiping the Deity, hearing *Śrīmad-Bhāgavatam,* associating among the devotees, *saṅkīrtana,* and living in Mathurā—are very important.

The sixty-four items of devotional service should include all of our activities of body, mind and speech. As stated in the beginning, the regulative principle of devotional service enjoins that all of our senses must be employed in the service of the Lord. Exactly how they can be thus employed is described in the above sixty-four items. Now, Śrīla Rūpa Gosvāmī will give evidence from different scriptures supporting the authenticity of many of these points.

7

Evidence Regarding Devotional Principles

Accepting the Shelter of a Bona Fide Spiritual Master

In the Eleventh Canto of *Śrīmad-Bhāgavatam,* Third Chapter, verse 21, Prabuddha tells Mahārāja Nimi, "My dear King, please know for certain that in the material world there is no happiness. It is simply a mistake to think that there is happiness here, because this place is full of nothing but miserable conditions. Any person who is seriously desirous of achieving real happiness must seek out a bona fide spiritual master and take shelter of him by initiation. The qualification of a spiritual master is that he must have realized the conclusions of the scriptures by deliberation and arguments and thus be able to convince others of these conclusions. Such great personalities who have taken shelter of the Supreme Godhead, leaving aside all material considerations, are to be understood as bona fide spiritual masters. Everyone should try to find such a bona fide spiritual master in order to fulfill his mission of life, which is to transfer himself to the plane of spiritual bliss."

The purport is that one should not accept as a spiritual master someone who is fool number one, who has no direction according to the scriptural injunctions, whose character is doubtful, who does not follow the principles of devotional service, or who has not conquered the influence of the six sense-gratifying agents. The six agents of sense gratification are the tongue, the genitals, the belly, anger, the mind and words. Anyone who has practiced controlling these six is permitted to make disciples all over the world. To accept such a spiritual master is the crucial point for advancement in spiritual life. One who is fortunate enough to come under the shelter of a bona fide spiritual master is sure to traverse the path of spiritual salvation without any doubt.

Accepting Initiation from the Spiritual Master and Receiving Instructions from Him

Sage Prabuddha continued to speak to the King as follows: "My dear King, a disciple has to accept the spiritual master not only as spiritual master, but also as the representative of the Supreme Personality of Godhead and the Supersoul. In other words, the disciple should accept the spiritual master as God, because he is the external manifestation of Kṛṣṇa. This is confirmed in every scripture, and a disciple should accept the spiritual master as such. One should learn *Śrīmad-Bhāgavatam* seriously and with all respect and veneration for the spiritual master. Hearing and speaking *Śrīmad-Bhāgavatam* is the religious process which elevates one to the platform of serving and loving the Supreme Personality of Godhead."

The attitude of the disciple should be to satisfy the bona fide spiritual master. Then it will be very easy for him to understand spiritual knowledge. This is confirmed in the *Vedas,* and Rūpa Gosvāmī will further explain that for a person who has unflinching faith in God and the spiritual master, everything becomes revealed very easily.

Serving the Spiritual Master with Faith and Confidence

Regarding serving the spiritual master, in the Eleventh Canto of *Śrīmad-Bhāgavatam,* Seventeenth Chapter, verse 27, it is stated by Lord Kṛṣṇa, "My dear Uddhava, the spiritual master must be accepted not only as My representative, but as My very self. He must never be considered on the same level with an ordinary human being. One should never be envious of the spiritual master, as one may be envious of an ordinary man. The spiritual master should always be seen as the representative of the Supreme Personality of Godhead, and by serving the spiritual master one is able to serve all the demigods."

Following in the Footsteps of Saintly Persons

In the *Skanda Purāṇa* it is advised that a devotee follow the past *ācāryas* and saintly persons, because by such following one can achieve the desired results, with no chance of lamenting or being baffled in his progress.

The scripture known as *Brahma-yāmala* states as follows: "If someone wants to pose himself as a great devotee without following the authorities of the revealed scriptures, then his activities will never help him to make progress in devotional service. Instead, he will simply create disturbances for the sincere students of devotional service." Those who do not strictly follow the principles of revealed scriptures are generally called *sahajiyās*—those who have imagined everything to be cheap, who have their own concocted ideas, and who do not follow the scriptural injunctions. Such persons are simply creating disturbances in the discharge of devotional service.

In this connection, an objection may be raised by those who are not in devotional service and who do not care for the revealed scriptures. An example of this is seen in Buddhist philosophy. Lord Buddha appeared in the family of a high-grade *kṣatriya* king, but his philosophy was not in accord with the Vedic conclusions and therefore was rejected. Under the patronage of a Hindu king, Mahārāja Aśoka, the Buddhist religion was spread all over India and the adjoining countries. However, after the appearance of the great stalwart teacher Śaṅkarācārya, this Buddhism was driven out beyond the borders of India.

The Buddhists or other religionists who do not care for revealed scriptures sometimes say that there are many devotees of Lord Buddha who show devotional service to Lord Buddha, and who therefore should be considered devotees. In answer to this argument, Rūpa Gosvāmī says that the followers of Buddha cannot be accepted as devotees. Although Lord Buddha is accepted as an incarnation of Kṛṣṇa, the followers of such incarnations are not very advanced in their knowledge of the *Vedas*. To study the *Vedas* means to come to the conclusion of the supremacy of the Personality of Godhead. Therefore any religious principle which denies the supremacy of the Personality of Godhead is not accepted and is called atheism. Atheism means defying the authority of the *Vedas* and decrying the great *ācaryas* who teach Vedic scriptures for the benefit of the people in general.

Lord Buddha is accepted as an incarnation of Kṛṣṇa in the *Śrīmad-Bhāgavatam,* but in the same *Śrīmad-Bhāgavatam* it is stated that Lord Buddha appeared in order to bewilder the atheistic class of men. Therefore his philosophy is meant for bewildering the atheists and should not be accepted. If someone asks, "Why should Kṛṣṇa propagate atheistic principles?" the answer is that it was the desire of the

Supreme Personality of Godhead to end the violence which was then being committed in the name of the *Vedas*. The so-called religionists were falsely using the *Vedas* to justify such violent acts as meat-eating, and Lord Buddha came to lead the fallen people away from such a false interpretation of the *Vedas*. Also, for the atheists Lord Buddha preached atheism so that they would follow him and thus be tricked into devotional service to Lord Buddha, or Kṛṣṇa.

Inquiring About Eternal Religious principles

In the *Nāradīya Purāṇa* it is said, "If one is actually very serious about devotional service, then all of his purposes will be served without any delay."

Being Prepared to Give Up Everything Material for Kṛṣṇa's Satisfaction

In the *Padma Purāṇa* it is stated, "For one who has given up his material sense enjoyment and has accepted the principles of devotional service, the opulence of Viṣṇuloka [the kingdom of God] is awaiting."

Residing in a Sacred Place

In the *Skanda Purāṇa* it is also said that for a person who has lived in Dvārakā for six months, for one month, or even for one fortnight, there is awaiting elevation to the Vaikuṇṭhalokas and all the profits of *sārūpya-mukti* (the privilege of having the same four-handed bodily features as Nārāyaṇa).

In the *Brahma Purāṇa* it is said, "The transcendental significance of Puruṣottama-kṣetra, which is the eighty-square-mile field of Lord Jagannātha, cannot be properly described. Even the demigods from higher planetary systems see the inhabitants of this Jagannātha Purī as having exactly the same bodily features possessed by one in Vaikuṇṭha. That is, the demigods see the inhabitants of Jagannātha Purī as being four-handed."

When there was a meeting of great sages at Naimiṣāraṇya, Sūta Gosvāmī was reciting *Śrīmad-Bhāgavatam*, and the importance of the Ganges was stated as follows: "The waters of the Ganges are always carrying the flavor of *tulasī* offered at the lotus feet of Śrī Kṛṣṇa, and as such the waters of the Ganges are ever flowing, spreading the glories of Lord Kṛṣṇa. Wherever the waters of the Ganges are flowing, all will be sanctified, both externally and internally."

Accepting Only What Is Necessary

In the *Nāradīya Purāṇa* it is directed, "One should not accept more than necessary if he is serious about discharging devotional service." The purport is that one should not neglect following the principles of devotional service, nor should one accept the rulings of devotional service which are more than what he can easily perform. For example, it may be said that one should chant the Hare Kṛṣṇa *mantra* at least one hundred thousand times daily on his beads. But if this is not possible, then one must minimize his chanting according to his own capacity. Generally, we recommend our disciples to chant at least sixteen rounds on their *japa* beads daily, and this should be completed. But if one is not even able to chant sixteen rounds, then he must make it up the next day. He must be sure to keep his vow. If he does not strictly follow this out, then he is sure to be negligent. That is offensive in the service of the Lord. If we encourage offenses, we shall not be able to make progress in devotional service. It is better if one fixes up a regulative principle according to his own ability and then follows that vow without fail. That will make him advanced in spiritual life.

Observing Fasting on Ekādaśī

In the *Brahma-vaivarta Purāṇa* it is said that one who observes fasting on Ekādaśī day is freed from all kinds of reactions to sinful activities and advances in pious life. The basic principle is not just to fast, but to increase one's faith and love for Govinda, or Kṛṣṇa. The real reason for observing fasting on Ekādaśī is to minimize the demands of the body and to engage our time in the service of the Lord by chanting or performing similar service. The best thing to do on fasting days is to remember the pastimes of Govinda and to hear His holy name constantly.

Offering Respect to the Banyan Trees

In the *Skanda Purāṇa* it is directed that a devotee should offer water to the *tulasī* plant and *āmalakī* trees. He should offer respect to the banyan tree (*aśvattha*), the cows and the *brāhmaṇas* and should serve the Vaiṣṇavas by offering them respectful obeisances and meditating upon them. All of these processes will help the devotee to diminish the reactions to his past sinful activities.

Giving Up the Company of Nondevotees

Lord Caitanya was once asked by one of His householder devotees what the general behavior of a Vaiṣṇava should be. In this connection, Lord Caitanya replied that a Vaiṣṇava should always give up the company of nondevotees. Then He explained that there are two kinds of nondevotees: one class is against the supremacy of Kṛṣṇa, and another class is too materialistic. In other words, those who are after material enjoyment and those who are against the supremacy of the Lord are called *avaiṣṇava,* and their company should be strictly avoided.

In the *Kātyāyana-saṁhitā* it is stated that even if one is forced to live within a cage of iron or in the midst of a blazing fire, he should accept this position rather than live with nondevotees who are through and through against the supremacy of the Lord. Similarly, in the *Viṣṇu-rahasya* there is a statement to the effect that one should prefer to embrace a snake, a tiger or an alligator rather than associate with persons who are worshipers of various demigods and who are impelled by material desire.

In the *Śrīmad-Bhāgavatam* it is instructed that one may worship a certain demigod if he is desirous of achieving some material gain. For example, one is advised to worship the sun-god if he is desirous of getting rid of a diseased condition. For a beautiful wife, one may worship Umā, the wife of Lord Śiva, and for advanced education one may worship Sarasvatī. There is a similar list for worshipers of all demigods, according to different material desires. But all of these worshipers, although they appear to be very good devotees of the demigods, are still considered to be nondevotees. They cannot be accepted as devotees.

The Māyāvādīs (impersonalists) say that one may worship any form of the Lord and that it doesn't matter, because one reaches the same destination anyway. But it is clearly stated in the *Bhagavad-gītā* that those who are worshipers of the demigods will ultimately reach only the planets of those demigods, while those who are devotees of the Lord

Himself will be promoted to the Lord's abode, the kingdom of God. So actually these persons who are worshipers of demigods have been condemned in the *Gītā*. It is described that due to their lusty desires they have lost their intelligence and have therefore taken to worshiping the different demigods. So in the *Viṣṇu-rahasya* these demigod worshipers are forcefully condemned by the statement that it is better to live with the most dangerous animals than to associate with these persons.

Not Accepting Unfit Disciples, Constructing Many Temples or Reading Many Books

Another stricture is that a person may have many disciples, but he should not act in such a way that he will be obliged to any of them for some particular action or some favor. And one should also not be very enthusiastic about constructing new temples, nor should one be enthusiastic about reading various types of books, save and except the ones which lead to the advancement of devotional service. Practically, if one very carefully reads *Bhagavad-gītā, Śrīmad-Bhāgavatam, Teachings of Lord Caitanya* and this *Nectar of Devotion*, that will give him sufficient knowledge to understand the science of Kṛṣṇa consciousness. One need not take the trouble of reading other books.

In the Seventh Canto of *Śrīmad-Bhāgavatam,* Thirteenth Chapter, verse 8, Nārada Muni, while discussing with Mahārāja Yudhiṣṭhira the various functions of the different orders in society, especially mentions rules for the *sannyāsīs,* those persons who have renounced this material world. One who has accepted the *sannyāsa* order of life is forbidden to accept as a disciple anyone who is not fit. A *sannyāsī* should first of all examine whether a prospective student is sincerely seeking Kṛṣṇa consciousness. If he is not, he should not be accepted. However, Lord Caitanya's causeless mercy is such that He advised all bona fide spiritual masters to speak about Kṛṣṇa consciousness everywhere. Therefore, in the line of Lord Caitanya even the *sannyāsīs* can speak about Kṛṣṇa consciousness everywhere, and if someone is seriously inclined to become a disciple, the *sannyāsī* always accepts him.

The one point is that without increasing the number of disciples, there is no propagation of the cult of Kṛṣṇa consciousness. Therefore, sometimes even at a risk, a *sannyāsī* in the line of Caitanya Mahāprabhu may accept even a person who is not thoroughly fit to become a disciple.

Later on, by the mercy of such a bona fide spiritual master, the disciple is gradually elevated. However, if one increases the number of disciples simply for some prestige or false honor, he will surely fall down in the matter of executing Kṛṣṇa consciousness.

Similarly, a bona fide spiritual master has no business reading many books simply to show his proficiency or to get popularity by lecturing in different places. One should avoid all these things. It is also stated that a *sannyāsī* should not be enthusiastic about constructing temples. We can see in the lives of various *ācāryas* in the line of Śrī Caitanya Mahāprabhu that they are not very enthusiastic about constructing temples. However, if somebody comes forward to offer some service, the same reluctant *ācāryas* will encourage the building of costly temples by such servitors. For example, Rūpa Gosvāmī was offered a favor by Mahārāja Mānsiṅgh, the commander-in-chief of Emperor Akbar, and Rūpa Gosvāmī instructed him to construct a large temple for Govindajī, which cost vast amounts of money.

So a bona fide spiritual master should not personally take any responsibility for constructing temples, but if someone has money and wants to spend it in the service of Kṛṣṇa, an *ācārya* like Rūpa Gosvāmī may utilize the devotee's money to construct a nice, costly temple for the service of the Lord. Unfortunately, it happens that someone who is not fit to become a spiritual master may approach wealthy persons to contribute for temple constructions. If such money is utilized by unqualified spiritual masters for living comfortably in costly temples without actually doing any preaching work, this is not acceptable. In other words, a spiritual master needn't be very enthusiastic for constructing temple buildings simply in the name of so-called spiritual advancement. Rather, his first and foremost activity should be to preach. In this connection, Śrīla Bhaktisiddhānta Sarasvatī Gosvāmī Mahārāja recommended that a spiritual master print books. If one has money, instead of constructing costly temples, one should spend his money for the publication of authorized books in different languages for propagating the Kṛṣṇa consciousness movement.

Straightforwardness in Ordinary Dealings and Equilibrium in Loss and Gain

There is a statement in the *Padma Purāṇa:* "Persons who are engaged in Kṛṣṇa consciousness should never be disturbed by some material gain or loss. Even if there is some material loss, one should not be perturbed, but should always think of Kṛṣṇa within himself." The purport is that every conditioned soul is always absorbed in thinking of materialistic activities; he has to free himself from such thoughts and transfer himself completely to Kṛṣṇa consciousness. As we have already explained, the basic principle of Kṛṣṇa consciousness is to always think of Kṛṣṇa. One should not be disturbed in material loss, but, rather, should concentrate his mind upon the lotus feet of the Lord.

A devotee should not be subjected to lamentation or illusion. There is the following statement in the *Padma Purāṇa:* "Within the heart of a person who is overpowered by lamentation or anger, there is no possibility of Kṛṣṇa's being manifested."

The Demigods

One should not neglect to offer due respect to the demigods. One may not be a devotee of demigods, but that does not mean that he should be disrespectful to them. For example, a Vaiṣṇava is not a devotee of Lord Śiva or Lord Brahmā, but he is duty-bound to offer all respects to such highly positioned demigods. According to Vaiṣṇava philosophy, one should offer respect even to an ant, so then what is there to speak of such exalted persons as Lord Śiva and Lord Brahmā?

In the *Padma Purāṇa* it is said, "Kṛṣṇa, or Hari, is the master of all demigods, and therefore He is always worshipable. But this does not mean that one should not offer respect to the demigods."

Not Giving Pain to Any Living Entity

This is the statement of *Mahābhārata:* "A person who does not disturb or cause painful action in the mind of any living entity, who treats everyone just like a loving father does his children, whose heart is so pure, certainly very soon becomes favored by the Supreme Personality of Godhead."

In so-called civilized society there is sometimes agitation against cruelty to animals, but at the same time regular slaughterhouses are always maintained. A Vaiṣṇava is not like that. A Vaiṣṇava can never support animal slaughter or even give pain to any living entity.

8

Offenses to Be Avoided

In the supplementary Vedic literature, there is the following list of thirty-two offenses in the matter of serving the Lord: (1) One should not enter the temple of the Deity in a car or palanquin or with shoes on the feet. (2) One should not fail to observe the various festivals for the pleasure of the Supreme Personality of Godhead, such as Janmāṣṭamī and Ratha-yātrā. (3) One should not avoid bowing down before the Deity. (4) One should not enter the temple to worship the Lord without having washed one's hands and feet after eating. (5) One should not enter the temple in a contaminated state. (According to Vedic scripture, if someone dies in the family the whole family becomes contaminated for some time, according to its status. For example, if the family is *brāhmaṇa* their contamination period is twelve days, for the *kṣatriyas* and *vaiśyas* it is fifteen days, and for *śūdras* thirty days.) (6) One should not bow down on one hand. (7) One should not circumambulate in front of Śrī Kṛṣṇa. (The process of circumambulating the temple is that one should begin circumambulating from the Deity's right-hand side of the temple and come round. Such circumambulation should be performed outside the temple structure at least three times daily.) (8) One should not spread his legs before the Deity. (9) One should not sit before the Deity holding the ankles, elbows or knees with one's hands. (10) One should not lie down before the Deity of Kṛṣṇa. (11) One should not accept *prasāda* before the Deity. (12) One should never speak a lie before the Deity. (13) One should not talk very loudly before the Deity. (14) One should not talk with others before the Deity. (15) One should not cry or howl before the Deity. (16) One should not quarrel or fight before the Deity. (17) One should not chastise anyone before the Deity. (18) One should not be charitable to beggars before the Deity. (19) One should not speak very harshly to others before the Deity. (20) One should not wear a fur blanket before the Deity. (21) One should not eulogize or praise anyone else before the Deity. (22) One should not speak any ill names before the Deity. (23) One should not pass air before the Deity.

(24) One should not fail to worship the Deity according to one's means. (In *Bhagavad-gītā* it is stated that the Lord is satisfied if some devotee offers Him even a leaf or a little water. This formula prescribed by the Lord is universally applicable, even for the poorest man. But that does not mean that one who has sufficient means to worship the Lord very nicely should also adopt this method and try to satisfy the Lord simply by offering water and a leaf. If he has sufficient means, he should offer nice decorations, nice flowers and nice foodstuffs and observe all ceremonies. It is not that one should try to satisfy the Supreme Lord with a little water and a leaf, and for himself spend all his money in sense gratification.) (25) One should not eat anything which is not offered first to Kṛṣṇa. (26) One should not fail to offer fresh fruit and grains to Kṛṣṇa, according to the season. (27) After food has been cooked, no one should be offered any foodstuff unless it is first offered to the Deity. (28) One should not sit with his back toward the Deity. (29) One should not offer obeisances silently to the spiritual master, or in other words, one should recite *aloud* the prayers to the spiritual master while offering obeisances. (30) One should not fail to offer some praise in the presence of the spiritual master. (31) One should not praise himself before the spiritual master. (32) One should not deride the demigods before the Deity.

This is a list of thirty-two offenses. Besides these, there are a number of offenses which are mentioned in the *Varāha Purāṇa*. They are as follows: (1) One should not touch the Deity in a dark room. (2) One should not fail to strictly follow the rules and regulations in worshiping the Deity. (3) One should not enter the temple of the Deity without first making some sound. (4) One should not offer any foodstuff to the Deity which has been seen by dogs or other lower animals. (5) One should not break silence while worshiping. (6) One should not pass urine or evacuate while engaged in worshiping. (7) One should not offer incense without offering some flower. (8) Useless flowers without any fragrance should not be offered. (9) One should not fail to wash his teeth very carefully every day. (10) One should not enter the temple directly after sexual intercourse. (11) One should not touch a woman during her menstrual period. (12) One should not enter the temple after touching a dead body. (13) One should not enter the temple wearing garments of red or blue color or garments which are unwashed. (14) One should not enter the temple after seeing a dead body. (15) One should not pass air within the temple. (16) One should not be angry within the temple. (17) One should not enter the temple after visiting a crematorium. (18) One should not belch before the Deity. So, until one has fully digested his food, he should not enter the temple. (19) One should not smoke marijuana, or *gañjā*. (20) One should not take opium or similar intoxicants. (21) One should not enter the Deity room or touch the body of the Deity after having smeared oil over his body. (22) One should not show disrespect to a scripture teaching about the supremacy of the Lord. (23) One should not introduce any opposing scripture. (24) One should not chew betel before the Deity. (25) One should not offer a flower which was kept in an unclean pot. (26) One should not worship the Lord while sitting on the bare floor; one must have a sitting place or carpet. (27) One should not touch the Deity before one has completed taking bath. (28) One should not decorate his forehead with the three-lined *tilaka*. (29) One should not enter the temple without washing his hands and feet.

Other rules are that one should not offer foodstuff which is cooked by a non Vaiṣṇava, one should not worship the Deity before a non-devotee, and one should not engage himself in the worship of the Lord while seeing a nondevotee. One should begin the worship of the demigod Gaṇapati, who drives away all impediments in the execution of devotional service. In the *Brahma-saṁhitā* it is stated that Gaṇapati worships the lotus feet of Lord Nṛsiṁhadeva and in that way has become auspicious for the devotees in clearing out all impediments. Therefore, all devotees should worship Gaṇapati. The Deities should not be bathed in water which has been touched by the nails or fingers. When a devotee is perspiring, he should not engage himself in worship ing the Deity. Similarly, there are many other prohibitions. For example, one should not cross or step over the flowers offered to the Deities, nor should one take a vow in the name of God. These are all different kinds of offenses in the matter of executing devotional service, and one should be careful to avoid them.

In the *Padma Purāṇa* it is stated that even a person whose life is completely sinful will be completely protected by the Lord if he simply surrenders unto Him. So it is accepted that one who surrenders unto the Supreme Personality of Godhead becomes free from all sinful reactions. And even when a person becomes an offender unto the Supreme Personality of Godhead Himself, he can still be delivered simply by taking shelter of the holy names of the Lord: Hare Kṛṣṇa, Hare Kṛṣṇa, Kṛṣṇa Kṛṣṇa, Hare Hare/ Hare Rāma, Hare Rāma, Rāma Rāma, Hare Hare. In other words, the chanting of Hare Kṛṣṇa is beneficial for eradicating all sins, but if one becomes an offender to the holy names of the Lord, then he has no chance of being delivered.

The offenses against the chanting of the holy name are as follows: (1) To blaspheme the devotees who have dedicated their lives for propagating the holy name of the Lord. (2) To consider the names of demigods like Lord Śiva or Lord Brahmā to be equal to, or independent of, the name of Lord Viṣṇu. (Sometimes the atheistic class of men take it that any demigod is as good as the Supreme Personality of Godhead, Viṣṇu. But one who is a devotee knows that no demigod, however great he may be, is independently as good as the Supreme Personality of Godhead. Therefore, if someone thinks that he can chant "Kālī, Kālī!" or "Durgā, Durgā!" and it is the same as Hare Kṛṣṇa, that is the greatest offense.) (3) To disobey the orders of the spiritual master. (4) To blaspheme the Vedic literature or literature in pursuance of the Vedic version. (5) To consider the glories of chanting Hare Kṛṣṇa to be imaginations. (6) To give some interpretation on the holy name of the Lord. (7) To commit sinful activities on the strength of the holy name of the Lord. (It should not be taken that because by chanting the holy name of the Lord one can be freed from all kinds of sinful reaction, one may continue to act sinfully and after that chant Hare Kṛṣṇa to neutralize his sins. Such a dangerous mentality is very offensive and should be avoided.) (8) To consider the chanting of Hare Kṛṣṇa one of the auspicious ritualistic activities offered in the *Vedas* as fruitive activities (*karma-kāṇḍa*). (9) To instruct a faithless person about the glories of the holy name. (Anyone can take part in chanting the holy name of the Lord, but in the beginning one should not be instructed about the transcendental potency of the Lord. Those who are too sinful cannot appreciate the transcendental glories of the Lord, and therefore it is better not to instruct them in this matter.) (10) To not have complete faith in the chanting of the holy names and to maintain material attachments, even after understanding so many instructions on this matter.

Every devotee who claims to be a Vaiṣṇava must guard against these offenses in order to quickly achieve the desired success.

9

Further Consideration of Devotional Principles

Blasphemy

One should not tolerate blasphemy of the Lord or His devotees. In this connection, in the Tenth Canto, Seventy-fourth Chapter, verse 40, of *Śrīmad-Bhāgavatam,* Śukadeva Gosvāmī tells Parīkṣit Mahārāja, "My dear King, if a person, after hearing blasphemous propaganda against the Lord and His devotees, does not go away from that place, he becomes bereft of the effect of all pious activities."

In one of Lord Caitanya's *Śikṣāṣṭaka* verses it is stated, "The devotee should be more tolerant than the tree and more submissive than the grass. He should offer all honor to others, but may not accept any honor for himself." In spite of Lord Caitanya's being so humble and meek as a devotee, when He was informed about injuries inflicted on the body of Śrī Nityānanda, He immediately ran to the spot and wanted to kill the offenders, Jagāi and Mādhāi. This behavior of Lord Caitanya's is very significant. It shows that a Vaiṣṇava may be very tolerant and meek, foregoing everything for his personal honor, but when it is a question of the honor of Kṛṣṇa or His devotee, he will not tolerate any insult.

There are three ways of dealing with such insults. If someone is heard blaspheming by words, one should be so expert that he can defeat the opposing party by argument. If he is unable to defeat the opposing party, then the next step is that he should not just stand there meekly, but should give up his life. The third process is followed if he is unable to execute the above-mentioned two processes, and this is that one must leave the place and go away. If a devotee does not follow any of the above-mentioned three processes, he falls down from his position of devotion.

Tilaka and Tulasī Beads

In the *Padma Purāṇa* there is a statement describing how a Vaiṣṇava should decorate his body with *tilaka* and beads: "Persons who put *tulasī* beads on the neck, who mark twelve places of their bodies as Viṣṇu temples with Viṣṇu's symbolic representations [the four items held in the four hands of Lord Viṣṇu—conch, mace, disc and lotus], and who have *viṣṇu-tilaka* on their foreheads, are to be understood as the devotees of Lord Viṣṇu in this world. Their presence makes the world purified, and anywhere they remain, they make that place as good as Vaikuṇṭha."

A similar statement is in the *Skanda Purāṇa,* which says, "Persons who are decorated with *tilaka,* or *gopī-candana,* and who mark their bodies all over with the holy names of the Lord, and on whose necks and breasts there are *tulasī* beads, are never approached by the Yamadūtas." The Yamadūtas are the constables of King Yama (the lord of death), who punishes all sinful men. Vaiṣṇavas are never called for by such constables of Yamarāja. In the *Śrīmad-Bhāgavatam,* in the narration of Ajāmila's deliverance, it is said that Yamarāja gave clear instructions to his assistants not to approach the Vaiṣṇavas. Vaiṣṇavas are beyond the jurisdiction of Yamarāja's activities.

The *Padma Purāṇa* also mentions, "A person whose body is decorated with the pulp of sandalwood, with paintings of the holy name of the Lord, is delivered from all sinful reactions, and after his death he goes directly to Kṛṣṇaloka to live in association with the Supreme Personality of Godhead."

Accepting Flower Garlands

The next instruction is that one should put on flower garlands which are offered to the Deity. In this connection, in the Eleventh Canto, Sixth Chapter, verse 46, of *Śrīmad-Bhāgavatam,* Uddhava says to Kṛṣṇa, "My dear Kṛṣṇa, I have taken things which You have used and enjoyed, such as garlands of flowers, scented oils, garments and ornaments, and I eat only the remnants of Your foodstuff, because I am Your menial servant. So, therefore, I am sure that I shall not be attacked by the spell of material energy." The purport of this verse is that for any person who simply follows these rules and regulations of decorating the body with the marks of *tilaka* of *gopī-candana* or sandalwood pulp, and who puts on the garlands which were offered to Kṛṣṇa, there is no question of being conquered by the spell of material energy. At the time of death, there is no question of such a person's being called by the constables of Yamarāja. Even if one does not accept all the Vaiṣṇava principles, but still takes the remnants of foodstuff offered to Kṛṣṇa, or *kṛṣṇa-prasāda,* he will gradually become qualified to rise to the platform of a Vaiṣṇava.

Similarly, in the *Skanda Purāṇa* Lord Brahmā tells Nārada, "My dear Nārada, anyone who puts on his neck the flower garland which was formerly used by Kṛṣṇa becomes relieved from all disease and reactions to sinful activities, and gradually he is liberated from the contamination of matter."

Dancing Before the Deity

In the *Dvārakā-māhātmya* the importance of dancing before the Deity is stated by Lord Kṛṣṇa as follows: "A person who is in a jubilant spirit, who feels profound devotional ecstasy while dancing before Me, and who manifests different features of bodily expression can burn away all the accumulated sinful reactions he has stocked up for many, many thousands of years." In the same book there is a statement by Nārada wherein he asserts, "From the body of any person who claps and dances before the Deity, showing manifestations of ecstasy, all the birds of sinful activities fly away upward." Just as by clapping the hands one can cause many birds to fly away, similarly the birds of all sinful activities which are sitting on the body can be made to fly away simply by dancing and clapping before the Deity of Kṛṣṇa.

Bowing Down in Honor of the Deity

In the *Nāradīya Purāṇa* there is a statement about bowing down and offering respect to the Deity. It is said there, "A person who has performed a great ritualistic sacrifice and a person who has simply offered his respectful obeisances by bowing down before the Lord cannot be held as equals." The person who has executed many great sacrifices will attain the result of his pious activities, but when such results are finished, he has to take birth again on the earthly planet; however, the person who has once offered respects, bowing down before the Deity, will not come back to this world, because he will go directly to the abode of Kṛṣṇa.

Standing Up to Receive the Lord

In the *Brahmāṇḍa Purāṇa* it is said, "A person who sees the Lord's Ratha-yātrā car festival and then stands up to receive the Lord can purge all kinds of sinful results from his body."

Following the Deity

A similar statement is there in the *Bhaviṣya Purāṇa,* in which it is said, "Even if born of a lowly family, a person who follows the Ratha-yātrā car when the Deities pass in front or from behind will surely be elevated to the position of achieving equal opulence with Viṣṇu."

Going to the Temple of Viṣṇu or to Places of Pilgrimage

It is stated in the *Purāṇas,* "Persons who attempt to visit the holy places of pilgrimage, like Vṛndāvana, Mathurā or Dvārakā, are actually glorified. By such traveling activities, they can pass over the desert of material existence."

In the *Hari-bhakti-sudhodaya* there is a statement about the benefit of visiting the temples of Lord Kṛṣṇa. As we have explained previously, in Vṛndāvana, Mathurā and Dvārakā the system is that all the devotees take advantage of visiting various temples situated in those holy places. It is stated in the *Hari-bhakti-sudhodaya,* "Persons who are impelled by pure devotional service in Kṛṣṇa consciousness and who therefore go to see the Deities of Viṣṇu in the temple will surely get relief from entering again into the prison house of a mother's womb." The conditioned soul forgets the trouble of living within the mother's womb during birth, but it is a very painful and terrible experience. In order to make an escape from this material condition, one is advised to visit a temple of Viṣṇu with devotional consciousness. Then one can very easily get out of the miserable condition of material birth.

Circumambulating the Temple of Viṣṇu

It is said in the *Hari-bhakti-sudhodaya,* "A person who is circumambulating the Deity of Viṣṇu can counteract the circumambulation of repeated birth and death in this material world." The conditioned soul is circumambulating through repeated births and deaths on account of his material existence, and this can be counteracted simply by circumambulating the Deity in the temple.

The Cāturmāsya ceremony is observed during the four months of the rainy season in India (approximately July, August, September and October), beginning from Śrāvaṇa. During these four months, saintly persons who are accustomed to travel from one place to another to propagate Kṛṣṇa consciousness remain at one place, usually a holy place of pilgrimage. During these times, there are certain special rules and regulations which are strictly followed. It is stated in the *Skanda Purāṇa* that during this period, if someone circumambulates the temple of Viṣṇu at least four times, it is understood that he has traveled all over the universe. By such circumambulation, one is understood to have seen all the holy places where the Ganges water is flowing, and by following the regulative principles of Cāturmāsya one can very quickly be raised to the platform of devotional service.

Arcanā

Arcanā means worship of the Deity in the temple. By executing this process one confirms himself to be not the body but spirit soul. In the Tenth Canto, Eighty-first Chapter, verse 19, of *Śrīmad-Bhāgavatam,* it is told how Sudāmā, an intimate friend of Kṛṣṇa's, while going to the house of a *brāhmaṇa,* murmured to himself, "Simply by worshiping Kṛṣṇa one can easily achieve all the results of heavenly opulence, liberation, supremacy over the planetary systems of the universe, all the opulences of this material world, and the mystic power of performing the *yoga* system."

The events leading to Sudāmā's murmuring this statement are as follows. Śrī Kṛṣṇa had ordered His friend Sudāmā to go to a *brāhmaṇa's* house and ask for some food. The *brāhmaṇas* were performing a great sacrifice, and Śrī Kṛṣṇa told Sudāmā to plead with them that He and Balarāma were feeling hungry and needed some food. When Sudāmā went there, the *brāhmaṇas* refused to offer anything, but the wives of the *brāhmaṇas,* upon hearing that Śrī Kṛṣṇa wanted some foodstuff, immediately took many palatable dishes and went to offer them to Śrī Kṛṣṇa. In the *Viṣṇu-rahasya,* also, it is stated, "Any person within this world who is engaged in the worship of Viṣṇu can very easily achieve the ever-blissful kingdom of God, known as Vaikuṇṭhaloka."

Rendering Service to the Lord

It is stated in the *Viṣṇu-rahasya,* "Any person who can arrange for service to the Lord in the same way that a king is given service by his attendants is surely elevated to the abode of Kṛṣṇa after death." Actually, in India the temples are just like royal palaces. They are not ordinary buildings, because the worship of Kṛṣṇa should be performed in just the way that a king is worshiped in his palace. So in Vṛndāvana there are many hundreds of temples wherein the Deity is worshiped exactly like a king. In the *Nāradīya Purāṇa* it is stated, "If person stays in the Lord's temple even for a few moments, he can surely achieve the transcendental kingdom of God."

The conclusion is that those who are rich men in society should construct beautiful temples and arrange for the worship of Viṣṇu, so that people may be attracted to visit such temples and thereby be offered the opportunity of dancing before the Lord or chanting the holy name of the Lord, or else of hearing the holy name of the Lord. In this way, everyone will be given the chance to elevate himself to the kingdom of God. In other words, even a common man, simply by visiting such a temple, will be able to attain the highest benedictions, not to mention the devotees who are constantly engaged in the service of the Lord in full Kṛṣṇa consciousness.

In this connection, there is a statement in the Fourth Canto, Twenty-first Chapter, verse 31, of the *Śrīmad-Bhāgavatam,* wherein King Pṛthu says to his subjects, "My dear citizens, please note that the Supreme Personality of Godhead, Hari, is actually the deliverer of all fallen, conditioned souls. No demigod can perform this act of delivering the conditioned souls, because the demigods themselves are conditioned. A conditioned soul cannot deliver another conditioned soul. Only Kṛṣṇa or His bona fide representative can deliver him. The Ganges water which is flowing down from the toe of Lord Viṣṇu falls upon the earthly planet and other planets and thereby delivers all the conditioned sinful living entities. So what need is there to speak of the deliverance of persons who are always engaged in the service of the Lord? There is no doubt about their liberation, even if they have stocks of sinful activities from many, many births." In other words, a person who is engaged in the worship of the Deities can minimize his stock of sinful reactions coming from many, many previous births. This process of worshiping the Deity has already been described, and one should try to follow these rules and regulations seriously.

Singing

In the *Liṅga Purāṇa* there is a statement about glorifying and singing about the Lord. It is said there, "A *brāhmaṇa* who is constantly engaged in singing the glories of the Lord is surely elevated to the same planet as the Supreme Personality of Godhead. Lord Kṛṣṇa appreciates this singing even more than the prayers offered by Lord Śiva."

Saṅkīrtana

When a person loudly chants the glories of the Lord's activities, qualities, form, etc., his chanting is called *saṅkīrtana*. *Saṅkīrtana* also refers to the congregational chanting of the holy name of the Lord.

In the *Viṣṇu-dharma* there is a statement glorifying this process of congregational chanting: "My dear King, this word *Kṛṣṇa* is so auspicious that anyone who chants this holy name immediately gets rid of the resultant actions of sinful activities from many, many births." That is a fact. There is the following statement in *Caitanya-caritāmṛta:* "A person who chants the holy name of Kṛṣṇa once can counteract the resultant actions of more sinful activities than he is able to perform." A sinful man can perform many, many sinful activities, but he is unable to perform so many that they cannot be wiped out by one single uttering of *Kṛṣṇa*.

In the Seventh Canto, Ninth Chapter, verse 18, of *Śrīmad-Bhāgavatam,* Mahārāja Prahlāda offers the following prayers to the Lord: "My dear Lord Nṛsiṁha, if I can be elevated to the position of Your servant, then it will be possible for me to hear about Your activities. You are the supreme friend, the supreme worshipable Deity. Your pastimes are transcendental, and simply by hearing of them one can counteract all his sinful activities. Therefore, I shall not care for all those sinful activities, because simply by hearing about Your pastimes I shall get out of all the contamination of material attachment."

There are many songs about the Lord's activities. For example, there is the *Brahma-saṁhitā,* sung by Lord Brahmā; *Nārada-pañcarātra,* sung by Nārada Muni; and *Śrīmad-Bhāgavatam,* sung by Śukadeva Gosvāmī. If these songs are heard by any person, he can easily get out of the clutches of material contamination. There should be no difficulty in hearing these songs of God. They are coming down from many, many millions of years ago, and people are still taking advantage of them. So why, at this time, should one not take full advantage and thus become liberated?

In the First Canto, Fifth Chapter, verse 22, of *Śrīmad-Bhāgavatam,* Nārada Muni tells his disciple Vyāsadeva, "My dear Vyāsa, you should know that persons who are engaged in executing austerities and penances, studying the *Vedas,* performing big sacrifices, chanting the hymns of the *Vedas,* speculating on transcendental knowledge and performing charitable functions have for all their auspicious activities simply to gain a place in the association of devotees and chant the glories of the Lord." It is indicated here that chanting about and glorifying the Lord is the ultimate activity of the living entity.

Japa

Chanting a *mantra* or hymn softly and slowly is called *japa,* and chanting the same mantra loudly is called *kīrtana.* For example, uttering the *mahā-mantra* (Hare Kṛṣṇa, Hare Kṛṣṇa, Kṛṣṇa Kṛṣṇa, Hare Hare/ Hare Rāma, Hare Rāma, Rāma Rāma, Hare Hare) very softly, only for one's own hearing, is called *japa.* Chanting the same mantra loudly for being heard by all others is called *kīrtana.* The *mahā-mantra* can be used for *japa* and *kīrtana* also. When *japa* is practiced it is for the personal benefit of the chanter, but when *kīrtana* is performed it is for the benefit of all others who may hear.

In the *Padma Purāṇa* there is a statement: "For any person who is chanting the holy name either softly or loudly, the paths to liberation and even heavenly happiness are at once open."

Submission

In the *Skanda Purāṇa* there is a statement about submission unto the lotus feet of the Lord. It is said there that those who are sober devotees can offer their submission to Kṛṣṇa in the following three ways: (1) *samprārthanātmikā,* very feelingly offering prayers; (2) *dainya-vodhikā,* humbly submitting oneself; (3) *lālasāmayī,* desiring some perfectional stage. This desiring some perfectional stage in spiritual life is not sense gratification. When one realizes something of his constitutional relationship with the Supreme Personality of Godhead, he understands his original position and wants to be reinstated in this position, either as friend, servant, parent or conjugal lover of Kṛṣṇa. That is called *lālasāmayī,* or very eagerly desiring to go to one's natural position. This *lālasāmayī* stage of submission comes in the stage of perfect liberation, which is technically called *svarūpa-siddhi,* when the living entity understands, by perfect spiritual advancement and revelation, his original relationship with the Lord.

In the *Padma Purāṇa* there is a statement of submission in feeling by devotees praying to the Lord: "My Lord, I know that young girls have natural affection for young boys, and that young boys have natural affection for young girls. I am praying at Your lotus feet that my mind may become attracted unto You in the same spontaneous way." The example is very appropriate. When a young boy or girl sees a member of the opposite sex there is a natural attraction, without the need for any introduction. Without any training there is a natural attraction due to the sex impulse. This is a material example, but the devotee is praying that he may develop a similar spontaneous attachment for the Supreme Lord, free from any desire for profit and without any other cause. This natural attraction for the Lord is the perfectional stage of self-realization.

In the same *Padma Purāṇa* there is a statement about submission in humbleness. It is stated there, "My dear Lord, there is no sinful living entity who is more of a sinner than myself. Nor is there a greater offender than myself. I am so greatly sinful and offensive that when I come to confess my sinful activities before You, I am ashamed." This is a natural position for a devotee. As far as the conditioned soul is concerned, there is no wonder that he has some sinful activities in his past life, and this should be admitted and confessed before the Lord. As soon as this is done, the Lord excuses the sincere devotee. But that does not mean that one should take advantage of the Lord's causeless mercy and expect to be excused over and over again, while he commits the same sinful activities. Such a mentality is only for shameless persons. Here it is clearly said, "When I come to confess my sinful activities I become ashamed." So if a person is not ashamed of his sinful activities and continues to commit the same sinful activities with the knowledge that the Lord will excuse him, that is a most nonsensical proposition. Such an idea is not accepted in any part of the Vedic literature. It is a fact that by chanting the holy name of the Lord one becomes washed clean of all sinful activities from his past life. But that does not mean that after being washed off, one should again begin sinful activities and expect to be washed again. These are nonsensical propositions and are not admitted in devotional service. Someone may think, "For a whole week I may commit sinful activities, and for one day I will go to the temple or church and admit my sinful activities so that I can become washed off and again begin my sinning." This is most nonsensical and offensive and is not acceptable to the author of *Bhakti-rasāmṛta-sindhu.*

In the *Nārada-pañcarātra* there is a statement of submission accompanied by the desire for perfection. The devotee says, "My dear Lord, when shall that day come when You will ask me to fan Your body, and according to Your pleasure, You will say, 'You just fan Me in this way'?" The idea in this verse is that the devotee is desiring to personally fan the body of the Supreme Personality of Godhead. That means that he is desiring to become the personal associate of the Supreme Lord. Of course, any devotee in any capacity, either as servant, friend or conjugal lover, always has direct association with the Lord. But according to his different individual taste, a person desires just one of these relationships. Here the devotee is desiring to become a servant of the Lord and desires to fan the Lord, as does His internal energy, Lakṣmī, the goddess of fortune. He also wishes that the Personality of Godhead will be pleased to give him directions as to how to fan. This submission with transcendental desire, or *lālasāmayī vijñapti,* is the highest perfectional stage of spiritual realization.

In the same *Nārada-pañcarātra,* there is another expression of submission, wherein the devotee says, "My dear Lord, O lotus-eyed one, when will that day come when on the bank of the Yamunā I shall become just like a madman and continue to chant Your holy name while incessant tears flow from my eyes?" This is another perfectional stage. Lord Caitanya also desired that "a moment will appear unto me as twelve years of time, and the whole world will appear to me as vacant on account of not seeing You, my dear Lord." One should feelingly pray and become eager to render his particular type of service to the Lord. This is the teaching of all great devotees, especially Lord Caitanya.

In other words, one should learn how to cry for the Lord. One should learn this small technique, and he should be very eager and actually cry to become engaged in some particular type of service. This is called *laulyam,* and such tears are the price for the highest perfection. If one develops this *laulyam,* or excessive eagerness for meeting and serving the Lord in a particular way, that is the price to enter into the kingdom of God. Otherwise, there is no material calculation for the value of the ticket by which one can enter the kingdom of God. The only price for such entrance is this *laulyam lālasāmayī,* or desire and great eagerness.

Reciting Notable Prayers

According to great learned scholars, the whole *Bhagavad-gītā* contains many authorized prayers, especially in the Eleventh Chapter, where Arjuna prays to the universal form of the Lord. Similarly, in the *Gautamīya-tantra* all the verses are called prayers. Again, in *Śrīmad-Bhāgavatam* there are hundreds of prayers to the Lord. So a devotee should select some of these prayers for his recitation. In *Skanda Purāṇa* the glories of these prayers are stated as follows: "Devotees whose tongues are decorated always with prayers to Lord Kṛṣṇa are always given respect even by the great saintly persons and sages, and such devotees are actually worshipable by the demigods."

Those who are less intelligent want to worship different demigods for some material gain rather than worship Kṛṣṇa. But here it is stated that a devotee who is always engaged in offering prayers to the Lord is worshipable even by the demigods themselves. The pure devotees have nothing to ask from any demigod; rather, the demigods are anxious to offer prayers to the pure devotees.

In the *Nṛsiṁha Purāṇa* it is stated, "Any person who comes before the Deity of Lord Kṛṣṇa and begins to chant different prayers is immediately relieved from all the reactions of sinful activities and becomes eligible, without any doubt, to enter into the Vaikuṇṭhaloka."

Partaking of Prasāda

There is this specific statement in the *Padma Purāṇa:* "A person who honors the *prasāda* and regularly eats it, not exactly in front of the Deity, along with *caraṇāmṛta* [the water offered to the lotus feet of the Lord, which is mixed with seeds of the *tulasī* tree], immediately can achieve the results of pious activities which are obtained through ten thousand performances of sacrificial rites."

Drinking Caraṇāmṛta

Caraṇāmṛta is obtained in the morning while the Lord is being washed before dressing. Scented with perfumes and flowers, the water comes gliding down through His lotus feet and is collected and mixed with yogurt. In this way this *caraṇāmṛta* not only becomes very tastefully flavored, but also has tremendous spiritual value. As described in the *Padma Purāṇa,* even a person who has never been able to give in charity, who has never been able to perform a great sacrifice, who has never been able to study the *Vedas,* who has never been able to worship the Lord—or, in other words, even one who has never done any pious activities—will become eligible to enter into the kingdom of God if he simply drinks the *caraṇāmṛta* which is kept in the temple. In the temple it is the custom that the *caraṇāmṛta* be kept in a big pot. The devotees who come to visit and offer respects to the Deity take three drops of *caraṇāmṛta* very submissively and feel themselves happy in transcendental bliss.

Smelling the Incense and Flowers Offered to the Deity

In the *Hari-bhakti-sudhodaya* there is a statement about the incense which is offered in the temple: "When the devotees smell the good fragrance of the incense which is offered to the Deity, they thus become cured of the poisonous effects of material contamination, as much as one becomes cured of a snakebite by smelling the prescribed medicinal herbs." The explanation of this verse is that there is an herb found in the jungles which expert persons know how to use to revive the consciousness of one who is bitten by a snake. Simply by smelling that herb one becomes immediately relieved of the poisonous effects of the snakebite. The same example is applicable: when a person comes to visit the temple and smells the incense offered to the Deity, he is cured at that time from all his material contamination.

Any devotee coming into the temple should always offer something to the Deity—fruit, flowers, incense, etc. If one cannot offer anything in cash, something else must be offered. In India the system is that all the ladies and gentlemen who come in the morning to visit the temple bring so many things. Even one morsel of rice or one morsel of flour can be offered. It is a regulative principle that one should not go to see a saintly person or the Deity in the temple without any offering. The offering may be very humble, or it may be priceless. Even a flower, a little fruit, a little water—whatever is possible—must be offered. So when a devotee comes to offer something to the Deity in the morning, he is sure to smell the good fragrance of the incense, and then at once he will become cleansed of the poisonous effect of material existence.

It is stated in the *Tantra-śāstra,* "If the smell of the garland which was offered to the Deity in the temple enters into a person's nostrils, immediately his bondage to sinful activities becomes cleared. And even if one has no sinful activities, still, by smelling such remnants of flowers, one can advance from Māyāvādī [impersonalist] to devotee." There are several instances of this, a prime one being the advancement of the four Kumāras. They were impersonalist Māyāvādīs, but after smelling the remnants of flowers and incense in the temple, they turned to become devotees. From the above verse it appears that the Māyāvādīs, or impersonalists, are more or less contaminated. They are not pure.

It is confirmed in *Śrīmad-Bhāgavatam,* "One who has not washed off all reactions of sinful activities cannot be a pure devotee. A pure devotee has no more doubts about the supremacy of the Personality of Godhead, and thus he engages himself in Kṛṣṇa consciousness and devotional service." A similar statement is in the *Agastya-saṁhitā:* just to purify the impurities of our nostrils, we should try to smell the remnants of flowers offered to Kṛṣṇa in the temple.

Touching the Deity

In the *Viṣṇu-dharmottara* there is a statement about touching the lotus feet of the Lord. It is said, "Only a person who is initiated as a Vaiṣṇava and is executing devotional service in Kṛṣṇa consciousness has the right to touch the body of the Deity." In India there was agitation during Gandhi's political movement because the lowborn classes of men like street-sweepers and *caṇḍālas* are prohibited, according to the Vedic system, from entering the temple. Due to their unclean habits they are prohibited, but at the same time they are given other facilities so they may be elevated to the highest grade of devotional service by association with pure devotees. A man born in any family is not barred, but he must be cleansed. That cleansing process must be adopted. Gandhi wanted to make them clean simply by stamping them with a fictitious name, *harijana* ("children of God"), and so there was a great tug-of-war between the temple owners and Gandhi's followers.

But anyway, the present law is the law of all scripture—that if anyone is purified he can enter into the temple. Actually, that is the position. Only one who is properly initiated, who is properly following the rules and regulations, can enter, and touch the Deity—not all. And one who touches the body of the Deity, following such regulative principles, is immediately delivered from the contamination of material sins, and all of his desires become fulfilled without delay.

Seeing the Deity

In the *Varāha Purāṇa* there is a statement praising the seeing of the Deity of Śrī Kṛṣṇa in the temple. A devotee says there, "My dear Vasundharā, any person who goes to Vṛndāvana and sees the Deity of Govindadeva is free from the courthouse of Yamarāja and is allowed to enter into the highest planetary system, in which reside the demigods." This means that even an ordinary person who goes to Vṛndāvana out of inquisitiveness and by chance sees the temple, especially that of Govindadeva, even if he is not elevated to the spiritual kingdom, is still assured promotion to the higher planetary systems. This means that simply by visiting the Deity of Govinda in Vṛndāvana one becomes highly elevated in pious life.

Observing Ārati and Celebrations of the Lord

In the *Skanda Purāṇa* there is the following description of the result of seeing *ārati* (worship) of the Deity: "If someone sees the face of the Lord while *ārati* is going on, he can be relieved of all sinful reactions coming from many, many thousands and millions of years past. He is even excused from the killing of a *brāhmaṇa* or similar prohibited activities.

As we have already explained, there are different ceremonies to be observed, such as the birthday of Kṛṣṇa, the birthday of Lord Rāmacandra, the birthday of some prominent Vaiṣṇavas, the ceremony of Jhulana-yātrā with the Lord sitting on a swing, and Dola-yātrā (the Lord's activities in the month of March). In all festivals the Lord is seated on a car, and the car moves through different streets of the city so that people may take advantage of visiting the Lord. In the *Bhaviṣya Purāṇa* it is said, "In such a ceremony, if even a *caṇḍāla* [dog-eater], simply out of curiosity, sees the Lord on the cart, he becomes counted as one of the associates of Viṣṇu."

In the *Agni Purāṇa* it is stated, "Any person who in gladness sees the worship of the Deity in the temple will obtain the results of *kriyā-yoga* which are described in the *Pañcarātra* scripture." *Kriyā-yoga* is a system of practice much like practical devotional service, but it is especially meant for the mystic *yogīs*. In other words, by this gradual process the mystic *yogīs* are eventually elevated to the devotional service of the Lord.

10

Techniques of Hearing and Remembering

Hearing

The beginning of Kṛṣṇa consciousness and devotional service is hearing, in Sanskrit called *śravaṇam*. All people should be given the chance to come and join devotional parties so that they may hear. This hearing is very important for progressing in Kṛṣṇa consciousness. When one links his ears to give aural reception to the transcendental vibrations, he can quickly become purified and cleansed in the heart. Lord Caitanya has affirmed that this hearing is very important. It cleanses the heart of the contaminated soul so that he becomes quickly qualified to enter into devotional service and understand Kṛṣṇa consciousness.

In the *Garuḍa Purāṇa* the stress on hearing is expressed very nicely. It is said there, "The state of conditioned life in the material world is just like that of a man lying unconscious, having been bitten by a snake. This is because both such unconscious states can be ended by the sound of a *mantra*." When a man is snake-bitten he does not die immediately, but first becomes unconscious and remains in a comatose condition. Anyone who is in the material world is also sleeping, as he is ignorant of his actual self or his actual duty and his relationship with God. So materialistic life means that one is bitten by the snake of *māyā*, illusion, and thus, without any Kṛṣṇa consciousness, is almost dead. Now, the so-called dead man bitten by a snake can be brought back to life by the chanting of some *mantra*. There are expert chanters of these *mantras* who can perform this feat. Similarly, one can be brought back into Kṛṣṇa consciousness from the deadly unconscious state of material life by hearing of the *mahā-mantra:* Hare Kṛṣṇa, Hare Kṛṣṇa, Kṛṣṇa Kṛṣṇa, Hare Hare/ Hare Rāma, Hare Rāma, Rāma Rāma, Hare Hare.

In the Fourth Canto of *Śrīmad-Bhāgavatam*, Twenty-ninth Chapter, verses 39–40, the importance of hearing of the pastimes of the Lord is stated by Śukadeva Gosvāmī to Mahārāja Parīkṣit: "My dear King, one should stay at a place where the great *ācāryas* [holy teachers] speak about the transcendental activities of the Lord, and one should give aural reception to the nectarean river flowing from the moonlike faces of such great personalities. If someone eagerly continues to hear such transcendental sounds, then certainly he will become freed from all material hunger, thirst, fear and lamentation, as well as all illusions of material existence."

Śrī Caitanya Mahāprabhu also recommended this process of hearing as a means of self-realization in the present Age of Kali. In this age it is very difficult to follow thoroughly the regulative principles and studies of the *Vedas* which were formerly recommended. However, if one gives aural reception to the sound vibrated by great devotees and *ācāryas,* that alone will give him relief from all material contamination. Therefore it is the recommendation of Caitanya Mahāprabhu that one should simply hear from authorities who are actually devotees of the Lord. Hearing from professional men will not help. If we hear from those who are actually self-realized, then the nectarean rivers, like those which are flowing on the moon planet, will flow into our ears. This is the metaphor used in the above verse.

As stated in *Bhagavad-gītā,* "A materialistic person can give up his material hankerings only by becoming situated in Kṛṣṇa consciousness." Unless one finds a superior engagement, he will not be able to give up his inferior engagement. In the material world everyone is engaged in the illusory activities of the inferior energy, but when one is given the opportunity to relish the activities of the superior energy performed by Kṛṣṇa, then he forgets all his lesser pleasures. When Kṛṣṇa speaks on the Battlefield of Kurukṣetra, to the materialistic person it appears that this is simply talk between two friends, but actually it is a river of nectar flowing down from the mouth of Śrī Kṛṣṇa. Arjuna gave aural reception to such vibrations, and thus he became freed from all the illusions of material problems.

In the Twelfth Canto of *Śrīmad-Bhāgavatam,* Third Chapter, verse 15, it is stated, "A person who desires unalloyed devotional service to Lord Kṛṣṇa, who is praised by transcendental sound vibrations, should always hear about His glorification and transcendental qualities. This will surely kill all kinds of inauspiciousness in the heart."

Expecting the Lord's Mercy

In the Tenth Canto, Fourteenth Chapter, verse 8, it is said, "My dear Lord, any person who is constantly awaiting Your causeless mercy to be bestowed upon him, and who goes on suffering the resultant actions of his past misdeeds, offering You respectful obeisances from the core of his heart, is surely eligible to become liberated, for it has become his rightful claim."

This statement of *Śrīmad-Bhāgavatam* should be the guide of all devotees. A devotee should not expect immediate relief from the reactions of his past misdeeds. No conditioned soul is free from such reactionary experiences, because material existence means continued suffering or enjoying of past activities. If one has finished his material activities then there is no more birth. This is possible only when one begins Kṛṣṇa conscious activities, because such activities do not produce reaction. Therefore, as soon as one becomes perfect in Kṛṣṇa conscious activities, he is not going to take birth again in this material world. A devotee who is not perfectly freed from the resultant actions should therefore continue to act in Kṛṣṇa consciousness seriously, even though there may be so many impediments. When such impediments arise he should simply think of Kṛṣṇa and expect His mercy. That is the only solace. If the devotee passes his days in that spirit, it is certain that he is going to be promoted to the abode of the Lord. By such activities, he earns his claim to enter into the kingdom of God. The exact word used in this verse is *dāya-bhak. Daya-bhāk* refers to a son's becoming the lawful inheritor of the property of the father. In a similar way, a pure devotee who is prepared to undergo all kinds of tribulations in executing Kṛṣṇa conscious duties becomes lawfully qualified to enter into the transcendental abode.

Remembrance

Some way or other, if someone establishes in his mind his continuous relationship with Kṛṣṇa, this relationship is called remembrance.

About this remembrance there is a nice statement in the *Viṣṇu Purāṇa*, where it is said, "Simply by remembering the Supreme Personality of Godhead all living entities become eligible for all kinds of auspiciousness. Therefore let me always remember the Lord, who is unborn and eternal." In the *Padma Purāṇa* the same remembrance is explained as follows: "Let me offer my respectful obeisances unto the Supreme Lord Kṛṣṇa, because if someone remembers Him, either at the time of death or during his span of life, he becomes freed from all sinful reactions."

Meditation

To meditate means to engage the mind in thinking of the form of the Lord, the qualities of the Lord, the activities of the Lord and the service of the Lord. Meditation does not mean anything impersonal or void. According to Vedic literature, meditation is always on the form of Viṣṇu.

In the *Nṛsiṁha Purāṇa* there is a statement about meditation on the form of the Lord. It is said there, "Meditation focusing on the lotus feet of the Supreme Personality of Godhead has been accepted as transcendental and beyond the experience of material pain and pleasure. By such meditation, even one who is grossly miscreant can be delivered from the sinful reactions of his life."

In the *Viṣṇu-dharma* there is a statement about meditation on the transcendental qualities of the Lord. It is said, "Persons who are constantly engaged in Kṛṣṇa consciousness, and who remember the transcendental qualities of the Lord, become free from all reactions to sinful activities, and after being so cleansed they become fit to enter into the kingdom of God." In other words, no one can enter into the kingdom of God without being freed from all sinful reactions. One can avoid sinful reactions simply by remembering the Lord's form, qualities, pastimes, etc.

In the *Padma Purāṇa* there is a statement about remembering the activities of the Lord: "A person who is always engaged in meditation on the sweet pastimes and wonderful activities of the Lord surely becomes freed from all material contamination."

In some of the *Purāṇas* the evidence is given that if someone is simply meditating on devotional activities, he has achieved the desired result and has seen face to face the Supreme Personality of Godhead. In this connection, there is a story in the *Brahma-vaivarta Purāṇa* that in the city of Pratiṣṭhānapura in South India there was once a *brāhmaṇa* who was not very well-to-do, but who was nevertheless satisfied in himself, thinking that it was because of his past misdeeds and by the desire of Kṛṣṇa that he did not get sufficient money and opulence. So he was not at all sorry for his poor material position, and he used to live very peacefully. He was very openhearted, and sometimes he went to hear some lectures delivered by great realized souls. At one such meeting, while he was very faithfully hearing about Vaiṣṇava activities, he was informed that these activities can be performed even by meditation. In other words, if a person is unable to actually perform Vaiṣṇava activities physically, he can meditate upon the Vaiṣṇava activities and thereby acquire all of the same results. Because the *brāhmaṇa* was not very well-to-do financially, he decided that he would simply meditate on grand, royal devotional activities, and he began this business thus:

Sometimes he would take his bath in the river Godāvarī. After taking his bath he would sit in a secluded place on the bank of the river, and by practicing the *yoga* exercises of *prāṇāyāma,* the usual breathing exercises, he would concentrate his mind. These breathing exercises are meant to mechanically fix the mind upon a particular subject. That is the result of the breathing exercises and also of the different sitting postures of *yoga*. Formerly, even quite ordinary persons used to know how to fix the mind upon the remembrance of the Lord, and so the *brāhmaṇa* was doing this. When he had fixed the form of the Lord in his mind, he began to imagine in his meditations that he was dressing the Lord very nicely in costly clothing, with ornaments, helmets and other paraphernalia. Then he offered his respectful obeisances by bowing down before the Lord. After finishing the dressing, he began to imagine that he was cleaning the temple very nicely. After cleansing the temple, he imagined that he had many water jugs made of gold and silver, and he took all those jugs to the river and filled them with the holy water. Not only did he collect water from the Godāvarī, but he collected from the Ganges, Yamunā, Narmadā and Kāverī. Generally a Vaiṣṇava, while worshiping the Lord, collects water from all these rivers by *mantra* chanting. This *brāhmaṇa,* instead of chanting some *mantra,* imagined that he was physically securing water from all these rivers in golden and silver waterpots. Then he collected all kinds of paraphernalia for worship—flowers, fruits, incense and sandalwood pulp. He collected everything to place before the Deity. All these waters, flowers and scented articles were then very nicely offered to the Deities to Their satisfaction. Then he offered *ārati,* and with the regulative principles he finished all these activities in the correct worshiping method.

He would daily execute similar performances as his routine work, and he continued to do so for many, many years. Then one day the *brāhmaṇa* imagined in his meditations that he had prepared some sweet rice with milk and sugar and offered the preparation to the Deity. However, he was not very satisfied with the offering because the sweet rice had been prepared recently and it was still very hot. (This preparation, sweet rice, should not be taken hot. The cooler the sweet rice, the better its taste.) So because the sweet rice had been prepared by the *brāhmaṇa* very recently, he wanted to touch it so that he could know whether it was fit for eating by the Lord. As soon as he touched the sweet rice pot with his finger, he immediately was burnt by the heat of the pot. In this way, his meditation broke. Now, when he looked at his finger, he saw that it was burnt, and he was wondering in astonishment how this could have happened. Because he was simply meditating on touching the hot sweet rice, he never thought that his finger would actually become burnt.

While he was thinking like this, in Vaikuṇṭha Lord Nārāyaṇa, seated with the goddess of fortune, Lakṣmī, began to smile humorously. On seeing this smiling of the Lord, all the goddesses of fortune attending the Lord became very curious and asked Lord Nārāyaṇa why He was smiling. The Lord, however, did not reply to their inquisitiveness, but instead immediately sent for the *brāhmaṇa.* An airplane sent from Vaikuṇṭha immediately brought the *brāhmaṇa* into Lord Nārāyaṇa's presence. When the *brāhmaṇa* was thus present before the Lord and the goddesses of fortune, the Lord explained the whole story. The *brāhmaṇa* was then fortunate enough to get an eternal place in Vaikuṇṭha in the association of the Lord and His Lakṣmīs. This shows how the Lord is all-pervading, in spite of His being locally situated in His abode. Although the Lord was present in Vaikuṇṭha, He was present also in the heart of the *brāhmaṇa* when he was meditating on the worshiping process. Thus, we can understand that things offered by the devotees even in meditation are accepted by the Lord, and they help one achieve the desired result.

11

Aspects of Transcendental Service

Servitorship

In the opinion of the *karmīs* (fruitive workers), offering the results of *karma* is called servitorship. But according to Vaiṣṇava *ācāryas* like Rūpa Gosvāmī, servitorship means constant engagement in some kind of service to the Lord.

In the *Skanda Purāṇa* it is said that those who are attached to ritualistic activities, the four orders of social life and the four orders of spiritual life are considered devotees. But when devotees are actually engaged in offering service to the Lord directly, these must be *bhāgavatas,* or pure devotees. Those who are engaged in fruitive activities, or prescribed duties according to the four orders of social and spiritual life, are not actually pure devotees. But still, because they are offering the result to the Lord, they are accepted as devotees. When one has no such desire, but acts spontaneously out of love of God, such a person must be accepted as a pure devotee. The conditioned souls who have come into contact with the material world are all more or less desirous of lording it over material nature. The system of *varṇāśrama* and the prescribed duties under this system are so designed that the conditioned soul may enjoy in the material world according to his desire for sense gratification and at the same time gradually become elevated to spiritual understanding. Under these prescribed duties of *varṇa* and *āśrama* there are many activities which belong to devotional service in Kṛṣṇa consciousness. Those devotees who are householders accept Vedic ritualistic performances as well as the prescribed duties of devotional service, because both are meant for satisfying Kṛṣṇa. When householder devotees perform some Vedic ritualistic duties, they do so to satisfy Kṛṣṇa. As we have previously discussed, any activity aiming at satisfying the Supreme Personality of Godhead is considered devotional service.

Śrīla Rūpa Gosvāmī describes one who is fit for becoming engaged in devotional service. He says that persons who are neophytes and who have developed a little love of Godhead are not interested in the activities of sense gratification, in proportion to their devotion. But if there is still some attraction for sense gratifying activities, then the result of such activities should be offered to Kṛṣṇa. This is also called engagement in the service of the Lord, with the Lord as the master and the worker as the servant.

In the *Nāradīya Purāṇa* there is a statement of how this servitorship is transcendental. It is said there that a person who is constantly engaged in devotional service by his body, mind and words, or even a person who is not practically engaged but is simply desiring to be so, is considered to be liberated.

Devotional Service in Friendship

Devotional service in friendship can be divided into two categories: the first is to act as the confidential servant of the Lord, and the other is to act as the well-wisher of the Lord. The devotee who has confidence in devotional service to the Lord systematically follows the rules and regulations, with the faith that he will achieve the platform of transcendental life. The second type of devotional friendship is to become a well-wisher of the Supreme Personality of Godhead. In *Bhagavad-gītā* it is said that the Lord accepts a preacher as the most dear servant. Anyone who is preaching the confidential message of the *Gītā* to the people in general is so dear to Kṛṣṇa that no one can be equal to him in human society.

In the *Mahābhārata,* Draupadī says, "My dear Govinda, Your promise is that Your devotee can never be vanquished. I believe in that statement, and therefore in all kinds of tribulations I simply remember Your promise, and thus I live." The purport is that Draupadī and her five husbands, the Pāṇḍavas, were put into severe tribulations by their cousin-brother Duryodhana, as well as by others. The tribulations were so severe that even Bhīṣmadeva, who was both a lifelong *brahmacārī* and a great warrior, would sometimes shed tears thinking of them. He was always surprised that although the Pāṇḍavas were so righteous and Draupadī was practically the goddess of fortune, and although Kṛṣṇa was their friend, still they had to undergo such severe tribulations. Though their tribulations were not ordinary, Draupadī was not discouraged. She knew that because Kṛṣṇa was their friend, ultimately they would be saved.

A similar statement is there in the Eleventh Canto of *Śrīmad-Bhāgavatam,* Second Chapter, verse 53, where Havis, the son of King Ṛṣabha, addresses Mahārāja Nimi: "My dear King, a person who never deviates even for a moment from engagement in service at the lotus feet of the Supreme Person (engagement which is sought even by great demigods like Indra), with firm conviction that there is nothing more worshipable or desirable than this, is called the first-class devotee."

Śrī Rūpa Gosvāmī says that a neophyte devotee who has simply developed a slight love of Godhead is certainly a prospective candidate for devotional service. When he becomes firmly fixed in such devotional service, that assured status becomes a confidential part of his devotional service.

Sometimes it is found that a pure devotee lies down in the temple of the Lord in order to serve Him as a confidential friend. Such friendly behavior of a devotee may be accepted as *rāgānugā,* or spontaneous. Although, according to regulative principles, no one can lie down in the temple of the Supreme Personality of Godhead, this spontaneous love of Godhead may be grouped under devotional service in friendship.

Surrendering Everything to the Lord

Regarding complete self-surrender, there is a nice description in the Eleventh Canto of *Śrīmad-Bhāgavatam,* Twenty-ninth Chapter, verse 34, where the Lord says, "A person who has completely surrendered unto Me and has completely given up all other activities is protected by Me personally, both in this life and in the next. In other words, I wish to help him become more and more advanced in spiritual life. Such a person is to be understood as having already achieved *sārṣṭi* [having equal opulences with the Supreme]." It is also confirmed in *Bhagavad-gītā* that as soon as a person surrenders unto the lotus feet of Kṛṣṇa, Kṛṣṇa takes charge of him and gives him a guarantee of protection from all sinful reactions. He also instructs from within, so that the devotee may very quickly make advancement toward spiritual perfection.

This self-surrender is called *ātma-nivedana.* According to different authorities, *self* is differently defined. *Self* is sometimes considered to refer to the spirit self, or soul, and *self* is sometimes considered to refer to the mind or to the body. Full self-surrender, therefore, means not only surrendering one's self as spirit soul, but also surrendering one's mind and body to the service of the Lord. Śrīla Bhaktivinoda Ṭhākura has sung a nice song in this connection. While offering himself as a fully surrendered soul, he said, "My mind, my household affairs, my body, whatever is in my possession, my dear Lord, I offer to You for Your service. Now You can do with them as You like. You are the supreme possessor of everything, so if You like You can kill me, or if You like You can give me protection. All authority belongs to You. I have nothing to claim as my own."

Śrī Yāmunācārya, in his prayers to the Lord, has expressed a similar idea in the following words: "My dear Lord, I may be living within some body as a human being or as a demigod, but whatever mode of life, I do not mind, because these bodies are simply by-products of the three modes of material nature, and I, who am in possession of these bodies, am surrendering myself unto You."

In the *Hari-bhakti-viveka,* there is a statement regarding how one can offer his body in self-surrender. There the devotee says, "My dear Lord, as a sold animal has no need to think about his maintenance and sustenance, so, because I have given up my body and soul unto You, I am no longer concerned with my maintenance and sustenance." In other words, one should not bother about his personal or family maintenance or sustenance. If one is actually surrendered in body and soul, he should always remember that his only concern is to be engaged in the service of the Lord.

Śrīla Rūpa Gosvāmī says that devotional service in friendship and devotional service in self-surrender are two difficult processes. Therefore such relationships with the Lord can very rarely be seen. Only for the advanced devotees are these two processes easily executed. The purport is that it is very rare to see surrender which is mixed with sincere ecstatic devotion. One must give himself completely to the will of the Lord.

Offering a Favorite Article

In the Eleventh Canto of *Śrīmad-Bhāgavatam,* Eleventh Chapter, verse 41, Lord Kṛṣṇa tells Uddhava, "My dear friend, if someone offers

Me the best thing in his possession, or anything which is very pleasing to him, he will be eternally benefited."

Performing All Endeavors for Kṛṣṇa

In the *Nārada-pañcarātra* there is a statement of how one can act in all spheres of life for the satisfaction of the Lord. It is stated there that a person who is actually in devotional service must be engaged in all kinds of activities—those prescribed in the revealed scriptures and also those which are accepted for livelihood. In other words, not only should a devotee engage himself in the prescribed duties of devotional service which are mentioned in the revealed scriptures, but he should also perform the duties of his practical life in Kṛṣṇa consciousness. For example, a devotee who has a great establishment or factory may offer the fruits of such a material possession for the service of the Lord.

Being a Surrendered Soul

In the *Hari-bhakti-vilāsa* there is the following statement about self-surrender: "My dear Lord, a person who has surrendered himself unto You, who is in firm conviction that he is Yours, and who actually acts in that way by his body, mind and words, can actually relish transcendental bliss."

In the *Nṛsiṁha Purāṇa,* Lord Nṛsiṁhadeva says, "Anyone who prays unto Me and takes shelter of Me becomes My ward, and I protect him always from all sorts of calamities."

Serving Trees Such as the Tulasī

In the *Skanda Purāṇa* there is a statement praising the *tulasī* tree as follows: "Let me offer my respectful obeisances unto the *tulasī* tree, which can immediately vanquish volumes of sinful activities. Simply by seeing or touching this tree one can become relieved from all distresses and diseases. Simply by offering obeisances to and pouring water on the *tulasī* tree, one can become freed from the fear of being sent to the court of Yamarāja [the King of death, who punishes the sinful]. If someone sows a *tulasī* tree somewhere, certainly he becomes devoted to Lord Kṛṣṇa. And when the *tulasī* leaves are offered in devotion at the lotus feet of Kṛṣṇa, there is the full development of love of Godhead."

In India all Hindus, even those not belonging to the Vaiṣṇava group, take special care of the *tulasī* tree. Even in great cities where it is very difficult to keep a *tulasī* tree, people are to be found very carefully keeping this plant. They water it and offer obeisances to it, because worship of the *tulasī* tree is very important in devotional service.

In the *Skanda Purāṇa* there is another statement about *tulasī,* as follows: "*Tulasī* is auspicious in all respects. Simply by seeing, simply by touching, simply by remembering, simply by praying to, simply by bowing before, simply by hearing about or simply by sowing this tree, there is always auspiciousness. Anyone who comes in touch with the *tulasī* tree in the above-mentioned ways lives eternally in the Vaikuṇṭha world."

12

Further Aspects of Transcendental Service

Hearing the Revealed Scriptures

According to Śrīla Rūpa Gosvāmī, any book which gives enlightenment in the matter of advancing in devotional service is considered to be revealed scripture. Śrīla Madhvācārya has also defined *revealed scriptures* as referring to books such as the *Rāmāyaṇa, Mahābhārata, Purāṇas, Upaniṣads, Vedānta*—and any other literature written in pursuance of such revealed scriptures.

In the *Skanda Purāṇa* there is this statement: "A person who is constantly engaged in reading literature enunciating the cultivation of Vaiṣṇava devotional service is always glorious in human society, and certainly Lord Kṛṣṇa becomes pleased with him. A person who very carefully keeps such literature at home and offers respectful obeisances to it becomes freed from all sinful reactions and ultimately becomes worshipable by the demigods."

It is also said to Nārada Muni, "My dear Nārada, a person who writes Vaiṣṇava literature and keeps such literature at home has Lord Nārāyaṇa always residing in his house."

In *Śrīmad-Bhāgavatam,* Twelfth Canto, Thirteenth Chapter, verse 15, it is stated, "*Śrīmad-Bhāgavatam* is the essence of all Vedānta philosophy. Any person who has become attached in some way or other to the reading of *Śrīmad-Bhāgavatam* cannot have any taste for reading any other literature. In other words, a person who has relished the transcendental bliss of *Śrīmad-Bhāgavatam* cannot be satisfied with mundane writings."

Residing in Mathurā

In the *Varāha Purāṇa* there is a statement praising the residential quarters of Mathurā. Lord Varāha tells the men of earth, "Any person who becomes attracted to places other than Mathurā will certainly be captivated by the illusory energy." In the *Brahmāṇḍa Purāṇa* it is said that all the results of traveling on all the pilgrimages within the three worlds can be achieved simply by touching the holy land of Mathurā. In many *śāstras* (scriptures) it is said that simply by hearing, remembering, glorifying, desiring, seeing or touching the land of Mathurā, one can achieve all desires.

Rendering Service to Devotees

In the *Padma Purāṇa,* there is a nice statement praising the service of the Vaiṣṇavas, or devotees. In that scripture Lord Śiva tells Pārvatī, "My dear Pārvatī, there are different methods of worship, and out of all such methods the worship of the Supreme Person is considered to be the highest. But even higher than the worship of the Lord is the worship of the Lord's devotees."

A similar statement is in the Third Canto, Seventh Chapter, verse 19, of *Śrīmad-Bhāgavatam:* "Let me become a sincere servant of the devotees, because by serving them one can achieve unalloyed devotional service unto the lotus feet of the Lord. The service of devotees diminishes all miserable material conditions and develops within one a deep devotional love for the Supreme Personality of Godhead."

In the *Skanda Purāṇa* there is a similar statement: "Persons whose bodies are marked with *tilaka,* symbolizing the conchshell, wheel, club and lotus—and who keep the leaves of *tulasī* on their heads, and whose bodies are always decorated with *gopī-candana*—even seen once, can help the seer be relieved from all sinful activities."

A similar statement is found in the First Canto, Nineteenth Chapter, verse 33, of *Śrīmad-Bhāgavatam:* "There is no doubt about one's becoming freed from all reactions to sinful activities after visiting a devotee or touching his lotus feet or giving him a sitting place. Even by remembering the activities of such a Vaiṣṇava, one becomes purified, along with one's whole family. And what, then, can be said of rendering direct service to him?"

In the *Ādi Purāṇa* there is the following statement by Lord Kṛṣṇa Himself, addressed to Arjuna: "My dear Pārtha, one who claims to be My devotee is not so. Only a person who claims to be the devotee of My devotee is actually My devotee." No one can approach the Supreme

Personality of Godhead directly. One must approach Him through His pure devotees. Therefore, in the system of Vaiṣṇava activities, the first duty is to accept a devotee as spiritual master and then to render service unto him.

Śrī Rūpa Gosvāmī affirms that all the quotations given in the *Bhakti-rasāmṛta-sindhu* from different scriptures are accepted by the great *ācāryas* and devotees of the Lord.

Serving the Lord According to One's Position

In the *Padma Purāṇa* there is a statement that one should perform the ceremonies for the Lord according to one's financial position. Everyone should observe the different ceremonies and celebrations of the Lord by all means.

Performing Devotional Service in Kārttika

One of the most important of these ceremonial functions is called Ūrja-vrata. Ūrja-vrata is observed in the month of Kārttika (October–November); especially in Vṛndāvana, there is a specific program for temple worship of the Lord in His Dāmodara form. "Dāmodara" refers to Kṛṣṇa's being bound with rope by His mother, Yaśodā. It is said that just as Lord Dāmodara is very dear to His devotees, so the month known as Dāmodara or Kārttika is also very dear to them.

The execution of devotional service during Ūrja-vrata in the month of Kārttika is especially recommended to be performed at Mathurā. This system is still followed by many devotees. They go to Mathurā or Vṛndāvana and stay there during the month of Kārttika specifically to perform devotional services during this period.

In the *Padma Purāṇa* it is said, "The Lord may offer liberation or material happiness to a devotee, but after some devotional service has been executed, particularly in Mathurā during the month of Kārttika, the devotees want only to attain pure devotional service unto the Lord." The purport is that the Lord does not award devotional service to ordinary persons who are not serious about it. But even such unserious persons who execute devotional service according to the regulative principles during the month of Kārttika, and within the jurisdiction of Mathurā in India, are very easily awarded the Lord's personal service.

Observing Festivals Celebrating the Lord's Activities

In the *Bhaviṣya Purāṇa* there is a statement about observing different ceremonies celebrating the Lord's appearance (birthday) and other transcendental activities. It is said, "My Lord Janārdana [Kṛṣṇa], please let us know the date when Your mother Devakī-devī gave birth to You. If You kindly inform us about this, then we shall observe a great celebration on this date. O killer of Keśī, we are souls one-hundred-percent surrendered unto Your lotus feet, and we wish only to please You with our ceremonies."

This statement of the *Bhaviṣya Purāṇa* gives evidence that by observing different functions in relationship with the Lord one is sure to become pleasing to the Lord.

Serving the Deity with Great Devotion

It is said in the *Ādi Purāṇa*, "A person who is constantly engaged in chanting the holy name and who feels transcendental pleasure, being engaged in devotional service, is certainly awarded the facilities of devotional service and is never given just *mukti* [liberation]."

Mukti means liberation from material contamination; when liberated, one does not have to take birth again in the material world. The impersonalists desire to merge into the spiritual existence, to end their individual existence, but according to *Śrīmad-Bhāgavatam, mukti* is only the beginning of one's becoming situated in his normal condition. The normal condition of every living entity is to be engaged in the devotional service of the Lord. From the statement of the *Ādi Purāṇa* it appears that a devotee is satisfied simply with being engaged in devotional service. He does not aspire for any liberation from material, conditional life. In other words, anyone who is engaged in devotional service is not in the material condition of life, although he may appear so.

Recitation of Śrīmad-Bhāgavatam Among Devotees

Śrīmad-Bhāgavatam is the desire tree of Vedic wisdom. *Veda* itself means "the aggregate of knowledge." And whatever knowledge is required for human society is perfectly presented in *Śrīmad-Bhāgavatam*. There are different branches of knowledge in the Vedic writings, including sociology, politics, medicine and military art. All these and other branches of knowledge are perfectly described in the *Vedas*. So, as far as spiritual knowledge is concerned, that is also perfectly described there, and *Śrīmad-Bhāgavatam* is considered to be the ripened fruit of this desire-fulfilling tree of the *Vedas.* A tree is honored by the production of its fruit. For example, a mango tree is considered very valuable because it produces the king of all fruits, the mango. When the mango fruit becomes ripened it is the greatest gift of that tree, and *Śrīmad-Bhāgavatam* is similarly held to be the ripened fruit of the Vedic tree. And as ripened fruit becomes more relishable when first touched by the beak of a parrot, or *śuka, Śrīmad-Bhāgavatam* has become more relishable by being delivered through the transcendental mouth of Śukadeva Gosvāmī.

Śrīmad-Bhāgavatam should be received in disciplic succession without any breakage. When a ripened fruit comes from the upper part of the tree onto the ground by the process of being handed down from a higher branch to a lower branch by persons in the tree, the fruit does not break. *Śrīmad-Bhāgavatam,* when received in the *paramparā* system, or disciplic succession, will likewise remain unbroken. It is stated in *Bhagavad-gītā* that the disciplic succession, or *paramparā,* is the way of receiving transcendental knowledge. Such knowledge must come down through the disciplic succession, through authorized persons who know the real purpose of the *śāstra.*

Śrī Caitanya Mahāprabhu recommended that one learn *Śrīmad-Bhāgavatam* from the mouth of the self-realized person called *bhāgavatam. Bhāgavata* means "in relationship with the Personality of Godhead [Bhagavān]." So the devotee is sometimes called *bhāgavatam,* and the book which is in relationship with devotional service to the Supreme Personality of Godhead is also called *Bhāgavatam.* Śrī Caitanya Mahāprabhu recommended that, in order to relish the real taste of *Śrīmad-Bhāgavatam,* one should take instruction from the person *bhāgavatam. Śrīmad-Bhāgavatam* is relishable even by a liberated person. Śukadeva Gosvāmī admitted that although he was liberated from within the very womb of his mother, it was only after relishing *Śrīmad-Bhāgavatam* that he became a great devotee. Thus, one who is desirous of advancing in Kṛṣṇa consciousness should relish the purport of *Śrīmad-Bhāgavatam* through the discussions of authorized devotees.

In *Śrīmad-Bhāgavatam,* Second Canto, First Chapter, verse 9, Śukadeva Gosvāmī admits that although he was very much attracted by the impersonal Brahman, when he heard the transcendental pastimes of the Supreme Personality of Godhead from the mouth of his father, Vyāsadeva, he became more attracted to *Śrīmad-Bhāgavatam*. The idea is that Vyāsadeva was also a self-realized soul, and his mature contribution of transcendental knowledge was delivered directly to Śukadeva Gosvāmī in the manner indicated.

Associating with Advanced Devotees

In *Śrīmad-Bhāgavatam,* First Canto, Eighteenth Chapter, verse 13, the importance of discussing *Śrīmad-Bhāgavatam* in the society of pure devotees was explained by Śaunaka Muni during the meeting at Naimiṣāraṇya, in the presence of Sūta Gosvāmī. Sūta Gosvāmī confirmed that if someone is fortunate enough to associate with a pure devotee of the Lord even for a moment, that particular moment is so valuable that even those pious activities which can promote one to the heavenly planets or give liberation from material miseries cannot compare to it. In other words, those who are attached to *Śrīmad-Bhāgavatam* do not care for any kind of benefit derived from elevation to the higher planetary kingdoms, or for the liberation which is conceived of by the impersonalists. As such, the association of pure devotees is so transcendentally valuable that no kind of material happiness can compare to it.

In the *Hari-bhakti-sudhodaya* there is a conversation between Prahlāda Mahārāja and his father, Hiraṇyakaśipu, in which Hiraṇyakaśipu addresses Prahlāda in this way: "My dear son, association is very important. It acts just like a crystal stone, which will reflect a flower or anything else which is put before it." Similarly, if we associate with the flowerlike devotees of the Lord, and if our hearts are crystal clear, then certainly the same action will be there. Another example given in this connection is that if a man is potent and if a woman is not diseased, then by their conjugation there will be conception. In the same way, if the recipient of spiritual knowledge and the deliverer of spiritual knowledge are sincere and bona fide, there will be good results.

Chanting the Holy Name of the Lord

The importance of chanting Hare Kṛṣṇa, Hare Kṛṣṇa, Kṛṣṇa Kṛṣṇa, Hare Hare/ Hare Rāma, Hare Rāma, Rāma Rāma, Hare Hare is very strongly stressed in the Second Canto, First Chapter, verse 11, of *Śrīmad-Bhāgavatam* in the following way. Śukadeva Gosvāmī tells

Mahārāja Parīkṣit, "My dear King, if one is spontaneously attached to the chanting of the Hare Kṛṣṇa *mahā-mantra,* it is to be understood that he has attained the highest perfectional stage." It is specifically mentioned that the *karmīs* who are aspiring after the fruitive results of their activities, the salvationists who are aspiring to become one with the Supreme Person, and the *yogīs* who are aspiring after mystic perfections can achieve the results of all perfectional stages simply by chanting the *mahā-mantra.* Śukadeva uses the word *nirṇītam,* which means "it has already been decided." He was a liberated soul and therefore could not accept anything which was not conclusive. So Śukadeva Gosvāmī especially stresses that it has already been concluded that one who has come to the stage of chanting the Hare Kṛṣṇa *mantra* with determination and steadiness must be considered to have already passed the trials of fruitive activities, mental speculation and mystic *yoga.*

The same thing is confirmed in the *Ādi Purāṇa* by Kṛṣṇa. While addressing Arjuna He says, "Anyone who is engaged in chanting My transcendental name must be considered to be always associating with Me. And I may tell you frankly that for such a devotee I become easily purchased."

In the *Padma Purāṇa* also it is stated, "The chanting of the Hare Kṛṣṇa *mantra* is present only on the lips of a person who has for many births worshiped Vāsudeva." It is further said in the *Padma Purāṇa,* "There is no difference between the holy name of the Lord and the Lord Himself. As such, the holy name is as perfect as the Lord Himself in fullness, purity and eternity. The holy name is not a material sound vibration, nor has it any material contamination." The holy name cannot, therefore, be chanted offenselessly by one who has failed to purify his senses. In other words, materialistic senses cannot properly chant the holy names of the Hare Kṛṣṇa *mahā-mantra.* But by adopting this chanting process, one is given a chance to actually purify himself, so that he may very soon chant offenselessly.

Caitanya Mahāprabhu has recommended that everyone chant the Hare Kṛṣṇa *mantra* just to cleanse the dust from the heart. If the dust of the heart is cleansed away, then one can actually understand the importance of the holy name. For persons who are not inclined to clean the dust from their hearts and who want to keep things as they are, it is not possible to derive the transcendental result of chanting the Hare Kṛṣṇa *mantra.* One should, therefore, be encouraged to develop his service attitude toward the Lord, because this will help him to chant without any offense. And so, under the guidance of a spiritual master, the disciple is trained to render service and at the same time chant the Hare Kṛṣṇa *mantra*. As soon as one develops his spontaneous service attitude, he can immediately understand the transcendental nature of the holy names of the *mahā-mantra*.

Living in Mathurā

In the *Padma Purāṇa* there is a statement about the importance of living at holy places like Mathurā or Dvārakā. It is stated there, "To travel to different places of pilgrimage means to attain emancipation from material bondage. This emancipation, however, is not the highest perfectional stage. After attaining this liberated stage, one has to become engaged in devotional service to the Lord. After attainment of the *brahma-bhūta* [liberation] stage, one can further advance to engagement in devotional service. So this attainment of transcendental loving devotional service to the Lord is the goal of life, and it can be achieved very easily for one who lives in Mathurā-maṇḍala even for a few seconds."

It is further said, "Who is that person who will not agree to worship the land of Mathurā? Mathurā can deliver all the desires and ambitions of the fruitive workers and of the salvationists, who desire to become one with the Supreme Brahman. Certainly Mathurā will deliver the desires of the devotees, who simply aspire to be engaged in the devotional service of the Lord." In the Vedic literature it is also stated, "How wonderful it is that simply by residing in Mathurā even for one day, one can achieve a transcendental loving attitude toward the Supreme Personality of Godhead! This land of Mathurā must be more glorious than Vaikuṇṭha-dhāma, the kingdom of God!"

13

Five Potent Forms of Devotional Service

Rūpa Gosvāmī has stated that five kinds of devotional activities—namely residing in Mathurā, worshiping the Deity of the Lord, reciting *Śrīmad-Bhāgavatam,* serving a devotee and chanting the Hare Kṛṣṇa *mantra*—are so potent that a small attachment for any one of these five items can arouse devotional ecstasy even in a neophyte.

Regarding worship of the form of the Lord, or Deity, Rūpa Gosvāmī has written the following verse: "My dear friend, if you still have any desire to enjoy the company of your friends within this material world, then don't look upon the form of Kṛṣṇa, who is standing on the bank of Keśī-ghāṭa [a bathing place in Vṛndāvana]. He is known as Govinda, and His eyes are very enchanting. He is playing upon His flute, and on His head there is a peacock feather. And His whole body is illuminated by the moonlight in the sky."

The purport of this verse is that if someone becomes attached to the *śrī-mūrti,* or Deity of Kṛṣṇa, by worshiping at home, then he will forget his relationships of so-called friendship, love and society. Thus it is the duty of every householder to install Deities of the Lord at home and to begin the process of worshiping along with all of his family members. This will save everyone from such unwanted activities as going to clubs, cinemas and dancing parties, and smoking, drinking, etc. All such nonsense will be forgotten if one stresses the worship of the Deities at home.

Rūpa Gosvāmī further writes, "My dear foolish friend, I think that you have already heard some of the auspicious *Śrīmad-Bhāgavatam,* which decries seeking the results of fruitive activities, economic development and liberation. I think that now it is certain that gradually the verses of the Tenth Canto of *Śrīmad-Bhāgavatam,* describing the pastimes of the Lord, will enter your ears and go into your heart."

In the beginning of *Śrīmad-Bhāgavatam* it is said that unless one has the ability to throw out, just like garbage, the fruitive results of ritualistic ceremonies, economic development and becoming one with the Supreme (or salvation), one cannot understand *Śrīmad-Bhāgavatam*. The *Bhāgavatam* deals exclusively with devotional service. Only one who studies *Śrīmad-Bhāgavatam* in the spirit of renunciation can understand the pastimes of the Lord which are described in the Tenth Canto. In other words, one should not try to understand the topics of the Tenth Canto, such as the *rāsa-līlā* (love dance), unless he has spontaneous attraction for *Śrīmad-Bhāgavatam*. One must be situated in pure devotional service before he can relish *Śrīmad-Bhāgavatam* as it is.

In the above two verses of Rūpa Gosvāmī there are some metaphorical analogies that indirectly condemn the association of materialistic society, friendship and love. People are generally attracted to society, friendship and love, and they make elaborate arrangements and strong endeavors to develop these material contaminations. But to see the *śrī-mūrtis* of Rādhā and Kṛṣṇa is to forget such endeavors for material association. Rūpa Gosvāmī composed his verse in such a way that he was seemingly praising the material association of friendship and love and was condemning the audience of *śrī-mūrti* or Govinda. This metaphorical analogy is constructed in such a way that things which seem to be praised are condemned, and things which are to be condemned are praised. The actual import of the verse is that one must see the form of Govinda if one at all wants to forget the nonsense of material friendship, love and society.

Śrīla Rūpa Gosvāmī has similarly described the transcendental nature of relishing topics which concern Kṛṣṇa. A devotee once said, "It is very astonishing that since I have seen this Personality of Godhead, who is washed by the tears of my eyes, there is shivering of my body, and He has made me a failure in executing my material duties. Since seeing Him, I cannot remain silently at home. I wish to go out to Him always." The purport of this statement is that as soon as one is fortunate enough to contact a pure devotee, one must be anxious immediately to hear about Kṛṣṇa, to learn about Kṛṣṇa, or, in other words, to become fully Kṛṣṇa conscious.

Similarly, there is a statement about hearing and chanting the *mahāmantra:* "It is said that saints have been able to hear the vibrating strings of the *vīṇā* in the hands of Nārada, who is always singing the glories of

Lord Kṛṣṇa. Now this same sound vibration has entered my ears, and I am always feeling the presence of the Supreme Personality. Gradually I am becoming bereft of all attachment for material enjoyment."

Again, Śrīla Rūpa Gosvāmī has described Mathurā-maṇḍala: "I remember the Lord standing by the banks of the Yamunā River, so beautiful amid the *kadamba* trees, where many birds are chirping in the gardens. And these impressions are always giving me transcendental realization of beauty and bliss." This feeling about Mathurā-maṇḍala and Vṛndāvana described by Rūpa Gosvāmī can actually be felt even by nondevotees. The places in the 168-square-mile district of Mathurā are so beautifully situated on the banks of the river Yamunā that anyone who goes there will never want to return to this material world. These statements by Rūpa Gosvāmī are factually realized descriptions of Mathurā and Vṛndāvana. All these qualities prove that Mathurā and Vṛndāvana are situated transcendentally. Otherwise, there would be no possibility of invoking our transcendental sentiments in these places. Such transcendental feelings are aroused immediately and without fail after one arrives in Mathurā or Vṛndāvana.

In these statements about devotional service, sometimes it may appear that the results have been overestimated, but actually there is no overestimation. Some devotees, as revealed scriptures give evidence, have had immediate results by such association, although this is not possible for all. For example, the Kumāras immediately became devotees simply by smelling the incense in the temple. Bilvamaṅgala Ṭhākura simply heard about Kṛṣṇa and then immediately gave up his beautiful girlfriend and started out for Mathurā and Vṛndāvana, where he became a perfect Vaiṣṇava. So these statements are not overestimations, nor are they stories. They are actual facts, but are true for certain devotees and do not necessarily apply to all. These descriptions, even if considered overestimations, must be taken as they are, in order to divert our attention from the fleeting material beauty to the eternal beauty of Kṛṣṇa consciousness. And for a person who is already in contact with Kṛṣṇa consciousness, the described results are not unusual.

Some scholars argue that simply by following the principles of *varṇa* and *āśrama* one can gradually rise to the perfections reached by practicing devotional service, but this argument is not accepted by the great authorities. Lord Caitanya also condemned this idea while He was talking with Rāmānanda Rāya about the gradual development of devotional service. He rejected the idea of the importance of *varṇāśrama-dharma* when it was put forward by Rāmānanda Rāya. He said that this advancement of *varṇa* and *āśrama* is merely external. There is a higher principle. In *Bhagavad-gītā* also the Lord says that one has to give up all other principles of elevation and take simply to the method of Kṛṣṇa consciousness. That will help one in achieving the highest perfection of life.

In the Eleventh Canto, Twentieth Chapter, verse 9, of *Śrīmad-Bhāgavatam,* the Lord Himself says, "One should execute the prescribed duties of *varṇa* and *āśrama* as long as he has not developed spontaneous attachment for hearing about My pastimes and activities." In other words, the prescribed forms of *varṇa* and *āśrama* are ritualistic ceremonies of religion intended for economic development, sense gratification or salvation. All of these things are recommended for persons who have not developed Kṛṣṇa consciousness; in fact, all such activities are recommended in the revealed scriptures only to bring one to the point of Kṛṣṇa consciousness. But one who has already developed spontaneous attachment for Kṛṣṇa does not require to execute the duties prescribed in the scriptures.

14

Devotional Qualifications

Some scholars recommend that knowledge and renunciation are important factors for elevating oneself to devotional service. But actually that is not a fact. Actually, the cultivation of knowledge or renunciation, which are favorable for achieving a footing in Kṛṣṇa consciousness, may be accepted in the beginning, but ultimately they may also come to be rejected, for devotional service is dependent on nothing other than the sentiment or desire for such service. It requires nothing more than sincerity.

It is the opinion of expert devotees that mental speculation and the artificial austerities of *yoga* practice may be favorable for becoming liberated from material contamination, but they will also make one's heart harder and harder. They will not help at all in the progress of devotional service. These processes are therefore not favorable for entering into the transcendental loving service of the Lord. Actually, Kṛṣṇa consciousness—devotional service itself—is the only way of advancing in devotional life. Devotional service is absolute; it is both the cause and the effect. The Supreme Personality of Godhead is the cause and effect of all that be, and to approach Him, the Absolute, the process of devotional service—which is also absolute—has to be adopted.

This is confirmed in *Bhagavad-gītā* by the Lord Himself: "One can understand Me only through devotional service." In beginning His teaching of the *Gītā,* the Lord said to Arjuna, "Because you are My devotee, I shall teach these secrets to you." Vedic knowledge means ultimately to understand the Supreme Lord, and the process of entering into His kingdom is devotional service. That is accepted by all authentic scriptures. Mental speculators neglect the process of devotional service, and by simply trying to defeat others in philosophical research they fail to develop the ecstasy of devotion.

In the Eleventh Canto, Twentieth Chapter, verse 31, of *Śrīmad-Bhāgavatam,* Kṛṣṇa says, "My dear Uddhava, for persons who are seriously engaged in My service, the cultivation of philosophical speculation and artificial renunciation are not very favorable. When a person becomes My devotee he automatically attains the fruits of the renunciation of material enjoyment, and he gets sufficient knowledge to understand the Absolute Truth." That is the test of advancement in devotional service. A devotee cannot be in darkness, because the Lord shows him special favor and enlightens him from within.

In the Eleventh Canto, Twentieth Chapter, verses 32 and 33, of *Śrīmad-Bhāgavatam* the Lord further instructs Uddhava, "My dear friend, the profits derived from fruitive activities, austerities, the culture of philosophical knowledge, renunciation, the practice of mystic *yoga,* charity and all similar auspicious activities are automatically achieved by My devotees—those who are simply attached to Me by loving service. These devotees have everything at their disposal, but they desire nothing outside of My devotional service. If ever a devotee should desire some material profit, like promotion to the heavenly planets, or some spiritual profit—to go to the Vaikuṇṭhas—by My causeless mercy his desires are very easily fulfilled."

Actually, a person who is developing Kṛṣṇa consciousness and still has some attachment to material enjoyment will soon be freed from such a tendency by regularly discharging devotional service under the instruction of a bona fide spiritual master.

Śrīla Rūpa Gosvāmī, then, recommends that one should not be attached to material sense enjoyment, but should accept everything enjoyable which is in relationship to Kṛṣṇa. For example, eating is necessary, and one wants some palatable dishes to satisfy his sense of taste. So in that case, for the satisfaction of Kṛṣṇa rather than for the satisfaction of the tongue, some palatable dishes may be prepared and offered to Kṛṣṇa. Then it is renunciation. Let the palatable dishes be prepared, but unless they are offered to Kṛṣṇa one should not accept them for eating. This vow of rejecting anything which is not offered to Kṛṣṇa is actually renunciation. And by such renunciation one is able to satisfy the demands of the senses.

The impersonalists, who try to avoid everything material, may undergo severe austerities, but they miss the opportunity of being engaged in the service of the Lord. Thus their renunciation is not sufficient for perfection. There are many instances where, following such artificial renunciation without any contact with devotional service, the impersonalist again fell down and became attracted to material contamination. There are many supposed renouncers even at the present moment who officially become *sannyāsīs,* or renouncers, and outwardly claim that spiritual existence is truth and material existence untruth. In this way, artificially they make a show of renunciation of the material world. However, because they cannot reach the point of devotional service, they fail to achieve the goal, and they again come back to material activities, such as philanthropic work and political agitation. There are many examples of so-called *sannyāsīs* who gave up the world as untruth but again came to the material world, because they were not seeking their real repose at the lotus feet of the Lord.

One should not give up anything which can be utilized in the service of the Lord. That is a secret of devotional service. Anything that can be utilized in advancing Kṛṣṇa consciousness and devotional service should be accepted. For instance, we are using many machines for the advancement of our present Kṛṣṇa consciousness movement, machines like typewriters, dictating machines, tape recorders, microphones and airplanes. Sometimes people ask us, "Why are you utilizing material products if you condemn the advancement of material civilization?" But actually we do not condemn. We simply ask people to do whatever they are doing in Kṛṣṇa consciousness. This is the same principle on which, in *Bhagavad-gītā,* Kṛṣṇa advised Arjuna to utilize his fighting abilities in devotional service. Similarly, we are utilizing these machines for Kṛṣṇa's service. With such sentiment for Kṛṣṇa, or Kṛṣṇa consciousness, we can accept everything. If the typewriter can be utilized for advancing our Kṛṣṇa consciousness movement, we must accept it. Similarly, the dictating machine or any other machine must be used. Our vision is that Kṛṣṇa is everything. Kṛṣṇa is the cause and effect, and nothing belongs to us. Kṛṣṇa's things must be used in the service of Kṛṣṇa. That is our vision.

This does not mean, however, that we should give up the principles of discharging devotional service or neglect abiding by the rules and regulations prescribed therein. In the neophyte stage of devotion one must follow all the principles, regulated by the authority of the spiritual master. The acceptance and rejection of things should always be in pursuance of the devotional principles; not that one can independently manufacture some idea of what should be accepted or rejected. The spiritual master as the visible manifestation of Kṛṣṇa is necessary, therefore, to direct the devotee on behalf of the Supreme Personality of Godhead.

The spiritual master must never be carried away by an accumulation of wealth or a large number of followers. A bona fide spiritual master will never become like that. But sometimes, if a spiritual master is not properly authorized and only on his own initiative becomes a spiritual master, he may be carried away by an accumulation of wealth and large numbers of disciples. His is not a very high grade of devotional service. If a person is carried away by such achievements, then his devotional service becomes slackened. One should therefore strictly adhere to the principles of disciplic succession.

A Kṛṣṇa conscious person, being naturally purified, has no need of developing any other purificatory process of thought or action. On account of his being highly elevated in Kṛṣṇa consciousness, he has already acquired all the good qualities and is following the rules and regulations prescribed for the mystic yogic process. Such rules are automatically practiced by the devotees. A concrete example is the quality of nonviolence, which is considered a good qualification. A devotee is naturally nonviolent and therefore doesn't have to practice nonviolence separately. Some people seek purification by joining a vegetarian movement, but a devotee is automatically a vegetarian. He doesn't need to practice separately in this matter or to join any society for vegetarians. He is automatically a vegetarian.

There are many other instances showing that a devotee needn't practice anything but Kṛṣṇa consciousness; all the good qualities of the demigods automatically develop within him. Those who are intentionally practicing to be vegetarians or to become nonviolent may have good qualifications by a material estimation, but these qualifications are not sufficient to make them devotees. A vegetarian is not necessarily a devotee, nor is a nonviolent person. But a devotee is automatically both vegetarian and nonviolent. We must conclude, therefore, that vegetarianism or nonviolence is not the cause of devotion.

In this connection, there is a story in the *Skanda Purāṇa* about a hunter who was converted into a great devotee under the instruction of Nārada Muni. When the hunter became a perfect devotee, he was not prepared to kill even an ant. Parvata Muni, a friend of Nārada's, saw the wonderful transformation of the hunter by devotional service and remarked, "My dear hunter, your unwillingness to kill even an ant is not very astonishing. Any person who develops the devotional attitude has *all* the good qualities automatically manifested in his person. A devotee is never a cause of distress to anyone."

Śrī Rūpa Gosvāmī affirms herein that purification of consciousness, purification of bodily activities, austerities, peace of mind, etc., all become automatically manifest in the person who is engaged in devotional service.

Śrī Rūpa Gosvāmī affirms herein that there are nine different kinds of devotional service, which are listed as hearing, chanting, remembering, serving, worshiping the Deity in the temple, praying, carrying out orders, serving Kṛṣṇa as a friend and sacrificing everything for Him. Each and every one of these processes is so powerful that if anyone follows even one single one of them, he can achieve the desired perfection without fail. For example, if one is attached simply to hearing about the Lord and another is attached to chanting the glories of the name, both will achieve their desired goal in devotional service. In the *Caitanya-caritāmṛta* this has been explained. One may execute one, two, three or all the different processes of devotional service, and at the ultimate end he will achieve the desired goal of being established in devotional service.

There are concrete examples of how a devotee discharged one of these services and achieved perfection. King Parīkṣit achieved the desired goal of life simply by hearing *Śrīmad-Bhāgavatam*. Śukadeva Gosvāmī achieved the desired goal of life simply by reciting *Śrīmad-Bhāgavatam*. Prahlāda Mahārāja became successful in his devotional service by always remembering the Lord. Lakṣmī, the goddess of fortune, was successful by engaging herself in massaging the lotus feet of the Lord. King Pṛthu became successful by worshiping in the temple. Akrūra became successful by offering prayers. Hanumān became successful by rendering personal service to Lord Rāmacandra. Arjuna became successful by being a friend of Kṛṣṇa. And Bali Mahārāja became successful simply by offering all of his possessions to Kṛṣṇa.

There are also examples of devotees who discharged all the different items together. In the Ninth Canto, Fourth Chapter, verses 18, 19 and 20, of *Śrīmad-Bhāgavatam*, there is a statement about Mahārāja Ambarīṣa, who followed every one of the devotional processes. In these verses, Śukadeva Gosvāmī says, "King Ambarīṣa first of all concentrated his mind on the lotus feet of Lord Kṛṣṇa and then engaged his speech in describing the pastimes and activities of the Lord. He engaged his hands in washing the temple of the Lord. He engaged his ears in hearing of the transcendental glories of the Lord. He engaged his eyes in seeing the beautiful Deity in the temple. He engaged his body in associating with the pure devotees of the Lord. [When you associate with someone you have to sit down together, eat together, etc.—and in this way the touch of your body with his body is inevitable. Ambarīṣa Mahārāja made his association only with pure devotees and did not allow his body to be touched by anyone else.] He engaged his nostrils in smelling the flowers and *tulasī* offered to Kṛṣṇa, and he engaged his tongue in tasting Kṛṣṇa *prasāda* [food prepared specifically for offering to the Lord, the remnants of which are taken by the devotees]. Mahārāja Ambarīṣa was able to offer very nice *prasāda* to Kṛṣṇa because he was a king and had no scarcity of finances. He used to offer Kṛṣṇa the most royal dishes and would then taste the remnants as *kṛṣṇa-prasāda*. There was no scarcity in his royal style, because he had a very beautiful temple wherein the Deity of the Lord was decorated with costly paraphernalia and offered high-grade food. So everything was available, and his engagement was always completely in Kṛṣṇa consciousness." The idea is that we should follow in the footsteps of great devotees. If we are unable to execute all the different items of devotional service, we must try to execute at least one of them, as exemplified by previous *ācāryas*. If we are engaged in the execution of all the items of devotional service, as was Mahārāja Ambarīṣa, then the perfection of devotional service is guaranteed from each one of these items. With the first complete engagement, one becomes automatically detached from material contamination, and liberation becomes the maidservant of the devotee. This idea is confirmed by Bilvamaṅgala Ṭhākura. If one develops unalloyed devotion to the Lord, liberation will follow the devotee as his maidservant.

Śrīla Rūpa Gosvāmī says that the regulative principles of devotional service are sometimes described by authorities as the path of serving the Lord in opulence.

15

Spontaneous Devotional Service

Examples of spontaneous devotional service can be easily seen in Kṛṣṇa's direct associates in Vṛndāvana. The spontaneous dealings of the residents of Vṛndāvana in relationship with Kṛṣṇa are called *rāgātmikā*. These beings don't have to learn anything about devotional service; they are already perfect in all regulative principles and have achieved the spontaneous loving service of the Supreme Personality of Godhead. For example, the cowherd boys who are playing with Kṛṣṇa do not have to learn by austerities or penances or yogic practice how to play with Him. They have passed all tests of regulative principles in their previous lives, and as a result they are now elevated to the position of direct association with Kṛṣṇa as His dear friends. Their spontaneous attitude is called *rāgātmikā-bhakti*.

Śrī Rūpa Gosvāmī has defined *rāgātmikā-bhakti* as spontaneous attraction for something while completely absorbed in thoughts in it, with an intense desire of love. Devotional service executed with such feelings of spontaneous love is called *rāgātmikā-bhakti*. Devotional service under the heading of *ragātmikā* can be further divided into two categories: one category is called "sensual attraction," and the other is called "relationship."

In this connection, there is a statement by Nārada Muni to Yudhiṣṭhira in the Seventh Canto, First Chapter, verse 30, of *Śrīmad-Bhāgavatam*. There Nārada says, "My dear King, there are many devotees who first become attracted to the Personality of Godhead for purposes of sense gratification, from being envious of Him, out of fear of Him or from desiring to associate affectionately with Him. Ultimately these attractions become freed from all material contamination, and gradually the worshiper develops spiritual love and achieves that ultimate goal of life desired by the pure devotee."

The *gopīs* may be considered to be examples of spontaneous love in sensual attraction. The *gopīs* are young girls, and Kṛṣṇa is a young boy. Superficially it seems that the *gopīs* are attracted to Kṛṣṇa on grounds of sex. Similarly, King Kaṁsa was attracted to Kṛṣṇa because of fear. Kaṁsa was always fearful of Kṛṣṇa, because it had been foretold that his sister's son, Kṛṣṇa, would kill him. Śiśupāla was also always envious of Kṛṣṇa. And the descendants of King Yadu, due to their family relationship with Kṛṣṇa, were always thinking of Him as one of their members. All of these different kinds of devotees have a spontaneous attraction for Kṛṣṇa, in different categories, and they achieve the same desired goal of life.

The attraction of the *gopīs* for Kṛṣṇa and the affection of the members of the Yadu dynasty are both accepted as spontaneous, or *rāgātmikā*. The attraction of Kaṁsa to Kṛṣṇa in fear and the attraction of Śiśupāla in envy are not accepted as devotional service, however, because their attitudes are not favorable. Devotional service should be executed only in a favorable frame of mind. Therefore, according to Śrīla Rūpa Gosvāmī, such attractions are not considered to be in devotional service. Again, he analyzes the affection of the Yadus. If it is on the platform of friendship, then it is spontaneous love, but if it is on the platform of regulative principles, then it is not. And only when affection comes to the platform of spontaneous love is it counted in the category of pure devotional service.

There may be some difficulty in understanding that both the *gopīs* and Kaṁsa achieved the same goal, so this point should be clearly understood, because the attitudes of Kaṁsa and Śiśupāla were different from that of the *gopīs*. Although in all these cases the focus is on the Supreme Personality of Godhead, and all of the devotees are elevated to the spiritual world, there is still a distinction between these two classes of souls. In the First Canto of *Śrīmad-Bhāgavatam* it is said that the Absolute Truth is one and that He is manifested as impersonal Brahman, Paramātmā (Supersoul) and Bhagavān (the Supreme Personality of Godhead). Here is a spiritual distinction. Although Brahman, Paramātmā and Bhagavān are the same-and-one Absolute Truth, devotees like Kaṁsa or Śiśupāla could attain only to the Brahman effulgence. They could not have realization of Paramātmā or Bhagavān. That is the distinction.

An analogy can be given with the sun globe and the sunshine: to remain in the sunshine does not mean one has gone to the sun globe. The temperature of the sun globe is different from the temperature of the sunshine. One who has gone through the sunshine in jet planes or in spaceships has not necessarily gone to the sun globe. Although the sunshine and the sun globe are actually one and the same, still there is a distinction, for one is the energy and one is the energetic source. The Absolute Truth and His bodily effulgence are in the same way simultaneously one and different. Kaṁsa and Śiśupāla attained to the Absolute Truth, but they were not allowed to enter into the Goloka Vṛndāvana abode. Impersonalists and the enemies of the Lord are, because of attraction to God, allowed to enter into His kingdom, but they are not allowed to enter into the Vaikuṇṭha planets or the Goloka Vṛndāvana planet of the Supreme Lord. To enter the kingdom and to enter the king's palace are not the same thing.

Śrīla Rūpa Gosvāmī is trying here to describe the different achievements of the impersonalists and the personalists. Generally, those who are impersonalists and are inimical to the Supreme Personality of Godhead get entrance only into the impersonal Brahman, when and if they reach spiritual perfection. The impersonalist philosophers are in one sense like the enemies of the Lord, because the out-and-out enemies of the Lord and the impersonalists are both allowed to enter only into the impersonal effulgence of the *brahmajyoti*. So it is to be understood that they are of similar classification. And actually the impersonalists are enemies of God, because they cannot tolerate the unparalleled opulence of the Lord. They try always to place themselves on the same level with the Lord. That is due to their envious attitude. Śrī Caitanya Mahāprabhu has proclaimed the impersonalists to be offenders of the Lord. The Lord is so kind, however, that even though they are His enemies, they are still allowed to enter into the spiritual kingdom and remain in the impersonal *brahmajyoti*, the undifferentiated light of the Absolute.

Sometimes an impersonalist may gradually elevate himself to the personal conception of the Lord. *Bhagavad-gītā* confirms this: "After many births and deaths, he who is actually in knowledge surrenders unto Me." By such surrender, an impersonalist can be elevated to the Vaikuṇṭhaloka (spiritual planet) where, as a surrendered soul, he attains bodily features like those of the Lord.

In the *Brahmāṇḍa Purāṇa* it is stated, "Those who have achieved liberation from material contamination and those who are demons and are killed by the Supreme Personality of Godhead become absorbed in the Brahman concept of life and reside in the spiritual sky of the *brahmajyoti*." That spiritual sky is far beyond the material sky, and it is confirmed also in *Bhagavad-gītā* that beyond this material sky there is another, eternal sky. The enemies and the impersonalists may be allowed to enter into this Brahman effulgence, but the devotees of Kṛṣṇa are promoted all the way to the spiritual planets. Because the pure devotees have developed their spontaneous love for the Supreme Personality of Godhead, they are allowed to enter into the spiritual planets to enjoy spiritual bliss in association with the Supreme Personality of Godhead.

In the Tenth Canto, Eighty-seventh Chapter, verse 23, of *Śrīmad-Bhāgavatam*, the *Vedas* personified address the Lord in this way: "My dear Lord, *yogīs* meditate upon Your localized feature, and thus they achieve the spiritual perfection of being merged in the impersonal *brahmajyoti*. Persons who treat You as an enemy achieve the same perfection without meditating. The *gopīs,* who are embraced by Your serpentine arms and who have such lusty attitudes, also achieve the same perfection. And as far as we are concerned, being different demigods in charge of the different parts of Vedic knowledge, we are always following in the footsteps of the *gopīs*. Thus we hope to attain the same perfection." By "the same perfection" we must always remember the example of the sun and the sunshine. Those who are impersonalists can merge into the sunshinelike *brahmajyoti,* whereas those who are in love with the Supreme Person enter into the supreme abode of the Lord, Goloka Vṛndāvana.

The "lusty attitude" of the *gopīs* does not refer to any sort of sex indulgence. Śrīla Rūpa Gosvāmī explains that this "lusty desire" refers to the devotee's particular attitude of association with Kṛṣṇa. Every devotee in his perfectional stage has a spontaneous attraction to the Lord. This attraction is sometimes called the "lusty desire" of the devotee. The lust is the devotee's excessive desire to serve the Lord in a particular capacity. Such a desire may seem to be a desire for enjoying the Lord, but actually the endeavor is to serve the Lord in that capacity. For example, a devotee may be desiring to associate with the Personality of Godhead as His cowherd friend. He will want to serve the Lord by assisting Him in controlling the cows in the pasturing ground. This may appear to be a desire to enjoy the company of the Lord, but actually it is spontaneous love, serving Him by assisting in managing the transcendental cows.

Sensual Attraction

This extreme desire to serve the Lord is manifest in the transcendental land of Vraja. And it is specifically manifested among the *gopīs*. The *gopīs'* love for Kṛṣṇa is so elevated that for our understanding it is sometimes explained as being "lusty desire."

The author of *Śrī Caitanya-caritāmṛta,* Kavirāja Kṛṣṇadāsa, has explained the distinction between lusty desire and the service attitude in this statement: "'Lusty desire' refers to the desire to gratify one's personal senses, and 'transcendental desire' refers to the desire for serving the senses of the Lord." In the material world there is no such thing as a lover's wanting to please the senses of his beloved. Actually, in the material world, everyone wants mainly to gratify his own personal senses. The *gopīs,* however, wanted nothing at all but to gratify the senses of the Lord, and there is no instance of this in the material world. Therefore the *gopīs'* ecstatic love for Kṛṣṇa is sometimes described by scholars as being like the "lusty desire" of the material world, but actually this should not be taken as a literal fact. It is simply a way of trying to understand the transcendental situation.

Great devotees up to the standard of Uddhava are very dear friends of the Lord, and they desire to follow in the footsteps of the *gopīs*. So the *gopīs'* love for Kṛṣṇa is certainly not material lusty desire. Otherwise, how could Uddhava aspire to follow in their footsteps? Another instance is Lord Caitanya Himself. After accepting the *sannyāsa* order of life, He was very, very strict about avoiding association with women, but still He taught that there is no better method of worshiping Kṛṣṇa than that conceived by the *gopīs*. Thus the *gopīs'* method of worshiping the Lord as if impelled by lusty desire was praised very highly even by Śrī Caitanya Mahaprabhu. This very fact means that although the attraction of the *gopīs* for Kṛṣṇa appears to be lusty, it is not in the least bit material. Unless one is fully situated in the transcendental position, the relationship of the *gopīs* with Kṛṣṇa is very difficult to understand. But because it appears to be just like ordinary dealings of young boys and girls, it is sometimes misinterpreted to be like the ordinary sex of this material world. Unfortunately, persons who cannot understand the transcendental nature of the loving affairs of the *gopīs* and Kṛṣṇa take it for granted that Kṛṣṇa's loving affairs with the *gopīs* are mundane transactions, and therefore they sometimes indulge in painting licentious pictures in some modernistic style.

On the other hand, the lusty desire of Kubjā is described by learned scholars as being "almost lusty desire." Kubjā was a hunchbacked woman who also wanted Kṛṣṇa with a great ecstatic love. But her desire for Kṛṣṇa was almost mundane, and so her love cannot be compared to the love of the *gopīs*. Her loving affection for Kṛṣṇa is called *kāma-prāyā,* or almost like the *gopīs'* love for Kṛṣṇa.

16

Spontaneous Devotion Further Described

Relationship

In the attitude of the denizens of Vṛndāvana, such as Nanda Mahārāja and Mother Yaśodā, is to be found the ideal transcendental concept of being the father and mother of Kṛṣṇa, the original Personality of Godhead. Factually, no one can become the father or mother of Kṛṣṇa, but a devotee's possession of such transcendental feelings is called love of Kṛṣṇa in a parental relationship. The Vṛṣṇis (Kṛṣṇa's relatives at Dvārakā) also felt like that. So spontaneous love of Kṛṣṇa in the parental relationship is found both among those denizens of Dvārakā who belonged to the dynasty of Vṛṣṇi and among the inhabitants of Vṛndāvana.

Spontaneous love of Kṛṣṇa as exhibited by the Vṛṣṇis and the denizens of Vṛndāvana is eternally existing in them. In the stage of devotional service where regulative principles are followed, there is no necessity of discussing this love, for it must develop of itself at a more advanced stage.

Eligibility for Spontaneous Devotional Service

Persons desiring to follow in the footsteps of such eternal devotees of the Lord as the Vṛṣṇis and Vṛndāvana denizens are called *rāgānugā* devotees, which means that they are trying to attain to the perfection of those devotees. These *rāgānugā* devotees do not follow the regulative principles of devotional service very strictly, but by spontaneous nature they become attracted to some of the eternal devotees such as Nanda or Yaśodā, and they try to follow in their footsteps spontaneously. There is a gradual development of the ambition to become like a particular devotee, and this activity is called *rāgānugā*.

We must always remember, however, that such eagerness to follow in the footsteps of the denizens of Vraja (Vṛndāvana) is not possible unless one is freed from material contamination. In following the regulative principles of devotional service, there is a stage called *anartha-nivṛtti,* which means the disappearance of all material contamination. Sometimes someone is found imitating such devotional love, but factually he is not freed from *anarthas,* or unwanted habits. It has been seen that a so-called devotee proclaims himself a follower of Nanda, Yaśodā or the *gopīs,* while at the same time his abominable attraction for mundane sex life is visible. Such a manifestation of divine love is mere imitation and has no value. When one is actually spontaneously attracted to the loving principles of the *gopīs,* there will be found no trace of any mundane contamination in his character.

Therefore, in the beginning, everyone should strictly follow the regulative principles of devotional service, according to the injunctions of the scriptures and the spiritual master. Only after the stage of liberation from material contamination can one actually aspire to follow in the footsteps of the devotees in Vṛndāvana.

It is said by Śrī Rūpa Gosvāmī, "When one is actually liberated from material contamination, he can always remember an eternal devotee in Vṛndāvana in order to love Kṛṣṇa in the same capacity. And developing such an aptitude, one will always live in Vṛndāvana, even within his mind." The purport is that if it is possible one should go and physically be present at Vrajabhūmi, Vṛndāvana, and be engaged always in the service of the Lord, following the devotees in Vraja-dhāma, the spiritual realm of Vraja. If it is not possible, however, to be physically present at Vṛndāvana, one can meditate anywhere upon living in that situation. Wherever he may be, one must always think about life in Vraja-dhāma and about following in the footsteps of a particular devotee in the service of the Lord.

A devotee who is actually advanced in Kṛṣṇa consciousness, who is constantly engaged in devotional service, should not manifest himself, even though he has attained perfection. The idea is that he should always continue to act as a neophyte devotee as long as his material body is there. Activities in devotional service under regulative principles must be followed even by the pure devotee. But when he realizes his actual position in relationship with the Lord, he can, along with the discharging of regulative service, think within himself of the Lord, under the guidance of a particular associate of the Lord, and develop his transcendental sentiments in following that associate.

In this connection, we should be careful about the so-called *siddha-praṇālī*. The *siddha-praṇālī* process is followed by a class of men who are not very authorized and who have manufactured their own way of devotional service. They imagine that they have become associates of the Lord simply by thinking of themselves like that. This external behavior is not at all according to the regulative principles. The so-called *siddha-praṇālī* process is followed by the *prākṛta-sahajiyās,* a pseudosect of so-called Vaiṣṇavas. In the opinion of Rūpa Gosvāmī, such activities are simply disturbances to the standard way of devotional service.

Śrī Rūpa Gosvāmī says that learned *ācāryas* recommend that we follow the regulative principles even after the development of spontaneous love for Kṛṣṇa. According to the regulative principles, there are nine departmental activities, as described above, and one should specifically engage himself in the type of devotional service for which he has a natural aptitude. For example, one person may have a particular interest in hearing, another may have a particular interest in chanting, and another may have a particular interest in serving in the temple. So these, or any of the other six different types of devotional service (remembering, serving, praying, engaging in some particular service, being in a friendly relationship or offering everything in one's possession), should be executed in full earnestness. In this way, everyone should act according to his particular taste.

Conjugal Love

Devotional service following in the footsteps of the *gopīs* of Vṛndāvana or the queens at Dvārakā is called devotional service in conjugal love. This devotional service in conjugal love can be divided into two categories. One is indirect conjugal love, the other direct. In both of these categories, one has to follow the particular *gopī* who is engaged in such service in Goloka Vṛndāvana. To be directly attached to the Supreme Personality of Godhead in conjugal love is technically called *keli*. This *keli* performance means to directly join with the Supreme Personality of Godhead. There are other devotees who do not wish direct contact with the Supreme Person, but who relish the conjugal loving affairs of the Lord with the *gopīs*. Such devotees enjoy simply by hearing of the activities of the Lord with the *gopīs*.

This development of conjugal love can be possible only with those who are already engaged in following the regulative principles of devotional service, specifically in the worship of Rādhā and Kṛṣṇa in the temple. Such devotees gradually develop a spontaneous love for the Deity, and by hearing of the Lord's exchange of loving affairs with the *gopīs,* they gradually become attracted to these pastimes. After this spontaneous attraction becomes highly developed, the devotee is placed in either of the above-mentioned categories.

This development of conjugal love for Kṛṣṇa is not manifested in women only. The material body has nothing to do with spiritual loving affairs. A woman may develop an attitude for becoming a friend of Kṛṣṇa, and, similarly, a man may develop the feature of becoming a *gopī* in Vṛndāvana. How a devotee in the form of a man can desire to become a *gopī* is stated in the *Padma Purāṇa* as follows: In days gone by there were many sages in Daṇḍakāraṇya. Daṇḍakāraṇya is the name of the forest where Lord Rāmacandra lived after being banished by His father for fourteen years. At that time there were many advanced sages who were captivated by the beauty of Lord Rāmacandra and who desired to become women in order to embrace the Lord. Later on, these sages appeared in Gokula Vṛndāvana when Kṛṣṇa advented Himself there, and they were born as *gopīs,* or girlfriends of Kṛṣṇa. In this way they attained the perfection of spiritual life.

The story of the sages of Daṇḍakāraṇya can be explained as follows. When Lord Rāmacandra was residing in Daṇḍakāraṇya, the sages who were engaged in devotional service there became attracted by His beauty and immediately thought of the *gopīs* at Vṛndāvana, who enjoyed conjugal loving affection with Kṛṣṇa. In this instance it is clear that the sages of Daṇḍakāraṇya desired conjugal love in the manner of the *gopīs,* although they were well aware of the Supreme Lord as both Kṛṣṇa and Lord Rāmacandra. They knew that although Rāmacandra was an ideal king and could not accept more than one wife, Lord Kṛṣṇa, being the full-fledged Personality of Godhead, could fulfill the desires of all of them in Vṛndāvana. These sages also concluded that the form of Lord Kṛṣṇa is more attractive than that of Lord Rāmacandra, and so they prayed to become *gopīs* in their future lives to be associated with

Kṛṣṇa. Lord Rāmacandra remained silent, and His silence shows that He accepted the prayers of the sages. Thus they were blessed by Lord Rāmacandra to have association with Lord Kṛṣṇa in their future lives. As a result of this benediction, they all took birth as women in the wombs of *gopīs* at Gokula, and as they had desired in their previous lives, they enjoyed the company of Lord Kṛṣṇa, who was present at that time in Gokula Vṛndāvana. The perfection of their human form of life was thus achieved by their generating a transcendental sentiment to share conjugal love with Lord Kṛṣṇa.

Conjugal love is divided into two classifications—namely, conjugal love as husband and wife and conjugal love as lover and beloved. One who develops conjugal love for Kṛṣṇa as a wife is promoted to Dvārakā, where the devotee becomes the queen of the Lord. One who develops conjugal love for Kṛṣṇa as a lover is promoted to Goloka Vṛndāvana, to associate with the *gopīs* and enjoy loving affairs with Kṛṣṇa there. We should note carefully, however, that this conjugal love for Kṛṣṇa, either as *gopī* or as queen, is not limited only to women. Even men can develop such sentiments, as was evidenced by the sages of Daṇḍakāraṇya. If someone simply desires conjugal love but does not follow in the footsteps of the *gopīs,* he is promoted to association with the Lord at Dvārakā.

In the *Mahā-kūrma Purāṇa* it is stated, "Great sages who were the sons of fire-gods rigidly followed the regulative principles in their desire to have conjugal love for Kṛṣṇa. As such, in their next lives they were able to associate with the Lord, the origin of all creation, who is known as Vāsudeva, or Kṛṣṇa, and all of them got Him as their husband."

Parenthood or Friendship

Devotees who are attracted to Kṛṣṇa as parents or as friends should follow in the footsteps of Nanda Mahārāja or Subala, respectively. Nanda Mahārāja is the foster father of Kṛṣṇa, and out of all of the friends of Kṛṣṇa, Subala is the most intimate in Vrajabhūmi.

In the development of becoming either the father or friend of the Lord, there are two varieties. One method is that one may try to become the father of the Lord directly, and the other is that one may follow Nanda Mahārāja and cherish the ideal of being Kṛṣṇa's father. Out of these two, the attempt to directly become the father of Kṛṣṇa is not recommended. Such a development can become polluted with Māyāvāda (impersonal) philosophy. The Māyāvādīs, or monists, think that they themselves are Kṛṣṇa, and if one thinks that he himself has become Nanda Mahārāja, then his parental love will become contaminated with the Māyāvāda philosophy. The Māyāvāda philosophical way of thinking is offensive, and no offender can enter into the kingdom of God to associate with Kṛṣṇa.

In the *Skanda Purāṇa* there is a story of an old man residing in Hastināpura, capital of the kingdom of the Pāṇḍus, who desired Kṛṣṇa as his beloved son. This old man was instructed by Nārada to follow in the footsteps of Nanda Mahārāja, and thus he achieved success.

There is a statement in the *Nārāyaṇa-vyūha-stava* prayers that persons who are always engaged in thinking of the Lord as their husband, friend, father or well-wisher are always worshipable by everyone. This spontaneous love for Kṛṣṇa can be developed only by the special mercy of Kṛṣṇa or His pure devotee. This process of devotional service is sometimes called *puṣṭi-mārga*. *Puṣṭi* means "nourishing," and *mārga* means "path." Such development of sentiment nourishes devotional service to the highest standard. Thus it is called the path of nourishment, or *puṣṭi-mārga*. The Vallabha-sampradāya, which belongs to the Viṣṇu Svāmī sect of Vaiṣṇava religion, worships Kṛṣṇa in this *puṣṭi-mārga*. Generally devotees in Gujarat worship Bāla Kṛṣṇa, under this heading of *puṣṭi-mārga*.

17

Ecstatic Love

By the process of executing regulated devotional service, one is actually elevated onto the transcendental stage, beyond the material modes of nature. At that time one's heart becomes illuminated like the sun. The sun is far above the planetary systems, and there is no possibility of its being covered by any kind of cloud; similarly, when a devotee is purified like the sun, from his pure heart there is a diffusion of ecstatic love which is more glorious than the sunshine. Only at that time is the attachment to Kṛṣṇa perfect. Spontaneously, the devotee becomes eager to serve the Lord in his ecstatic love. At this stage the devotee is on the platform of *uttama-adhikārī,* perfect devotion. Such a devotee has no agitation from material affections and is interested only in the service of Rādhā and Kṛṣṇa.

To clarify, in the previous chapters the symptoms of devotional service were explained along with instructions as to how we may execute devotional service with our present senses and gradually rise to the platform of ecstasy in spontaneous love. And the two kinds of devotional service—namely devotional service through regulative principles and through spontaneous love—were discussed. Within the stage of the regulative principles of devotional service there are two divisions—namely executive and effective. This effective portion of devotional service is called *bhāva,* or ecstasy. In this connection, there is a statement in the *tantras* that ecstasy is the first symptom of pure love for the Personality of Godhead, and in that stage one is sometimes found shedding tears or shivering. Not always are these symptoms manifest, but occasionally. When King Ambarīṣa was put into difficulty by Durvāsā, he began to think of the lotus feet of the Lord, and thus there were some changes in his body, and tears were falling from his eyes. These symptoms are activities of ecstasy. They are visible in the shivering of the body and the shedding of tears. After the outward appearance of these ecstatic symptoms, they stay within the mind, and continuation of the ecstasy is called *samādhi*. This stage of appreciation becomes the cause of future exchanges of loving affairs with Kṛṣṇa.

Elevation to this stage of ecstasy can be possible in two ways. One way is by constant association with pure devotees. The other way is by the special mercy of Kṛṣṇa or by the mercy of a pure devotee of Kṛṣṇa. Elevation to the ecstatic stage of life is generally attained through association with pure devotees, while elevation to that stage by the special mercy of Kṛṣṇa or His devotee is very rare. The purport is that one should execute devotional service rigidly in the association of devotees so that there will be certainty in raising oneself to that ecstatic position. In special cases, of course, there is special favor from Kṛṣṇa, and although we should always expect that, we should not sit idly and simply wait for Kṛṣṇa's special mercy; the regular duties must be performed. It is just as when, sometimes, it is found that a person who never attended school or college may be recognized as a great scholar, or an honorary degree from great universities may be offered to him. But this does not mean that one should avoid school and expect to automatically receive an honorary degree from some university. Similarly, one should devoutly execute the regulative principles of devotional service and at the same time hope for Kṛṣṇa's favor or for His devotee's favor.

An example of rising to the stage of ecstatic love by executing the regulative principles of devotional service is given in the life story of Nārada, which is described to Vyāsadeva in *Śrīmad-Bhāgavatam*. Nārada tells there of his previous life and how he developed to the stage of ecstatic love. He was engaged in the service of great devotees and used to hear their talks and songs. Because he had the opportunity to hear these pastimes and songs of Kṛṣṇa from the mouths of pure devotees, he became very attracted within his heart. Because he had become so eager to hear these topics, he gradually developed within himself an ecstatic love for Kṛṣṇa. This ecstatic love is prior to the pure love of Kṛṣṇa, because in the next verse Nārada confirms that by the gradual process of hearing from the great sages he developed love of Godhead. In that connection, Nārada continues to say in the First Canto, Fifth Chapter, verse 28, of the *Bhāgavatam*, "First I passed my days in the association of the great sages during the rainy autumn season. Every morning and evening I heard them while they were singing and chanting the Hare Kṛṣṇa *mantra*, and thus my heart gradually became purified. As soon as I heard them with great attention, the influence of the modes of material ignorance and passion disappeared, and I became firmly fixed in devotional service to the Lord."

This is a practical example of how one can develop to the stage of ecstatic love simply by the association of pure devotees. It is essential, therefore, that one constantly associate with pure devotees who are engaged morning and evening in chanting the Hare Kṛṣṇa *mantra*. In this way one will get the chance to purify his heart and develop this ecstatic pure love for Kṛṣṇa.

This statement is also confirmed in the Third Canto, Twenty-fifth Chapter, verse 25, of *Śrīmad-Bhāgavatam,* where Lord Kapila says, "My dear mother, when a person is actually in association with pure devotees, the sublime potency of My devotional service can be experienced." In other words, when a pure devotee speaks, his words act upon the hearts of the audience. What is the secret of hearing and chanting? A professional speaker cannot impress transcendental ecstasy within the hearts of the listeners. However, when a realized soul who is engaged in the service of the Lord is speaking, he has the potency to inject spiritual life within the audience. One should, therefore, seek the association of such pure, unalloyed devotees, and by such association and service a neophyte devotee will certainly develop attachment, love and devotion for the Supreme Personality of Godhead.

In the *Padma Purāṇa* there is the story of a neophyte devotee who, in order to raise herself to the ecstatic platform, danced all night to invoke the Lord's grace upon her.

Sometimes, however, it is found that without undergoing any devotional process, one all of a sudden develops devotion for Lord Kṛṣṇa. This sudden development of the devotional attitude in a person must be understood as a special mercy of Kṛṣṇa or of His devotee. This apparently accidental development of ecstatic feelings through the causeless mercy of Kṛṣṇa can be divided into three groups: simply by speaking, simply by glancing and simply by good wishes.

In the *Nāradīya Purāṇa* there is a statement about development of ecstatic love simply by speaking. Lord Kṛṣṇa said to Nārada, "O best of the *brāhmaṇas,* I wish that you may develop unalloyed devotional service to Me, which is full of transcendental bliss and all auspiciousness."

In the *Skanda Purāṇa* there is a statement about developing ecstatic love toward Kṛṣṇa simply by glancing. It is stated there, "When the inhabitants of Jāṅgala Province saw the Personality of Godhead, Kṛṣṇa, they were so stricken with feeling that they could not withdraw their glance from Him."

As far as heartfelt wishes are concerned, there is a statement in the *Śuka-saṁhitā* where Nārada tells Śrīla Vyāsadeva, "You have a son who is the greatest devotee of the Personality of Godhead, and I can observe that without any following of the regulative principles of devotional service, he is already enriched with many of the symptoms achieved by the execution of devotional service after many, many births."

As for ecstatic love of Kṛṣṇa, there is a statement in the Seventh Canto, Fourth Chapter, verse 36, of *Śrīmad-Bhāgavatam,* in which Nārada addresses King Yudhiṣṭhira, "My dear King, it is very difficult to describe the character of Prahlāda. He developed a natural attraction for Kṛṣṇa, and whatever I can explain about his character will simply be an arrangement of words; his actual character is impossible to describe." This means that Nārada himself admitted that the natural development of Prahlāda's ecstatic love was by the grace of Lord Kṛṣṇa.

This natural attraction for Kṛṣṇa on the part of Prahlāda was developed simply by the mercy of Nārada. When Prahlāda Mahārāja was within the womb of his mother, she was being sympathetically instructed by Nārada about the science of devotional service, and at the same time Nārada was wishing that the child within the womb could also take advantage of the instructions. Because Nārada, an authorized devotee and great associate of the Personality of Godhead, was desiring auspiciousness for Prahlāda Mahārāja, he developed all the characteristics of a high-grade devotee. This is called natural attraction. It is caused by the special grace of the Personality of Godhead or by the special grace of a great devotee like Nārada.

There is a statement in the *Skanda Purāṇa* wherein Parvata Muni tells Nārada, "My dear Nārada, of all saintly persons you are so great and glorious that simply by your good wishes a lowborn hunter also has become a great, elevated devotee of Lord Kṛṣṇa."

This ecstatic love for Kṛṣṇa can be divided into five divisions, which will be described by Śrī Rūpa Gosvāmī later on.

18

Character of One in Ecstatic Love

Rūpa Gosvāmī next describes the characteristics of a person who has actually developed his ecstatic love for Kṛṣṇa. The characteristics are as follows:

(1) He is always anxious to utilize his time in the devotional service of the Lord. He does not like to be idle. He wants service always, twenty-four hours a day, without deviation.

(2) He is always reserved and perseverant.

(3) He is always detached from all material attraction.

(4) He does not long for any material respect in return for his activities.

(5) He is always certain that Kṛṣṇa will bestow His mercy upon him.

(6) He is always very eager to serve the Lord faithfully.

(7) He is very much attached to the chanting of the holy names of the Lord.

(8) He is always eager to describe the transcendental qualities of the Lord.

(9) He is very pleased to live in a place where the Lord's pastimes are performed, e.g., Mathurā, Vṛndāvana or Dvārakā.

Utilization of Time

An unalloyed devotee who has developed ecstatic love for Kṛṣṇa is always engaging his words in reciting prayers to the Lord. Within the mind he is always thinking of Kṛṣṇa, and with his body he either offers obeisances by bowing down before the Deity or engages in some other service. During these ecstatic activities he sometimes sheds tears. In this way his whole life is engaged in the service of the Lord, with not a moment wasted on any other engagement.

Perseverance

When a person is undisturbed even in the presence of various causes of disturbance, he is called reserved and perseverant. An example of this perseverance and reservation is found in the behavior of King Parīkṣit as described in the First Canto, Nineteenth Chapter, verse 15, of *Śrīmad-Bhāgavatam*. The King says there to all the sages present before him at the time of his death, "My dear *brāhmaṇas,* you should always accept me as your surrendered servant. I have come to the bank of the Ganges just to devote my heart and soul unto the lotus feet of Lord Kṛṣṇa. So please bless me, that mother Ganges may also be pleased with me. Let the curse of the *brāhmaṇa's* son fall upon me—I do not mind. I only request that at the last moment of my life all of you will kindly chant the holy name of Viṣṇu, so that I may realize His transcendental qualities."

This example of Mahārāja Parīkṣit's behavior, his remaining patient even at the last point of his life, his undisturbed condition of mind, is an example of reservation. This is one of the characteristics of a devotee who has developed ecstatic love for Kṛṣṇa.

Detachment

The senses are always desiring sense enjoyment, but when a devotee develops transcendental love for Kṛṣṇa his senses are no longer attracted by material desires. This state of mind is called detachment. There is a nice example of this detachment in connection with the character of King Bharata. In the Fifth Canto, Fourteenth Chapter, verse 43, of *Śrīmad-Bhāgavatam* it is stated, "Emperor Bharata was so attracted by the beauty of the lotus feet of Kṛṣṇa that even in his youthful life he gave up all kinds of attachments to family, children, friends, kingdom, etc., as though they were untouchable stools."

Emperor Bharata provides a typical example of detachment. He had everything enjoyable in the material world, but he left it. This means that detachment does not mean artificially keeping oneself aloof and apart from the allurements of attachment. Even in the presence of such allurements, if one can remain unattracted by material attachments, he is called detached. In the beginning, of course, a neophyte devotee must try to keep himself apart from all kinds of alluring attachments, but the real position of a mature devotee is that even in the presence of all allurements, he is not at all attracted. This is the actual criterion of detachment.

Pridelessness

When a devotee, in spite of possessing all the qualities of pure realization, is not proud of his position, he is called prideless. In the *Padma Purāṇa* it is stated that King Bhagīratha was the emperor above all other kings, yet he developed such ecstatic love for Kṛṣṇa that he became a mendicant and went out begging even to the homes of his political enemies and untouchables. He was so humble that he respectfully bowed down before them.

There are many similar instances in the history of India. Even very recently, about two hundred years ago or less, one big landlord known as Lāl Bābu, a Calcutta landholder, became a Vaiṣṇava and lived in Vṛndāvana. He was also begging from door to door, even at the homes of his political enemies. Begging involves being ready to be insulted by persons to whose home one has come. That is natural. But one has to tolerate such insults for the sake of Kṛṣṇa. The devotee of Kṛṣṇa can accept any position in the service of Kṛṣṇa.

Great Hope

The strong conviction that one will certainly receive the favor of the Supreme Personality of Godhead is called in Sanskrit *āśā-bandha*. *Āśā-bandha* means to continue to think, "Because I'm trying my best to follow the routine principles of devotional service, I am sure that I will go back to Godhead, back to home."

In this connection, one prayer by Rūpa Gosvāmī is sufficient to exemplify this hopefulness. He says, "I have no love for Kṛṣṇa, nor for the causes of developing love of Kṛṣṇa—namely, hearing and chanting. And the process of *bhakti-yoga,* by which one is always thinking of Kṛṣṇa and fixing His lotus feet in the heart, is also lacking in me. As far as philosophical knowledge or pious works are concerned, I don't see any opportunity for me to execute such activities. But above all, I am not even born of a nice family. Therefore I must simply pray to You, Gopījana-vallabha [Kṛṣṇa, maintainer and beloved of the *gopīs*]. I simply wish and hope that some way or other I may be able to approach Your lotus feet, and this hope is giving me pain, because I think myself quite incompetent to approach that transcendental goal of life." The purport is that under this heading of *āśā-bandha,* one should continue to hope against hope that some way or other he will be able to approach the lotus feet of the Supreme Lord.

Eagerness for Achieving the Desired Success

When one is sufficiently eager to achieve success in devotional service, that eagerness is called *samutkaṇṭhā*. This means "complete eagerness." Actually this eagerness is the price for achieving success in Kṛṣṇa consciousness. Everything has some value, and one has to pay the value before obtaining or possessing it. It is stated in the Vedic literature that to purchase the most valuable thing, Kṛṣṇa consciousness, one has to develop intense eagerness for achieving success. This intense eagerness is very nicely expressed by Bilvamaṅgala Ṭhākura in his book *Kṛṣṇa-karṇāmṛta*. He says, "I am eagerly waiting to see that boy of Vṛndāvana whose bodily beauty is captivating the whole universe, whose eyes are always bounded by black eyebrows and expanded like lotus petals, and who is always eagerly glancing over His devotees and therefore moving slightly here and there. His eyes are always moist, His lips are colored like copper, and through those lips there comes a sound vibration which drives one madder than a mad elephant. I want so much to see Him at Vṛndāvana!"

Attachment to Chanting the Holy Names of the Lord

In the same *Kṛṣṇa-karṇāmṛta* there is another statement, about the chanting of Rādhārāṇī. It is said by one of the associates of Rādhārāṇī, "O Lord Govinda, the girl who is the daughter of King Vṛṣabhānu is now shedding tears, and She is anxiously chanting Your holy name—'Kṛṣṇa! Kṛṣṇa!'"

Eagerness to Describe the Lord's Transcendental Qualities

Attachment for chanting the glories of the Lord is also expressed in the *Kṛṣṇa-karṇāmṛta* as follows: "What shall I do for Kṛṣṇa, who is pleasing beyond all pleasurable conceptions, and who is naughtier than all restless boys? The idea of Kṛṣṇa's beautiful activities is attracting my heart, and I do not know what I can do!"

Attraction for Living in a Place Where Kṛṣṇa Has His Pastimes

In the book *Padyāvalī* by Rūpa Gosvāmī there is the following statement about Vṛndāvana: "In this place the son of Mahārāja Nanda used to live with His father, who was king of all cowherd men. In this place Lord Kṛṣṇa broke the cart in which the Śakaṭāsura demon was concealed. At this place Dāmodara, who can cut the knot of our material existence, was tied up by His mother, Yaśodā."

A pure devotee of Lord Kṛṣṇa resides in the district of Mathurā or Vṛndāvana and visits all the places where Kṛṣṇa's pastimes were performed. At these sacred places Kṛṣṇa displayed His childhood activities with the cowherd boys and Mother Yaśodā. The system of circumambulating all these places is still current among devotees of Lord Kṛṣṇa, and those coming to Mathurā and Vṛndāvana always feel transcendental pleasure. Actually, if someone goes to Vṛndāvana, he will immediately feel separation from Kṛṣṇa, who performed such nice activities when He was present there.

Such attraction for remembering Kṛṣṇa's activities is known as attachment for Kṛṣṇa. There are impersonalist philosophers and mystics, however, who by a show of devotional service want ultimately to merge into the existence of the Supreme Lord. They sometimes try to imitate a pure devotee's sentiment for visiting the holy places where Kṛṣṇa had His pastimes, but they simply have a view for salvation, and so their activities cannot be considered attachment.

It is said by Rūpa Gosvāmī that the attachment exhibited by pure devotees for Kṛṣṇa cannot possibly be perfected in the hearts of fruitive workers (*karmīs*) or mental speculators, because such attachment in pure Kṛṣṇa consciousness is very rare and not possible to achieve even for many liberated persons. As stated in *Bhagavad-gītā,* liberation from material contamination is the stage at which devotional service can be achieved. For a person who simply wants to have liberation and to merge into the impersonal *brahmajyoti,* attachment to Kṛṣṇa is not possible to acquire. This attachment is very confidentially kept by Kṛṣṇa and is bestowed only upon pure devotees. Even ordinary devotees cannot have such pure attachment for Kṛṣṇa. Therefore, how is it possible for success to be achieved by persons whose hearts are contaminated by the actions and reactions of fruitive activities and who are entangled by various types of mental speculation?

There are many so-called devotees who artificially think of Kṛṣṇa's pastimes known as *aṣṭa-kālīya-līlā.* Sometimes one may artificially imitate these, pretending that Kṛṣṇa is talking with him in the form of a boy, or else one may pretend that Rādhārāṇī and Kṛṣṇa both have come to him and are talking with him. Such characteristics are sometimes exhibited by the impersonalist class of men, and they may captivate some innocent persons who have no knowledge in the science of devotional service. However, as soon as an experienced devotee sees all of these caricatures, he can immediately evaluate such rascaldom. If such a pretender is sometimes seen possessing imitative attachment to Kṛṣṇa, that will not be accepted as real attachment. It may be said, however, that such attachment gives the pretender hope that he may eventually rise onto the actual platform of pure devotional service.

This imitative attachment can be divided into two headings—namely, shadow attachment and *parā* (transcendental) attachment. If someone, without undergoing the regulative principles of devotional service or without being guided by a bona fide spiritual master, shows such imitative attachment, this is called shadow attachment. Sometimes it is found that a person actually attached to material enjoyment or salvation has the good fortune to associate with pure devotees while they are engaged in chanting the holy name of the Lord. By the good grace of the Lord one may also cooperate and join in the chanting. At that time, simply by the association of such pure devotees, the moonlike rays from their hearts reflect on him, and by the influence of the pure devotees he may show some likeness of attachment caused by inquisitiveness, but this is very flickering. And if by the manifestation of such shadow attachment one feels the disappearance of all material pangs, then it is called *parā* attachment.

Such shadow attachment or *parā* attachment can develop if one associates with a pure devotee or visits holy places like Vṛndāvana or Mathurā, and if an ordinary man develops such attachment for Kṛṣṇa and fortunately performs devotional activities in the association of pure devotees, he can also rise to the platform of pure devotional service. The conclusion is that transcendental attachment is so powerful that if such attachment is seen manifested even in some common man, by the association of a pure devotee it can bring one to the perfectional stage. But such attachment for Kṛṣṇa cannot be invoked in a person without his being sufficiently blessed by the association of pure devotees.

As attachment can be invoked by the association of pure devotees, so attachment can also be extinguished by offenses committed at the lotus feet of pure devotees. To be more clear, by the association of pure devotees attachment for Kṛṣṇa can be aroused, but if one commits offenses at the lotus feet of a devotee, one's shadow attachment or *parā* attachment can be extinguished. This extinguishing is like the waning of the full moon, which gradually decreases and at last becomes dark. One should therefore be very careful while associating with pure devotees to guard against committing an offense at their lotus feet.

Transcendental attachment, either shadow or *parā,* can be nullified by different degrees of offenses at the lotus feet of pure devotees. If the offense is very serious, then one's attachment becomes almost nil, and if the offense is not very serious, one's attachment can become second class or third class.

If someone becomes attached to the principles of salvation or to merging into the existence of the *brahmajyoti,* his ecstasies gradually diminish into shadow and *parā* attachment or else transform into the principles of *ahaṅgrahopāsanā*. This *ahaṅgrahopāsanā* describes a living entity when he begins spiritual realization by identifying himself with the Supreme Lord. This state of self-realization is technically known as monism. The monist thinks himself one with the Supreme Lord. Thus, because he does not differentiate between himself and the Supreme Lord, it is his view that by worshiping himself he is worshiping the supreme whole.

Sometimes it is found that a neophyte is taking part in chanting and dancing very enthusiastically, but within himself he is under the impression that he has become one with the supreme whole. This conception of monism is completely different from pure, transcendental devotional service. If, however, it is seen that a person has developed a high standard of devotion without having undergone even the regulative principles, it is to be understood that his status of devotional service was achieved in a former life. For some reason or another it had been temporarily stopped, most probably by an offense committed at the lotus feet of a devotee. Now, with a good second chance, it has again begun to develop. The conclusion is that steady progress in devotional service can be attained only in the association of pure devotees.

If one can gradually advance his status in devotional service, this is understood to be due to the causeless mercy of Kṛṣṇa Himself. If a person is completely detached from material enjoyment and has developed pure ecstatic devotion, even if he is sometimes accidentally found not living up to the standard of devotional service, one should not be envious of him. It is confirmed also in *Bhagavad-gītā* that a devotee who has unflinching faith in and devotion to the Lord, even if sometimes found to be accidentally deviated from pure devotional characteristics, should still be counted among the pure. Unflinching faith in devotional service, in Lord Kṛṣṇa and in the spiritual master makes one highly elevated in the activities of devotional service.

In the *Nṛsiṁha Purāṇa* it is stated, "If a person has completely engaged his mind, body and activities in the service of the Supreme Godhead, but externally he is found to be engaged in some abominable activities, these abominable activities will surely be very quickly vanquished by the influence of his staunch devotional force." The example is given that on the full moon there are some spots which may appear to be pockmarks. Still, the illumination spread by the full moon cannot be checked. Similarly, a little fault in the midst of volumes of devotional service is not at all to be counted as a fault. Attachment for Kṛṣṇa is transcendental bliss. Amid unlimited volumes of transcendental bliss, a spot of some material defect cannot act in any way.

19

Devotional Service in Pure Love of God

When one's desire to love Kṛṣṇa in one's particular relationship becomes intensified, this is known as pure love of Godhead. In the beginning a devotee is engaged in the regulative principles of devotional service by the order of his spiritual master. When one thereby becomes completely purified of all material contamination, there develops an attachment and taste for devotional service. This taste and attachment, when gradually intensified in the course of time, becomes love. The word *love* can be actually applied only in relationship with the Personality of Godhead. In the material world, love is not applicable at all. What goes on under the name of love in the material world is nothing but lust. There is a gulf of difference between love and lust, like the difference between gold and iron. In the *Nārada-pañcarātra* it is clearly stated that when lust is completely transferred to the Supreme Godhead and the concept of kinship is completely reposed in Him, such is accepted as pure love of God by great authorities like Bhīṣma, Prahlāda, Uddhava and Nārada.

Great authorities like Bhīṣma have explained that love of Godhead means completely giving up all so-called love for any other person. According to Bhīṣma, love means reposing one's affection completely upon one person, withdrawing all affinities for any other person. This pure love can be transferred to the Supreme Personality of Godhead under two conditions—out of ecstasy and out of the causeless mercy of the Supreme Personality of Godhead Himself.

Ecstasy

Ecstatic love of Godhead can be potently invoked simply by following the rules and regulations of devotional service as they are prescribed in scriptures, under the direction of a bona fide spiritual master. In the Eleventh Canto, Second Chapter, verse 40, of *Śrīmad-Bhāgavatam,* this ecstatic love, born of the execution of regulative devotional service, is explained: "A devotee, in the course of executing the regulative principles of devotional service, develops his natural Kṛṣṇa consciousness, and being thus softened at heart he chants and dances like a madman. While performing chanting of the holy name of the Lord, he sometimes cries, sometimes talks wildly, sometimes sings and sometimes—without caring for any outsider—dances like a madman."

In the *Padma Purāṇa* there is a statement about ecstatic love born of spontaneous affection. Candrakānti, a celebrated fair-faced girl, rigidly observed celibacy in order to obtain Kṛṣṇa as her husband. She always engaged herself in meditating on the transcendental form of the Lord and always chanted the glories of the Lord. She did not desire to accept anyone else as her husband. She had firmly decided that only Lord Kṛṣṇa would be her husband.

The Lord's Extraordinary Mercy

When a devotee is found to be always associated with the Lord in ecstatic love, it is to be understood that such a position has been awarded by the Lord Himself out of His causeless extraordinary mercy. An example of such extraordinary mercy is given in the Eleventh Canto, Twelfth Chapter, verse 7, of *Śrīmad-Bhāgavatam,* wherein Lord Kṛṣṇa tells Uddhava, "The *gopīs* in Vṛndāvana did not study the *Vedas* to achieve Me. Nor had they ever been in holy places of pilgrimage. Nor did they devoutly execute any regulative principle. Nor did they undergo any kind of austerity. It is simply by My association that they have attained the highest perfection of devotional service."

From the example of Candrakānti as found in the *Padma Purāṇa* and from the example of the *gopīs* as found in *Śrīmad-Bhāgavatam,* it appears that a devotee who always thinks of Kṛṣṇa and who always chants His glories in ecstatic love, regardless of his condition, will attain the highest perfection of unalloyed devotional love due to Lord Kṛṣṇa's extraordinary mercy. This is confirmed in the *Nārada-pañcarātra:* "If a person worships, adores and loves Hari, the Supreme Lord, he should be understood to have finished all kinds of austerities, penances and similar processes for self-realization. On the other hand, if after undergoing all types of austerities, penances and mystic *yoga* practices one does not develop such love for Hari, then all his performances are to be considered a useless waste of time. If someone always sees Kṛṣṇa inside and out, then it is to be understood that he has surpassed all austerities and penances for self-realization. And if, after executing all kinds of penances and austerities, one cannot always see Kṛṣṇa inside and out, then he has executed his performances uselessly."

Spontaneous attraction to Kṛṣṇa, which is said to be due to the extraordinary mercy of the Lord, can be placed under two headings: one is profound veneration for the greatness of the Lord, and the other is one's being automatically attracted to Kṛṣṇa without any extraneous consideration. In the *Nārada-pañcarātra* it is said that if on account of profound veneration for the greatness of the Supreme Lord one attains a great affection and steady love for Him, one is certainly assured of attaining the four kinds of Vaiṣṇava liberation—namely achieving the same bodily features as the Lord, achieving the same opulence as the Lord, dwelling on the planet where the Lord is residing, and attaining eternal association with the Lord. The Vaiṣṇava liberation is completely different from the Māyāvāda liberation, which is simply a matter of being merged into the effulgence of the Lord.

In the *Nārada-pañcarātra* pure, unalloyed devotional service is explained as being without any motive for personal benefit. If a devotee is continuously in love with Lord Kṛṣṇa and his mind is always fixed upon Him, that devotional attitude will prove to be the only means of attracting the attention of the Lord. In other words, a Vaiṣṇava who is incessantly thinking of the form of Lord Krsna is to be known as a pure Vaiṣṇava.

Generally, a devotee who has achieved the causeless mercy of the Lord on account of following the strict rules and regulations of devotional service becomes attracted by the supreme greatness of the Lord, by the transcendental beauty of the Lord and by the spontaneous execution of devotional service. To be more clear, by executing the regulative principles of devotional service one can fully appreciate the transcendental beauty of the Lord. In any case, such exalted positions are possible only by the extraordinary mercy of the Lord upon the devotee.

Association with Pure Devotees

Although many different processes for developing love of Godhead have been explained so far, Śrīla Rūpa Gosvāmī now gives us a general description of how one can best achieve such a high position. The beginning of ecstatic love of Godhead is basically faith. There are many societies and associations of pure devotees, and if someone with just a little faith begins to associate with such societies, his advancement to pure devotional service is rapid. The influence of a pure devotee is such that if someone comes to associate with him with a little faith, one gets the chance of hearing about the Lord from authoritative scriptures like *Bhagavad-gītā* and *Śrīmad-Bhāgavatam*. Thus, by the mercy of the Lord, who is situated in everyone's heart, one gradually develops his faith in the descriptions of such authoritative scriptures. This is the first stage of association with pure devotees. In the second stage, after one becomes a little advanced and mature, he automatically offers to follow the principles of devotional service under the guidance of the pure devotee and accepts him as the spiritual master. In the next stage, under the guidance of the spiritual master, the devotee executes regulative devotional service, and as a result of such activities, he becomes freed from all unwanted occupations. When he is freed from unwanted occupations, his faith becomes steadily fixed, and he develops a transcendental taste for devotional service, then attachment, then ecstasies, and in the last stage there is pure love of Godhead. These are the different stages of the development of pure love.

Only the most fortunate persons can achieve such success in life. Those who are simply academic students of the Vedic scriptures cannot appreciate how such a development takes place. In the *Nārada-pañcarātra* Lord Śiva therefore tells Pārvatī, "My dear supreme goddess, you may know from me that any person who has developed the ecstasy of love for the Supreme Personality of Godhead, and who is always merged in transcendental bliss on account of this love, cannot even perceive the material distress or happiness coming from the body or mind."

The affection and the dealings of love that are different branches of the original tree of love precede many varieties of affectionate manifestations that will not be discussed here. These different manifestations have been described by Sanātana Gosvāmī in his *Bhāgavatāmṛta*. Although the subject of such affections and dealings of love is very confidential, Sanātana Gosvāmī has described them very explicitly.

Śrī Rūpa Gosvāmī thus concludes the first division of the *Bhakti-rasāmṛta-sindhu,* offering up his treatise for the transcendental pleasure of Sanātana Gosvāmī, who has established the transcendental beauty, and of Gopāla Bhaṭṭa Gosvāmī, Śrī Raghunātha Bhaṭṭa Gosvāmī and Raghunātha dāsa Gosvāmī. It appears from this statement that the great Śrīla Jīva Gosvāmī was not yet active when *Bhakti-rasāmṛta-sindhu* was written.

Thus ends the Bhaktivedanta summary study of the first division of Bhakti-rasāmṛta-sindhu, *up to the descriptions of ecstatic love of Godhead, which are to follow next.*

PART TWO

20

Transcendental Mellow

In this second division of *Bhakti-rasāmṛta-sindhu* the author offers his respectful obeisances unto "Sanātana." This Sanātana can be interpreted as either Śrī Kṛṣṇa Himself or as Sanātana Gosvāmī, the elder brother and spiritual master of Rūpa Gosvāmī. In the case where "Sanātana" is accepted to mean Śrī Kṛṣṇa, the obeisances are offered to Kṛṣṇa because He is naturally so beautiful and because He is the killer of the demon Agha. If it is interpreted to mean Sanātana Gosvāmī, then it is because he is so greatly favored by Rūpa Gosvāmī, being always served by him, and because he is the annihilator of all kinds of sinful activities. In this division of *Bhakti-rasāmṛta-sindhu* the author wants to describe the general symptoms of the transcendental mellow (loving mood) of discharging devotional service.

In this division of *Bhakti-rasāmṛta-sindhu* there are five general topics: (1) *vibhāva*—special symptoms or causes of ecstasy, (2) *anubhāva*—subsequent ecstasy, (3) *sāttvika-bhāva*—constitutional or existential ecstasy, (4) *vyabhicāri-bhāva*—aggressive ecstasy and (5) *sthāyi-bhāva*—fervent or continuous ecstasy.

The word *rasa*, used in the *Bhakti-rasāmṛta-sindhu*, is understood by different persons differently because the exact English equivalent is very difficult to find. But as we have seen our spiritual master translate this word *rasa* into "mellow," we shall follow in his footsteps and also translate the word in that way.

The particular loving mood or attitude relished in the exchange of love with the Supreme Personality of Godhead is called *rasa*, or mellow. The different types of *rasa*, when combined together, help one to taste the mellow of devotional service in the highest degree of transcendental ecstasy. Such a position, although entirely transcendental to our experience, will be explained in this section as far as possible, following in the footsteps of Śrīla Rūpa Gosvāmī.

Without relishing some sort of mellow, or loving mood, in one's activities, no one can continue to perform such activities. Similarly, in the transcendental life of Kṛṣṇa consciousness and devotional service there must be some mellow, or specific taste, from the service. Generally this mellow is experienced by chanting, hearing, worshiping in the temple and being engaged in the service of the Lord. So when a person feels transcendental bliss; that is called "relishing the mellow." To be more clear, we may understand that the various feelings of happiness derived from discharging devotional service may be termed the "mellows" of devotional service.

This relishing of transcendental mellow in discharging devotional service cannot be experienced by all classes of men, because this sweet loving mood is developed only from one's previous life's activities or by the association of unalloyed devotees. As explained above, association with pure devotees is the beginning of faith in devotional service. Only by developing such faith in the association of a pure devotee, or by having in one's previous life executed devotional activities, can one actually relish the mellow of devotional service. In other words, this transcendental bliss is not to be enjoyed by any common man unless he is so extraordinarily fortunate as to be in association with devotees or to be continuing his previous birth's devotional activities.

The gradual process of development to the stage of devotional service is explained in *Śrīmad-Bhāgavatam*, First Canto: "The beginning is to hear about Lord Kṛṣṇa in the association of devotees who have themselves cleansed their hearts by association. Hearing about the transcendental activities of the Lord will result in one's feeling transcendental bliss always." It is also explained in *Bhagavad-gītā* that for one who has actually come to the spiritual platform, the first symptom visible will be that he is always joyful. This joyous life is attained by one's reaction to reading *Bhagavad-gītā* or *Śrīmad-Bhāgavatam,* or else from associating with persons who are very interested in the spiritual life of Kṛṣṇa consciousness—specifically those who have made the determination to achieve the favor of Govinda by being engaged in transcendental loving service at His lotus feet. Being encouraged by such a feeling, one who is constantly engaged in discharging the regulative principles of devotional service in such a way as to please the Supreme Personality of Godhead develops two principles of compelling force, which come under the heading of *vibhāva*. Thus one enjoys transcendental bliss.

There are several origins or causes for this compulsive love of Kṛṣṇa, such as Kṛṣṇa Himself, the devotees of Kṛṣṇa, and Kṛṣṇa's playing on the flute. The effect is sometimes loving and sometimes stunted.

There are eight transcendental symptoms found in the body during ecstasy, and all of them are possible only by a mixture of the abovementioned five ecstatic divisions. Without some mixture of these five ecstatic principles, one cannot relish transcendental bliss. The cause or basis for relishing transcendental mellow is exactly what we mean by *vibhāva*. This *vibhāva* is divided into two—namely, basic and impelling, or impetus-giving. In the *Agni Purāṇa* the description of *vibhāva* is given as follows: "The basis from which ecstatic love is born is called *vibhāva*, which is divided into two—basic and impelling." In other words, there are two kinds of ecstatic love. The object of basic ecstatic love is Kṛṣṇa and His devotee. Lord Kṛṣṇa is the object of basic ecstatic love, and His pure devotee, a reservoir of such love, is the object of impelling ecstatic love. Impelling ecstatic love, then, is that love which develops when one sees an object which reminds him of Kṛṣṇa.

Lord Kṛṣṇa, who is the possessor of inconceivable potencies and qualities of transcendental knowledge and bliss, is the basic cause of ecstatic love. Lord Kṛṣṇa also becomes the reservoir (impetus) of ecstatic love by His different incarnations and expansions. In *Śrīmad-Bhāgavatam* there is a statement in connection with the *brahma-vimohana-līlā* which demonstrates something of this impelling or impetus-giving feature of ecstatic love. When Brahmā was deluded by Kṛṣṇa, who expanded Himself into so many cowherd boys, calves and cows, Kṛṣṇa's elder brother, Śrī Baladeva (a direct expansion of Krsna Himself), felt astonishment and said, "How wonderful it is that My ecstatic love for Kṛṣṇa is again being attracted to so many cowherd boys, calves and cows!" He was struck with wonder by thinking in this way. This is one of the examples in which Kṛṣṇa Himself becomes the object and reservoir of ecstatic love in the impelling aspect.

21

Qualities of Śrī Kṛṣṇa

Personal features can be divided into two: one feature is covered, and the other feature is manifested. When Kṛṣṇa is covered by different kinds of dress, His personal feature is covered. There is an example of His covered personal feature in *Śrīmad-Bhāgavatam* in connection with His *dvārakā-līlā* (His residence in Dvārakā as its king). Sometimes Lord Kṛṣṇa began to play by dressing Himself like a woman. Seeing this form, Uddhava said, "How wonderful it is that this woman is attracting my ecstatic love exactly as Lord Kṛṣṇa does. I think she must be Kṛṣṇa covered by the dress of a woman!"

One devotee praised the bodily features of Kṛṣṇa when he saw the Lord in His manifested personal feature. He exclaimed, "How wonderful is the personal feature of Lord Kṛṣṇa! How His neck is just like a conchshell! His eyes are so beautiful, as though they themselves were encountering the beauty of a lotus flower. His body is just like the *tamāla* tree, very blackish. His head is protected with a canopy of hair. There are the marks of Śrīvatsa on His chest, and He is holding His conchshell. By such beautiful bodily features, the enemy of the demon Madhu has appeared so pleasing that He can bestow upon me transcendental bliss simply by my seeing His transcendental qualities."

Śrīla Rūpa Gosvāmī, after consulting various scriptures, has enumerated the transcendental qualities of the Lord as follows: (1) beautiful features of the entire body; (2) marked with all auspicious characteristics; (3) extremely pleasing; (4) effulgent; (5) strong; (6) ever youthful; (7) wonderful linguist; (8) truthful; (9) talks pleasingly; (10) fluent; (11) highly learned; (12) highly intelligent; (13) a genius; (14) artistic; (15) extremely clever; (16) expert; (17) grateful; (18) firmly determined; (19) an expert judge of time and circumstances; (20) sees and speaks on the authority of the *Vedas*, or scriptures; (21) pure; (22) self-controlled; (23) steadfast;

(24) forbearing; (25) forgiving; (26) grave; (27) self-satisfied; (28) possessing equilibrium; (29) magnanimous; (30) religious; (31) heroic; (32) compassionate; (33) respectful; (34) gentle; (35) liberal; (36) shy; (37) the protector of surrendered souls; (38) happy; (39) the well-wisher of devotees; (40) controlled by love; (41) all-auspicious; (42) most powerful; (43) all-famous; (44) popular; (45) partial to devotees; (46) very attractive to all women; (47) all-worshipable; (48) all-opulent; (49) all-honorable; (50) the supreme controller. The Supreme Personality of Godhead has all these fifty transcendental qualities in fullness as deep as the ocean. In other words, the extent of His qualities is inconceivable.

As parts and parcels of the Supreme Lord, the individual living entities can also possess all of these qualities in minute quantities, provided they become pure devotees of the Lord. In other words, all of the above transcendental qualities can be present in the devotees in minute quantity, whereas the qualities in fullness are always present in the Supreme Personality of Godhead.

Besides these, there are other transcendental qualities which are described by Lord Śiva to Pārvatī in the *Padma Purāṇa,* and in the First Canto of *Śrīmad-Bhāgavatam* in connection with a conversation between the deity of the earth and the King of religion, Yamarāja. It is said therein, "Persons who are desirous of becoming great personalities must be decorated with the following qualities: truthfulness, cleanliness, mercy, perseverance, renunciation, peacefulness, simplicity, control of the senses, equilibrium of the mind, austerity, equality, forbearance, placidity, learning, knowledge, detachment, opulence, chivalry, influence, strength, memory, independence, tactfulness, luster, patience, kindheartedness, ingenuity, gentility, mannerliness, determination, perfection in all knowledge, proper execution, possession of all objects of enjoyment, gravity, steadiness, faithfulness, fame, respectfulness and lack of false egotism." Persons who are desiring to become great souls cannot be without any of the above qualities, so we can know for certain that these qualities are found in Lord Kṛṣṇa, the supreme soul.

Besides all of the above-mentioned fifty qualities, Lord Kṛṣṇa possesses five more, which are sometimes partially manifested in the persons of Lord Brahmā or Lord Śiva. These transcendental qualities are as follows: (51) changeless; (52) all-cognizant; (53) ever fresh; (54) *sac-*

cid-ānanda (possessing an eternal blissful body); (55) possessing all mystic perfections.

Kṛṣṇa also possesses five other qualities, which are manifest in the body of Nārāyaṇa, and they are listed as follows. (56) He has inconceivable potency. (57) Uncountable universes generate from His body. (58) He is the original source of all incarnations. (59) He is the giver of salvation to the enemies whom He kills. (60) He is the attractor of liberated souls. All these transcendental qualities are manifest wonderfully in the personal feature of Lord Kṛṣṇa.

Besides these sixty transcendental qualities, Kṛṣṇa has four more, which are not manifest even in the Nārāyaṇa form of Godhead, what to speak of the demigods or living entities. They are as follows. (61) He is the performer of wonderful varieties of pastimes (especially His childhood pastimes). (62) He is surrounded by devotees endowed with wonderful love of Godhead. (63) He can attract all living entities all over the universes by playing on His flute. (64) He has a wonderful excellence of beauty which cannot be rivaled anywhere in the creation.

Adding to the list these four exceptional qualities of Kṛṣṇa, it is to be understood that the aggregate number of qualities of Kṛṣṇa is sixty-four. Śrīla Rūpa Gosvāmī has attempted to give evidences from various scriptures about all sixty-four qualities present in the person of the Supreme Lord.

1. Beautiful Bodily Features

Any comparison of the different parts of the Lord's body to different material objects cannot factually be a complete comparison. Ordinary persons, who cannot understand how exalted are the bodily features of the Lord, are simply given a chance to understand by a material comparison. It is said that Kṛṣṇa's face is as beautiful as the moon, His thighs are powerful just like the trunks of elephants, His arms are just like two pillars, His palms are expanded like lotus flowers, His chest is just like a doorway, His hips are dens, and the middle of His body is a terrace.

2. Auspicious Characteristics

There are certain characteristics of different limbs which are considered to be very auspicious and are fully present in the body of the Lord.

In this connection, one friend of Nanda Mahārāja, speaking about Lord Kṛṣṇa's auspicious bodily symptoms, said, "My dear King of the cowherds, I can find thirty-two auspicious symptoms on the body of your son! I am wondering how this boy could have taken His birth in a family of cowherd men." Generally, when Lord Kṛṣṇa appears He does so in a family of *kṣatriyas* (kings), as did Lord Rāmacandra, and sometimes in a family of *brāhmaṇas*. But Kṛṣṇa accepted the role of son to Mahārāja Nanda, despite the fact that Nanda belonged to the *vaiśya* community. The business of the *vaiśya* community is trade, commerce and the protection of cows. Therefore his friend, who may have been born into a *brāhmaṇa* family, expressed his wonder at how such an exalted child could take birth in a family of *vaiśyas*. Anyway, he pointed out the auspicious signs on the body of Kṛṣṇa to the boy's foster father.

He continued, "This boy has a reddish luster in seven places—His eyes, the palms of His hands, the soles of His feet, His palate, His lips, His tongue and His nails. A reddish luster in these seven places is considered to be auspicious. Three parts of His body are very broad: His waist, forehead and chest. Three parts of His body are short: His neck, thighs and genitals. Three parts of His body are very deep: His voice, intelligence and navel. There is highness in five parts of His body: His nose, arms, ears, forehead and thighs. In five parts of His body there is fineness: His skin, the hairs on His head and on the other parts of His body, His teeth and His fingertips. The aggregate of all these bodily features is manifest only in the bodies of great personalities."

The fate lines on the palm are also considered to be auspicious bodily symptoms. In this connection, one old *gopī* informed King Nanda, "Your son possesses various wonderful fate lines on His palms. There are the signs of lotus flowers and wheels on His palms, and on His soles there are the signs of a flag, a thunderbolt, a fish, a rod for controlling elephants, and a lotus flower. Please observe how auspicious these signs are!"

3. Pleasing

Beautiful bodily features which automatically attract the eyes are called *rucira* (pleasing). Kṛṣṇa possesses this attractive feature of *rucira* in His personal features. In the Third Canto, Second Chapter, verse 13, of *Śrīmad-Bhāgavatam,* there is a statement about this. "The Supreme Personality of Godhead, in His pleasing dress, appeared at the scene of the sacrificial arena when King Yudhiṣṭhira was performing the Rājasūya sacrifice. All important personalities from different parts of the universe had been invited to the sacrificial arena, and all of them, upon beholding Kṛṣṇa there, considered that the Creator had ended all of His craftsmanship in the creation of this particular body of Kṛṣṇa."

It is said that the transcendental body of Kṛṣṇa resembles the lotus flower in eight parts—namely His face, His two eyes, His two hands, His navel and His two feet. The *gopīs* and inhabitants of Vṛndāvana used to see the luster of lotus flowers everywhere, and they could hardly withdraw their eyes from such a vision.

4. Effulgent

The effulgence pervading the universe is considered to be the rays of the Supreme Personality of Godhead. The supreme abode of Kṛṣṇa is always throwing off the effulgence known as *brahmajyoti,* and that effulgence is emanating from His body.

The luster of the hosts of jewels fixed on the chest of the Lord can defeat even the luster of the sun, and still, when compared with the bodily luster of the Lord, that crest of jewels appears to be only as bright as one of the stars in the sky. Therefore the transcendental influence of Kṛṣṇa is so great that it can defeat anyone. When Kṛṣṇa was present in the sacrificial arena of His enemy King Kaṁsa, the wrestlers present, although appreciating the softness of the body of Śrī Kṛṣṇa, were afraid and perturbed when they thought of engaging with Him in battle.

5. Strong

A person who has extraordinary bodily strength is called *balīyān*. When Kṛṣṇa killed Ariṣṭasura, some of the *gopīs* said, "My dear friends, just see how Kṛṣṇa has killed Ariṣṭāsura! Although he was stronger than a mountain, Kṛṣṇa plucked him up just like a piece of cotton and threw him away without any difficulty!" There is another passage wherein it is said, "O my dear devotees of Lord Kṛṣṇa, may the left hand of Lord Kṛṣṇa, which has lifted Govardhana Hill like a ball, save you from all dangers."

6. Ever Youthful

Kṛṣṇa is beautiful at His different ages—namely His childhood, His boyhood and His youth. Out of these three, His youth is the reservoir of all pleasures and is the time when the highest varieties of devotional service are acceptable. At that age, Kṛṣṇa is full with all transcendental qualities and is engaged in His transcendental pastimes. Therefore, devotees have accepted the beginning of His youth as the most attractive feature in ecstatic love.

At this age Kṛṣṇa is described as follows: "The force of Kṛṣṇa's youth was combined with His beautiful smile, which defeated even the beauty of the full moon. He was always nicely dressed, in beauty surpassing even Cupid, and He was always attracting the minds of the *gopīs,* who were thereby always feeling pleasure."

7. Wonderful Linguist

Rūpa Gosvāmī says that a person who knows the languages of different countries, especially the Sanskrit language, which is spoken in the cities of the demigods—as well as other worldly languages, including those of the animals—is called a wonderful linguist. It appears from this statement that Kṛṣṇa can also speak and understand the languages of the animals. An old woman in Vṛndāvana, present at the time of Kṛṣṇa's pastimes, once stated in surprise, "How wonderful it is that Kṛṣṇa, who owns the hearts of all the young girls of Vrajabhūmi, can nicely speak the language of Vrajabhūmi with the *gopīs,* while in Sanskrit He speaks with the demigods, and in the language of the animals He can even speak with the cows and buffalo! Similarly, in the language of the Kashmir Province, and with the parrots and other birds, as well as in most common languages, Kṛṣṇa is so expressive!" She inquired from the *gopīs* as to how Kṛṣṇa had become so expert in speaking so many different types of languages.

8. Truthful

A person whose word of honor is never broken is called truthful. Kṛṣṇa once promised Kuntī, the mother of the Pāṇḍavas, that He would bring her five sons back from the Battlefield of Kurukṣetra. After the battle was finished, when all the Pāṇḍavas had come home, Kuntī praised Kṛṣṇa because His promise was so nicely fulfilled. She said, "Even the sunshine may one day become cool and the moonshine one day become hot, but still Your promise will not fail." Similarly, when Kṛṣṇa, along with Bhīma and Arjuna, went to challenge Jarāsandha, He plainly told

Jarāsandha that He was the eternal Kṛṣṇa, present along with two of the Pāṇḍavas. The story is that both Kṛṣṇa and the Pāṇḍavas—in this case Bhīma and Arjuna—were *kṣatriyas* (warrior-kings). Jarāsandha was also a *kṣatriya* and was very charitable toward the *brāhmaṇas*. Thus Kṛṣṇa, who had planned to fight with Jarāsandha, went to him with Bhīma and Arjuna in the dress of *brāhmaṇas*. Jarāsandha, being very charitable toward the *brāhmaṇas,* asked them what they wanted, and they expressed their desire to fight with him. Then Kṛṣṇa, dressed as a *brāhmaṇa,* declared Himself to be the same Kṛṣṇa who was the King's eternal enemy.

9. Pleasing Talker

A person who can speak sweetly even with his enemy just to pacify him is called a pleasing talker. Kṛṣṇa was such a pleasing talker that after defeating His enemy Kāliya in the water of the Yamunā, He said, "My dear King of the snakes, although I have given you so much pain, please do not be dissatisfied with Me. It is My duty to protect these cows, which are worshiped even by the demigods. Only in order to save them from the danger of your presence have I been obliged to banish you from this place."

Kāliya was residing within the water of the Yamunā, and as a result the back portion of that river had become poisoned. Thus so many cows who had drunk the water had died. Therefore Kṛṣṇa, even though He was only four or five years old, dipped Himself into the water, punished Kāliya very severely and then asked him to leave the place and go elsewhere.

Kṛṣṇa said at that time that the cows are worshiped even by the demigods, and He practically demonstrated how to protect the cows. At least people who are in Kṛṣṇa consciousness should follow in His footsteps and give all protection to the cows. Cows are worshiped not only by the demigods. Kṛṣṇa Himself worshiped the cows on several occasions, especially on the days of Gopāṣṭamī and Govardhana-pūjā.

10. Fluent

A person who can speak meaningful words and with all politeness and good qualities is called *vāvadūka,* or fluent. There is a nice statement in *Śrīmad-Bhāgavatam* regarding Kṛṣṇa's speaking politely. When Kṛṣṇa politely bade His father, Nanda Mahārāja, to stop the ritualistic offering of sacrifice to the rain god, Indra, a wife of one village cowherd man became captivated. She later thus described the speaking of Kṛṣṇa to her friends: "Kṛṣṇa was speaking to His father so politely and gently that it was as if He were pouring nectar into the ears of all present there. After hearing such sweet words from Kṛṣṇa, who will not be attracted to Him?"

Kṛṣṇa's speech, which contains all good qualities in the universe, is described in the following statement by Uddhava: "The words of Kṛṣṇa are so attractive that they can immediately change the heart of even His opponent. His words can immediately solve all of the questions and problems of the world. Although He does not speak very long, each and every word from His mouth contains volumes of meaning. These speeches of Kṛṣṇa are very pleasing to my heart."

11. Highly Learned

When a person is highly educated and acts strictly on moral principles, he is called highly learned. A person conversant in different departments of knowledge is called educated, and because he acts on moral principles, he is called morally stout. Together, these two factors constitute learning.

Kṛṣṇa's receiving education from Sāndīpani Muni is described by Śrī Nārada Muni as follows: "In the beginning, Lord Brahmā and others are like clouds of evaporated water from the great ocean of Kṛṣṇa. In other words, Brahmā first received the Vedic education from Kṛṣṇa, as the clouds receive water from the ocean. That Vedic education or instruction which was spoken by Brahmā to the world was then reposed upon the mountain of Sāndīpani Muni. Sāndīpani Muni's instructions to Kṛṣṇa are like a reservoir of water on the mountain, which flows as a river and goes again to mix with the source, the ocean of Kṛṣṇa." To be more clear, the idea is that Kṛṣṇa actually cannot be instructed by anyone, just as the ocean does not receive water from any source but itself. It only appears that the rivers are pouring water into the ocean. So it is clear that Brahmā received his education from Kṛṣṇa, and from Brahmā, via the disciplic succession, this Vedic instruction was distributed. Sāndīpani Muni is likened to the river which is flowing down again to that same original ocean of Kṛṣṇa.

The Siddhas, the inhabitants of Siddhaloka (where all are born with fully developed mystic powers), and the Cāraṇas, the inhabitants of a similar planet, pray to Kṛṣṇa as follows: "My Lord Govinda, the goddess of learning is decorated with fourteen kinds of educational ornaments, her intelligence is all-pervading within the four departments of the *Vedas,* her attention is always on the lawbooks given by great sages like Manu, and she is appareled in six kinds of expert knowledge—namely Vedic evidence, grammar, astrology, rhetoric, vocabulary and logic. Her constant friends are the supplements of the *Vedas,* the *Purāṇas,* and she is decorated with the final conclusion of all education. And now she has acquired an opportunity to sit with You as a class friend in school, and she is now engaged in Your service."

Kṛṣṇa, the Supreme Personality of Godhead, does not require any education, but He gives a chance to the goddess of learning to serve Him. Being self-sufficient, Kṛṣṇa does not require the service of any living entity, although He has many devotees. It is because Kṛṣṇa is so kind and merciful that He gives everyone the opportunity to serve Him, as though He required the service of His devotees.

Regarding His moral principles, it is stated in *Śrīmad-Bhāgavatam* that Kṛṣṇa is ruling over Vṛndāvana as death personified to the thieves, as pleasing bliss to the pious, as the most beautiful Cupid to the young girls and as the most munificent personality to the poor men. He is as refreshing as the full moon to His friends, and to His opponents He is the annihilating fire generated from Lord Śiva. Kṛṣṇa is therefore the most perfect moralist in His reciprocal dealings with different kinds of persons. When He is death personified to the thieves, it is not that He is without moral principles or that He is cruel; He is still kind, because to punish thieves with death is to exhibit the highest quality of moral principles. In *Bhagavad-gītā,* also, Kṛṣṇa says that He deals with different kinds of persons according to their dealings with Him. Kṛṣṇa's dealings with devotees and with nondevotees, although different, are equally good. Because Kṛṣṇa is all-good, His dealings with everyone are always good.

12. Highly Intelligent

A man is called intelligent if he has a sharp memory and fine discretion. As far as Kṛṣṇa's memory is concerned, it is said that when He was studying in the school of Sāndīpani Muni in Avantīpura, He showed such a sharp memory that by once taking instructions from the teacher He immediately became perfect in any subject. Actually, His going to the school of Sāndīpani Muni was to show the people of the world that however great or ingenious one may be, he must go to higher authorities for general education. However great one may be, he must accept a teacher or spiritual master.

Kṛṣṇa's fine discretion was exhibited when He was fighting with the untouchable king who attacked the city of Mathurā. According to Vedic rites, those who are untouchable are not to be touched by the *kṣatriya* kings, not even for killing. Therefore, when the untouchable king seized the city of Mathurā, Kṛṣṇa did not think it wise to kill him directly with His own hand. Still the king had to be killed, and therefore Kṛṣṇa decided with fine discretion that He should flee from the battlefield so that the untouchable king would chase Him. He could then lead the king to the mountain where Mucukunda was lying asleep. Mucukunda had received a benediction from Kārttikeya to the effect that when he awoke from his sleep, whomever he might see would at once be burnt to ashes. Therefore Kṛṣṇa thought it wise to lead the untouchable king to that cave, so that the king's presence would awaken Mucukunda and he would at once be burnt to ashes.

13. Genius

A person is called a genius when he can refute any kind of opposing element with newer and newer arguments. In this connection there is a statement in *Padyāvalī* which contains the following conversation between Kṛṣṇa and Rādhā. One morning, when Kṛṣṇa came to Rādhā, Rādhā asked Him, "My dear Keśava, where is Your *vāsa* at present?" The Sanskrit word *vāsa* has three meanings: one meaning is residence, one meaning is fragrance, and another meaning is dress.

Actually Rādhārāṇī inquired from Kṛṣṇa, "Where is Your dress?" But Kṛṣṇa took the meaning as residence, and He replied to Rādhārāṇī, "My dear captivated one, at the present moment My residence is in Your beautiful eyes."

To this Rādhārāṇī replied, "My dear cunning boy, I did not ask You about Your residence. I inquired about Your dress."

Kṛṣṇa then took the meaning of *vāsa* as fragrance and said, "My dear fortunate one, I have just assumed this fragrance in order to be associated with Your body."

Śrīmatī Rādhārāṇī again inquired from Kṛṣṇa, "Where did You pass Your night?" The exact Sanskrit word used in this connection was *yāminyāmuṣitaḥ*. *Yāminyām* means "at night," and *uṣitaḥ* means "pass." Kṛṣṇa, however, divided the word *yāminyāmuṣitaḥ* into two separate words, namely *yāminyā* and *muṣitaḥ*. By dividing this word into two, it came out to mean that He was kidnapped by Yāminī, or night. Kṛṣṇa therefore replied to Rādhārāṇī, "My dear Rādhārāṇī, is it possible that night can kidnap Me?" In this way He was answering all of the questions of Rādhārāṇī so cunningly that He gladdened this dearest of the *gopīs*.

14. Artistic

One who can talk and dress himself very artistically is called *vidagdha*. This exemplary characteristic was visible in the personality of Śrī Kṛṣṇa. It is spoken of by Rādhārāṇī as follows: "My dear friend, just see how Kṛṣṇa has nicely composed songs and how He dances and speaks funny words and plays on His flute, wearing such nice garlands. He has dressed Himself in such an enchanting way, as though He had defeated all kinds of players at the chessboard. He lives wonderfully at the topmost height of artistic craftsmanship."

15. Clever

A person who can perform various types of work at once is called clever. In this connection one of the *gopīs* said, "My dear friends, just see the clever activities of Śrī Kṛṣṇa! He has composed nice songs about the cowherd boys and is pleasing the cows. By the movement of His eyes He is pleasing the *gopīs*, and at the same time He is fighting with demons like Ariṣṭāsura. In this way, He is sitting with different living entities in different ways, and He is thoroughly enjoying the situation."

16. Expert

Any person who can quickly execute a very difficult task is called expert. About the expertise of Kṛṣṇa there is a statement in the Tenth Canto, Fifty-ninth Chapter, verse 17, of *Śrīmad-Bhāgavatam*, wherein

Śukadeva Gosvāmī tells Mahārāja Parīkṣit, "O best of the Kurus, Śrī Kṛṣṇa cut to pieces all the different weapons used by different fighters." Formerly, fighting was done by releasing different kinds of arrows. One party would release a certain arrow, and the other party had to defeat it by counteracting it with another arrow. For example, one party might release an arrow which would cause water to pour from the sky, and to counteract this the opposing party would have to release an arrow which could immediately turn the water into clouds. So from this statement it appears that Kṛṣṇa was very expert in counteracting the enemy's arrows. Similarly, at the *rāsa* dance, each and every *gopī* requested that Kṛṣṇa individually become her partner, and Kṛṣṇa immediately expanded Himself into so many Kṛṣṇas in order to be coupled with each and every *gopī*. The result was that each *gopī* found Kṛṣṇa by her side.

17. Grateful

Any person who is conscious of his friend's beneficent activities and never forgets his service is called grateful. In the *Mahābhārata,* Kṛṣṇa says, "When I was away from Draupadī, she cried with the words '*He govinda!*' This call for Me has put Me in her debt, and that indebtedness is gradually increasing in My heart!" This statement by Kṛṣṇa gives evidence of how one can please the Supreme Lord simply by addressing Him, "*He kṛṣṇa! He govinda!*"

The *mahā-mantra* (Hare Kṛṣṇa, Hare Kṛṣṇa, Kṛṣṇa Kṛṣṇa, Hare Hare/ Hare Rāma, Hare Rāma, Rāma Rāma, Hare Hare) is also simply an address to the Lord and His energy. So to anyone who is constantly engaged in addressing the Lord and His energy, we can imagine how much the Supreme Lord is obliged. It is impossible for the Lord to ever forget such a devotee. It is clearly stated in this verse that anyone who addresses the Lord immediately attracts the attention of the Lord, who always remains obliged to him.

Another instance of Kṛṣṇa's feeling of obligation is stated in connection with His dealings with Jāmbavān. When the Lord was present as Lord Rāmacandra, Jāmbavān, the great king of the monkeys, rendered very faithful service to Him. When the Lord again appeared as Lord Kṛṣṇa, He married Jāmbavān's daughter and paid him all the respect that is usually given to superiors. Any honest person is obliged to his friend if some service has been rendered unto Him. Since Kṛṣṇa is the supreme honest personality, how can He forget an obligation to His servitor?

18. Determined

Any person who observes regulative principles and fulfills his promises by practical activity is called determined. As far as the Lord's determination is concerned, there is an example in His dealings in the *Hari-vaṁśa*. This is in connection with Lord Kṛṣṇa's fighting the King of heaven, Indra, who was forcibly deprived of the *pārijāta* flower. *Pārijāta* is a kind of lotus flower grown on the heavenly planets. Once, Satyabhāmā, one of Kṛṣṇa's queens, wanted that lotus flower, and Kṛṣṇa promised to deliver it; but Indra refused to part with his *pārijāta* flower. Therefore there was a great fight, with Kṛṣṇa and the Pāṇḍavas on one side and all of the demigods on the other. Ultimately, Kṛṣṇa defeated all of them and took the *pārijāta* flower, which He presented to His queen. So, in regard to that occurrence, Kṛṣṇa told Nārada Muni, "My dear great sage of the demigods, now you can declare to the devotees in general, and to the nondevotees in particular, that in this matter of taking the *pārijāta* flower, all the demigods—the Gandharvas, the Nāgas, the demon Rākṣasas, the Yakṣas, the Pannagas—tried to defeat Me, but none could make Me break My promise to My queen."

There is another promise by Kṛṣṇa in *Bhagavad-gītā* to the effect that His devotee will never be vanquished. So a sincere devotee who is always engaged in the transcendental loving service of the Lord should know for certain that Kṛṣṇa will never break His promise. He will always protect His devotees in every circumstance.

Kṛṣṇa showed how He fulfills His promise by delivering the *pārijāta* flower to Satyabhāmā, by saving Draupadī from being insulted and by freeing Arjuna from the attacks of all enemies.

The promise of Kṛṣṇa that His devotees are never vanquished had also previously been admitted by Indra when he was defeated in the *govardhana-līlā*. When Kṛṣṇa stopped the villagers of Vraja (Vṛndāvana) from worshiping Indra, Indra became angry and therefore inundated Vṛndāvana with continuous rain. Kṛṣṇa, however, protected all of the citizens and animals of Vṛndāvana by lifting Govardhana Hill, which served as an umbrella. After the incident was over, Indra surrendered to Kṛṣṇa with many prayers, in which he admitted, "By Your lifting Govardhana Hill and protecting the citizens of Vṛndāvana, You have kept Your promise that Your devotees are never to be vanquished."

19. Expert Judge of Time and Circumstances

Kṛṣṇa was very expert in dealing with people according to circumstances, country, time and paraphernalia. How He could take advantage of a particular time, circumstance and person is expressed by Him while talking to Uddhava about His *rāsa* dance with the *gopīs*. He says, "The most opportune time is the full-moon night in autumn, like tonight. The best place within the universe is Vṛndāvana, and the most beautiful girls are the *gopīs*. So, My dear friend Uddhava, I think I should now take advantage of all these circumstances and engage Myself in the *rāsa* dance."

20. Seer by the Authority of the Scriptures

A person who acts exactly according to the tenets of scripture is called *śāstra-cakṣus*. *Śāstra-cakṣus* means one who sees through the eyes of the authorized scriptures. Actually, any man of knowledge and experience should see everything through these books. For example, with our naked eye we perceive the sun globe simply as some glaring substance, but when we see through authorized books of science and other literature, we can understand how much greater the sun globe is than this earth and how powerful it is. So seeing things through the naked eye is not actually seeing. Seeing things through the authorized books or authorized teachers is the correct way to see. So, although Kṛṣṇa is the Supreme Personality of Godhead and can see all that is past, present and future, to teach the people in general He used to always refer to the scriptures. For example, in *Bhagavad-gītā*, although Kṛṣṇa was speaking as the supreme authority, He still mentioned and quoted *Vedānta-sūtra* as authority. There is a statement in *Śrīmad-Bhāgavatam* wherein a person jokingly says that Kṛṣṇa, the enemy of Kaṁsa, is known as the seer through the *śāstras*. In order to establish His authority, however, He is now engaged in seeing the *gopīs*, whereby the *gopīs* are becoming maddened.

21. Pure

There are two kinds of supreme purity. When one type is possessed, one is able to deliver a sinful person. When the other type is possessed, one does not do anything which is impure. A person who possesses either of these qualities is called supremely pure. Kṛṣṇa is both; He can deliver all sinful conditioned souls, and at the same time, He never does anything by which He can be contaminated.

In this connection, Vidura, while trying to detach his elder brother, Dhṛtarāṣṭra, from his familial attachments, said, "My dear brother, you just fix your mind on the lotus feet of Kṛṣṇa, who is worshiped with beautiful, erudite verses by great sages and saintly persons. Kṛṣṇa is the supreme deliverer among all deliverers. Undoubtedly there are great demigods like Lord Śiva and Lord Brahmā, but their positions as deliverers depend always upon the mercy of Kṛṣṇa." Therefore Vidura advised his elder brother, Dhṛtarāṣṭra, to concentrate his mind and worship only Kṛṣṇa. If one simply chants the holy name of Kṛṣṇa, this holy name will rise within one's heart like the powerful sun and will immediately dissipate all the darkness of ignorance. Vidura advised Dhṛtarāṣṭra to therefore think always of Kṛṣṇa, so that the volumes of contaminations due to sinful activities would be washed off immediately. In *Bhagavad-gītā* also Kṛṣṇa is addressed by Arjuna as *paraṁ brahma paraṁ dhāma pavitram*—the supreme pure. There are many other instances exhibiting Kṛṣṇa's supreme purity.

22. Self-controlled

A person who can control his senses fully is called *vaśī,* or self-controlled. In this connection it is stated in *Śrīmad-Bhāgavatam,* "All the sixteen thousand wives of Kṛṣṇa were so exquisitely beautiful that their smiling and shyness were able to captivate the minds of great demigods like Lord Śiva. But still they could not even agitate the mind of Kṛṣṇa, in spite of their attractive feminine behavior." Every one of the thousands of wives of Kṛṣṇa was thinking that Kṛṣṇa was captivated by her feminine beauty, but this was not the case. Kṛṣṇa is therefore the supreme controller of the senses, and this is admitted in *Bhagavad-gītā,* where He is addressed as Hṛṣīkeśa—the master of the senses.

23. Steadfast

A person who continues to work until his desired goal is achieved is called steadfast.

There was a fight between Kṛṣṇa and King Jāmbavān, and Kṛṣṇa was to take the valuable Syamantaka jewel from the King. The King tried to hide himself in the forest, but Kṛṣṇa would not become discouraged. Kṛṣṇa finally got the jewel by seeking out the King with great steadfastness.

24. Forbearing

A person who tolerates all kinds of troubles, even though such troubles appear to be unbearable, is called forbearing.

When Kṛṣṇa was residing at the place of His spiritual master, He did not mind taking all troubles in rendering service to His *guru,* although His body was very soft and delicate. It is the duty of the disciple to execute all services unto the spiritual master, despite all kinds of difficulties. The disciple living at the residence of the spiritual master has to go begging from door to door and bring everything back to the spiritual master. When *prasāda* is being served, the spiritual master is supposed to call each and every disciple to come eat. If by chance the spiritual master forgets to call a disciple to partake of the *prasāda,* it is enjoined in the scriptures that the student should fast on that day rather than accept food on his own initiative. There are many such strictures. Sometimes, also, Kṛṣṇa went to the forest to collect dry wood for fuel.

25. Forgiving

A person who can tolerate all kinds of offenses from the opposite party is known to be forgiving.

Lord Kṛṣṇa's forgiving quality is described in the *Śiśupāla-vadha* in connection with His forbidding the killing of Śiśupāla. King Śiśupāla was the monarch of the Cedi kingdom, and although he happened to be a cousin of Kṛṣṇa's, he was always envious of Him. Whenever they would meet, Śiśupāla would try to insult Kṛṣṇa and call Him ill names as much as possible. In the arena of the Rājasūya sacrifice of Mahārāja Yudhiṣṭhira, when Śiśupāla began to call Lord Kṛṣṇa ill names, Kṛṣṇa did not care and remained silent. Some of the people at the arena were prepared to kill Śiśupāla, but Kṛṣṇa restricted them. He was so forgiving. It is said that when there is a thundering sound in the clouds, the mighty lion immediately replies with his thundering roar. But the lion doesn't care when all the foolish jackals begin to make their less important sounds.

Śrī Yāmunācārya praises Kṛṣṇa's power of forgiveness with the following statement: "My dear Lord Rāmacandra, You are so merciful to have excused the crow's clawing on the nipples of Jānakī simply because of his bowing down before You." Once Indra, the King of heaven, assumed the form of a crow and attacked Sītā (Jānakī), Lord Rāmacandra's wife, by striking her on the breast. This was certainly an insult to the universal mother, Sītā, and Lord Rāmacandra was immediately prepared to kill the crow. But because later on the crow bowed down before the Lord, the Lord excused his offense. Śrī Yāmunācārya further says in his prayer that the forgiving power of Lord Kṛṣṇa is even greater than that of Lord Rāmacandra, because Śiśupāla was always in the habit of insulting Kṛṣṇa—not only in one lifetime, but continually throughout three lives. Still, Kṛṣṇa was so kind that He gave Śiśupāla the salvation of merging into His existence. From this we can understand that the goal of the monist to merge into the effulgence of the Supreme is not a very difficult problem. Persons like Śiśupāla who are consistently inimical to Kṛṣṇa can also get this liberation.

26. Grave

A person who does not express his mind to everyone, or whose mental activity and plan of action are very difficult to understand, is called grave. After Lord Śrī Kṛṣṇa had been offended by Brahmā, Brahmā prayed to Him to be excused. But in spite of his offering nice prayers to Kṛṣṇa, Brahmā could not understand whether Kṛṣṇa was satisfied or still dissatisfied. In other words, Kṛṣṇa was so grave that He did not take the prayers of Brahmā very seriously. Another instance of Kṛṣṇa's gravity is found in connection with His loving affairs with Rādhārāṇī. Kṛṣṇa was always very silent about His loving affairs with Rādhārāṇī, so much so that Baladeva, Kṛṣṇa's elder brother and constant companion, could not understand the transformations of Kṛṣṇa on account of His gravity.

27. Self-satisfied

A person who is fully satisfied in himself, without any hankering, and who is not agitated even in the presence of serious cause for distress, is called self-satisfied.

An example of Kṛṣṇa's self-satisfaction was exhibited when He, Arjuna and Bhīma went to challenge Jarāsandha, the formidable king of Magadha, and Kṛṣṇa gave all credit to Bhīma for the killing of Jarāsandha. From this we can understand that Kṛṣṇa never cares at all for fame, although no one can be more famous.

An example of His not being disturbed was shown when Śiśupāla began to call Him ill names. All the kings and *brāhmaṇas* assembled at the sacrificial arena of Mahārāja Yudhiṣṭhira became perturbed and immediately wanted to satisfy Kṛṣṇa by offering nice prayers. But all these kings and *brāhmaṇas* could not discover any disturbance in Kṛṣṇa's person.

28. Possessing Equilibrium

A person who is unaffected by attachment and envy is said to possess equilibrium.

An example of Kṛṣṇa's equilibrium is given in the Tenth Canto, Sixteenth Chapter, verse 33, of *Śrīmad-Bhāgavatam* in connection with His chastising Kāliya, the hundred-headed serpent. While Kāliya was being severely punished, all of his wives appeared before the Lord and prayed as follows: "Dear Lord, You have descended to punish all kinds of demoniac living creatures. Our husband, this Kāliya, is a greatly sinful creature, and so Your punishment for him is quite appropriate. We know that Your punishment for Your enemies and Your dealings with Your sons are both the same. We know that it is in thinking of the future welfare of this condemned creature that You have chastised him."

In another prayer it is said, "My dear Lord Kṛṣṇa, best of all the Yadu dynasty, You are so impartial that if even Your enemy is qualified, You will reward him; and if one of Your sons is a culprit, You will chastise him. This is Your business, because You are the supreme author of the universes. You have no partiality. If anyone finds any partiality in Your characteristics, he is surely mistaken."

29. Magnanimous

Any person who is very charitably disposed is called magnanimous.

When Kṛṣṇa was reigning over Dvārakā, He was so magnanimous

and charitably disposed that there was no limit to His charity. In fact, so great was His charity in Dvārakā that even the spiritual kingdom, with all of its opulence of *cintāmaṇi* (touchstone), desire trees and *surabhi* cows, was surpassed. In the spiritual kingdom of Lord Kṛṣṇa, named Goloka Vṛndāvana, there are *surabhi* cows which give unlimited quantities of milk. There are desire trees from which anyone can take all kinds of fruits, as much as he may desire. The land is made of touchstone, which when touched to iron will transform it into gold. In other words, although in the spiritual kingdom, the abode of Kṛṣṇa, everything is wonderfully opulent, still when Kṛṣṇa was in Dvārakā His charity exceeded the opulences of Goloka Vṛndāvana. Wherever Kṛṣṇa is present, the limitless opulence of Goloka Vṛndāvana is automatically present.

It is also stated that while Lord Kṛṣṇa was living in Dvārakā, He expanded Himself into 16,108 forms, and each and every expansion resided in a palace with a queen. Not only was Kṛṣṇa happily living with His queens in those palaces, but He was giving in charity from each palace an aggregate number of 13,054 cows completely decorated with nice clothing and ornaments. From each of Kṛṣṇa's 16,108 palaces, these cows were being given in charity by Kṛṣṇa every day. No one can estimate the value of such a large number of cows given in charity, but that was the system of Kṛṣṇa's daily affairs while He was reigning in Dvārakā.

30. Religious

A person who personally practices the tenets of religion as they are enjoined in the *śāstras* and who also teaches others the same principles is called religious. Simply professing a kind of faith is not a sign of religiousness. One must act according to religious principles, and by his personal example he should teach others. Such a person is to be understood as religious.

When Kṛṣṇa was present on this planet, there was no irreligion. In this connection, Nārada Muni once addressed Kṛṣṇa jokingly, "My dear Lord of the cowherd boys, Your bulls [bulls are the representation of religion], while eating grass from the pasturing ground and moving on their four legs, have certainly eaten up all the grass of irreligion!" In other words, by the grace of Kṛṣṇa, religious principles were so well cared for that hardly any irreligious activities could be found.

It is said that because Kṛṣṇa was constantly performing various types of sacrifices and was inviting the demigods from the higher planetary systems, the demigods were almost always absent from their consorts. Therefore the wives of the demigods, regretting the absence of their husbands, began to pray for the appearance of Lord Buddha, Kṛṣṇa's ninth incarnation, who appears in the Age of Kali. In other words, instead of being pleased that Lord Kṛṣṇa had come, they began to pray for Lord Buddha, who is the ninth incarnation, because Lord Buddha stopped the ritualistic ceremonies and sacrifices recommended in the *Vedas* in order to discourage animal-killing. The demigods' wives thought that if Lord Buddha appeared, all kinds of sacrifices would be stopped, and thus their husbands would not be invited to such ceremonies and would not be separated from them.

Sometimes it is inquired, "Why don't the demigods from higher planetary systems come to this earth planet nowadays?" The plain answer is that since Lord Buddha appeared and began to deprecate the performance of sacrifice in order to stop animal-killing on this planet, the process of offering sacrifices has been stopped, and the demigods do not care to come here anymore.

22

Qualities of Kṛṣṇa Further Explained

31. Heroic

A person who is very enthusiastic in military activities and expert in releasing different kinds of weapons is called heroic.

Regarding Kṛṣṇa's heroism in fighting, there is the following statement: "My dear killer of the enemy, just as the elephant while taking bath in the lake destroys all the lotus stems within the water by swinging its trunk, so simply by moving Your arms, which are compared to the trunks of elephants, You have killed so many lotuslike enemies."

Regarding Kṛṣṇa's expertise in releasing weapons, when Jarāsandha and thirteen divisions of soldiers attacked Kṛṣṇa's army, they were unable to hurt even one soldier on the side of Kṛṣṇa. This was due to Kṛṣṇa's expert military training. This is unique in the history of military art.

32. Compassionate

A person who is unable to bear another's distress is called compassionate.

Kṛṣṇa's compassion for distressed persons was exhibited when He released all of the kings imprisoned by Magadhendra. While dying, Grandfather Bhīṣma prayed to Kṛṣṇa and described Him as the sun which eradicated darkness. The kings imprisoned by Magadhendra were put into dark cells, and when Kṛṣṇa appeared there, the darkness immediately disappeared, just as if the sun had risen. In other words, although Magadhendra was able to imprison so many kings, upon the appearance of Kṛṣṇa they were all released. Kṛṣṇa released the kings out of His sincere compassion for them.

Kṛṣṇa's compassion was also exhibited when Grandfather Bhīṣma was lying on the bed of arrows which had been shot through his body. While lying in this position, Bhīṣma was very anxious to see Kṛṣṇa, and thus Kṛṣṇa appeared there. Upon seeing the pitiable condition of Bhīṣma, Kṛṣṇa began speaking with tears in His eyes. Not only was He shedding tears, but He also forgot Himself in His compassion. Therefore, instead of offering obeisances to Kṛṣṇa directly, devotees offer obeisances to His compassionate nature. Actually, because Kṛṣṇa is the Supreme Personality of Godhead, it is very difficult to approach Him. But the devotees, taking advantage of His compassionate nature, which is represented by Rādhārāṇī, always pray to Rādhārāṇī for Kṛṣṇa's compassion.

33. Respectful

A person who shows adequate respect to a spiritual master, a *brāhmaṇa* and an old person is to be understood as being respectful.

When superior persons assembled before Kṛṣṇa, Kṛṣṇa first of all offered respect to His spiritual master, then to His father, and then to His elder brother, Balarāma. In this way Lord Kṛṣṇa, the lotus-eyed, was completely happy and pure at heart in all of His dealings.

34. Gentle

Any person who neither becomes impudent nor exhibits a puffed-up nature is called gentle.

The example of Kṛṣṇa's gentle behavior was manifested when He was coming to the arena of the Rājasūya sacrifice arranged by Mahārāja Yudhiṣṭhira, Kṛṣṇa's older cousin. Mahārāja Yudhiṣṭhira knew that Kṛṣṇa was the Supreme Personality of Godhead, and he was attempting to get down from his chariot to receive Kṛṣṇa. But before Yudhiṣṭhira could get down, Lord Kṛṣṇa got down from His own chariot and immediately fell at the feet of the King. Even though Kṛṣṇa is the Supreme Personality of Godhead, He never forgets to show social etiquette in His dealings.

35. Liberal

Any person who is by his natural behavior very mild is called liberal.

A statement by Uddhava after the Syamantaka jewel plundering confirms that Kṛṣṇa is so kind and favorable that if a servitor is accused even of great offenses, Kṛṣṇa does not take this into consideration. He simply considers the service that is rendered by His devotee.

36. Shy

A person who sometimes exhibits humility and bashfulness is called shy.

As described in the *Lalita-mādhava,* Kṛṣṇa's shyness was manifested when He lifted Govardhana Hill by the little finger of His left hand. All of the *gopīs* were observing Kṛṣṇa's wonderful achievement, and Kṛṣṇa was also smiling at seeing the *gopīs.* When Kṛṣṇa's glance went over the breasts of the *gopīs,* His hand began to shake, and upon seeing His hand shake, all of the cowherd men underneath the hill became a little disturbed. Then there was a tumultuous roaring sound, and they all began to pray to Kṛṣṇa for safety. At this time Lord Balarāma was smiling, thinking that these cowherd men had been frightened by the shaking of Govardhana Hill. But, seeing Balarāma smile, Kṛṣṇa thought that Balarāma had understood His mind in observing the breasts of the *gopīs,* and He immediately became bashful.

37. Protector of Surrendered Souls

Kṛṣṇa is the protector of all surrendered souls.

Some enemy of Kṛṣṇa's was enlivened with the thought that he needn't fear Kṛṣṇa, because if he simply surrendered unto Him, Kṛṣṇa would give him all protection. Kṛṣṇa is sometimes compared to the moon, which does not hesitate to distribute its soothing rays, even on the houses of the *caṇḍālas* and other untouchables.

38. Happy

Any person who is always joyful and untouched by any distress is called happy.

As far as Kṛṣṇa's enjoyment is concerned, it is stated that the ornaments which decorated the bodies of Kṛṣṇa and His queens were beyond the dreams of Kuvera, the treasurer of the heavenly kingdom. The constant dancing before the doors of Kṛṣṇa's palaces was not to be imagined even by the demigods in the heavenly kingdom. In the heavenly kingdom, Indra always sees the dancing of the society girls. But even Indra could not imagine how beautiful were the dances being performed at the gates of Kṛṣṇa's palaces. *Gaurī* means "white woman," and Lord Śiva's wife is called Gaurī. The beautiful women residing within the palaces of Kṛṣṇa were so much whiter than Gaurī that they were compared to the moonshine, and they were constantly visible to Kṛṣṇa. Therefore, no one can be enjoying more than Kṛṣṇa. The conception of enjoyment is beautiful women, ornaments and riches. And all of these were fabulously present in the palaces of Kṛṣṇa, defeating even the imagination of Kuvera, Lord Indra or Lord Śiva.

Not even a slight distress can touch Kṛṣṇa. Once some of the *gopīs* went to the place where the *brāhmaṇas* were performing sacrifices and said, "Dear wives of the *brāhmaṇas,* you must know that not even a slight smell of distress can touch Kṛṣṇa. He knows no loss, He knows no defamation, He has no fear, He has no anxiety, and He does not know calamity. He is simply encircled by the dancers of Vraja and is enjoying their company in the *rāsa* dance."

39. Well-wisher of His Devotees

It is said of Kṛṣṇa's devotees that if they offer even a little water or a *tulasī* leaf in devotion to Lord Viṣṇu, Lord Viṣṇu is so kind that He will sell Himself to them.

Kṛṣṇa's favoritism toward His devotees was exhibited in His fight with Bhīṣma. When Grandfather Bhīṣma was lying at the point of death on the bed of arrows, Kṛṣṇa was present before him, and Bhīṣma was remembering how Kṛṣṇa had been kind to him on the battlefield. Kṛṣṇa had promised that in the Battle of Kurukṣetra He would not even touch a weapon to help either side; He would remain neutral. Although Kṛṣṇa was Arjuna's charioteer, He had promised that He would not help Arjuna by using any weapons. But one day Bhīṣma, in order to nullify Kṛṣṇa's promise, exhibited his fighting spirit so magnificently against Arjuna that Kṛṣṇa was obliged to get down from His chariot. Taking up a broken chariot wheel, He ran toward Grandfather Bhīṣma as a lion runs toward an elephant to kill it. Grandfather Bhīṣma remembered this scene, and he later praised Kṛṣṇa for His glorious favoritism toward His devotee, Arjuna, even at the risk of breaking His own promise.

40. Controlled by Love

Kṛṣṇa becomes obliged to the loving spirit of the devotee and not exactly to the service rendered. No one can serve Kṛṣṇa completely. He is so complete and self-sufficient that He has no need of any service from the devotee. It is the devotee's attitude of love and affection for Kṛṣṇa that makes Him obliged. A very nice example of this obligatory behavior was manifested when Sudāmā Vipra went to Kṛṣṇa's palace. Sudāmā Vipra had been a class friend of Kṛṣṇa's, and due to his poverty he was induced by his wife to see Kṛṣṇa to request some aid. When Sudāmā Vipra reached Kṛṣṇa's palace, Kṛṣṇa received him very well, and both He and His wife washed the feet of Sudāmā Vipra, showing respect to the *brāhmaṇa*. Remembering His loving affairs with Sudāmā in their childhood, Kṛṣṇa began to shed tears while receiving him.

Another instance of Kṛṣṇa's obligation to His devotee is described in the Tenth Canto, Ninth Chapter, verse 18, of *Śrīmad-Bhāgavatam,* where Śukadeva Gosvāmī tells King Parīkṣit, "My dear King, when Mother Yaśodā was perspiring, tired of trying to bind Kṛṣṇa up with rope, Kṛṣṇa agreed to allow her to bind Him." Kṛṣṇa, as a child, was disturbing His mother by His naughty activities, and she wanted to bind Him up. Mother Yaśodā brought some rope from the house and tried to tie up the child, but she could not tie a knot due to the shortness of the rope. She tied together many ropes, but when she finished still the rope was too short. After a while she felt very tired and began to perspire. At that time Kṛṣṇa agreed to be bound up by His mother. In other words, no one can bind Kṛṣṇa by any means other than love. He is bound only by obligation to His devotees, because of their ecstatic love for Him.

41. All-auspicious

A person who is always engaged in auspicious welfare activities for everyone is known as all-auspicious.

After the disappearance of Lord Kṛṣṇa from this planet, Uddhava began to remember the activities of the Lord and said, "Kṛṣṇa satisfied all great sages by His wonderful pastimes. He demolished all of the demoniac activities of the cruel royal order, protected all pious men and killed all cruel fighters on the battlefield. Therefore He is all-auspicious for all men."

42. Most Powerful

A person who can always put his enemy into calamities is called powerful.

When Kṛṣṇa was present on this planet, just as the powerful sun drives all darkness to take shelter in caves, He drove away all of His enemies, who fled like owls to take shelter beyond His sight.

43. All-famous

A person who becomes well known due to his spotless character is called famous.

It is stated that the diffusion of Kṛṣṇa's fame is like the moonshine, which turns darkness into light. In other words, if Kṛṣṇa consciousness is preached all over the world, the darkness of ignorance and the anxiety of material existence will turn into the whiteness of purity, peacefulness and prosperity.

When the great sage Nārada was chanting the glories of the Lord, the bluish line on the neck of Lord Śiva disappeared. Upon seeing this, Gaurī, the wife of Lord Śiva, suspected Lord Śiva of being someone else disguised as her husband, and out of fear she immediately left his company. Upon hearing the chanting of Kṛṣṇa's name, Lord Balarāma saw that His dress had become white, although He was generally accustomed to a bluish dress. And the cowherd girls saw all of the water of the Yamunā River turn into milk, so they began to churn it into butter. In other words, by the spreading of Kṛṣṇa consciousness, or the glories of Kṛṣṇa, everything became white and pure.

44. Popular

Any person who is very dear to people in general is called a popular man.

As for Kṛṣṇa's popularity, there is a statement in the First Canto, Eleventh Chapter, verse 9, of *Śrīmad-Bhāgavatam,* that deals with His returning home from the capital of Hastināpura. While He had been absent from Dvārakā at the Battle of Kurukṣetra, all the citizens of Dvārakā had become morose. Then, when He returned, the citizens joyfully received Him and said, "Dear Lord, while You were absent from the city, we passed our days in the darkness of night. As in the darkness of night every moment appears to be a long duration of time, so while You were gone every moment appeared to us like millions of years. Your separation is completely unbearable to us." This statement shows how popular Kṛṣṇa was all over the country.

A similar incident occurred when Kṛṣṇa entered the arena of sacrifice arranged by King Kaṁsa for His death. As soon as He entered the place, all the sages began to cry, "Jaya! Jaya! Jaya!" (which means "Victory!"). Kṛṣṇa was a boy at that time, and all the sages offered their respectful blessings to Him. The demigods who were present also began to offer beautiful prayers to Kṛṣṇa. And the ladies and girls present expressed their joy from all corners of the arena. In other words, there was no one in that particular place with whom Kṛṣṇa was not very popular.

45. Partiality to Devotees

Although Kṛṣṇa is the Supreme Personality of Godhead and is therefore not partial to anyone, it is stated in *Bhagavad-gītā* that He has special attraction for a devotee who worships His name in love and affection. When Kṛṣṇa was on this planet, one devotee expressed his feeling in this way: "My dear Lord, if You had not appeared on this planet, then the *asuras* [demons] and atheists would have surely created havoc against the activities of the devotees. I cannot imagine the magnitude of such devastation prevented by Your presence." From the very beginning of His appearance, Kṛṣṇa was the greatest enemy of all demoniac persons, although Kṛṣṇa's enmity toward the demons is actually comparable to His friendship with the devotees. This is because any demon who is killed by Kṛṣṇa receives immediate salvation.

46. Very Attractive to All Women

Any person who has special qualifications becomes immediately very attractive to women.

A devotee made the following statement about the queens of Dvāraka: "How shall I describe the glories of the queens of Dvārakā, who were personally engaged in the service of the Lord? The Lord is so great that simply by chanting His name all the great sages like Nārada can enjoy transcendental bliss. So what can be said about those queens, who were at every moment seeing the Lord and serving Him personally?" Kṛṣṇa had 16,108 wives in Dvārakā, and each and every one of them was attracted to Kṛṣṇa just as iron is attracted by a magnet. There is a statement by a devotee: "My dear Lord, You are just like a magnet, and all the damsels of Vraja are just like iron: in whichever direction You are moving they are following You, as iron is attracted by magnetic force."

47. All-worshipable

A person who is respected and worshiped by all kinds of human beings and demigods is called *sarvārādhya,* or all-worshipable.

Kṛṣṇa is worshiped not only by all living entities, including the great demigods like Lord Śiva and Lord Brahmā, but also by Viṣṇu expansions (forms of Godhead) such as Baladeva and Śeṣa. Baladeva is a direct expansion of Kṛṣṇa, but He still accepts Kṛṣṇa as worshipable. When Kṛṣṇa appeared in the arena of the Rājasūya sacrifice organized by Mahārāja Yudhiṣṭhira, to all present, including great sages and demigods, Kṛṣṇa became the cynosure, the center of attraction, and everyone offered Him respects.

48. All-opulent

Kṛṣṇa is full in all opulences—namely strength, wealth, fame, beauty, knowledge and renunciation. When Kṛṣṇa was present in Dvārakā, His family, which is known as the Yadu dynasty, consisted of 560 million members. And all of these family members were very obedient and faithful to Kṛṣṇa. There were more than 900,000 big palatial buildings there to house all the people, and everyone in them respected Kṛṣṇa as the most worshipable. Devotees were astonished to see the opulence of Kṛṣṇa.

This was verified by Bilvamaṅgala Ṭhākura when in *Kṛṣṇa-karṇāmṛta* he addressed Kṛṣṇa thus: "My dear Lord, what can I say about the opulence of Your Vṛndāvana? Simply the ornaments on the legs of the damsels of Vṛndāvana are more than *cintāmaṇi,* and their dresses are as good as the heavenly *pārijāta* flowers. And the cows exactly resemble the *surabhi* cows in the transcendental abode. Therefore Your opulence is just like an ocean that no one can measure."

49. All-honorable

A person who is chief among all important persons is called all-honorable.

When Kṛṣṇa was living at Dvārakā, demigods like Lord Śiva, Lord Brahmā, Indra the King of heaven and many others used to come to visit Him. The doorkeeper, who had to manage the entrance of all these demigods, one very busy day said, "My dear Lord Brahmā and Lord Śiva, please sit down on this bench and wait. My dear Indra, please desist from reading your prayers. This is creating a disturbance. Please wait silently. My dear Varuṇa, please go away. And my dear demigods, do not waste your time uselessly. Kṛṣṇa is very busy; He cannot see you!"

50. The Supreme Controller

There are two kinds of controllers, or lords: one who is independent is called controller, and one whose orders cannot be neglected by anyone is called controller.

Regarding Kṛṣṇa's complete independence and lordship, *Śrīmad-Bhāgavatam* says that although Kāliya was a great offender, Kṛṣṇa still favored him by marking his head with His lotus feet, whereas Lord Brahmā, although having prayed to Kṛṣṇa with so many wonderful verses, still could not attract Him.

This contradictory treatment by Kṛṣṇa is just befitting His position, because in all the Vedic literature He is described as the complete independent. In the beginning of *Śrīmad-Bhāgavatam* the Lord is described as *svarāṭ,* which means "completely independent." That is the position of the Supreme Absolute Truth. The Absolute Truth is not only sentient, but is also completely independent.

As for Kṛṣṇa's orders not being neglected by anyone, in *Śrīmad-Bhāgavatam,* Third Canto, Second Chapter, verse 21, Uddhava tells Vidura, "Lord Kṛṣṇa is the master of the three modes of material nature. He is the enjoyer of all opulences, and therefore there is no one equal to or greater than Him." All the great kings and emperors used to come before Him, offer their gifts and pay obeisances with their helmets at the feet of the Lord. One devotee said, "My dear Kṛṣṇa, when You order Brahmā, 'Now you may create the universe,' and when You order Lord Śiva, 'Now you dissolve this material manifestation,' You are in this way creating and dissolving the material creation Yourself. Simply by Your orders and by Your partial representation of Viṣṇu, You are maintaining the universes. In this way, O Kṛṣṇa, O enemy of Kaṁsa, there are so many Brahmās and Śivas who are simply carrying out Your orders."

51. Changeless

Kṛṣṇa does not change His constitutional position, not even when He appears in this material world. Ordinary living entities have their constitutional spiritual positions covered. They appear in different bodies, and under the different bodily concepts of life they act. But Kṛṣṇa does not change His body. He appears in His own body and is therefore not affected by the modes of material nature. In the First Canto, Eleventh Chapter, verse 38, of *Śrīmad-Bhāgavatam* it is stated that the special prerogative of the supreme controller is that He is not at all affected by the modes of nature. The practical example of this is that devotees who are under the protection of the Lord are also not affected by material nature. To overcome the influence of material nature is very difficult, but the devotees or the saintly persons who are under the protection of the Lord are not affected. So what need is there to speak of the Lord Himself? To be more clear, although the Lord sometimes appears in this material world, He has nothing to do with the modes of material nature, and He acts with full independence in His transcendental position. This is the special quality of the Lord.

52. All-cognizant

Any person who can understand the feelings of all persons and incidents in all places at all times is called all-cognizant.

A nice example of the all-cognizant quality of the Lord is described in *Śrīmad-Bhāgavatam,* First Canto, Fifteenth Chapter, verse 11, in connection with Durvāsā Muni's visit to the house of the Pāṇḍavas in the forest. Following a calculated plan, Duryodhana sent Durvāsā Muni and his ten thousand disciples to be guests of the Pāṇḍavas in the forest. Duryodhana arranged for Durvāsā and his men to reach the place of the Pāṇḍavas just when the Pāṇḍavas' lunchtime ended, so that the Pāṇḍavas would be caught without sufficient means to feed such a large number of guests. Knowing Duryodhana's plan, Kṛṣṇa came to the Pāṇḍavas and asked their wife, Draupadī, if there were any remnants of food which she could offer to Him. Draupadī offered Him a container in which there was only a little fragment of some vegetable preparation, and Kṛṣṇa at once ate it. At that moment all of the sages accompanying Durvāsā were taking bath in the river, and when Kṛṣṇa felt satisfaction from eating Draupadī's offering, they also felt satisfaction, and their hunger was gone. Because Durvāsā and his men were unable to eat anything more, they went away without coming into the house of the Pāṇḍavas. In this way the Pāṇḍavas were saved from the wrath of Durvāsā. Duryodhana had sent them because he knew that since the Pāṇḍavas would not be able to receive such a large number, Durvāsā would become angry, and the Pāṇḍavas would be cursed. But Kṛṣṇa saved them from this calamity by His trick and by His all-cognizant quality.

53. Ever Fresh

Kṛṣṇa is always remembered, and His name is always chanted by millions of devotees, but the devotees never become satiated. Instead of becoming disinterested in thinking of Kṛṣṇa and in chanting His holy name, the devotees get newer and newer impetus to continue the process. Therefore Kṛṣṇa is ever fresh. Not only Kṛṣṇa Himself, but also Kṛṣṇa's knowledge is ever fresh. *Bhagavad-gītā,* which was imparted five thousand years ago, is still being read repeatedly by many, many men, and still new light is always being found in it. Therefore, Kṛṣṇa and His name, fame, qualities—and everything in relationship with Him—is ever fresh.

All the queens at Dvārakā were goddesses of fortune. It is said in *Śrīmad-Bhāgavatam,* First Canto, Eleventh Chapter, verse 33, that the goddesses of fortune are very fickle and restless, so no one can consistently captivate them. Thus one's luck will always change sometime. Yet the goddesses of fortune could not leave Kṛṣṇa for even a moment when they were residing with Him at Dvārakā. This means that Kṛṣṇa's attraction is ever fresh. Even the goddesses of fortune cannot leave His company.

Regarding Kṛṣṇa's attractive features being ever fresh, there is a statement by Rādhārāṇī in the *Lalita-mādhava* in which Kṛṣṇa is compared to the greatest sculptor, because He is expert in chiseling at the chastity of women. In other words, although chaste women may follow the rules and regulations of Vedic principles to become ever faithful to their husbands, Kṛṣṇa is able to break their stonelike chastity with the chisel of His beauty. Most of the girlfriends of Kṛṣṇa were married, but because Kṛṣṇa was their friend before their marriages, they could not forget His attractive features, which were always fascinating to them, even after their marriages.

54. Sac-cid-ānanda-vigraha

Kṛṣṇa's transcendental body is eternal, full of knowledge and bliss. *Sat* means ever-existing for all time and in all places; in other words, all-pervading in time and space. *Cit* means full of knowledge. Kṛṣṇa has nothing to learn from anyone. He is independently full of all knowledge. *Ānanda* means the reservoir of all pleasure. The impersonalists are seeking to merge into the Brahman effulgence of eternity and knowledge, but the major portion of the absolute pleasure which is in Kṛṣṇa is avoided by them. One can enjoy the transcendental blissfulness of merging into the Brahman effulgence after being freed from the contamination of material illusion, false identification, attachment, detachment and material absorption. These are the preliminary qualifications of a person who can realize Brahman. It is stated in *Bhagavad-gītā* that one has to become full of joyfulness; this is not exactly joyfulness, but a sense of freedom from all anxieties. Freedom from all anxieties may be the first principle of joyfulness, but it is not actual joyfulness. Those who realize the self, or become *brahma-bhūta,* are only preparing themselves for the platform of joyfulness. That joyfulness can be actually achieved only when one comes into contact with Kṛṣṇa. Kṛṣṇa consciousness is so complete that it includes the transcendental pleasure derived from impersonal or Brahman realization. Even the impersonalist will become attracted to the personal form of Kṛṣṇa, known as Śyāmasundara.

It is confirmed by the statement of *Brahma-saṁhitā* that the Brahman effulgence is the bodily ray of Kṛṣṇa; the Brahman effulgence is simply an exhibition of the energy of Kṛṣṇa. Kṛṣṇa is the source of the Brahman effulgence, as He Himself confirms in *Bhagavad-gītā*. From this we can conclude that the impersonal feature of the Absolute Truth is not the ultimate end; Kṛṣṇa is the ultimate end of the Absolute Truth.

The members of the Vaiṣṇava schools therefore never try to merge into the Brahman effulgence in their pursuit of spiritual perfection. They accept Kṛṣṇa as the ultimate goal of self-realization. Therefore Kṛṣṇa is called Parabrahman (the Supreme Brahman) or Parameśvara (the supreme controller). Śrī Yāmunācārya has prayed as follows: "My dear Lord, I know that the gigantic universe and gigantic space and time within the universe are covered by the ten layers of the material elements, each layer ten times larger than the previous one. The three material modes of nature, the Garbhodakaśāyī Viṣṇu, the Kṣīrodakaśāyī Viṣṇu, the Mahā-Viṣṇu, and beyond them the spiritual sky and its spiritual planets, known as Vaikuṇṭhas, and the Brahman effulgence in that spiritual sky—all of these taken together are nothing but a small exhibition of Your potency."

55. Possessing All Mystic Perfections

There are many standards of perfection. The highest material perfections, obtained by perfect *yogīs,* are listed as eight: to become the smallest of the small, to become the greatest of the great, etc. All of these material perfections, as well as all spiritual perfections, can be found fully in Kṛṣṇa's personality.

56. Kṛṣṇa's Inconceivable Potencies

Kṛṣṇa is present everywhere, not only within the universe, not only within the hearts of all living entities, but also within every atom. In the prayers of Queen Kuntī we find mention of this inconceivable potency of Kṛṣṇa. While Kṛṣṇa was talking with Kuntī, He simultaneously entered the womb of Uttarā, who was in danger due to the atomic weapon of Aśvatthāmā. Kṛṣṇa can illusion even Lord Brahmā and Lord Śiva, and He can protect all surrendered devotees from the reactions of sinful activities. These are some of the examples of His inconceivable potencies.

Śrīla Rūpa Gosvāmī therefore offers his obeisances unto Kṛṣṇa by saying, "Kṛṣṇa, who is present as a human being, has as His mere shadow the whole material nature. He has expanded Himself into so many cows, calves and cowherd boys, and He has again manifested Himself in all of them as the four-handed Nārāyaṇa. He has taught millions of Brahmās self-realization, and thus He is worshipable not only by the heads of all universes, but by everyone else also. Therefore let me always accept Him as the Supreme Personality of Godhead."

When Indra was defeated by Kṛṣṇa in the matter of taking the *pārijāta* plant from heaven, Nārada met Indra and criticized him, "O Indra, great King of heaven, Kṛṣṇa has already defeated Lord Brahmā and Lord Śiva. So what can be said of an insignificant demigod like you?" Nārada Muni, of course, was criticizing Indra jokingly, and Indra enjoyed it. In Nārada's statement it is confirmed that Kṛṣṇa was able to illusion even Lord Brahmā and Lord Śiva, as well as Indra. So there is no question of Kṛṣṇa's power to do the same to lesser living entities.

A description of Kṛṣṇa's power in minimizing the sufferings of sinful reactions is given in *Brahma-saṁhitā* as follows: "Beginning from the great King of heaven down to the ant, everyone is undergoing the reactions of past deeds. But a devotee of Kṛṣṇa is relieved from such reactions by the grace of Kṛṣṇa." This was clearly proved when Kṛṣṇa went to the place of Yamarāja, the Lord of death, to reclaim the dead son of His teacher. Kṛṣṇa's teacher had requested Kṛṣṇa to bring back his dead son, and to do so Kṛṣṇa went to the place of Yamarāja to claim that soul, who had been brought there by Yamarāja and was being kept under his control. Kṛṣṇa immediately ordered Yamarāja, "Be benefited by My order and return that soul unto Me!" The purport of this incident is that even a person who is under the regulative principles of the laws of nature, and is therefore punishable by Yamarāja under these laws, can be granted complete immunity by the grace of Kṛṣṇa.

Kṛṣṇa's inconceivable potencies have been described by Śukadeva Gosvāmī as follows: "Kṛṣṇa is bewildering my intelligence because, although He is unborn, He has appeared as the son of Nanda Mahārāja. He is all-pervading, but still He is held on the lap of Yaśodā. In spite of His being all-pervasive, He has become limited by the love of Yaśodā. Although He has innumerable forms, still He is moving as one Kṛṣṇa before His father and mother, Nanda and Yaśodā." In the *Brahma-saṁhitā* also it is said that although Kṛṣṇa is eternally living in Goloka Vṛndāvana, His transcendental abode, He is still present everywhere, even within the atoms.

57. Kṛṣṇa's Body Generates Innumerable Universes

In the Tenth Canto, Fourteenth Chapter, verse 11, of *Śrīmad-Bhāgavatam,* Lord Brahmā says, "My dear Lord, false ego, intelligence, mind, sky, air, fire, water and earth are the material ingredients of this universe, which can be compared to a gigantic pot. In that gigantic pot my body is of insignificant measurement, and even though one of the many universes is created by me, innumerable universes are coming and going from the pores of Your body, just as atomic particles are seen flickering in the sunlight. I think I am very, very insignificant before You, and I am therefore begging Your pardon. Please be merciful toward me."

If one takes account of only one universe, he will find so many combinations of wonderful things within, because there are innumerable planets, innumerable residences and places of demigods. The diameter of the universe is four billion miles, and it is infested with many unfathomable regions known as Pātālas, or lower planetary systems. Although Kṛṣṇa is the origin of all this, He can always be seen in Vṛndāvana, exhibiting His inconceivable potencies. So who can adequately worship such an all-powerful Lord, possessed of such inconceivable energy?

58. The Original Source of All Incarnations

Jayadeva Gosvāmī, in his *Gīta-govinda,* has sung as follows: "The Lord has saved the *Vedas* in His form as a fish, and He has borne the whole universe on His back in the form of a tortoise. He has picked up this earthly planet from the water in the form of a boar. He has killed Hiraṇyakaśipu in the form of Nṛsiṁha. He has cheated Mahārāja Bali in the form of Vāmana. He has annihilated all the dynasties of the *kṣatriyas* in the form of Paraśurāma. He has killed all the demons in the form of Lord Rāma. He has accepted the great plow in the form of Balarāma. He has annihilated all the atheistic persons in the form of Kalki. And He has saved all the poor animals in the form of Lord Buddha."* These are some of the descriptions of the incarnations emanating from Kṛṣṇa, and from *Śrīmad-Bhāgavatam* it is understood that innumerable incarnations are always coming out from the body of Kṛṣṇa, just like waves in the ocean. No one can even count how many waves there are, and similarly no one can count how many incarnations are coming from the Lord's body.

59. Kṛṣṇa Gives Salvation to the Enemies That He Kills

Another name for salvation is *apavarga*. *Apavarga* is the opposite of *pavarga,* or the various miserable conditions of material existence. The word *pa-varga* indicates the combination of five Sanskrit letters: *pa, pha, ba, bha* and *ma.* These letters are the first letters of the words for five different conditions, as described below. The first letter, *pa,* comes from the word *parābhava,* which means "defeat." In this material struggle for existence, we are simply meeting defeat. Actually, we

*All of these incarnations of Godhead are described in the author's *Śrīmad-Bhāgavatam,* First Canto, Chapter Three.

have to conquer birth, death, disease and old age, and because there is no possibility of overcoming all these miserable conditions, due to the illusion of *māyā* we are simply meeting with *parābhava,* or defeat. The next letter, *pha,* is taken from the word *phena*. *Phena* is the foam which is found on the mouth when one is very tired (as is commonly observed with horses). The letter *ba* comes from the word *bandha,* or bondage. *Bha* is taken from the word *bhīti,* or fearfulness. *Ma* is taken from the word *mṛti,* or death. So the word *pavarga* signifies our struggle for existence and our meeting with defeat, exhaustion, bondage, fearfulness and, at last, death. *Apavarga* means that which can nullify all of these material conditions. Kṛṣṇa is said to be the giver of *apavarga,* the path of liberation.

For the impersonalists and the enemies of Kṛṣṇa, liberation means merging into the Supreme. The demons and the impersonalists do not care for Kṛṣṇa, but Kṛṣṇa is so kind that He gives this liberation even to His enemies and to the impersonalists. There is the following statement in this connection: "O Murāri [Kṛṣṇa]! How wonderful it is that although the demons, who were always envious of the demigods, have failed to penetrate Your military phalanx, they have penetrated the region of *mitra,* the sun globe." The word *mitra* is used metaphorically. *Mitra* means "the sun globe," and *mitra* also means "friend." The demons who opposed Kṛṣṇa as enemies wanted to penetrate His military phalanx, but instead of doing this, they died in battle, and the result was that they penetrated the planet of Mitra, or the sun planet. In other words, they entered into the Brahman effulgence. The example of the sun planet is given here because the sun is ever-illuminating, like the spiritual sky, where there are innumerable illuminating Vaikuṇṭha planets. The enemies of Kṛṣṇa were killed, and instead of penetrating Kṛṣṇa's phalanx, they entered into the friendly atmosphere of the spiritual effulgence. That is the mercy of Kṛṣṇa, and therefore He is known as the deliverer of His enemies also.

60. The Attractor of Liberated Souls

There are many examples of how Kṛṣṇa attracted even great liberated souls like Śukadeva Gosvāmī and the Kumāras. In this connection the following statement was given by the Kumāras: "How wonderful it is that although we are completely liberated, free from desire and situated at the stage of *paramahaṁsa,* we are still aspiring to taste the pastimes of Rādhā and Kṛṣṇa."

61. Performer of Wonderful Activities

In the *Bṛhad-vāmana Purāṇa,* the Lord says, "Although I have many fascinating pastimes, whenever I think of the *rāsa-līlā,* which I perform with the *gopīs,* I become eager to have it again."

One devotee has said, "I know about Nārāyaṇa, the husband of the goddess of fortune, and I also know about many other incarnations of the Lord. Certainly all the pastimes of such incarnations are exciting to my mind, but still the pastimes of the *rāsa-līlā* performed by Lord Kṛṣṇa Himself are wonderfully increasing my transcendental pleasure."

62. Kṛṣṇa Is Surrounded by Loving Devotees

When we speak of Kṛṣṇa, Kṛṣṇa is not alone. "Kṛṣṇa" means His name, His qualities, His fame, His friends, His paraphernalia, His entourage—all of these are included. When we speak of a king, it is to be understood that he is surrounded by ministers, secretaries, military commanders and many other people. Similarly, Kṛṣṇa is not impersonal. In His Vṛndāvana *līlā* especially, He is surrounded by the *gopīs,* the cowherd boys, His father, His mother and all the inhabitants of Vṛndāvana.

In the Tenth Canto, Thirty-first Chapter, verse 15, of *Śrīmad-Bhāgavatam,* the *gopīs* lament, "My dear Kṛṣṇa, during the daytime when You go out into the forest of Vṛndāvana with Your cows, we consider one moment to be twelve years, and it is very difficult for us to pass the time. And again when You come back at the end of the day, by seeing Your beautiful face we are so much attracted that we are unable to stop looking upon You constantly. At these times, when there is occasional blinking of our eyelids, we condemn the creator, Lord Brahmā, as a dunce, because he does not know how to make perfect eyes!" In other words, the *gopīs* were disturbed by the blinking of their eyes, because for the moment that their eyes were closed they could not see Kṛṣṇa. This means that the *gopīs'* love for Kṛṣṇa was so great and ecstatic that they were disturbed by even His momentary absence. And when they saw Kṛṣṇa, they were also disturbed. This is a paradox.

One *gopī*, expressing herself to Kṛṣṇa, says, "When we meet You at night, we consider the duration of night to be very small. And why speak of only this night? Even if we had a night of Brahmā* we would consider it a very short time!" We get an idea of Brahmā's day from the following statement of *Bhagavad-gītā* (8.17): "By human calculation, a thousand *yuga* cycles taken together is Brahmā's one day. And such also is the duration of his night." The *gopīs* said that even if they could have that duration of night, it would still not be sufficient for their meeting with Kṛṣṇa.

63. Kṛṣṇa's Attractive Flute

In the Tenth Canto, Thirty-fifth Chapter, verse 15, of *Śrīmad-Bhāgavatam,* the *gopīs* tell Mother Yaśodā, "When your son plays on His flute, Lord Śiva, Lord Brahmā and Indra—although they are supposed to be the greatest learned scholars and personalities—all become bewildered. Although they are all very great personalities, by hearing the sound of Kṛṣṇa's flute they humbly bow down and become grave from studying the sound vibrated."

In his book *Vidagdha-mādhava,* Śrī Rūpa Gosvāmī thus describes the vibration of Kṛṣṇa's flute: "The sound vibration created by the flute of Kṛṣṇa wonderfully stopped Lord Śiva from playing his *ḍiṇḍima* drum, and the same flute has caused great sages like the four Kumāras to become disturbed in their meditation. It has caused Lord Brahmā, who was sitting on the lotus flower for the creative function, to become astonished. And Anantadeva, who was calmly holding all the planets on His hoods, was moving in this way and that due to the transcendental vibration from Kṛṣṇa's flute, which penetrated through the covering of this universe and reached to the spiritual sky."

64. Kṛṣṇa's Exquisite Beauty

In the Third Canto, Second Chapter, verse 12, of *Śrīmad-Bhāgavatam,* Uddhava tells Vidura, "My dear sir, Kṛṣṇa's form was most wonderful when He appeared on this planet and exhibited the potency of His internal energy. His wonderfully attractive form was present during His pastimes on this planet, and by His internal potency He exhibited

*4,320,000,000 solar years equals twelve hours, or one night, of Brahmā.

His opulences, which are striking to everyone. His personal beauty was so great that there was no necessity for His wearing ornaments on His body. In fact, instead of the ornaments' beautifying Kṛṣṇa, Kṛṣṇa's beauty enhanced the ornaments."

Regarding the attractiveness of Kṛṣṇa's bodily beauty and the sound vibration of His flute, in the Tenth Canto, Twenty-ninth Chapter, verse 40, of *Śrīmad-Bhāgavatam,* the *gopīs* address Kṛṣṇa as follows: "Although our attitude toward You resembles loving affairs with a paramour, we cannot but wonder at how no woman can maintain her chastity upon hearing the vibration from Your flute. And not only women, but even stronghearted men are subject to falling down from their position at the sound of Your flute. In fact, we have seen that in Vṛndāvana even the cows, the deer, the birds, the trees—everyone—has been enchanted by the sweet vibration of Your flute and the fascinating beauty of Your person."

In Rūpa Gosvāmī's *Lalita-mādhava,* it is said, "One day Kṛṣṇa happened to see the shadow of His beautiful form reflected on the jeweled foreground. Upon seeing this bodily reflection, He expressed His feelings: 'How wonderful it is that I have never seen such a beautiful form! Although it is My own form, still, like Rādhārāṇī, I am trying to embrace this form and enjoy celestial bliss.'" This statement shows how Kṛṣṇa and His shadow reflection are one and the same. There is no difference between Kṛṣṇa and His shadow reflection, nor between Kṛṣṇa and His picture. That is the transcendental position of Kṛṣṇa.

The above statements describe some of the wonderful reservoirs of pleasure within Kṛṣṇa, as well as the transcendental qualities of His personality. The transcendental qualities of Kṛṣṇa are compared to the ocean: no one can estimate the length and breadth of the ocean. But as one can understand the ocean's contents simply by testing one drop of it, so these statements will give us some understanding of Kṛṣṇa's transcendental position and qualities.

In the Tenth Canto, Fourteenth Chapter, verse 7, of *Śrīmad-Bhāgavatam,* Lord Brahmā says, "My dear Lord, the inconceivable qualities, beauties and activities which You have revealed by Your presence on this planet cannot be calculated by any material measurement. If one even tries to imagine, 'Kṛṣṇa may be like this,' that is also impossible. The day may come when the material scientist, after many, many births or after many, many years, will be able to estimate the atomic constitution of the whole world, or he may be able to count the atomic fragments that permeate the sky, or he may even give an estimate of all the atoms within the universe, but still he will never be able to count the transcendental qualities in Your reservoir of transcendental bliss."

23

Kṛṣṇa's Personality

Śrīla Rūpa Gosvāmī states that although Lord Kṛṣṇa is the reservoir of unlimited pleasure and the greatest leader of all, He is still dependent upon His devotees in three ways. According to the emotional status of the devotee, the Supreme Personality of Godhead is appreciated in three ways: as the most perfect, as very perfect and as perfect. When He exhibits Himself in fullness, He is appreciated by great learned scholars as most perfect. When He exhibits Himself in lesser degrees, He is called very perfect. And when He exhibits still less, He is called perfect. This means that Kṛṣṇa is appreciated for three degrees of perfection. These three degrees of perfection are especially exhibited as follows: when He is in Goloka Vṛndāvana His transcendental qualities are exhibited as most perfect, when He is in Mathurā He exhibits His qualities as very perfect, and when He is in Dvārakā He exhibits His qualities as perfect.

Kṛṣṇa's personality is analyzed as *dhīrodātta, dhīra-lalita, dhīra-praśānta* and *dhīroddhata*. If one asks how a personality can be beheld in four quite opposing ways, the answer is that the Lord is the reservoir of all transcendental qualities and activities. Therefore, His different aspects can be analyzed according to the exhibition of His limitless variety of pastimes, and as such there is no contradiction.

Dhīrodātta

A *dhīrodātta* is a person who is naturally very grave, gentle, forgiving, merciful, determined, humble, highly qualified, chivalrous and physically attractive.

In this connection, the following statement given by Indra, the King of heaven, is very significant: "My dear Lord, I admit that I have committed great offenses unto You, but I cannot express my feelings of regret, being bewildered at seeing Your extraordinary chivalrous spirit, Your endeavor to protect Your devotees, Your determination, Your steadiness in lifting the great hill of Govardhana, Your beautiful bodily features and Your astonishing characteristic of being pleased simply by accepting the prayers of Your devotees and offenders."

The above statement by the King of heaven is an exact corroboration of Kṛṣṇa's being *dhīrodātta*. Many learned scholars have agreed to also accept Lord Rāmacandra as *dhīrodātta,* but all of Lord Rāmacandra's qualities are also included in the character of Lord Kṛṣṇa.

Dhīra-lalita

A person is called *dhīra-lalita* if he is naturally very funny, always in full youthfulness, expert in joking and free from all anxieties. Such a *dhīra-lalita* personality is generally found to be domesticated and very submissive to his lover. This *dhīra-lalita* trait in the personality of Kṛṣṇa is described by Yajña-patnī, the wife of one of the *brāhmaṇas* who were performing sacrifices in Vṛndāvana. She tells her friends, "One day Śrīmatī Rādhārāṇī, accompanied by Her associates, was taking rest in Her garden, and at that time Lord Śrī Kṛṣṇa arrived in that assembly. After sitting down, He began to narrate very impudently about His previous night's pastimes with Rādhārāṇī. While He was speaking in that way, Rādhārāṇī became very embarrassed. She was feeling ashamed and was absorbed in thought, and Kṛṣṇa took the opportunity to mark Her breasts with different kinds of *tilaka*. Kṛṣṇa proved Himself to be very expert in that art." In this way Kṛṣṇa, as *dhīra-lalita,* was enjoying His youthful proclivities in the company of the *gopīs.*

Generally, those who are expert in writing drama choose to call Cupid the ideal *dhīra-lalita,* but we can more perfectly find in the personality of Kṛṣṇa all the characteristics of *dhīra-lalita.*

Dhīra-praśānta

A person who is very peaceful, forbearing, considerate and obliging is called *dhīra-praśānta*. This *dhīra-praśānta* trait of Kṛṣṇa was exhibited in His dealings with the Pāṇḍavas. On account of the Pāṇḍavas' faithful devotion to the Lord, He agreed to become their charioteer, their advisor, their friend, their messenger and sometimes their bodyguard. Such is an example of the result of devotional service toward Viṣṇu. When Kṛṣṇa was speaking to Mahārāja Yudhiṣṭhira about religious principles, He demonstrated Himself to be a great learned scholar, but because He accepted the position of younger cousin to Yudhiṣṭhira, He was speaking in a very gentle tone which enhanced His beautiful bodily features. The movements of His eyes and the mode of His speech proved that He was very, very expert in giving moral instruction. Sometimes, Mahārāja Yudhiṣṭhira is also accepted by learned scholars as *dhīra-praśānta.*

Dhīroddhata

A person who is very envious, proud, easily angered, restless and complacent is called *dhīroddhata* by learned scholars. Such qualities were visible in the character of Lord Kṛṣṇa, because when He was writing a letter to Kālayavana, Kṛṣṇa addressed him as a sinful frog. In His letter Kṛṣṇa advised Kālayavana that he should immediately go and find some dark well for his residence, because there was a black snake named Kṛṣṇa who was very eager to devour all such sinful frogs. Kṛṣṇa reminded Kālayavana that He could turn all the universes to ashes simply by looking at them.

The above statement by Kṛṣṇa seems apparently to be of an envious nature, but according to different pastimes, places and times this quality is accepted as a great characteristic. Kṛṣṇa's *dhīroddhata* qualities have been accepted as great because Kṛṣṇa uses them only to protect His devotees. In other words, even undesirable traits may also be used in the exchange of devotional service.

Sometimes Bhīma, the second brother of the Pāṇḍavas, is also described as *dhīroddhata.*

Once, while fighting with a demon who was appearing as a deer, Kṛṣṇa challenged him in this way: "I have come before you as a great elephant named Kṛṣṇa. You must leave the battlefield, accepting defeat, or else there is death awaiting you." This challenging spirit of Kṛṣṇa's is not contradictory to His sublime character; because He is the Supreme Being, everything is possible in His character.

There is a nice statement in the *Kūrma Purāṇa* about these contradictory traits of the Supreme Personality of Godhead. It is stated there that the Supreme Person is neither very fat nor very thin; He is always transcendental to material qualities, and yet His bodily luster is blackish. His eyes are reddish, He is all-powerful, and He is equipped with all different kinds of opulences. Contradictory traits in Kṛṣṇa's person are not at all surprising; one should not consider the characteristics of Kṛṣṇa, the Supreme Personality of Godhead, to be actually contradictory. One should try to understand the traits of Kṛṣṇa from authorities and try to understand how these characteristics are employed by the supreme will of the Lord.

In the *Mahā-varāha Purāṇa* it is confirmed that the transcendental bodies of the Supreme Personality of Godhead and His expansions are all existing eternally. Such bodies are never material; they are completely spiritual and full of knowledge. They are reservoirs of all transcendental qualities. In the *Viṣṇu-yāmala-tantra* there is a statement that because the Personality of Godhead and His expanded bodies are always full of knowledge, bliss and eternity, they are always free from the eighteen kinds of material contaminations—illusion, fatigue, errors, roughness, material lust, restlessness, pride, envy, violence, disgrace, exhaustion, untruth, anger, hankering, dependence, desire to lord it over the universe, seeing duality and cheating.

Regarding all of the above-mentioned statements, it is understood that the Mahā-Viṣṇu is the source of all incarnations in the material world. But because of His greater, extraordinary opulence, we can understand that the son of Nanda Mahārāja is the source of the Mahā-Viṣṇu also. This is confirmed in the *Brahma-saṁhitā,* wherein it is stated, "Let me offer my respectful obeisances unto Govinda, whose partial representation is the Mahā-Viṣṇu." The gigantic form of the Mahā-Viṣṇu is the source of generation for innumerable universes. Innumerable universes are coming out of His exhaling breath, and the same universes are going back in with His inhaling breath. This Mahā-Viṣṇu is also a plenary portion of a portion of Kṛṣṇa.

24
Further Traits of Śrī Kṛṣṇa

After describing the different opulences of Kṛṣṇa, Śrīla Rūpa Gosvāmī tries to further describe the transcendental beauties and qualities of the Lord as decorated, enjoying, pleasing, dependable, steady and predominating. He is also described as a meticulous dresser and a magnanimous personality. These are generally considered to be the qualities of great personalities.

Decorated

It is said that a person is great if he is decorated with the qualities of being very merciful toward the unfortunate, very powerful, superior, chivalrous, enthusiastic, expert and truthful. These decorations were manifested in the character of Kṛṣṇa during His *govardhana-līlā*. At that time the whole tract of land in Vṛndāvana was being disturbed by the rains sent by Indra, as described elsewhere. At first Kṛṣṇa thought, "Let Me retaliate against this vengeance of Indra by destroying his heavenly kingdom," but later on, when He thought of the insignificance of the King of heaven, Kṛṣṇa changed His mind and felt merciful toward Indra. No one is able to tolerate the wrath of Kṛṣṇa, so instead of retaliating against Indra, He simply showed His compassion for His friends in Vṛndāvana by lifting the whole of Govardhana Hill to protect them.

Enjoying

When a person is seen to be always happy and is accustomed to speak smilingly, he is considered to be in the mode of enjoyment. This trait was found in Kṛṣṇa when He appeared at the sacrificial arena of King Kaṁsa. It is described that the lotus-eyed Kṛṣṇa entered among the wrestlers without being impolite to them, glanced over them with determination and seemed to them just like an elephant attacking some plants. Even while speaking to them, Kṛṣṇa was still smiling, and in this way He stood valiantly upon the wrestling dais.

Pleasing

When one's characteristics are very sweet and desirable, his personality is called pleasing. An example of Kṛṣṇa's pleasing nature is described as follows: "One day while Kṛṣṇa was awaiting the arrival of Śrīmatī Rādhārāṇī by the bank of the Yamunā, He began to make a garland of *kadamba* flowers. In the meantime, Śrīmatī Rādhārāṇī appeared there, and at that time Murāri [Kṛṣṇa], the enemy of Mura, glanced over Rādhārāṇī very sweetly."

Dependable

Any person who is reliable in all circumstances is called dependable. In this connection Rūpa Gosvāmī says that even the demons were relying upon the dependability of Kṛṣṇa, because they were confident that Kṛṣṇa would never attack them without due cause. Therefore, with faith and confidence they used to live with their doors wide open. And the demigods, although afraid of the demons, were confident of the protection of Kṛṣṇa. Therefore, even in the midst of danger they were engaged in sportive activities. Persons who had never undergone the reformatory ritualistic ceremonies of the *Vedas* were confident that Kṛṣṇa would accept only faith and devotion, and so they were engaged in Kṛṣṇa consciousness and were freed from all anxieties. In other words, all kinds of men, from the demigods down to the uncultured, can rely on the causeless mercy of the Supreme Lord.

Steady

A person who is not disturbed even in a situation of reverses is called steady. This steadiness was observed in Kṛṣṇa in connection with His chastising the demon known as Bāṇa. The Bāṇa demon had many hands, and Kṛṣṇa was cutting off these hands one after another. This Bāṇa was a great devotee of Lord Śiva and the goddess Durgā. Thus, when Bāṇa was being chastised, Lord Śiva and Durgā became very furious at Kṛṣṇa. But Kṛṣṇa did not care for them.

Predominating

A person who can affect the mind of everyone is called predominating. As far as Kṛṣṇa's predomination is concerned, in the Tenth Canto, Forty-third Chapter, verse 17, of *Śrīmad-Bhāgavatam,* Kṛṣṇa is described thus by Śukadeva Gosvāmī to King Parīkṣit: "My dear King, Kṛṣṇa is a thunderbolt to the wrestlers; to the common man He is the most beautiful human being; to the young girls He is just like Cupid; to the cowherd men and women He is the most intimate relative; to the impious kings He is the supreme ruler; to His parents, Nanda and Yaśodā, He is just a baby; to Kaṁsa, the King of Bhoja, He is death personified; to the dull and stupid He is just like a stone; to the *yogīs* He is the Supreme Absolute Truth; and to the Vṛṣṇis He is the Supreme Personality of Godhead. In such a predominating position, Kṛṣṇa appeared in that arena along with His older brother, Balarāma." When Kṛṣṇa, the reservoir of all mellows, was present in the arena of Kaṁsa, He appeared differently to the different persons who were related to Him in different mellows. It is stated in *Bhagavad-gītā* that He appears to every person according to one's relationship with Him.

Sometimes learned scholars describe "predominating" to mean a person intolerant of being neglected. This peculiarity in Kṛṣṇa was visible when Kaṁsa was insulting Mahārāja Nanda. Vasudeva was asking Kṛṣṇa's assistance in killing Kaṁsa, and Kṛṣṇa was glancing over Kaṁsa with longing eyes, just like a prostitute, and was just preparing to jump at the King.

Meticulous Dresser

A person who is very fond of dressing himself is called *lalita,* or a meticulous dresser. This characteristic was found in Kṛṣṇa in two ways: sometimes He used to decorate Śrīmatī Rādhārāṇī with various marks, and sometimes, when He was preparing to kill demons like Ariṣṭāsura, He would take care to arrange His belt very nicely.

Magnanimous

Persons who can give themselves to anyone are called magnanimous. No one could be more magnanimous than Kṛṣṇa, because He is always prepared to give Himself completely to His devotee. Even to one who is not a devotee, Kṛṣṇa in His form of Lord Caitanya is prepared to give Himself and to grant deliverance.

Although Kṛṣṇa is independent of everyone, out of His causeless mercy He is dependent upon Garga Ṛṣi for religious instruction; for learning the military art He is dependent upon Sātyaki; and for good counsel He is dependent upon His friend Uddhava.

25

Devotees of Kṛṣṇa

A person who is always absorbed in Kṛṣṇa consciousness is called a devotee of Kṛṣṇa. Śrīla Rūpa Gosvāmī says that all the transcendental qualities discussed previously are also found in the devotees of Kṛṣṇa. The devotees of Kṛṣṇa can be classified into two groups: those who are cultivating devotional service in order to enter into the transcendental kingdom and those who are already in the perfectional stage of devotional service.

A person who has attained the stage of attraction for Kṛṣṇa and who is not freed from the material impasse, but who has qualified himself to enter into the kingdom of God, is called *sādhaka. Sādhaka* means one who is cultivating devotion in Kṛṣṇa consciousness. The description of such a devotee is found in the Eleventh Canto, Second Chapter, verse 46, of *Śrīmad-Bhāgavatam.* It is said there that a person who has unflinching faith in and love for the Personality of Godhead, who is in friendship with devotees of Kṛṣṇa, and who is very merciful to the ignorant, raising them to the standard of devotional service, and who is uninterested in nondevotees, is considered to be situated in the position of cultivating devotional service.

When one is found shedding tears by hearing of the pastimes of the Lord, it is to be understood that the blazing fire of material existence will be extinguished by such watering. When there is shivering of the body and the hairs of the body stand up, it is to be understood that the devotee is nearing perfection. An example of a *sādhaka* cultivating devotional service is Bilvamaṅgala Ṭhākura.

When a devotee is never tired of executing devotional service and is always engaged in Kṛṣṇa conscious activities, constantly relishing the transcendental mellows in relationship with Kṛṣṇa, he is called perfect. This perfectional stage can be achieved in two ways: one may achieve this stage of perfection by gradual progress in devotional service, or one may become perfect by the causeless mercy of Kṛṣṇa, even though he has not executed all the details of devotional service.

There is the following nice statement in the Third Canto, Fifteenth Chapter, verse 25, of the *Śrīmad-Bhāgavatam,* describing a devotee who achieves perfection by regularly executing devotional service: A person who is freed from the false egotism of material existence, or an advanced mystic, is eligible to enter into the kingdom of God, known as Vaikuṇṭha. Such a mystic becomes so joyful by constant execution of the regulative principles of devotional service that he thereby achieves the special favor of the Supreme Lord. Yamarāja, the mighty superintendent of death, is afraid to go near such a devotee; so we can imagine the potency of advanced devotional service, especially when devotees sit together and engage in talking of the pastimes of the Supreme Personality of Godhead. Those devotees express their feelings in such a way that they automatically melt with ecstasy, and many transcendental symptoms become manifested in their bodies. Anyone desiring advancement in devotional service must follow in the footsteps of such devotees.

Prahlāda Mahārāja said that no one can attain the perfectional stage of devotional service without bowing down before exalted devotees. Learned sages like Mārkaṇḍeya Ṛṣi attained perfection in devotional service simply by executing such regulative principles of service.

A person's achieving perfection in devotional service simply by the causeless mercy of the Lord is explained in *Śrīmad-Bhāgavatam* in connection with the *brāhmaṇas* and their wives who were engaged in performing *yajña,* or sacrifice. When the wives of the *brāhmaṇas* were favored by Lord Kṛṣṇa and immediately attained the ecstasy of love of Godhead, their husbands said, "How wonderful it is that although these women have undertaken no reformatory performances such as accepting the sacred thread, have not resided in the monasteries of the spiritual master, have not observed the strict principles of celibacy, have not undergone any austerities and have not philosophized upon the observance of ritualistic ceremonies, they still have attained the favor of Kṛṣṇa, which is aspired after even by great mystics! How wonderful it is that these women have attained such perfection, while we, although *brāhmaṇas* who have performed all the reformatory activities, cannot attain to this advanced stage!"

There is a similar statement by Nārada, addressed to Śukadeva Gosvāmī: "My dear Śukadeva Gosvāmī, you never took the trouble to reside under the care of a spiritual master, and yet you have attained such a great status of transcendental knowledge. You never took the trouble to undergo severe austerities, and still, how wonderful it is that you have been situated in the most perfect stage of love of Godhead."

Śukadeva Gosvāmī and the wives of the *brāhmaṇas* performing *yajña* are vivid examples of devotees who achieved the perfectional stage of devotional service by the grace of the Supreme Personality of Godhead.

Eternal Perfection

Persons who have achieved eternal, blissful life exactly on the level of Śrī Kṛṣṇa, and who are able to attract Lord Kṛṣṇa by their transcendental loving service, are called eternally perfect. The technical name is *nitya-siddha.* There are two classes of living entities—namely, *nitya-siddha* and *nitya-baddha.* The distinction is that the *nitya-siddhas* are eternally Kṛṣṇa conscious without any forgetfulness, whereas the *nitya-baddhas,* or eternally conditioned souls, are forgetful of their relationship with Kṛṣṇa.

The position of the *nitya-siddhas* is explained in the *Padma Purāṇa* in connection with the narration of the Supreme Personality of Godhead and Satyabhāmā-devī. The Lord tells Satyabhāmā, "My dear Satyabhāmā-devī, I have descended to this earthly planet by the request of Lord Brahmā and other demigods. Those who are born into this family of Yadu are all My eternal associates. My dear wife, you should not consider that My associates are ever separated from Me; they are My personal expansions, and as such, you must know that they are almost as powerful as I am. Because of their transcendental qualities, they are very, very dear to Me, as I am very, very dear to them." Anyone who becomes exhilarated by hearing of the pastimes of Lord Kṛṣṇa when He was present on this earth with His associates is to be understood as *nitya-siddha,* eternally perfect.

In the Tenth Canto, Fourteenth Chapter, verse 32, of *Śrīmad-Bhāgavatam* there is this statement: "How wonderful are the fortunate residents of Vṛndāvana, such as Nanda and the other cowherd men. The Supreme Personality of Godhead, the Supreme Brahman, has actually become their intimate friend!"

A similar statement is there in the Tenth Canto, Twenty-sixth Chapter, verse 10, of *Śrīmad-Bhāgavatam*. When Lord Kṛṣṇa lifted Govardhana Hill, the cowherd men, under the protection of Lord Kṛṣṇa, became struck with wonder and went to Nanda Mahārāja and inquired from him, "My dear Nanda Mahārāja, how is it that we are so intensely attached to Kṛṣṇa and that Kṛṣṇa is also so affectionately attached to us? Does it mean that He is the Supersoul of everyone?"

All of the residents of Vṛndāvana and Dvārakā—namely, the cowherd men and the members of the Yadu family—are eternally perfect devotees of the Lord. As the Lord descends by His causeless mercy upon this planet, so, in order to help in the pastimes of the Lord, these devotees also come here. They are not ordinary living entities or conditioned souls; they are ever-liberated persons, associates of the Personality of Godhead. And just as Lord Kṛṣṇa behaves like an ordinary man when He descends to this planet, so the members of the Yadu dynasty and the residents of Vṛndāvana execute activities just like ordinary men. But they are not ordinary men; they are as liberated as Lord Kṛṣṇa Himself.

In the *Padma Purāṇa, Uttara-khaṇḍa* section, it is stated, "Just as Lord Rāmacandra descends along with Lakṣmaṇa (an expansion of Saṅkarṣaṇa) and Bharata (an expansion of Pradyumna), so the members of the Yadu dynasty and the cowherd men of Vṛndāvana also descend with Lord Kṛṣṇa in order to join in the transcendental pastimes of the Lord. When the Supreme Lord returns to His eternal abode, His associates return with Him to their respective places. As such, these ever-liberated Vaiṣṇavas are not bound by the material laws of birth and death."

As stated in *Bhagavad-gītā* by the Lord Himself, His birth, deeds and activities are all transcendental. Similarly, the birth, deeds and activities of the associates of the Lord are also transcendental. And as it is an offense to consider oneself to be Kṛṣṇa, so it is offensive to consider oneself to be Yaśodā, Nanda or any other associate of the Lord. We should always remember that they are transcendental; they are never conditioned souls.

It is described that Kṛṣṇa, the enemy of Kaṁsa, has sixty-four transcendental qualities, and all of the ever-liberated souls who accompany the Lord have the first fifty-five of the qualities, without any doubt. Such devotees are related to the Supreme Personality of Godhead in any of five transcendental mellows—namely neutrality, servitorship, friendship, parenthood and conjugal love. These relationships with the Lord are eternal, and therefore *nitya-siddha* devotees do not have to strive to attain the perfectional stage by executing regulative devotional principles. They are eternally qualified to serve Kṛṣṇa.

26

Stimulation for Ecstatic Love

Some things which give impetus or stimulation to ecstatic love of Kṛṣṇa are His transcendental qualities, His uncommon activities, His smiling features, His apparel and garlands, His flute, His buffalo horn, His leg bells, His conchshell, His footprints, His places of pastimes (such as Vṛndāvana), His favorite plant (*tulasī*), His devotee and the periodical occasions for remembering Him. One such occasion for remembering Kṛṣṇa is Ekādaśī, which comes twice a month on the eleventh day of the moon, both waning and waxing. On that day all the devotees remain fasting throughout the night and continuously chant the glories of the Lord.

Kṛṣṇa's Transcendental Qualities, His Uncommon Activities and His Smile

As far as Kṛṣṇa's transcendental qualities are concerned, they can be divided into three groups: qualities pertaining to His transcendental body, qualities pertaining to His transcendental speech and qualities pertaining to His transcendental mind.

Kṛṣṇa's age, His transcendental bodily features, His beauty and His mildness are qualities pertaining to His body. There is no difference between Kṛṣṇa and His body, and therefore the transcendental features pertaining to His body are the same as Kṛṣṇa Himself. But because these qualities stimulate the devotee's ecstatic love, they have been analyzed as separate causes of that love. To be attracted by the qualities of Kṛṣṇa means to be attracted by Kṛṣṇa Himself, because there is no real distinction between Kṛṣṇa and His qualities. Kṛṣṇa's name is also Kṛṣṇa. Kṛṣṇa's fame is also Kṛṣṇa. Kṛṣṇa's entourage is also Kṛṣṇa. Kṛṣṇa and everything related with Kṛṣṇa which gives stimulation to love of Kṛṣṇa are all Kṛṣṇa, but for our understanding these items may be considered separately.

Kṛṣṇa is the reservoir of all transcendental pleasure. Therefore, the impetuses to love of Kṛṣṇa, although seemingly different, are not actually distinct from Kṛṣṇa Himself. In the technical Sanskrit terms, such qualities as Kṛṣṇa's name and fame are accepted both as reservoirs of and as stimulation for love of Kṛṣṇa.

Kṛṣṇa's age is considered in three periods: from His appearance day to the end of His fifth year is called *kaumāra,* from the beginning of the sixth year up to the end of the tenth year is called *paugaṇḍa,* and from the eleventh to the end of the fifteenth year is called *kaiśora*. After the beginning of the sixteenth year, Kṛṣṇa is called a *yauvana,* or a youth, and this continues with no change.

As far as Kṛṣṇa's transcendental pastimes are concerned, they are mostly executed during the *kaumāra, paugaṇḍa* and *kaiśora* periods. His affectionate pastimes with His parents are executed during His *kaumāra* age. His friendship with the cowherd boys is exhibited during the *paugaṇḍa* period. And His friendship with the *gopīs* is exhibited during the age of *kaiśora*. Kṛṣṇa's pastimes at Vṛndāvana are finished by the end of His fifteenth year, and then He is transferred to Mathurā and Dvārakā, where all other pastimes are performed.

Śrīla Rūpa Gosvāmī gives us a vivid description of Kṛṣṇa as the reservoir of all pleasure in his *Bhakti-rasāmṛta-sindhu*. Here are some parts of that description.

Kṛṣṇa's *kaiśora* age may be divided into three parts. In the beginning of His *kaiśora* age—that is, at the beginning of His eleventh year—the luster of His body becomes so bright that it becomes an impetus for ecstatic love. Similarly, there are reddish borders around His eyes, and a growth of soft hairs on His body. In describing this early stage of His *kaiśora* age, Kundalatā, one of the residents of Vṛndāvana, said to her friend, "My dear friend, I have just seen an extraordinary beauty appearing in the person of Kṛṣṇa. His blackish bodily hue appears just like the *indranīla* jewel. There are reddish signs on His eyes, and small soft hairs are coming out on His body. The appearance of these symptoms has made Him extraordinarily beautiful."

In this connection, in the Tenth Canto, Twenty-first Chapter, verse 5, of *Śrīmad-Bhāgavatam,* Śukadeva Gosvāmī tells King Parīkṣit, "My dear King, I shall try to describe how the minds of the *gopīs* became absorbed in thought of Kṛṣṇa. The *gopīs* would meditate on Kṛṣṇa's dressing Himself just like a dancing actor and entering the forest of Vṛndāvana, marking the ground with His footprints. They meditated on Kṛṣṇa's having a helmet with a peacock feather and wearing earrings on His ears and yellow-gold–colored garments covered with jewels and pearls. They also meditated on Kṛṣṇa's blowing His flute and on all the cowherd boys' singing of the glories of the Lord." That is the description of the meditation which the *gopīs* used to perform.

Sometimes the *gopīs* would think about His soft nails, His moving eyebrows and His teeth, which were catechu-colored from chewing pan. One description was given by a *gopī* to her friend: "My dear friend, just see how the enemy of Agha has assumed such wonderful features! His brows are just like the bow of Cupid, and they are moving just as though they were dancing. The tips of His nails are so soft—it is as if they were dried bamboo leaves. His teeth are reddish, and so it appears that He has assumed a feature of anger. Under the circumstances, where is the chance for a young girl not to be attracted by such beautiful features and not to be afraid of becoming a victim to such beauty?"

Kṛṣṇa's attractive features are also described by Vṛndā, the *gopī* after whom Vṛndāvana was named. She told Kṛṣṇa, "My dear Mādhava, Your newly invented smile has so captivated the hearts of the *gopīs* that they are simply unable to express themselves! As such, they have become bewildered and will not talk with others. All of these *gopīs* have become so affected that it is as if they had offered three sprinkles of water upon their lives. In other words, they have given up all hope for their living condition." According to the Indian system, when a person is dead there is a sprinkling of water on the body. Thus, the statement of Vṛndā shows that the *gopīs* were so enchanted by the beauty of Kṛṣṇa that because they could not express their minds, they had decided to commit suicide.

When Kṛṣṇa arrived at the age of thirteen to fourteen years, His two arms and chest assumed an unspeakable beauty, and His whole form became simply enchanting. When Kṛṣṇa attained thirteen years of age, His two thighs were challenging the trunks of elephants, His rising chest was trying to come to peace talks with doors of jewels, and His two arms were minimizing the value of the bolts found on doors. Who can describe the wonderful beauty of these features of Kṛṣṇa? The special beauty of Kṛṣṇa's body was His mild smiling, His restless eyes and His world-enchanting songs. These are the special features of this age.

There is a statement in this connection that Kṛṣṇa, on arriving at this age, manifested such beautiful bodily features that His restless eyes became the playthings of Cupid, and His mild smile resembled the newly grown lotus flower. The enchanting vibration of His songs became a great impediment to the young girls, who were supposed to remain chaste and faithful to their husbands.

At this age Kṛṣṇa enjoyed the *rāsa-līlā,* exhibiting His power of joking with the cowherd girls and enjoying their company in the bushes of the gardens by the bank of the Yamunā.

In this connection there is the following statement: "Throughout the whole tract of land known as Vṛndāvana there were the footprints of Kṛṣṇa and the *gopīs,* and in some places peacock feathers were strewn about. In some places there were nice beddings in the bushes of the Vṛndāvana gardens, and in some places there were piles of dust due to the group-dancing of Govinda and the *gopīs.*" These are some of the features which are due to the different pastimes invented by Śrī Kṛṣṇa in the place known as Vṛndāvana.

There is the following statement by one *gopī,* describing Kṛṣṇa's attractive feature during this age: "My dear friend, just see how all of a sudden in the sky of Kṛṣṇa there is a powerful rising sun and how this rising sun is minimizing the rays of our chastity moon. Our attraction for Kṛṣṇa is so intense that it is drying up the lotus flower of our discrimination, and we are losing our senses in deciding whether we shall continue as chaste women or be victimized by the beauty of Kṛṣṇa. My dear friend, I think that we have lost all hope of life!"

In the *kaiśora* age, beginning from the eleventh year and continuing up to the end of the fifteenth year, Kṛṣṇa's arms, legs and thighs became marked with three divisional lines. At that time Kṛṣṇa's chest challenged a hill of *marakata* jewels, His arms challenged pillars of the *indranīla* jewel, the three lines of His waist challenged the waves of the river Yamunā, and His thighs challenged beautiful bananas. One *gopī* said, "With all these exquisite features of His body, Kṛṣṇa is too extraordinarily beautiful, and therefore I am always thinking of Him to protect me, because He is the killer of all demons."

The idea expressed in this statement is that the *gopīs* were comparing their attraction for Kṛṣṇa to an attack by demons; and to counteract their attraction for the beauty of Kṛṣṇa, they were also turning to

Kṛṣṇa hopefully, because He is the killer of all kinds of demons. In other words, they were perplexed, because on one hand they were attracted by the beauty of Kṛṣṇa, and on the other they needed Kṛṣṇa to drive away the demon of such attraction.

This *kaiśora* age can be translated as adolescence. At the end of this period all the *gopīs* said, "Kṛṣṇa is the killer of the attraction of Cupid, and as such He disturbs the patience of all newly married girls. Kṛṣṇa's bodily features have become so exquisite—it is as if they were all manifesting an artistic sense of the highest sort. His dancing eyes have dimmed the brilliance of the most expert dancer, and so there is no longer any comparison to the beauty of Kṛṣṇa." Learned scholars therefore describe the features of His body at this time as *nava-yauvana,* newly invented youthfulness. At this stage of Kṛṣṇa's bodily features, the conjugal loving affairs with the *gopīs* and similar pastimes become very prominent.

There are six features of conjugal loving affairs, called peacemaking, picking a quarrel, going to meet one's lover, sitting together, separation and support. Lord Kṛṣṇa expanded an empire of these six features, of which He was the ruling prince. Somewhere He was picking quarrels with the young girls, somewhere He was scratching them with the nails of parrots, somewhere He was busy going to visit the *gopīs,* and somewhere He was negotiating through cowherd friends to take shelter of the *gopīs.*

Some of the *gopīs* addressed Him thus: "Dear Kṛṣṇa, because of Your adolescent age, You have just become the spiritual master of these young girls, and You are teaching them to whisper among themselves. You are teaching them to offer solemn prayers, as well as training them to cheat their husbands and to join You in the gardens at night, without caring for the instructions of their superiors. You are enthusing them by the vibration of Your enchanting flute; and, as their teacher, You are teaching them all the intricacies of loving affairs."

It is said that even when Kṛṣṇa was a boy of five He manifested such youthful energies, but learned scholars do not explain them because of the absence of suitable age. Kṛṣṇa was beautiful because every part of His body was perfectly arranged without any defect. Such perfect bodily features of Kṛṣṇa are described as follows: "My dear enemy of Kaṁsa, Your broad eyes, Your rising chest, Your two pillarlike arms and the thin middle portion of Your body are always enchanting to every lotus-eyed beautiful girl." The ornaments on the body of Kṛṣṇa were not actually enhancing His beauty, but just the reverse—the ornaments were beautified by Kṛṣṇa.

A person is called mild when he cannot even bear the touch of the most soft thing. It is described that every part of Kṛṣṇa's body was so soft that even at the touch of newly grown leaves, the color of the touched part of His skin would change. At this *kaiśora* age, Kṛṣṇa's endeavors were always bent toward arranging the *rāsa* dance, as well as toward killing the demons in the forest of Vṛndāvana. While Kṛṣṇa was engaged in enjoyment with the boys and girls within the forest of Vṛndāvana, Kaṁsa used to send his associates to kill Kṛṣṇa, and Kṛṣṇa would show His prowess by killing them.

Kṛṣṇa's Apparel and Garlands

Generally, there are four kinds of garments on the body of Kṛṣṇa: His shirt, turban, belt and wearing garments. In Vṛndāvana, He used to put on reddish garments, with a golden shirt on His body and an orange-colored turban on His head. The different kinds of belts, combined with His enchanting smile, used to always increase the transcendental bliss of His associates. This dress of Kṛṣṇa is described as gorgeous. As a baby elephant is sometimes dressed in colorful clothing, so Kṛṣṇa's gorgeousness was manifested by decoration with such colorful clothing on the different parts of His body.

Ākalpa refers to the texture of Kṛṣṇa's hair, His nicely dressed body anointed with sandalwood pulp and decorated with flower garlands, His *tilaka* and His chewing pan. Kṛṣṇa was decorated constantly in this *ākalpa* process. Kṛṣṇa's hair was sometimes decorated with flowers placed on the middle of His head, or else it was reaching down to His back. In this way Kṛṣṇa dressed His hair differently at different times. As for the ointment on His body, the pulp of sandalwood generally appeared to be white, and when it was mixed with saffron dye it appeared to be yellow.

Kṛṣṇa used to put a *vaijayantī* garland around His neck. This *vaijayantī* garland is made of flowers of at least five different colors. Such a garland was always long enough to touch Kṛṣṇa's knees or feet. Besides this garland of flowers, there were other kinds of flower garlands too—sometimes decorating His head, sometimes hanging around His neck and chest. Artistic paintings with sandalwood pulp and colored sandalwood were also to be found on the body of Kṛṣṇa.

One *gopī* addressed her friend and began to praise the bodily features of Kṛṣṇa. She praised His blackish complexion, the reddish color of chewing pan enhancing His beauty hundreds of times, the curling hair on His head, the red spots of *kuṅkuma** on His body and the *tilaka* on His forehead.

His helmet, His earrings, His necklace, His four garments, the bangles on His hands, the rings on His fingers, His ankle bells and His flute—these are the different features of Kṛṣṇa's ornaments. Kṛṣṇa, the enemy of Agha, always looked beautiful with His incomparable helmet, His earrings made of diamonds, His necklace of pearls, His bangles, His embroidered garments and the beautiful rings on His fingers.

Kṛṣṇa is sometimes called *vana-mālī*. *Vana* means "forest," and *mālī* means "gardener," so *vana-mālī* refers to one who extensively uses flowers and garlands on different parts of His body. Kṛṣṇa was dressed like this not only in Vṛndāvana but also on the Battlefield of Kurukṣetra. Seeing such colorful dress and the garlands of different flowers, some great sages prayed, "Lord Kṛṣṇa was going to the Battlefield of Kurukṣetra not to fight, but to grace all of the devotees with His presence."

Kṛṣṇa's Flute

As far as His flute is concerned, it is said that the vibration of this wonderful instrument was able to break the meditation of the greatest sages. Kṛṣṇa was thus challenging Cupid by advertising His transcendental glories all over the world.

There are three kinds of flutes used by Kṛṣṇa. One is called *veṇu*, one is called *muralī*, and the third is called *vaṁśī*. *Veṇu* is very small, not more than six inches long, with six holes for whistling. *Muralī* is about eighteen inches long with a hole at the end and four holes on the body of the flute. This kind of flute produces a very enchanting sound. The *vaṁśī* flute is about fifteen inches long, with nine holes on its body. Kṛṣṇa used to play on these three flutes occasionally when they were needed. Kṛṣṇa has a longer *vaṁśī*, which is called *mahānandā*, or

**Kuṅkuma* is a sweetly scented reddish powder which is thrown on the bodies of worshipable persons.

sammohinī. When it is still longer it is called *ākarṣiṇī*. When it is even longer it is called *ānandinī*. The *ānandinī* flute is very pleasing to the cowherd boys and is technically named *vaṁśulī*. These flutes were sometimes bedecked with jewels. Sometimes they were made of marble and sometimes of hollow bamboo. When the flute is made of jewels it is called *sammohinī*. When made of gold, it is called *ākarṣiṇī*.

Kṛṣṇa's Buffalo Horn

Kṛṣṇa used a buffalo horn as a bugling instrument. This instrument was always highly polished and circled with gold bands, and on the middle there was a hole. Regarding these instruments, there is a metaphorical statement about a *gopī* named Tārāvalī. It is said that Tārāvalī was bitten by the most venomous snake of Kṛṣṇa's flute. Then, in order to neutralize the poisonous effect, she drank the milk produced by the buffalo horn in the hand of Kṛṣṇa. But instead of decreasing the poisonous effect, it increased it a thousand times. The *gopī* was thus put into the most miserable poisoned condition.

The Attraction of Kṛṣṇa's Leg Bells

A certain *gopī* once stated to her friend, "My dear friend, when I heard the sound of the leg bells of Śrī Kṛṣṇa, I immediately started to go out of the house to see Him. But most regrettably, my superiors were present just before me at that time, and I could not go out."

Kṛṣṇa's Conchshell

Kṛṣṇa's conchshell is known as Pāñcajanya. This Pāñcajanya conch is also mentioned in *Bhagavad-gītā*. Kṛṣṇa sounded it before the Battle of Kurukṣetra. It is said that when Lord Kṛṣṇa blows on His transcendental conchshell, the wives of the demons become subject to abortions, and the wives of the demigods become blessed with all auspiciousness. In this way, the sound of Kṛṣṇa's conchshell used to vibrate and circulate all over the world.

Kṛṣṇa's Footprints

It is stated in *Śrīmad-Bhāgavatam* that when Akrūra, who drove Kṛṣṇa from Vṛndāvana to Mathurā, saw the footprints of Kṛṣṇa on the land of Vṛndāvana, his ecstatic love for Kṛṣṇa increased so much that the hairs on his body stood up. His eyes became overflooded with tears, and in such ecstasy he jumped out of the chariot and fell down on the ground and began to chant, "How wonderful this is! How wonderful this is!"

Similar feelings were expressed by the *gopīs* when they were going to the bank of the Yamunā and saw Kṛṣṇa's footprints in the dust. When Kṛṣṇa walked on the ground of Vṛndāvana, the marks of His sole (flag, thunderbolt, fish, a rod for controlling elephants, and a lotus flower) would be imprinted upon the dust of the land. The *gopīs* became overwhelmed simply at seeing those marks on the ground.

Kṛṣṇa's Places of Pastimes

One devotee has exclaimed, "Oh, I have not as yet visited the wonderful places where the pastimes of the Lord were performed. But simply by hearing the name of Mathurā I have become overwhelmed with joy!"

Kṛṣṇa's Favorite Plant: Tulasī

Lord Kṛṣṇa is very fond of *tulasī* leaves and buds. Because *tulasī* buds are usually offered up to the lotus feet of Kṛṣṇa, a devotee once prayed to the *tulasī* buds to give him some information about the lotus feet of the Lord. The devotee expected that the *tulasī* buds would know something about the glories of Lord Śrī Kṛṣṇa's lotus feet.

Kṛṣṇa's Devotees

One may sometimes become overwhelmed with joy by seeing a devotee of the Lord. When Dhruva Mahārāja saw two associates of Narayaṇa approaching him, he immediately stood up out of sincere respect and devotion and remained before them with folded hands; but because of his ecstatic love, he could hardly offer them a proper reception.

There is a statement by a *gopī* who addressed Subala, a friend of Kṛṣṇa: "My dear Subala, I know that Kṛṣṇa is your friend and that you always enjoy smiling and joking with Him. The other day I saw you both standing together. You were keeping your hand upon Kṛṣṇa's shoulder, and both of you were joyfully smiling. When I saw the two of you standing like that in the distance, my eyes at once became overflooded with tears."

Special Days for Remembering Kṛṣṇa

There are many statements about the festive days in connection with Kṛṣṇa's different activities. One of these festive days is Janmāṣṭamī, the day of Kṛṣṇa's birth. This Janmāṣṭamī day is the most opulent festival day for the devotees, and it is still observed with great pomp in every Hindu house in India. Sometimes even the devotees of other religious groups take advantage of this auspicious day and enjoy the performance of the ceremony of Janmāṣṭamī. Ecstatic love for Kṛṣṇa is also aroused on the days of Ekādaśī, which are other festive days in connection with Kṛṣṇa.

27

Symptoms of Ecstatic Love

The bodily symptoms manifested by a devotee in expressing ecstatic love for Kṛṣṇa are called *anubhāva*. Practical examples of *anubhāva* are as follows: dancing, rolling on the ground, singing very loudly, stretching the body, crying loudly, yawning, breathing very heavily, neglecting the presence of others, drooling, laughing like a madman, wheeling the head and belching. When there is an extraordinary excess of ecstatic love, with all of these bodily symptoms manifested, one feels relieved transcendentally.

These symptoms are divided into two parts: one is called *śīta*, and the other is called *kṣepaṇa*. When there is yawning, the symptoms are called *śīta*, and when there is dancing they are called *kṣepaṇa*.

Dancing

While watching the *rāsa* dance performed by Lord Kṛṣṇa and the *gopīs*, Lord Śiva beheld the beautiful face of Kṛṣṇa and immediately began to dance and beat upon his small *diṇḍima* drum. While Lord Śiva was dancing in ecstasy, his eldest son, Gaṇeśa, joined him.

Rolling on the Ground

In the Third Canto, First Chapter, verse 32, of *Śrīmad-Bhāgavatam*, Vidura inquires from Uddhava, "My dear friend, is Akrūra in an auspicious condition? Not only is he a learned scholar and sinless, but he is also a devotee of Lord Kṛṣṇa. He has such ecstatic love for Kṛṣṇa that I have seen him rolling upon Kṛṣṇa's footprints in the dust as if bereft of all sense." Similarly, one *gopī* gave a message to Kṛṣṇa that Rādhārāṇī, because of Her separation from Him and because of Her enchantment with the aroma of His flower garlands, was rolling on the ground, thereby bruising Her soft body.

Singing Loudly

One *gopī* informed Kṛṣṇa that when Śrīmatī Rādhārāṇī was singing about His glories, She enchanted all of Her friends in such a way that they became stonelike and dull. At the same time, the nearby stones began to melt away in ecstatic love.

When Nārada Muni was chanting the Hare Kṛṣṇa *mantra,* he chanted so loudly that it was apprehended that Lord Nṛsiṁha had appeared. Thus all the demons began to flee in different directions.

Stretching the Body

It is said that sometimes when Nārada, the carrier of the *vīṇā,* remembers his Lord Kṛṣṇa in great ecstasy, he begins to stretch his body so vigorously that his sacred thread gives way.

Crying Loudly

A *gopī* once said to Kṛṣṇa, "My dear son of Nanda Mahārāja, by the sound of Your flute Śrīmatī Rādhārāṇī has become full of lamentation and fear, and thus, with a faltering voice, She is crying like a *kurarī* bird."

It is described that by hearing the vibration of Kṛṣṇa's flute, Lord Śiva becomes very puzzled and begins to cry so loudly into space that the demons become vanquished and the devotees become overwhelmed with joy.

Yawning

It is said that when the full moon rises, the lotus petals become expanded. Similarly, when Kṛṣṇa used to appear before Rādhārāṇī, Her face, which is compared to the lotus flower, would expand by Her yawning.

Breathing Heavily

As far as breathing heavily is concerned, it is stated, "Lalitā [one of the *gopīs*] is just like a *cātakī* bird, which only takes water falling directly from the rain cloud and not from any other source." In this statement Kṛṣṇa is compared to the dark cloud, and Lalitā is compared to the *cātakī* bird seeking only Kṛṣṇa's company. The metaphor continues to say, "As a heavy wind sometimes disperses a mighty cloud, so the heavy breath from Lalitā's nostrils caused her to miss Kṛṣṇa, who had disappeared by the time she recovered herself."

Neglecting the Presence of Others

As far as neglecting the presence of others is concerned, the wives of the *brāhmaṇas* who were performing sacrifices at Vṛndāvana left home as soon as they heard that Kṛṣṇa was nearby. They left their homes without caring for their learned husbands. The husbands began to discuss this among themselves: "How wonderful is the attraction for Kṛṣṇa that it has made these women leave us without any care!" This is the influence of Kṛṣṇa. Anyone who becomes attracted to Kṛṣṇa can be relieved from the bondage of birth and death, which can be compared to the locked-up homes that were neglected by the wives of the *brāhmaṇas*.

In the *Padyāvalī* there is a statement by some devotees: "We shall not care for any outsiders. If they should deride us, we shall still not care for them. We shall simply enjoy the transcendental mellow of chanting Hare Kṛṣṇa, and thus we shall roll on the ground and dance ecstatically. In this way we shall eternally enjoy transcendental bliss."

Drooling

As an example of the running down of saliva from the mouth, it is stated that sometimes when Nārada Muni was chanting the Hare Kṛṣṇa *mantra*, he remained stunned for a while, and saliva oozed from his mouth.

Laughing like a Madman

When a devotee laughs very loudly like a madman, it is done out of an extraordinary agitation of ecstatic love within the heart. Such mad laughing is an expression of the condition of the heart which is technically called *aṭṭa-hāsa*. When a devotee becomes affected with this mental condition, his love is expressed through the lips. The laughing sounds, coming one after another, are compared to flowers falling from the creeper of devotion which grows within the heart of the devotee. In the *Caitanya-caritāmṛta* devotional service to the Lord is also compared to a creeper which rises up to the lotus feet of Kṛṣṇa in Goloka Vṛndāvana.

Wheeling of the Head

One *gopī* told her friend, "It appears that Lord Kṛṣṇa, the enemy of the demon Agha, has released from His mouth a whirlwind which is acting on your head and is gradually proceeding to do the same to the other lotus-eyed *gopīs*."

Belching

Sometimes belching also becomes a symptom of ecstatic love for Kṛṣṇa. There is evidence of this in Paurṇamāsī's address to one crying associate of Rādhārāṇī: "My dear daughter, don't be worried because Śrīmatī Rādhārāṇī is belching. I am about to offer a remedial measure for this symptom. Do not cry so loudly. This belching is not due to indigestion; it is a sign of ecstatic love for Kṛṣṇa. I shall arrange to cure this belching symptom immediately. Don't be worried." This statement by Paurṇamāsī is evidence that ecstatic love for Kṛṣṇa is sometimes manifested through belching.

Sometimes trembling of the whole body and hemorrhaging from some part of the body are also manifested in response to ecstatic love for Kṛṣṇa, but such symptoms are very rare, and therefore Śrīla Rūpa Gosvāmī does not discuss any further on this point.

28

Existential Ecstatic Love

When a devotee is always intensely affected by love for Kṛṣṇa in a direct relationship with Him—or even a little apart from Him—his status is called existential ecstatic love. The symptoms originating from such existential ecstatic love are divided into three headings—namely moist, burnt and dried-up.

Moist existential ecstatic love aroused in connection with Kṛṣṇa is divided into two: direct and indirect. Rādhārāṇī was weaving a garland of *kunda* flowers, and upon hearing the vibration of Kṛṣṇa's flute, She immediately stopped Her work. This is an example of direct moistened existential ecstatic love. Indirect moistened existential ecstatic love is described in the following statement: Kṛṣṇa, who is also called Puruṣottama, is to the eyes of Mother Yaśodā just like the cloud is to the eyes of the *cātakī* bird. When Kṛṣṇa had been brought to Mathurā, Mother Yaśodā, being very anxious and angry, began to rebuke the King of Mathurā.

Burnt existential ecstatic love is divided into three, and one example is as follows: One day, Mother Yaśodā was dreaming that the gigantic demon Pūtanā was lying on the courtyard of her house, and she immediately became anxious to seek out Kṛṣṇa.

When there are manifestations of ecstatic symptoms in the body of a nondevotee, these are called dried-up symptoms of ecstatic love. The nondevotees are actually materialistic, but in contact with some pure devotee, they sometimes may manifest some symptoms of ecstasy. Devotional scholars call these dried-up symptoms.

There are eight symptoms of existential ecstatic love: becoming stunned, perspiring, standing of the hairs on the body, faltering of the voice, trembling of the body, changing of bodily colors, shedding of tears and devastation.

The scientific explanation of these eight symptoms is given by Rūpa Gosvāmī as follows. When the vital force of life is in contact with the earth, one is stunned. When the same force comes into contact with water, there is the shedding of tears. When the same force comes into contact with fire, there is perspiration. When the force comes into contact with the sky, there is complete devastation. And when that force comes into contact with the air, there is trembling, failing of the voice and standing of the hairs on the body.

These symptoms are sometimes manifested internally and sometimes externally. The pure devotee always feels such symptomatic expressions within himself, but being afraid of outsiders he does not generally manifest them externally.

Becoming Stunned

The symptom of being stunned is caused by ecstatic tribulation, fearfulness, astonishment, lamentation and anger. This symptom is exhibited by a stoppage of talking, a stoppage of movement, a feeling of voidness and an extreme feeling of separation.

When Uddhava was describing Kṛṣṇa's pastimes to Vidura, he said, "One day the *gopīs* became stunned when Kṛṣṇa, in the dress of a gardening maid, entered the greenhouse and enlivened them with joking and laughter. Then when Kṛṣṇa left the greenhouse, the *gopīs* were seeing Kṛṣṇa so ecstatically that it was as though both their minds and eyes were following Him." These symptoms signify that although the *gopīs'* business was not finished, they had become stunned with ecstatic love.

Another example of being stunned took place when Kṛṣṇa was surrounded by various wrestlers in the sacrificial arena of Kaṁsa. His mother, Devakī*, then became stunned, and her eyes dried up when she saw Kṛṣṇa among the wrestlers.

There is also an example of the astonishment of Lord Brahmā. It is explained in the Tenth Canto, Thirteenth Chapter, verse 56, of *Śrīmad-Bhāgavatam,* that when Brahmā understood that this cowherd boy was

---

*Devakī was the natural mother of Kṛṣṇa, His father being Vasudeva. In order to protect the divine baby from Devakī's brother, Kaṁsa, Vasudeva delivered Kṛṣṇa to Nanda and Mother Yaśodā in Vṛndāvana, and it was there that He exhibited His childhood pastimes. At sixteen years of age He returned to Mathurā (where Devakī had given birth to Him) and vanquished Kaṁsa in the arena mentioned here. See the author's *Kṛṣṇa,* as well as his *Śrīmad-Bhāgavatam,* for further details.

the Supreme Personality of Godhead Himself, he became stunned. All of his sensory activities stopped when he saw all the cowherd boys again, along with Kṛṣṇa. Lord Brahmā was so stunned that he appeared to be a golden statue with four heads. Also, when the residents of Vraja found that Kṛṣṇa had lifted Govardhana Hill with His left hand, they became stunned.

Astonishment caused by lamentation was exemplified when Kṛṣṇa was entering into the belly of the Bakāsura demon and all the demigods from higher planets became stunned with lamentation. A similar example of becoming stunned was visible in Arjuna when he saw that Aśvatthāmā was attempting to release his *brahmāstra** at Kṛṣṇa.

Perspiring

An example of perspiring because of jubilation is described in *Śrīmad-Bhāgavatam.* One *gopī* addressed Rādhārāṇī thus: "My dear Rādhārāṇī, You are rebuking the sunshine unnecessarily, but I can understand that You are perspiring only because of Your becoming too lusty at seeing Kṛṣṇa."

Perspiration caused by fearfulness was exhibited by Raktaka, one of the servants of Kṛṣṇa. One day Kṛṣṇa dressed Himself just like Abhimanyu, the husband of Rādhārāṇī. Abhimanyu did not like Rādhārāṇī's association with Kṛṣṇa, and therefore when Raktaka saw Kṛṣṇa in the dress of Abhimanyu and thus mistook His identity, he began to strongly rebuke Him. As soon as Raktaka finally understood that it was Kṛṣṇa in the dress of Abhimanyu, he began perspiring. This perspiration was caused by fearfulness.

Perspiration due to anger was exhibited by Garuḍa, the eagle who is the carrier of Viṣṇu. Once the heavenly king, Indra, was sending torrents of rain over Vṛndāvana. Garuḍa was observing the incident from above the clouds, and because of his anger, he began perspiring.

Standing of Hairs on the Body

The standing up of hair on the body was manifested when Mother Yaśodā found within Kṛṣṇa's mouth all of the universal planetary systems. She had asked Kṛṣṇa to open His mouth wide just to see whether

* The *brahmāstra* was a nuclear weapon controlled by *mantra,* or sound vibration.

He had eaten dirt. But when Kṛṣṇa opened His mouth, she saw not only the entire earth, but also many other planets within His mouth. This caused a standing up of the hair on her body.

The standing up of hair on the body resulting from jubilation is described in the Tenth Canto, Thirtieth Chapter, verse 10, of *Śrīmad-Bhāgavatam,* in connection with the *gopīs* engaged in the *rāsa* dance. During this *rāsa* dance Kṛṣṇa disappeared all of a sudden with Rādhārāṇī, and the *gopīs* began to search Him out. At that time they addressed the earth and said, "Dear earthly planet, how many austerities and penances you must have undergone to have the lotus feet of Kṛṣṇa always touching your surface. I think that you must be very jubilant, because the trees and plants, which are just like hairs on your body, are standing up so gloriously. May we ask when you first got these symptoms? Have you been enjoying this jubilation since you were touched by the incarnation Vāmana or since you were delivered by the incarnation Varāha?"

Kṛṣṇa would sometimes perform mock fighting along with the cowherd boys. When Kṛṣṇa blew His horn in this mock fighting, Śrīdāmā, who was on the opposing side, felt his bodily hairs stand up. Similarly, when Arjuna saw Kṛṣṇa in His gigantic universal form, there was a standing of the hairs on his body.

Faltering of the Voice

When Kṛṣṇa was going to Mathurā on the chariot driven by Akrūra, Yaśodā and all the *gopīs* came to try to forbid Him to pass and to block His way. At that time Rādhārāṇī was so perturbed that in a faltering voice She requested Mother Yaśodā to please stop Akrūra.

Faltering of the voice resulting from wonder was exhibited by Brahmā. It is said in *Śrīmad-Bhāgavatam,* Tenth Canto, Thirteenth Chapter, verse 64, that after bowing down before Lord Kṛṣṇa, when Brahmā began to rise he prayed to the Lord in a faltering voice.

In the Tenth Canto, Twenty-ninth Chapter, verse 30, another example of faltering of the voice was exhibited by the *gopīs* when they came to Kṛṣṇa, desiring to dance with Him. Kṛṣṇa asked them to go back to their husbands and homes. The *gopīs* apparently became very angry and began to talk to Kṛṣṇa with faltering voices.

In the Tenth Canto, Thirty-ninth Chapter, verses 56 and 57, of *Śrīmad-Bhāgavatam,* a faltering voice due to jubilation was exhibited by Akrūra when he was shown all of the Vaikuṇṭha planets resting within the river Yamunā. When Akrūra understood that Kṛṣṇa was the Supreme Personality of Godhead, he bowed his head to Kṛṣṇa's lotus feet and with folded hands began to pray in a faltering voice.

There are also examples of faltering of the voice caused by fearfulness. One of Kṛṣṇa's friends praised Him thus: "My dear friend, Your flute was given to Your servant Patrī, and when I asked him to return it he began speaking in a faltering voice, and his complexion became yellow."

Trembling

When Kṛṣṇa was trying to capture the demon Śaṅkha, Rādhārāṇī began trembling out of fearfulness. Similar trembling of the body was exhibited in Sahadeva, the younger brother of Nakula. When Śiśupāla was vehemently blaspheming the Lord, Sahadeva began to tremble out of anger.

Trembling of the body was also exhibited by Rādhārāṇī out of tribulation. Rādhārāṇī trembled as She told one of the *gopīs,* "Don't joke with this disappointing boy! Please ask Him not to approach Me, because He is always the cause of all grief for us."

Changing of Bodily Color

Sometimes, due to great aggrievement caused by the dealings of Kṛṣṇa, the body changes color. The *gopīs* therefore addressed the Lord thus: "Dear Kṛṣṇa, due to separation from You, all of the denizens of Vṛndāvana have changed their color. And because of this change of color even the great sage Nārada was thinking of Vṛndāvana as a white island in the ocean of milk."

When Kṛṣṇa and Balarāma were present in the arena of Kaṁsa, Kaṁsa's body changed color. Similarly, Indra's face changed color when he saw that Kṛṣṇa was protecting all the denizens of Vraja by lifting Govardhana Hill. If the color change takes place due to excessive jubilation, the hue turns red. Because such a change of color is so rare, Śrīla Rūpa Gosvāmī does not further discuss this point.

Tears

Out of jubilation, anger or separation there may be the pouring down of tears from the eyes. When such tears are very cold they are due to jubilation, and when they are due to anger the tears become hot. In all cases there is a severe movement of the eyes, and the eyes generally become reddish. There is also an itching sensation which causes the sufferer to rub his eyes.

When the lotus-eyed Rukmiṇī, the first queen of Kṛṣṇa in Dvārakā, was shedding tears out of ecstatic jubilation, she did not like the tears. There is a passage in the *Hari-vaṁśa* wherein Satyabhāmā begins to shed tears because of her great affection for Kṛṣṇa.

An example of shedding tears because of anger was exhibited by Bhīma when he saw that Śiśupāla was insulting Kṛṣṇa in the Rājasūya arena of sacrifice. Bhīma wanted to kill Śiśupāla immediately, but because Kṛṣṇa did not order him to do so, he became morose with anger. It is described that there were hot tears covering his eyes, as a thin cloud sometimes covers the evening moon. In the evening, when the moon is slightly covered by a thin cloud, it looks very nice, and when Bhīma was shedding tears on account of his anger, he also looked very nice.

In the Tenth Canto of *Śrīmad-Bhāgavatam,* Sixtieth Chapter, verse 23, there is a nice example of Rukmiṇī's shedding tears of lamentation. When Kṛṣṇa and Rukmiṇī were talking, Rukmiṇī became frightened of separation from Kṛṣṇa, and therefore she began scratching the earth with her red, lotuslike nails. Because she was shedding tears, the black ointment from her eyes was dripping, along with the tears, onto her breasts, which were covered with *kuṅkuma* powder. Rukmiṇī was so aggrieved that her voice was choked up.

Devastation

When a person is confused by simultaneous happiness and tribulation and does not know what to do, this state of confusion is called *pralaya,* or devastation. In this condition of *pralaya* one sometimes falls down on the ground, and all the symptoms of ecstatic love become manifest. When the *gopīs* were searching after Kṛṣṇa and all of a sudden He came out from the bushes and creepers, all of them became stunned and almost senseless. In this state the *gopīs* appeared very beautiful. This is an example of *pralaya,* or devastation, in happiness.

There are also instances of *pralaya* in distress. One such example is described in the Tenth Canto, Thirty-ninth Chapter, verse 15, of *Śrīmad-Bhāgavatam,* wherein Śukadeva Gosvāmī tells King Parīkṣit, "My dear King, when the *gopīs* were missing Kṛṣṇa, they were so much absorbed in meditation upon Him that all of their senses stopped functioning, and they lost all bodily sense. It was as though they had become liberated from all material conditions."

Degrees of Ecstatic Symptoms

Out of the many ecstatic symptoms of the body, the symptom of being stunned is especially significant. According to the degree of being stunned, the vital force within the body becomes agitated, and due to such a state, the other ecstatic loving symptoms sometimes become altered. These transcendental ecstatic symptoms gradually develop, and in the course of such development they are sometimes called smoky, sometimes called blazing, and sometimes called shining. These three degrees are experienced for many, many years, and they extend to different parts of the body. Unlike the shedding of tears and faltering of the voice, the condition of being stunned is spread all over the body. The shedding of tears and faltering of the voice are simply localized symptoms.

The shedding of tears, however, sometimes makes the eyes become swollen and whitish, and sometimes the lenses of the eyes become differently focused. Faltering of the voice may sometimes cause choking in the throat and extreme anxiety. As the different symptoms of these ecstatic manifestations are localized, they are accompanied by different local reactions; e.g., when the throat is choked up because of a faltering voice, there may be a sound like "*ghura.*" Such sounds choke the voice, and with extreme mental anxiety they may be manifest in different ways. All these symptoms are listed under the dried-up existential condition known as smoky, and they are exhibited in different ways.

Sometimes, while participating in ceremonies celebrating Kṛṣṇa's pastimes, or in the society of devotees, there is dancing ecstasy. Such sentiments are called blazing.

None of the above symptoms can be manifested without the basic principle of strong attachment for Kṛṣṇa. In the smoky condition of such ecstatic expressions, the symptoms could otherwise be hidden. This type of symptom was experienced by Priest Gargamuni, who was performing some ritualistic ceremony in the house of Nanda Mahārāja. When he heard about Kṛṣṇa's killing of the Aghāsura demon, there were some tears visible in his eyes, his throat was trembling, and perspiration covered his whole body. In this way Priest Gargamuni's beautiful face assumed a nice condition.

When several such ecstatic symptoms are visible, the condition is called blazing. For example, one of Kṛṣṇa's friends told Him, "My dear friend, as soon as I heard the sound of Your flute from within the forest, my hands became almost motionless, and my eyes became full of tears—so much so, in fact, that I could not recognize Your peacock feather. My thighs became almost completely stunned so that I could not move even an inch. Therefore, my dear friend, I must acknowledge the wonderful vibration of Your transcendental flute."

Similarly, one *gopī* said to another, "My dear friend, when I heard the sound of Kṛṣṇa's flute, I tried to hide myself from the reaction of the vibrations. But still I could not check the trembling of my body, and therefore all of my friends in the house could detect my attachment for Kṛṣṇa without any doubt."

When the ecstatic symptoms cannot be checked and they simultaneously appear in four or five different categories, this stage of ecstatic love is called shining. The example is cited, in this connection, that when the sage Nārada saw Lord Kṛṣṇa standing before him, his body became so stunned that he stopped playing on his *vīṇā*. Because of his faltering voice, he could not offer any prayers to Kṛṣṇa, and his eyes filled with tears. Thus, Nārada's ability to see Kṛṣṇa was also obstructed.

When similar symptoms were manifest in the body of Śrīmatī Rādhārāṇī, some of Her friends criticized Her: "Dear friend, You are blaming the aroma of the flowers for the tears in Your eyes. You are rebuking the air for the standing of the hairs on Your body. And You are cursing Your walking in the forest for Your thighs' being stunned. But Your faltering voice reveals the cause to be different: it is just Your attachment for Kṛṣṇa!"

Śrīla Rūpa Gosvāmī remarks that when various symptoms become manifest very prominently, the devotee's condition may be called the brightest. For example, a friend of Kṛṣṇa addressed Him as follows: "My dear Pītāmbara, because of separation from You all the residents of Goloka Vṛndāvana are perspiring. They are lamenting with different words, and their eyes have become moistened with tears. Actually, all of them are in great confusion."

There is a supreme symptom of ecstatic love which is called *mahābhāva*. This *mahābhāva* expression was possible only in Rādhārāṇī, but later on when Śrī Kṛṣṇa Caitanya appeared in order to feel the mode of love of Rādhārāṇī, He also expressed all of the symptoms of *mahābhāva*. Śrī Rūpa Gosvāmī says in this connection that when the symptoms of ecstatic love become the most bright, that stage is accepted as *mahābhāva*.

Śrīla Rūpa Gosvāmī further analyzes the ecstatic loving expression into four divisions which are called *sāttvikābhāsā*.

Sometimes impersonalists, who are not actually in devotional service, may also exhibit such symptoms of ecstatic love, but this is not accepted as actual ecstasy. It is a reflection only. For example, sometimes in Vārāṇasī, a holy city for impersonalist scholars, there may be seen a *sannyāsī* crying from hearing the glories of the Lord. Impersonalists also sometimes chant the Hare Kṛṣṇa *mantra* and dance, but their aim is not to serve the Lord. It is to become one with the Lord and merge into His existence. Rūpa Gosvāmī therefore says that even if the reactions to chanting are manifested in the impersonalist's body, they should not be considered to be symptoms of actual attachment, but reflections only, just like the sun reflected in a dark room through some polished glass. The chanting of Hare Kṛṣṇa, however, is so nice and transcendental that it will eventually melt even the hearts of persons who are impersonalists. Rūpa Gosvāmī says that the impersonalists' symptoms are simply reflections of ecstatic love, not the real thing.

Sometimes it is found that when staunch logicians, without any trace of devotional service and without actually understanding the transcendental glories of the Lord, sit down to hear the glories of the Lord, they appear to be melting and shedding tears. In this connection there is a statement by a devotee who addresses the Lord thus: "My dear Mukunda, I cannot properly express the glories of Your pastimes. Even when the nondevotees hear of Your glorious pastimes they become affected and shed tears and start to tremble." Such nondevotees are not actually melted; they are hardhearted. But the influence of the glories of the Lord is so great that even the nondevotees sometimes shed tears.

Sometimes it is found that a nondevotee who has practically no taste for Kṛṣṇa and who follows no rules or regulations can, by practice, make a show of devotional symptoms, even crying in an assembly of devotees. This shedding of tears is not actually an ecstatic loving expression, however. It is done simply by practice. Although there is no need to describe these reflections of ecstatic love, Rūpa Gosvāmī gives some instances where there is no actual devotional service and such expressions are manifested.

29

Expressions of Love for Kṛṣṇa

There are some bodily symptoms which express overwhelming ecstatic love (*vyabhicāri-bhāva*). They are counted at thirty-three as follows: disappointment, lamentation, humility, guilt, fatigue, intoxication, pride, doubt, apprehension, intense emotion, madness, forgetfulness, disease, confusion, death, laziness, inertness, bashfulness, concealment, remembrance, argumentativeness, anxiety, thoughtfulness, endurance, happiness, eagerness, violence, haughtiness, envy, impudence, dizziness, sleepiness and alertness.

Disappointment

When one is forced to act in a way which is forbidden, or to refrain from acting in a way which is proper, he becomes regretful and thinks himself dishonored. At that time there is a sense of disappointment. In this kind of disappointment one becomes full of anxiety, sheds tears, changes bodily color, feels humility and breathes heavily.

When Kṛṣṇa, in punishing the Kāliya serpent, appeared to have drowned Himself in the poisonous water of the Yamunā, Nanda Mahārāja addressed Yaśodā-devī thus: "My dear wife, Kṛṣṇa has gone deep into the water, and so there is no longer any need to maintain our bodies, which are so full of sinful activities! Let us also enter into the poisonous water of the Yamunā and compensate for the sinful activities of our lives!" This is an instance of severe shock, wherein the devotee becomes greatly disappointed.

When Kṛṣṇa left Vṛndāvana, Subala, His intimate friend, decided to leave also. While leaving, Subala was contemplating that without Kṛṣṇa there was no longer any pleasure to be found in Vṛndāvana. The analogy is given that as the bees go away from a flower that has no honey, Subala left Vṛndāvana when he found that there was no longer any relishable transcendental pleasure there.

In *Dāna-keli-kaumudī* Śrīmatī Rādhārāṇī addresses one of Her friends in this manner: "My dear friend, if I cannot hear of the glorious activities of Kṛṣṇa, it is better for Me to become deaf. And because I am now unable to see Him, it would be good for Me to be a blind woman." This is another instance of disappointment due to separation from Kṛṣṇa.

There is a statement in the *Hari-vaṁśa* wherein Satyabhāmā, one of the queens of Kṛṣṇa in Dvārakā, tells her husband, "My dear Kṛṣṇa, since I heard Nārada glorifying Rukmiṇī before You, I can understand that there is no need of any talking about myself!" This is an instance of disappointment caused by envy. Rukmiṇī and Satyabhāmā were co-wives, and because Kṛṣṇa was husband of both, there naturally was some feminine envy between them. So when Satyabhāmā heard the glories of Rukmiṇī, she was envious of her and thus became disappointed.

In the Tenth Canto, Fifty-first Chapter, verse 47, of the *Śrīmad-Bhāgavatam,* there is this statement: "My dear Kṛṣṇa, I cannot say that it is only other people who are implicated in material existence, because I too am much entangled with the bodily concept of life. I am always too anxious about my family, home, wife, wealth, land and kingdom. And because I have been so maddened by this material atmosphere, I am thinking now that my life has been simply spoiled." This statement is an instance of disappointment caused by lamentation.

According to Bharata Muni, this disappointment is inauspicious. But there are other learned scholars who have accepted such disappointment as being in the mood of neutrality and as being a preservative of ecstatic love.

Lamentation

When one is unsuccessful in achieving his desired goal of life, when one finds no fulfillment in his present occupation, when one finds himself in reversed conditions and when one feels guilt—at such a time one is said to be in a state of lamentation.

In this condition of lamentation one becomes questioning, thoughtful, tearful, regretful and heavy-breathed. His bodily color changes, and his mouth becomes dry.

One aged devotee of Kṛṣṇa addressed Him in this way: "My dear Kṛṣṇa, O killer of the demon Agha, my body is now invalid due to old age. I cannot speak very fluently, my voice is faltering, my mind is not strong, and I am often attacked by forgetfulness. But, my dear Lord, You are just like the moonlight, and my only real regret is that for want of any taste for Your pleasant shining I did not advance myself in Kṛṣṇa consciousness." This statement is an instance of lamentation due to one's being unable to achieve his desired goal.

One devotee said, "This night I was dreaming of collecting various flowers from the garden, and I was thinking of making a garland to offer to Kṛṣṇa. But I am so unfortunate that all of a sudden my dream was over, and I could not achieve my desired goal!" This statement is an instance of lamentation resulting from nonfulfillment of one's duties.

When Nanda Mahārāja saw his foster son Kṛṣṇa embarrassed in the sacrificial arena of Kaṁsa, he said, "How unfortunate I am that I did not keep my son bolted within a room. Unfortunately, I have brought Him to Mathurā, and now I see that He's embarrassed by this giant elephant named Kuvalaya. It is as though the moon of Kṛṣṇa were eclipsed by the shadow of the earth." This is an instance of lamentation caused by reversed conditions.

In the Tenth Canto, Fourteenth Chapter, verse 9, of the *Śrīmad-Bhāgavatam* there is a statement by Brahmā: "My dear Lord, just see my impudence! You are the unlimited, the original Personality of Godhead, the Supersoul—and You rule over the most perfect illusory energies! And just see my impudence! I wanted to supersede You by my own personal power, and I was very puffed up with this tiny power of mine. Just as a simple spark from a fire cannot do any harm to the fire, so my bewildering potency was completely unsuccessful in thwarting Your superior illusory power. Therefore I find myself to be most insignificant and think of myself as a most useless person." This statement by Brahmā is an instance of lamentation caused by committing an offense.

Humility

A sense of weakness caused by distress, fear or offensiveness is called humility. In such a humble condition one becomes talkative, small in heart, dirty in mind, full of anxiety and inactive.

In the Tenth Canto, Fifty-first Chapter, verse 57, of the *Śrīmad-Bhāgavatam,* there is the following statement by King Mucukunda: "My dear Lord, because of my bad deeds in the past I am everlastingly aggrieved. I am always suffering from my desires, but still my senses are never satisfied with material enjoyments. Somehow or other, by Your grace, I am now in a peaceful condition because I have taken shelter of Your lotus feet, which are always free from all lamentation, fear and death. O supreme protector, O supreme soul! O supreme controller! Kindly give me Your protection. I am so much embarrassed." This statement by Mucukunda is an instance of humility resulting from a severely miserable condition of material existence.

When Uttarā was attacked by the *brahmāstra* of Aśvatthāmā, she became afraid of losing her child, Mahārāja Parīkṣit, who was still within the womb. She immediately surrendered to Kṛṣṇa and said, "My dear Lord, kindly save my child! I do not mind if I myself must be killed by the *brahmāstra* of Aśvatthāmā." This is an instance of humility caused by fear.

In the Tenth Canto, Fourteenth Chapter, verse 10, of the *Śrīmad-Bhāgavatam,* Lord Brahmā says, "O infallible one! I am born in the mode of passion, and therefore I have been falsely proud of being the creator of this material world. My false pride was just like dense darkness, and in this darkness I had become blind. In my blindness I was considering myself a competitor to You, the Supreme Personality of Godhead. But, my dear Lord, even though I am accepted as the creator of this universe, I am eternally Your servant. Therefore, kindly always be compassionate toward me and excuse me in that way." This statement by Brahmā is another instance of humility resulting from committing an offense.

Sometimes there is humility due to shyness. For example, when Kṛṣṇa stole all of the garments from the *gopīs* while they were bathing in the river, all of them begged Kṛṣṇa not to commit this injustice upon them. The *gopīs* addressed Him thus: "Dear Kṛṣṇa, we know that You are the son of Nanda Mahārāja and that You are the most beloved of all Vṛndāvana. And You are very much loved by us also! But why are You giving us this trouble? Kindly return our garments. Just see how we are trembling from the severe cold!" This humility was due to their shyness from being naked before Kṛṣṇa.

Guilt

When a person blames himself for committing an inappropriate action, his feeling is called guilt.

One day Śrīmatī Rādhārāṇī was churning yogurt for Kṛṣṇa. At that time the jeweled bangles on Her hands were circling around, and She was also chanting the holy name of Kṛṣṇa. All of a sudden She thought, "I am chanting the holy name of Kṛṣṇa, and My superiors—My mother-in-law and My sister-in-law—may hear Me!" By this thought Rādhārāṇī became overanxious. This is an instance of feeling guilty because of devotion to Kṛṣṇa.

One day the beautiful-eyed Śrīmatī Rādhārāṇī entered into the forest to collect some flowers to prepare a garland for Kṛṣṇa. While collecting the flowers, She became afraid that someone might see Her, and She felt some fatigue and weakness. This is an instance of guilty feelings caused by labor for Kṛṣṇa.

There is a statement in *Rasa-sudhākara* that after passing the night with Kṛṣṇa, Rādhārāṇī became so weak that She was unable to get up from bed. When Kṛṣṇa took Her hand to help Her, Rādhārāṇī felt guilty about having passed the night with Him.

Fatigue

One feels fatigue after walking a long distance, after dancing and after sexual activity. In this kind of fatigue there is dizziness, perspiration, inactivity of the limbs, yawning and very heavy breathing.

One day Yaśodā was chasing Kṛṣṇa in the yard after He had offended her. After a while, Yaśodā became very fatigued, and therefore she was perspiring, and her bunched hair became loosened. This is an instance of becoming fatigued because of working too much.

Sometimes all of the cowherd friends of Kṛṣṇa, along with Balarama, danced together in some ceremony. At these times the garlands on their necks would move, and the boys would begin to perspire. Their whole bodies became wet from their ecstatic dancing. This is an instance of fatigue caused by dancing.

In *Śrīmad-Bhāgavatam,* Tenth Canto, Thirty-third Chapter, verse 20, it is said that after enjoying loving affairs with Kṛṣṇa by dancing, embracing and kissing, the *gopīs* would sometimes become very tired, and Kṛṣṇa, out of His causeless mercy and compassion, would smear their faces with His lotus hands. This is an example of fatigue caused by laboring in the *rāsa* dance.

Intoxication

When one becomes arrogant with false prestige due to drinking intoxicants or being too lustful, the voice becomes faulty, the eyes become swollen, and there are symptoms of redness on the body. There is a statement in the *Lalita-mādhava* that Lord Baladeva,* intoxicated from drinking excessive quantities of honey, once began to address the ants, "O you kings of the ants! Why are you hiding yourselves in these holes?" At the same time He also addressed the King of heaven, "O King Indra! You plaything of Śacī! Why are you laughing? I am now prepared to smash the whole universe, and I know that Kṛṣṇa will not be angry with Me." Then He addressed Kṛṣṇa, "My dear Kṛṣṇa, tell Me immediately why the whole world is trembling and why the moon has become elongated! And O you members of the Yadu dynasty, why are you laughing at Me? Please give Me back My liquors made of honey from the *kadamba* flower!" Śrīla Rūpa Gosvāmī prays that Lord Balarāma will be pleased with all of us while He is thus talking just like an intoxicated person.

In this state of intoxication, Balarāma felt tired and lay down for rest. Generally, those who are exalted personalities lie down when they feel intoxicated, whereas those who are mediocre laugh and sing during intoxication, and those who are lowly use vulgar language and sometimes cry. Such intoxication is manifested according to different ages and mentalities. Śrīla Rūpa Gosvāmī does not describe further in this direction because there is no necessity for such a discussion.

There is another description of the symptoms of intoxication in the person of Śrī Rādhārāṇī after She saw Kṛṣṇa. Sometimes She was walking hither and thither, sometimes She was laughing, sometimes She was covering Her face, sometimes She was talking without any meaning, and sometimes She was praying to Her associate *gopīs*. Seeing these symptoms in Rādhārāṇī, the *gopīs* began to talk among themselves:

---

*Baladeva, or Balarāma, is the older brother of Kṛṣṇa. He is an expansion of the Godhead Himself, and therefore to be considered an incarnation of God, as explained in the *Śrīmad-Bhāgavatam*.

"Just see how Rādhārāṇī has become intoxicated simply by seeing Kṛṣṇa before Her!" This is an instance of ecstatic love in intoxication.

Pride

Expressions of ecstatic love in pride may be the result of excessive wealth, exquisite beauty, a first-class residence or the attainment of one's ideal goal. One is also considered proud when he does not care about the neglect of others.

Bilvamaṅgala Ṭhākura said, "My dear Kṛṣṇa, You are leaving me, forcibly getting out of my clutches. But I shall be impressed by Your strength only when You can go forcibly from the core of my heart." This is an instance of feeling pride in ecstatic love for Kṛṣṇa.

Once during the *rāsa* dance, when Rādhārāṇī left the arena and Kṛṣṇa went to seek Her out, one of the dear friends of Rādhārāṇī addressed Kṛṣṇa thus: "My dear Kṛṣṇa, You have been very much obliging in serving the form of our Śrī Rādhārāṇī, and now You have left all the other *gopīs* to search for Her. Please allow me to inquire how You want Her to treat You." This is an instance of feeling pride on account of exquisite beauty.

Sometimes Rādhārāṇī felt pride within Herself and said, "Although the cowherd boys prepare nice flower garlands for Kṛṣṇa, when I present My garland to Him, He becomes struck with wonder and immediately accepts it and puts it on His heart."

Similarly, in the Tenth Canto, Second Chapter, verse 33, of *Śrīmad-Bhāgavatam,* Lord Brahmā says, "My dear Madhusūdana, persons who are pure devotees of Your Lordship actually feel Your ecstatic friendship, and as such they are never vanquished by enemies. They know they are always protected by You, and so they can matter-of-factly pass over the heads of their enemies without any care." In other words, one who has taken complete shelter under the lotus feet of the Lord is always proud of being able to conquer all enemies.

One weaver at Mathurā addressed Kṛṣṇa in this way: "My dear King of Vṛndāvana, I have become so proud of Your causeless mercy upon me that I do not even count upon the mercy of the Lord of Vaikuṇṭha, which is sought after by many great sages in deep meditation." In other words, although the *yogīs* and great sages sit in meditation upon Lord Viṣṇu, who is residing in Vaikuṇṭha, a devotee of Kṛṣṇa is so proud that he does not consider such meditation to be very valuable. This feeling of pride is due to one's having achieved the highest goal of life—Kṛṣṇa.

Doubt

After Lord Brahmā had stolen all of the calves, cows and cowherd boys from Kṛṣṇa, he was trying to go away. But all of a sudden he became doubtful about his stealing affairs and began to watch on all sides with his eight eyes. Lord Brahmā has four heads, and therefore he has eight eyes. This is an instance of ecstatic love in doubt, caused by stealing.

Similarly, just to please Kṛṣṇa, Akrūra stole the Syamantaka *maṇi,* a stone which can produce unlimited quantities of gold, but later on he repented his stealing. This is another instance of ecstatic love for Kṛṣṇa in doubt caused by stealing.

When the King of heaven, Indra, was causing torrents of rain to fall on the land of Vraja, he was advised to surrender himself at the lotus feet of Kṛṣṇa. At that time Indra's face became very dark because of doubt.

Apprehension

When a person becomes disturbed in his heart by seeing lightning in the sky, by seeing a ferocious animal or by hearing a tumultuous sound, his state of mind is called apprehensive. In such a state of apprehension, one tries to take shelter of something which provides safety. There may be standing of the hairs on the body, trembling of the body and sometimes the committing of mistakes. And sometimes the body may become stunned.

In the *Padyāvalī* there is the following statement: "My dear friend, Kṛṣṇa's residence in the demoniac circle at Mathurā, under the supremacy of the king of demons, Kaṁsa, is causing me much worry." This is one instance of apprehending some danger to Kṛṣṇa in ecstatic love for Him.

When Vṛṣāsura appeared in Vṛndāvana as a bull, all of the *gopīs* became greatly affected with fear. Being perturbed in that way, they began to embrace the *tamāla* trees. This is an instance of fear caused by a ferocious animal and of the search for shelter while remembering Kṛṣṇa in ecstatic love. Upon hearing the jackals crying in the forest of Vṛndāvana, Mother Yaśodā sometimes became very careful about keeping Kṛṣṇa under her vigilance, fearing that Kṛṣṇa might be attacked by them. This is an instance of ecstatic love for Kṛṣṇa in fear caused by a tumultuous sound. This kind of fear is a little different from being actually afraid. When one is afraid of something, he can still think of past and future. But when there is this kind of ecstatic apprehension, there is no scope for such thinking.

Intense Emotion

Emotion is caused by something very dear, by something very detestable, by fire, by strong wind, by strong rainfall, by some natural disturbance, by the sight of a big elephant or by the sight of an enemy. When there is emotion caused by seeing something very dear, one can speak very swiftly and use kind words. When there is emotion caused by seeing something detestable, one cries very loudly. When there is emotion caused by seeing fire, one tries to flee. There may also be trembling of the body, closing of the eyes and tears in the eyes. When one becomes emotional on account of a strong wind, one tries to run very swiftly and rubs his eyes. When one is emotional because of rainfall, one takes an umbrella, and there is tension in his body. When there is emotion due to a sudden disturbance, one's face becomes discolored, one becomes struck with wonder, and there is trembling of the body. If there is emotion from seeing an elephant, one may jump and show various signs of fear, and sometimes one may keep looking behind him. When there is emotion due to the presence of an enemy, one looks for a fatal weapon and tries to escape.

When Kṛṣṇa returned from the forest of Vṛndāvana, Mother Yaśodā was so emotional from seeing her son that milk began to flow from her breasts. This is an instance of emotion caused by seeing a dear object.

In the Tenth Canto, Twenty-third Chapter, verse 18, of *Śrīmad-Bhāgavatam,* Śukadeva Gosvāmī informs King Parīkṣit, "My dear King, the wives of the *brāhmaṇas* were usually very much attached to the glorification of Kṛṣṇa, and they were always anxious to get an opportunity to see Him. Because of this, when they heard that Kṛṣṇa was nearby, they became very anxious to see Him and immediately left their homes." This is an instance of emotional activity caused by the presence of someone very dear.

When Pūtanā, the demoniac witch, was struck down and killed by Kṛṣṇa, Mother Yaśodā was struck with wonder and began to cry emotionally, "Oh, what is this? What is this?" When she saw that her dear baby Kṛṣṇa was playing on the chest of the dead demoniac woman, Mother Yaśodā, at a loss what to do, began to walk this way and that. This is an instance of being emotional on account of seeing something ghastly.

When Kṛṣṇa uprooted the two *arjuna* trees and Yaśodā heard the sound of the trees crashing down, she became overcome with emotion and simply stared upward, being too bewildered to know what else to do. This is an instance of being emotional from hearing a tumultuous sound.

When there was a forest fire in Vṛndāvana, all the cowherd men assembled together and desperately appealed to Kṛṣṇa for protection. This is an instance of emotion caused by fire.

The whirlwind demon known as Tṛṇāvarta once carried Kṛṣṇa off from the ground and blew Him around, along with some very big trees. At that time, Mother Yaśodā could not see her son, and she was so disturbed that she began to walk this way and that. This is an instance of emotion caused by severe wind.

In the Tenth Canto, Twenty-fifth Chapter, verse 11, of *Śrīmad-Bhāgavatam,* there is a description of Indra's causing severe torrents of rain at Vṛndāvana. All the cows and cowherd boys became so afflicted by the wind and cold that they all gathered together to take shelter under the lotus feet of Kṛṣṇa. This is an instance of emotion caused by severe rainfall.

There were severe torrents of hail when Kṛṣṇa was staying in the forest of Vṛndāvana, and the elderly persons bade Him, "Kṛṣṇa, don't You move now! Even persons who are stronger and older than You cannot move, and You are just a little boy. So please stay still!" This is an instance of emotion caused by heavy hailing.

When Kṛṣṇa was chastising Kāliya in the poisonous water of the Yamunā, Mother Yaśodā began to speak emotionally: "Oh, see how the earth appears to be trembling! There appears to be an earth tremor, and in the sky meteors are flying here and there! My dear son has entered into the poisonous water of the Yamunā. What shall I do now?" This is an instance of emotion resulting from a natural disturbance.

In the arena of Kaṁsa, when Kṛṣṇa was attacked by big elephants, all of the ladies present began to address Him in this way: "My dear boy—please leave this place immediately! Please leave this place immediately! Don't You see the big elephants coming to attack You? Your innocent gazing upon them is causing us too much perturbation!" Kṛṣṇa then told Mother Yaśodā, "My dear mother, don't be perturbed by the appearance of the elephants and horses that are so forcibly coming and raising dust, causing blindness to these lotus-eyed women. Let even the Keśī demon come before Me; My arms will still be adequate for victory. So please don't be perturbed."

In the *Lalita-mādhava,* a friend tells Mother Yaśodā, "How wonderful it is that when the Śaṅkhacūḍa demon—as vast and strong as a great hill—attacked your Cupid-like beautiful son, there was no one present in Vṛndāvana to help. And yet the demon was killed by your little son. It appears to be due to the result of severe penances and austerities in your past lives that your son was saved in this way."

In the same *Lalita-mādhava* there is an account of Kṛṣṇa's kidnapping Rukmiṇī at her royal marriage ceremony. At that time all of the princes present began to converse among themselves, saying, "We have our elephants, horses, chariots, bows, arrows and swords, so why should we be afraid of Kṛṣṇa? Let us attack Him! He is nothing but a lusty cowherd boy! He cannot take away the princess in this way! Let us all attack Him!" This is an instance of emotion caused by the presence of enemies.

Śrīla Rūpa Gosvāmī is trying to prove by the above examples that in relationship with Kṛṣṇa there is no question of impersonalism. All personal activities are there in relationship with Kṛṣṇa.

Madness

Śrīla Bilvamaṅgala Ṭhākura prays in his book as follows: "Let Śrīmatī Rādhārāṇī purify the whole world, because She has surrendered Herself completely unto Kṛṣṇa. Out of Her ecstatic love for Him, She sometimes acted just like an addled person and attempted to churn yogurt, although there was no yogurt in the pot. And seeing this, Kṛṣṇa became so enchanted by Rādhārāṇī that He began to milk a bull instead of a cow." These are some of the instances of insanity or madness in connection with the loving affairs of Rādhā and Kṛṣṇa. In *Śrīmad-Bhāgavatam* it is said that when Kṛṣṇa entered the poisonous waters of the Yamunā, Śrīmatī Yaśodā-devī went insane. Instead of searching for curative herbs, she began to speak to the trees as if they were snake chanters. With folded hands she began to bow down to the trees, asking them, "What is the medicinal herb which can check Kṛṣṇa's dying from this poisonous water?" This is an instance of insanity caused by some great danger.

How a devotee can be in a state of insanity because of ecstatic love is described in the Tenth Canto, Thirtieth Chapter, verse 4, of *Śrīmad-Bhāgavatam,* wherein the *gopīs* were searching for Kṛṣṇa in the forests of Vṛndāvana. The *gopīs* were loudly singing the glories of Kṛṣṇa and wandering from one forest to another in search of Him. They knew that Kṛṣṇa is not localized but all-pervading. He is in the sky, He is in the water, He is in the air, and He is the Supersoul in everyone's heart. Thus the *gopīs* began to inquire from all kinds of trees and plants about the Supreme Personality of Godhead. This is an instance of ecstatic madness on the part of devotees.

Similarly, there are symptoms of diseases caused by ecstatic love. This condition is credited by learned scholars as being *mahābhāva.* This highly elevated condition is also called *divyonmāda,* or transcendental madness.

Forgetfulness

When Kṛṣṇa was absent from Vṛndāvana and was staying in Mathurā, Śrīmatī Rādhārāṇī sent news to Him that His mother, the Queen of Vraja, was feeling such separation from Him that there was foam coming from her mouth, like the foam on the shore of the ocean. And sometimes she was raising her arms like the waves of the ocean, and because of her intense feelings of separation, she was rolling on the ground and creating a tumultuous roaring sound. And sometimes she was remaining completely silent, like a calm sea. These symptoms of separation from Kṛṣṇa are called *apasmāra,* or forgetfulness. One completely forgets his position when he manifests these symptoms in ecstatic love.

Another message was once sent to Kṛṣṇa informing Him that after He had killed Kaṁsa, one of Kaṁsa's demon friends had gone insane. This demon was foaming at the mouth, waving his arms and rolling on the ground. This demoniac demonstration is in relationship with Kṛṣṇa in a ghastly humor. This mellow or flavor is one of the indirect relationships with Kṛṣṇa. The first five kinds of relationships are called direct, and the other seven are called indirect. Some way or other, the demon must have had some relationship with Kṛṣṇa, because these symptoms developed when he heard that Kṛṣṇa had already killed Kaṁsa. Śrīla Rūpa Gosvāmī remarks that there is also transcendental excellence in this kind of symptom.

Disease

When Kṛṣṇa was absent from Vṛndāvana and was staying at Mathurā, some of His friends informed Him, "Dear Kṛṣṇa, because of their separation from You, the inhabitants of Vraja are so afflicted that they appear to be diseased. Their bodies are feverish, and they cannot move properly. They are simply lying down on the ground and breathing heavily."

In the Tenth Canto, Twelfth Chapter, verse 44, of *Śrīmad-Bhāgavatam,* Mahārāja Parīkṣit asked about Lord Ananta, and upon hearing this question, Śukadeva Gosvāmī began to show symptoms of collapsing. Yet he checked himself and answered King Parīkṣit's question in a mild voice. This collapsing condition is described as a feverish state resulting from ecstatic pleasure.

There is another statement in *Śrīmad-Bhāgavatam* telling of the damsels of Vraja meeting Kṛṣṇa at the sacred place of Kurukṣetra, many years after their childhood pastimes. When they met in that sacred place, all the *gopīs* became stunned by the occurrence of a solar eclipse. Their breathing, blinking of the eyes and all similar activities stopped, and they stood before Kṛṣṇa just like statues. This is another instance of a diseased condition resulting from exuberant transcendental pleasure.

30

Further Features of Ecstatic Love for Kṛṣṇa

Confusion

There is the following statement in the *Haṁsadūta:* "One day when Śrīmatī Rādhārāṇī was feeling much affliction because of Her separation from Kṛṣṇa, She went to the bank of the Yamunā with some of Her friends. There Rādhārāṇī saw a cottage wherein She and Kṛṣṇa had experienced many loving pleasures, and by remembering those incidents She immediately became overcome with dizziness. This dizziness was very prominently visible." This is an instance of confusion caused by separation.

Similarly, there is a statement describing confusion caused by fearfulness. These symptoms were exhibited by Arjuna when he saw Kṛṣṇa's universal form on the Battlefield of Kurukṣetra. His confusion was so strong that his bow and arrows fell from his hand and he could not perceive anything clearly.

Death

Once the Bakāsura demon assumed the shape of a very big heron and opened his mouth in order to swallow Kṛṣṇa and all the cowherd boys. When Kṛṣṇa was entering into the demon's mouth, Balarāma and the other cowherd boys almost fainted and appeared as though they had no life. Even if devotees are illusioned by some ghastly scene or by any accidental occurrence, they never forget Kṛṣṇa. Even in the greatest danger they can remember Kṛṣṇa. This is the benefit of Kṛṣṇa consciousness: even at the time of death, when all the functions of the body become dislocated, the devotee can remember Kṛṣṇa in his innermost consciousness, and this saves him from falling down into material existence. In this way Kṛṣṇa consciousness immediately takes one from the material platform to the spiritual world.

In this connection there is a statement about persons who died at Mathurā: "These persons had a slight breathing exhilaration, their eyes were wide open, the colors of their bodies were changed, and they began to utter the holy name of Kṛṣṇa. In this condition they gave up their material bodies." These symptoms are prior manifestations of death.

Laziness

When, because of self-satisfaction or dislike of excessive labor, a person does not perform his duty in spite of having the energy, he is called lazy. This laziness also is manifested in ecstatic love of Kṛṣṇa. For example, when some *brāhmaṇas* were requested by Nanda Mahārāja to circumambulate Govardhana Hill, they told him that they were more interested in offering benedictions than in circumambulating Govardhana Hill. This is an instance of laziness caused by self-satisfaction.

Once when Kṛṣṇa, along with His cowherd boyfriends, was having a mock battle, Subala showed the symptoms of fatigue. Kṛṣṇa immediately told His other friends, "Subala is feeling too fatigued from mock-fighting with Me. So please do not disturb him any more by inviting him to fight." This is an instance of laziness caused by dislike of excessive labor.

Inertness

In the Tenth Canto, Twenty-first Chapter, verse 13, of *Śrīmad-Bhāgavatam,* there is an appreciation by the *gopīs* of the inertia of the cows in Vṛndāvana. The *gopīs* saw that the cows were hearing the sweet songs vibrated by Kṛṣṇa's flute and were appearing to be drinking the nectar of these transcendental sounds. The calves were stunned, and they forgot to drink the milk from the milk bags. Their eyes seemed to be embracing Kṛṣṇa, and there were tears in their eyes. This is an instance of inertia resulting from hearing the transcendental vibrations of Kṛṣṇa's flute.

When Lakṣmaṇā became disturbed upon hearing words against Kṛṣṇa, she remained inert and did not move her eyelids. This is another example of inertia caused by hearing.

In the Tenth Canto, Seventy-first Chapter, verse 39, of *Śrīmad-*

Bhāgavatam, there is an account of King Yudhiṣṭhira's bewilderment after his bringing Kṛṣṇa into his home with the greatest respect. King Yudhiṣṭhira was very much bewildered because of his transcendental pleasure at having Kṛṣṇa present in his house. In fact, while receiving Kṛṣṇa, King Yudhiṣṭhira forgot himself. This is an instance of inertia resulting from the ecstasy of seeing Kṛṣṇa.

There is another instance in the Tenth Canto, Thirty-ninth Chapter, verse 36, of *Śrīmad-Bhāgavatam.* When Kṛṣṇa was going to Mathurā, all of the *gopīs* were standing behind Kṛṣṇa, and upon seeing the chariot leaving, they stood there stunned and did not move. They remained like that until the flag of the chariot and the dust thrown up by its wheels became invisible.

Kṛṣṇa was once addressed by His friend thus: "My dear Mukunda [Kṛṣṇa], due to their being separated from You, the cowherd boys are standing just like neglected Deities in the house of a professional *brāhmaṇa.*" There is a class of professional *brāhmaṇas* who take to Deity worship as a means of earning their livelihood. *Brāhmaṇas* in this class are not very interested in the Deity; they are interested mainly in the money they can earn as holy men. So the Deities worshiped by such professional *brāhmaṇas* are not properly decorated, Their dress is not changed, and Their bodies are not cleaned. They look dirty and are not very attractive. Actually, Deity worship should be done very carefully: the dress should be changed daily, and as far as possible there should be ornaments. Everything should be so clean that the Deity is attractive to all visitors. Here the example is given of the Deities in the house of a professional *brāhmaṇa* because such Deities are not at all attractive. The friends of Kṛṣṇa, in the absence of Kṛṣṇa, were appearing like such neglected Deities.

Bashfulness

When Rādhārāṇī was first introduced to Kṛṣṇa, She felt very bashful. One of Her friends addressed Her in this way: "My dear friend, You have already sold Yourself and all Your beauty to Govinda. Now You should not be bashful. Please look upon Him cheerfully. One who has sold an elephant to another person should not make a miserly quarrel about selling the trident which controls the elephant." This kind of bashfulness is due to a new introduction in ecstatic love with Kṛṣṇa.

The heavenly King, Indra, upon being defeated in his fight with Kṛṣṇa for possession of the *pārijāta* flower, became very bashful because of his defeat. He was standing before Kṛṣṇa, bowing down his head, when Kṛṣṇa said, "All right, Indra, you can take this *pārijāta* flower. Otherwise, you will not be able to show your face before your wife, Śacīdevī." Indra's bashfulness was due to defeat. In another instance, Kṛṣṇa began to praise Uddhava for his various high qualifications. Upon being praised by Kṛṣṇa, Uddhava also bowed down his head bashfully.

In the *Hari-vaṁśa,* Satyabhāmā, feeling slighted by Rukmiṇī's high position, said, "My dear Kṛṣṇa, the Raivataka Mountain is always full of spring flowers, but when I have become persona non grata to You, what is the use of my observing them?" This is an instance of bashfulness resulting from being defeated.

Concealment

There is a symptom of ecstatic love known as concealment, or trying to hide one's real mental condition by externally showing another attitude. In this state of mind one tries to hide his mind by looking away in different directions, by unnecessarily trying for something which is impossible, or by using words which cover one's real thoughts. According to *ācāryas* expert in the study of psychological activities, these attempts at hiding one's real affections are another part of ecstatic feeling for Kṛṣṇa.

In the Tenth Canto, Thirty-second Chapter, verse 15, of *Śrīmad-Bhāgavatam,* Śukadeva Gosvāmī states, "My dear King, the *gopīs* were always beautiful and decorated with confidential smiles and alluring garments. In their movements, intended to give impetus to lusty feelings, they would sometimes press Kṛṣṇa's hand on their laps, and sometimes they would keep His lotus feet on their breasts. After doing this, they would talk with Kṛṣṇa as if they were very angry with Him."

There is another instance of this concealment in ecstatic love. When Kṛṣṇa, the supreme joker, planted the *pārijāta* tree in the courtyard of Satyabhāmā, Rukmiṇī, the daughter of King Vidarbha, became very angry, but due to her natural gentle behavior, she did not express anything. No one could understand Rukmiṇī's real mental condition. This is an instance of competitive concealment.

There is another instance in the First Canto, Eleventh Chapter, verse

32, of *Śrīmad-Bhāgavatam*. After entering Dvārakā, Kṛṣṇa was received in different ways by different members of His family. Upon seeing their husband from a distance, the queens of Dvārakā immediately embraced Him within their minds and slowly glanced over Him. As Kṛṣṇa came nearer, they pushed their sons forward to embrace Him. Others were trying, out of shyness, not to shed tears, but they still could not keep the tears from gliding down. This is an instance of concealment caused by shyness.

On another occasion, when Śrīmatī Rādhārāṇī thought that Kṛṣṇa was involved with another woman, She addressed Her friend in this manner: "My dear friend, as soon as I think of Kṛṣṇa the cowherd boy attached to some other woman, I become stricken with fear, and the hairs on My body stand up. I must be very careful that Kṛṣṇa not see Me at such times." This is an instance of concealment caused by shyness and diplomatic behavior.

It has been stated, "Although Śrīmatī Rādhārāṇī developed a deep loving affection for Kṛṣṇa, She hid Her attitude in the core of Her heart so that others could not detect Her actual condition." This is an instance of concealment caused by gentleness.

Once when Kṛṣṇa and His cowherd friends were enjoying friendly conversation, Kṛṣṇa began to address His associates in casual language. At that time Kṛṣṇa's servant Patrī was also enjoying the conversation. But then, remembering his position of servitude, Patrī bowed down before his master, and with great respect and control, he stifled his smiling. This subdued smiling is an instance of concealment caused by a respectful attitude.

Remembrance

There are many symptoms of ecstatic love caused by remembering Kṛṣṇa. For example, one friend of Kṛṣṇa informed Him, "My dear Mukunda, just after observing a bluish cloud in the sky, the lotus-eyed Rādhārāṇī immediately began to remember You. And simply by observing this cloud She became lusty for Your association." This is an instance of remembering Kṛṣṇa in ecstatic love because of seeing something resembling Him. Kṛṣṇa's bodily complexion is very similar to the bluish hue of a cloud, so simply by observing a bluish cloud, Śrīmatī Rādhārāṇī remembered Him.

One devotee said that even when he was not very attentive he would sometimes, seemingly out of madness, remember the lotus feet of Kṛṣṇa within his heart. This is an instance of remembrance resulting from constant practice. In other words, devotees who are constantly thinking of the lotus feet of Kṛṣṇa, even if they are momentarily inattentive, will see the figure of Lord Kṛṣṇa appearing within their hearts.

Argumentativeness

Madhumaṅgala was an intimate friend of Kṛṣṇa coming from the *brāhmaṇa* community. Kṛṣṇa's friends were mostly cowherd boys belonging to the *vaiśya* community, but there were others who belonged to the *brāhmaṇa* community. Actually, in Vṛndāvana the *vaiśya* community and the *brāhmaṇa* community are considered prominent. This Madhumaṅgala one day addressed Kṛṣṇa in this fashion: "My dear friend, I can see that You are not aware of the peacock feathers that are falling on the ground, and at the same time You are unmindful of the flower garlands which are offered to You. I think I can guess the reason for Your absentmindedness when I see Your two eyes flying over to the eyes of Śrīmatī Rādhārāṇī, just like black drones flying to lotus flowers." This is an instance of an argumentative suggestion in ecstatic love.

Once while Kṛṣṇa was out walking, one of the associates of Rādhārāṇī told Her, "My dear friend, do You think that this walking personality is a *tamāla* tree?* If He is a *tamāla* tree, then how is it possible for Him to walk and be so beautiful? Then, this personality might be a cloud. But if He's a cloud, then where is the beautiful moon within? Under the circumstances, I think it may be granted that this person is the same enchanting Personality of Godhead by whose flute vibration the three worlds are captivated. He must be the same Mukunda who is standing before Govardhana Hill." This is another instance of an argumentative presentation of ecstatic love.

Anxiety

In the Tenth Canto, Twenty-ninth Chapter, verse 29, of *Śrīmad-Bhāgavatam,* when Kṛṣṇa asked all the *gopīs* to go back to their homes,

* The *tamāla* tree is always described as being the same color as Kṛṣṇa.

they did not like it. Because of their grief at this, they were sighing heavily, and their beautiful faces appeared to be drying up. In this condition they remained, without making a sound. They began to draw lines on the ground with their toes, and with their tears they washed the black ointment from their eyes onto their breasts, which were covered with red *kuṅkuma* powder. This is an instance of anxiety in ecstatic love.

One of the friends of Kṛṣṇa once informed Him, "My dear killer of the demon Mura, Your kind and gentle mother is very anxious because You have not returned home, and with great difficulty she has passed the evening constantly sitting on the balcony of Your home. It is certainly astonishing how You could forget Your mother while You are off somewhere engaged in Your playful activities!" This is another instance of deep anxiety in ecstatic love.

When Mother Yaśodā was very anxiously waiting for Kṛṣṇa to return from Mathurā, Mahārāja Nanda gave her this solace: "My dear Yaśodā, please don't be worried. Please dry your beautiful lotuslike face. There is no need for you to breathe so hotly. I will go immediately with Akrūra to the palace of Kaṁsa and get your son back for you." Here is an instance of anxiety in ecstatic love caused by Kṛṣṇa's awkward position.

Thoughtfulness

In the *Vaiśākha-māhātmya* section of the *Padma Purāṇa* a devotee states that though in some of the eighteen *Purāṇas* the process of glorifying Lord Viṣṇu is not mentioned and the glorifying of some demigod is offered, such glorification must be continued for millions of years. For when one studies the *Purāṇas* very scrutinizingly, he can see that ultimately Lord Viṣṇu is the Supreme Personality of Godhead. This is an instance of ecstatic love developed out of thoughtfulness.

In the Tenth Canto, Sixtieth Chapter, verse 39, of *Śrīmad-Bhāgavatam,* there is an account of Rukmiṇī-devī's writing a letter to Kṛṣṇa requesting Him to kidnap her before her marriage to another person. At that time the specific attachment of Rukmiṇī for Kṛṣṇa was expressed by Rukmiṇī as follows: "My dear Lord Kṛṣṇa, Your transcendental glories are chanted by great sages who are free from material contamination, and in exchange for such glorification You are so kind that You freely distribute Yourself to such devotees. As one can elevate oneself simply by Your grace, so also by Your direction alone one may be lost to all benedictions, under the influence of eternal time. Therefore I have selected Your Lordship as my husband, brushing aside personalities like Brahmā and Indra—not to mention others." Rukmiṇī enhanced her love for Kṛṣṇa simply by thinking of Him. This is an instance of thoughtfulness in ecstatic love.

Endurance

When a person is fully satisfied due to attaining knowledge, transcending all distress or achieving his desired goal of life in transcendental devotional service to God, his state of endurance or steady-mindedness is called *dhṛti.* At this stage one is not perturbed by any amount of loss, nor does anything appear to be unachieved by him.

According to the opinion of Bhartṛhari, a learned scholar, when a person is elevated to this state of endurance, he thinks as follows: "I do not wish to be a highly posted government servant. I shall prefer to remain naked, without proper garments. I shall prefer to lie down on the ground without any mattress. And despite all these disadvantages, I shall refuse to serve anyone, even the government." In other words, when one is in ecstatic love with the Personality of Godhead, he can endure any kind of disadvantages calculated under the material concept of life.

Nanda Mahārāja, the father of Kṛṣṇa, used to think, "In my pasturing ground the goddess of fortune is personally present, and I possess more than ten hundred thousand cows, which loiter here and there. And above all, I have a son like Kṛṣṇa, who is such a powerful, wonderful worker. Therefore, even though I am a householder, I am feeling so satisfied!" This is an instance of mental endurance resulting from the absence of all distress.

In another instance a devotee says, "I am always swimming in the nectarean ocean of the pastimes of the Personality of Godhead, and as such I have no more attraction for religious rituals, economic development, sense gratification or even the ultimate salvation of merging into the existence of Brahman." This is an instance of the mind's endurance due to achieving the best thing in the world. The best thing in the world is absorption in Kṛṣṇa consciousness.

Happiness

It is described in the *Viṣṇu Purāṇa* that when Akrūra came to take

Kṛṣṇa and Balarāma to Mathurā, just by seeing Their faces he became so cheerful that all over his body there were symptoms of ecstatic love. This state is called happiness.

It is stated in the Tenth Canto, Thirty-third Chapter, verse 11, of *Śrīmad-Bhāgavatam,* "Upon seeing that Kṛṣṇa's arm was placed on her shoulder, one of the *gopīs* engaged in the *rāsa* dance became so ecstatically happy that she kissed Kṛṣṇa on His cheek." This is an instance of feeling happiness because of achieving a desired goal.

Eagerness

In the Tenth Canto, Seventy-first Chapter, verse 33, of *Śrīmad-Bhāgavatam,* it is said, "When Kṛṣṇa first came from His kingdom, Dvārakā, to Indraprastha,* the young females of the city became so eager to see Him that even at night, when they were lying down with their husbands, they could not restrain their eagerness. Even though they were not properly dressed and although their hair was loose and there were many household duties to perform, they still gave up everything and immediately went into the street to see Kṛṣṇa." This is an instance of eagerness in ecstatic love.

In his book *Stavāvalī,* Śrī Raghunātha dāsa Gosvāmī has prayed for the mercy of Rādhārāṇī, who was so captivated by the flute vibrations of Kṛṣṇa that She immediately asked information of His whereabouts from residents in the Vṛndāvana forest. Upon first seeing Kṛṣṇa, She was filled with such ecstatic love and pleasure that She began to scratch Her ears. The damsels of Vraja and Rādhārāṇī were very expert in talking cunningly, so as soon as they saw Kṛṣṇa they began their talkings; and Kṛṣṇa, pretending to go for some flowers for them, immediately left that place and entered into a mountain cave. This is another instance of eager loving exchanges on the parts of both the *gopīs* and Kṛṣṇa.

Violence

When Kṛṣṇa was fighting with the Kāliya snake by dancing on his heads, Kāliya bit Kṛṣṇa on the leg. At that time Garuḍa became infuriated and began to murmur, "Kṛṣṇa is so powerful that simply by His thundering voice the wives of Kāliya have had miscarriages. Because

* Indraprastha is the present-day Delhi.

my Lord has been insulted by this snake, I wish to devour him immediately, but I cannot do so in the presence of my Lord, because He may become angry with me." This is an instance of eagerness to act in ecstatic love as a result of dishonor to Kṛṣṇa.

When Śiśupāla objected to the worship of Kṛṣṇa in the Rājasūya arena at a sacrifice organized by Mahārāja Yudhiṣṭhira, Sahadeva, the younger brother of Arjuna, said, "A person who cannot tolerate the worship of Kṛṣṇa is my enemy and is possessed of a demoniac nature. Therefore I wish to strike my left foot upon his broad head, just to punish him more strongly than the wand of Yamarāja!" Then Baladeva began to lament like this: "Oh, all auspiciousness to Lord Kṛṣṇa! I am so surprised to see that the condemned descendants of the Kuru dynasty, who so unlawfully occupied the throne of the Kuru kingdom, are criticizing Kṛṣṇa with diplomatic devices. Oh, this is intolerable!" This is another instance of eagerness caused by dishonor to Kṛṣṇa.

Haughtiness, Resulting in Dishonorable Words

In the *Vidagdha-mādhava,* Jaṭilā, the mother-in-law of Rādhārāṇī, began to criticize Kṛṣṇa in this way: "Kṛṣṇa, You are standing here, and Rādhārāṇī, who has just been married to my son, is also standing here. Now I know both of You very well, so why should I not be very anxious to protect my daughter-in-law from Your dancing eyes?" This is an instance of dishonorable words used to indirectly criticize Kṛṣṇa.

Similarly, some of the *gopīs* once began to address Kṛṣṇa with these dishonorable words: "My dear Kṛṣṇa, You are a first-class thief. So please leave this place immediately. We know You love Candrāvalī more than us, but there is no use in praising her in our presence! Kindly do not contaminate the name of Rādhārāṇī in this place!" This is another instance of dishonorable words cast upon Kṛṣṇa in ecstatic love.

There is another statement in the Tenth Canto, Thirty-first Chapter, verse 16, of *Śrīmad-Bhāgavatam.* When all the *gopīs* came out of their homes to meet Kṛṣṇa in the Vṛndāvana forest, Kṛṣṇa refused to accept them and asked them to go home, giving them some moral instruction. At that time the *gopīs* spoke as follows: "Dear Kṛṣṇa, there is extreme distress in being out of Your presence, and there is extreme happiness simply in seeing You. Therefore we have all left our husbands, relatives, brothers and friends and have simply come to You, being captivated by the sound of Your transcendental flute. O infallible one, You had better know the reason for our coming here. In plain words, we are here simply because we have been captivated by the sweet sound of Your flute. We are all beautiful girls, and You are so foolish that You are rejecting our association. We do not know anyone, other than Yourself, who would miss this opportunity to associate with young girls in the dead of night!" This is another instance of indirect insults used against Kṛṣṇa in ecstatic love.

Envy

In the *Padyāvalī,* one of the friends of Rādhārāṇī once addressed Her thus: "My dear friend, please do not be too puffed up because Kṛṣṇa has decorated Your forehead with His own hand. It may be that Kṛṣṇa is yet attracted by some other beautiful girl. I see that the decoration on Your forehead is very nicely made, and so it appears that Kṛṣṇa was not too disturbed in painting it. Otherwise, He could not have painted such exact lines!" This is an instance of envy caused by Rādhā's good fortune.

In the Tenth Canto, Thirtieth Chapter, verse 30, of *Śrīmad-Bhāgavatam,* there is the following statement: "When the *gopīs* were searching for Kṛṣṇa and Rādhā before the *rāsa* dance, they thus began to speak among themselves: 'We have seen the footprints of Kṛṣṇa and Rādhā on the ground of Vṛndāvana, and they are giving us great pain, because although Kṛṣṇa is everything to us, that girl is so cunning that She has taken Him away alone and is enjoying His kissing without sharing Him with us!'" This is another instance of envy of the good fortune of Śrīmatī Rādhārāṇī.

Sometimes when the cowherd boys used to play in the forests of Vṛndāvana, Kṛṣṇa would play on one side, and Balarāma would play on another. There would be competition and mock fighting between the two parties, and when Kṛṣṇa's party was defeated by Balarāma, the boys would say, "If Balarāma's party remains victorious, then who in the world can be weaker than ourselves?" This is another instance of envy in ecstatic love.

Impudence

In the Tenth Canto, Fifty-second Chapter, verse 41, of *Śrīmad-Bhāgavatam,* Rukmiṇī addresses Kṛṣṇa in a letter as follows: "My dear unconquerable Kṛṣṇa, my marriage day is fixed for tomorrow. I request that You come to the city of Vidarbha without advertising Yourself. Then have Your soldiers and commanders suddenly surround and defeat all the strength of the King of Magadha, and by thus adopting the methods of the demons, please kidnap and marry me."

According to the Vedic system there are eight kinds of marriages, one of which is called *rākṣasa-vivāha. Rākṣasa-vivāha* refers to kidnapping a girl and marrying her by force. This is considered to be a demoniac method. When Rukmiṇī was going to be married to Śiśupāla by the choice of her elder brother, she wrote the above letter to Kṛṣṇa requesting Him to kidnap her. This is an instance of impudence in ecstatic love for Kṛṣṇa.

One of the *gopīs* said, "May Kṛṣṇa's sweet flute be washed away by the waves of the Yamunā, and let it fall into the ocean! The sweet sound of that flute is so impudent that it makes us lose all composure before our superiors."

Dizziness

Every evening at sunset Kṛṣṇa used to return from the pasturing ground where He herded cows. Sometimes when Mother Yaśodā could not hear the sweet vibration of His flute she would become very anxious, and because of this she would feel dizzy. Thus, dizziness caused by anxiety in ecstatic love for Kṛṣṇa is also possible.

When Yaśodā had tied Kṛṣṇa up one time, she began to think, "Kṛṣṇa's body is so soft and delicate. How could I have tied Him with rope?" Thinking this, her brain became puzzled, and she felt dizziness.

The *gopīs* were advised by their superiors to bolt the doors at night, but they were so carefree that they did not carry out this order very rigidly. Sometimes, by thinking of Kṛṣṇa, they became so confident of being out of all danger that they would lie down at night in the courtyards of their houses. This is an instance of dizziness in ecstatic love due to natural affection for Kṛṣṇa.

It may be questioned why devotees of Kṛṣṇa should be attacked by dizziness, which is usually considered a sign of the mode of ignorance. To answer this question, Śrī Jīva Gosvāmī has said that the devotees of Lord Kṛṣṇa are always transcendental to all the modes of material nature; when they feel dizziness or go to sleep, they are not considered to be sleeping under the modes of nature, but are accepted as being in a trance of devotional service. There is an authoritative statement in the *Garuḍa Purāṇa* about mystic *yogīs* who are under the direct shelter of the Supreme Personality of Godhead: "In all three stages of their consciousness—namely wakefulness, dreaming and deep sleep—the devotees are absorbed in thought of the Supreme Personality of Godhead. Therefore, in their complete absorption in thought of Kṛṣṇa, they do not sleep."

Sleepiness

Once Lord Baladeva began to talk in His sleep as follows: "O lotus-eyed Kṛṣṇa, Your childhood adventures are manifest simply according to Your own will. Therefore, please immediately dispose of the stubborn pride of this Kāliya serpent." By saying this, Lord Baladeva astonished the assembly of the Yadus and made them laugh for some time. Then, yawning so hard as to make ripples on His abdomen, Lord Baladeva, the bearer of the plow, returned to His deep sleep. This is an instance of sleepiness in ecstatic love.

Alertness

A devotee once stated, "I have already conquered the mode of ignorance, and I am now on the platform of transcendental knowledge. Therefore I shall be engaged only in searching after the Supreme Personality of Godhead." This is an instance of alertness in ecstatic love. Transcendental alertness is possible when the illusory condition is completely overcome. At that stage, when in contact with any reaction of material elements, such as sound, smell, touch or taste, the devotee realizes the transcendental presence of the Supreme Personality of Godhead. In this condition the ecstatic symptoms (e.g., standing of the hair on the body, rolling of the eyeballs and getting up from sleep) are persistently visible.

When Śrīmatī Rādhārāṇī first saw Kṛṣṇa, She suddenly became conscious of all transcendental happiness, and the functions of Her different limbs were stunned. When Lalitā, Her constant companion, whispered into Her ear the holy name of Kṛṣṇa, Rādhārāṇī immediately opened Her eyes wide. This is an instance of alertness caused by hearing the sound of Kṛṣṇa's name.

One day, in a joking mood, Kṛṣṇa informed Rādhārāṇī, "My dear

Rādhārāṇī, I am going to give up Your company." Upon saying this, He immediately disappeared, and because of this Rādhārāṇī became so afflicted that the hue of Her body changed, and She immediately fell down upon the ground of Vṛndāvana. She had practically stopped breathing, but when She smelled the fragrance of the flowers on the ground, She awoke in ecstasy and got up. This is an instance of transcendental alertness caused by smelling.

When Kṛṣṇa was touching the body of one *gopī,* the *gopī* addressed her companion thus: "My dear friend, whose hand is this touching my body? I had become very afraid after seeing the dark forest on the bank of the Yamunā, but suddenly the touch of this hand has saved me from hysterical fits." This is an instance of alertness caused by touching.

One of the *gopīs* informed Kṛṣṇa, "My dear Kṛṣṇa, when You disappeared from the arena of the *rāsa* dance, our most dear friend, Rādhārāṇī, immediately fell on the ground and lost consciousness. But after this, when I offered Her some of Your chewed betel nut remnants, She immediately returned to consciousness with jubilant symptoms in Her body." This is an instance of alertness caused by tasting.

One night Śrīmatī Rādhārāṇī was talking in a dream. "My dear Kṛṣṇa," She said, "please do not play any more jokes on Me! Please stop! And please don't touch My garments either. Otherwise I shall inform the elderly persons, and I shall disclose all of Your naughty behavior." While She was talking like this in a dream, She suddenly awoke and saw some of Her superiors standing before Her. Thus Rādhārāṇī became ashamed and bowed Her head. This is an instance of alertness after awakening from sleep.

There is another instance of this. A messenger from Kṛṣṇa came to Śrīmatī Rādhārāṇī while She was sleeping, and Rādhārāṇī immediately awakened. Similarly, when Kṛṣṇa began to blow on His flute in the night, all of the *gopīs,* the beautiful daughters of the cowherd men, immediately got up from their sleep. There is a very beautiful comparison made in this connection: "The lotus flower is sometimes surrounded by white swans, and sometimes it is surrounded by black wasps who are collecting its honey. When there is a thundering in the sky, the swans go away, but the black wasps stay to enjoy the lotus flowers." The *gopīs'* sleeping condition is compared to the white swans, and the sound of

Kṛṣṇa's flute is compared to a black wasp. When Kṛṣṇa's flute sounded, the white swans, which represent the sleeping condition of the *gopīs,* were immediately vanquished, and the black wasp sound of the flute began to enjoy the lotus flower of the *gopīs'* beauty.

One must see the Deity with great devotion." (p. 56) This instruction is one of the basic rinciples of Deity worship, which is an essential part of the science of God realization.

Though the devotee was only meditating on touching the hot sweet rice, when his meditatio
broke he saw that his finger was actually burnt. (p. 94) This illustrates the absolute natu
of Kṛṣṇa consciousness. By the proper practice of meditation one can directly experience th
presence of Kṛṣṇa.

“These cowherd boys are now playing with the Supreme Person as though they are on an equal level!” (p. 321) By practicing the science of devotional service, one comes to the perfectional stage of being promoted to the spiritual world and there attains the direct association of Lord Kṛṣṇa, the Supreme Personality of Godhead.

"Even the impersonalists will become attracted to the form of Kṛṣṇa, known as Śyāmasundara." (p. 186) The transcendental form of the Lord is not material. It is composed of the spiritua elements of eternal existence (*sat*), full knowledge (*cit*), and complete bliss (*ānanda*). It als possesses unlimited opulences.

We have seen that in Vṛndāvana even the cows, the deer, the birds, trees—everyone—as been enchanted by the sweet vibration of Your flute and the fascinating beauty of your erson." (p. 193) In His transcendental abode, Kṛṣṇa reveals Himself to His pure devotees, wakening within them deeper and deeper love for Him and causing them to experience ever-ıcreasing ecstasy.

"In enjoying Kṛṣṇa's attitude of stealing butter very stealthily, Mother Yaśoda experience the ecstasy of maternal love." (p. 346) All Kṛṣṇa's devotees experience their own uniqu sentiments of ecstatic love for Him, and the Lord performs different pastimes to enhan their particular relationships.

ecause of her ecstatic love for Him, Kṛṣṇa allowed Mother Yaśodā to bind Him with ropes. p. 179) Yaśodā experiences spiritual love for Kṛṣṇa that resembles the affection a mother eels for her child. After catching Him stealing butter, she dutifully chastises her naughty ranscendental son.

Sometimes Kṛṣṇa's younger friends would assist Mother Yaśodā in dressing Him. (p. 323
The spiritual world is full of ever-increasing love for the Supreme Lord. There is no way t
measure the love and devotion Kṛṣṇa's devotees feel for Him.

"When Kṛṣṇa was chastising Kāliya-nāga in the Yamunā River, the big snake wrapped his coils all over Kṛṣṇa's body." (p. 373) Kṛṣṇa performed this pastime to increase the ecstatic spiritual emotions of His devotees, who felt unlimited transcendental anxiety for His safety. In the spiritual world, devotees experience all varieties of emotions.

When the *gopīs* saw the fearful giant bull, out of the madness of love they embraced the *tamāla* trees, whose hue resembles Kṛṣṇa's complexion. (p. 240) The *gopīs* are the most intimate devotees of Kṛṣṇa and exhibit the highest love of God. Sometimes the intensity of their love causes them to act in transcendental madness.

Kṛṣṇa playfully impersonated Abhimanyu, the so-called husband of Rādhārāṇī. (p. 362) As part of His confidential amorous pastimes, Kṛṣṇa sometimes acts in joking ways to increase the love of the *gopīs*.

ŚĀNTA-RASA (Neutral Love of God)

When the *yogī* sees the eternal form of Viṣṇu and appreciates the Lord's beauty in awe and veneration, he is situated in the neutral stage of love of God. (pp. 286–87) The science of devotional service (*bhakti-yoga*) analyzes direct love of God in five main categories called *rasas,* or tastes.

DĀSYA-RASA (Transcendental Affection—Servitude)

The followers of Kṛṣṇa who live in the transcendental city of Dvārakā are all great devotees who are constantly engaged in varied personal service of the Lord. (pp. 297–98) Each soul possesses a unique loving relationship with Kṛṣṇa. When devotees return to the spiritual world, they serve Kṛṣṇa in their particular *rasa*.

SAKHYA-RASA (Fraternal Devotion)

Kṛṣṇa's friends would immediately come and try to relieve His fatigue in different ways (p. 324) Kṛṣṇa's divine energy, *yogamāyā,* causes His intimate devotees to forget that He i actually God, thus allowing them to experience pure love for Him in the *rasa* of friendship.

VĀTSALYA-RASA (Parenthood)

'Mahārāja Nanda addressed his wife, 'My dear Yaśodā, how wonderful Kṛṣṇa looks, and ıow He is increasing my transcendental bliss more and more!" (p. 345) Kṛṣṇa is the supreme njoyer, and He takes pleasure in all the varieties of love His confidential devotees offer Him.

MĀDHURYA-RASA (Devotional Service in Conjugal Love)
The intimate mellow of devotion to the Supreme in conjugal love is exhibited by Rādhā an Kṛṣṇa, but such feelings are not at all material. (p. 353) Only when a person frees himsel from all lusty desires for material sense enjoyment can he understand pure love of God in th conjugal *rasa*.

31

Additional Symptoms

ll the previously mentioned thirty-three symptoms of ecstatic love are alled *vyabhicārī,* or disturbing. All these symptoms refer to apparently isturbed conditions, but even in such disturbed conditions there is cute ecstatic love for Kṛṣṇa. These symptoms, however, can be divided nto three groups: first class, second class and third class. There are nany disturbing symptoms in ecstatic love, such as envy, anxiety, pride, ealousy, coming to a conclusion, cowardliness, forgiveness, impatience, ankering, regret, doubtfulness and impudence. These are included in ie thirty-three conditions of ecstatic love. Śrīla Rūpa Gosvāmī has ery nicely analyzed the different kinds of disturbing symptoms, and al-hough it is very difficult to find the exact English equivalents for many anskrit words used here, his analysis will now be presented.

When one becomes malicious upon seeing another's advancement of ife, his state of mind is generally called envy. When one becomes fright-ned at seeing a lightning bolt in the sky, that fearfulness brings on nxiety. Therefore, fearfulness and anxiety may be taken as one. One's esire to hide his real mentality is called *avahitthā,* or concealment, nd a desire to exhibit superiority is called pride. Both of these may be lassified under pretension. In a pretentious attitude both *avahitthā* and ride are to be found. One's inability to tolerate an offense committed y another is called *amarṣa,* and one's inability to tolerate the opu-ence of another is called jealousy. Jealousy and *amarṣa* are both caused y intolerance. One's ability to establish the correct import of a word nay be called conclusiveness. And before such a conclusive determina-on of import, there must be thoughtful consideration. Therefore, the ct of consideration is present during the establishment of a conclusion. Vhen one presents himself as ignorant, his attitude is called humil-y, and when there is absence of enthusiasm it is called cowardice.

Therefore, in humility, there is sometimes cowardice also. When the mind is steadfast it is called enduring, and one's ability to tolerate others offenses is also called endurance. Therefore, forgiveness and endurance can be synonymous. Anxiousness for time to pass is called impatience and when one sees something wonderful one is said to be struck with wonder. Impatience may be caused by being struck with wonder, and so impatience and being struck with wonder can be synonymous. When anxiety is in its dormant stage it is called hankering. Therefore, anxiety and hankering can also be synonymous. When one becomes regretful for some offense, his feeling is called bashfulness. In this way, bashfulness and regret can be synonymous. Doubtfulness is one of the aspects of argument. After exhibiting impudence one becomes restless Therefore restlessness and impudence can be synonymous.

When all such symptoms are included in ecstatic love, they are called *sañcārī*, or continuously existing ecstatic symptoms. All of these symptoms are transcendental, and they are exhibited in different ways acting and interacting under different conditions. They are like the reciprocation of love between the lover and beloved.

When a person is envious or defamed, there may be a change in the color of the body. This may be classified as *vibhāva*, or subecstasy Sometimes illusion, collapse and strong anxiety are also considered to be *vibhāva*. When there are many such symptoms, they can simply be grouped together under ecstatic love.

Śrīla Rūpa Gosvāmī says that fright, sleep, fatigue, laziness and the madness of intoxication are sometimes grouped under continuous symptoms of ecstatic love, and they are due to a strong attraction.

False argument, determination, steadiness, remembrance, joyfulness ignorance, humility and unconsciousness are also different symptoms of ecstatic love. Dependence is also grouped under ecstatic love, and this can be divided into superior dependence and inferior dependence The direct differentiations between superior and inferior dependence are ascertained by Rūpa Gosvāmī and will be presented in due course

One devotee exclaimed, "Oh, I cannot see the district of Mathurā Even though by simply hearing the name of Mathurā the hairs of my body are standing up, I cannot see the place. So of what use are my eyes?" This statement reveals a strong anxiety to see the district of Mathurā resulting from a strong attachment to Kṛṣṇa. There is another instance of this strong attachment for Kṛṣṇa expressed by Bhīma when he began to murmur, "My arms are just like thunderbolts, but despite these arms I could not smash Śiśupāla while he was blaspheming Kṛṣṇa. Therefore, of what use are these strong arms?" In this instance Bhīma became angry, and being influenced by such anger, his hopelessness became a cause for strong attachment to Kṛṣṇa. This instance can be described as strong attachment for Kṛṣṇa in anger.

When Arjuna witnessed the universal form of Kṛṣṇa, whose dazzling teeth were practically devouring the very existence of the universe, Arjuna's mouth became dried up. At that time Arjuna forgot himself and could not understand that he was Arjuna, Kṛṣṇa's friend, although he was always dependent upon Kṛṣṇa's mercy. This incident is an example of inferior dependence.

Sometimes ghastly activities also support strong ecstatic love for Kṛṣṇa. This state of mind is called ecstatic fearfulness under illusion. In the Tenth Canto, Twenty-third Chapter, verse 40, of *Śrīmad-Bhāgavatam,* there is the following statement by the *brāhmaṇas* who were performing sacrifices: "We have all been born into three advantageous conditions: we are in high *brāhmaṇa* families, we have ceremoniously received the sacred thread, and we are also properly initiated by a spiritual master. But, alas, in spite of all these advantages, we are condemned. Even our observance of *brahmacarya* is condemned." The *brāhmaṇas* thus began to condemn their own activities. They realized that in spite of being so elevated by birth, education and culture, they still were under the spell of the illusory energy. They also admitted that even great *yogīs* who are not devotees of the Lord are covered by the influence of material energy. This kind of hopelessness felt by the *brāhmaṇas* who were performing ritualistic ceremonies shows practically no attachment for Kṛṣṇa. There is another hopelessness, however, which shows attachment for Kṛṣṇa. When the bull demon attacked the damsels of Vraja, they began to cry out, "Dear Kṛṣṇa—please save us! We are now gone!" This is hopelessness with attachment for Kṛṣṇa.

When the Keśī demon was assassinated by Kṛṣṇa, Kaṁsa became hopeless. He said, "Keśī-daitya was as dear to me as my own life, but he has been killed by some cowherd boy who is crude, uneducated and ignorant in fighting. Even though I have defeated the King of heaven without difficulty, still I do not know the value of life." Because this hopelessness has a slight touch of attraction for Kṛṣṇa, it is considered to be a reflection of ecstatic love in hopelessness.

Kaṁsa once rebuked Akrūra by saying, "You are such a fool that you are accepting a cowherd boy to be the Supreme Personality of Godhead simply because He has defeated some harmless water snake! The boy may have lifted one pebble called Govardhana Hill, but what is more surprising than that is your statement that this boy is the Personality of Godhead!" This is an instance of a maliciously opposing element caused by hopelessness in ecstatic love for Kṛṣṇa.

One devotee tried to console a *kadamba* tree when the tree was lamenting because Kṛṣṇa had not touched even its shadow. The devotee said, "My dear *kadamba* tree, do not be worried. Just after defeating the Kāliya snake in the Yamunā River, Kṛṣṇa will come and satisfy your desire." This is an instance of inappropriate hopelessness in ecstatic love for Kṛṣṇa.

Garuḍa the eagle, the carrier of Viṣṇu, once said, "Who can be more pure than I? Where is there a second bird like me, so able and competent? Kṛṣṇa may not like me, He may not wish to join my party, but still He has to take advantage of my wings!" This is an instance of hopelessness in the neutral mood of ecstatic love.

The symptoms of ecstatic love are sometimes grouped under four headings—namely generation, conjunction, aggregation and satisfaction.

Kṛṣṇa once told Rādhārāṇī, "My dear friend, when You tried to meet Me alone in the morning, Your friend Mekhalā remained hungry with envy. Just look at her!" When Kṛṣṇa was joking with Rādhārāṇī in this way, Rādhārāṇī moved Her beautiful eyebrows crossly. Rūpa Gosvāmī prays that everyone may become blessed by this movement of Śrīmatī Rādhārāṇī's eyebrows. This is an instance of the generation of malice in ecstatic love of Kṛṣṇa.

One night, after the Pūtanā demon had been killed, baby Kṛṣṇa could be seen playing upon her breast. Upon seeing this, Yaśodā became stunned for some time. This is an example of a conjunction of various symptoms of ecstatic love. The conjunction can be auspicious or inauspicious. That the Pūtanā demon had been killed was auspicious, but that Kṛṣṇa was playing on her breast in the dead of night, with no one to help Him in case of trouble, was inauspicious. Yaśodā was caught between auspiciousness and inauspiciousness.

After Kṛṣṇa had just learned to walk, He was going in and out of the house very frequently. Yaśodā became surprised and said, "This child is too restless and cannot be controlled! He is incessantly going about the neighborhood of Gokula [Vṛndāvana], and then He is coming back inside the house. I see that the child is very fearless, but in spite of His fearlessness, I am becoming more and more afraid of His falling into some danger." This again is an instance of the conjunction of two opposing elements: the child was very fearless, but at the same time Yaśodā was becoming fearful of some danger. Here danger is the cause, and Yaśodā's feelings are in a conjunction of two opposing symptoms. In other words, Yaśodā was feeling both happiness and doubt, or growing fear.

When Devakī, the mother of Kṛṣṇa, saw her son very jubilant in the presence of the wrestlers in Kaṁsa's arena, two kinds of tears were simultaneously gliding down her cheeks: sometimes her tears were warm, and sometimes they were cold. This is an instance of a conjunction of jubilation and lamentation due to different causes of ecstatic love.

Once when Śrīmatī Rādhārāṇī was standing on the bank of the Yamunā River in the forest of Vṛndāvana, She was attacked by Kṛṣṇa, who was stronger than She. Although She externally expressed a disturbed mood from this incident, within Herself She was smiling and feeling great satisfaction. Externally She moved Her eyebrows and made a show of rejecting Kṛṣṇa. In this mood Rādhārāṇī looked very beautiful, and Śrīla Rūpa Gosvāmī glorifies Her beauty. This is an instance of exhibiting varying feelings in ecstatic love, although the cause is one only—Kṛṣṇa.

Sometimes there were great festivals in the house of Nanda Mahārāja, and all of the inhabitants of Vṛndāvana would assemble for these festivals. During one such festival, Śrīmatī Rādhārāṇī was seen wearing a golden necklace given Her by Kṛṣṇa. This was immediately detected by Mother Yaśodā as well as by Rādhārāṇī's mother, because the necklace was too long for Rādhārāṇī's neck. At the same time Rādhārāṇī could see Kṛṣṇa nearby, as well as Her own husband, Abhimanyu. So all of these things combined to make Rādhārāṇī feel very much ashamed, and with Her face shriveled She began to look very beautiful. In this case there was a combination of bashfulness, anger, jubilation and lamentation. This is an instance of an aggregate of symptoms of ecstatic love.

Kaṁsa once said, "What harm can this boy do to me? He has no power." The next moment Kaṁsa was informed that all of his friends had been killed by the boy. Then Kaṁsa began to think in perplexity, "Shall I go immediately and surrender unto Him? But how can a great warrior do this?" The next moment he thought, "Why should *I* be afraid of *Him*? There are still so many wrestlers standing to support me." But the next moment he began to consider, "The boy is certainly not common, because He has lifted Govardhana Hill with His left hand. So what can I do in this connection? Let me go to Vṛndāvana and inflict pains on all the residents there. But still I cannot even go out, because my heart is trembling from fear of this boy!" This condition of Kaṁsa's mind reveals an instance of pride, lamentation, humility, determination, remembrance, doubtfulness, anger and fear. Actually eight different symptoms comprised the mental condition of Kaṁsa. This is another instance of an aggregate of symptoms in hopeless ecstatic love.

One householder devotee once said, "My Lord, I am so wretched that these two eyes are never desiring to see the glorious city of Mathurā. Therefore, my eyes are actually condemned. I am nicely educated, but my education has simply been used in government service. I have not considered formidable time, stronger than anything else, which creates and annihilates everything. To whom shall I leave all of my wealth and fortune? I am becoming older and older. What shall I do? Shall I execute devotional service from here at home? This I cannot do, because my mind is being attracted by the transcendental land of Vṛndāvana."

This is an instance of hopelessness, pride, doubt, patience, lamentation, determination and eagerness—an aggregation of seven different symptoms in ecstatic love for Kṛṣṇa.

There is a proverb in Sanskrit which says, "Disappointment gives rise to the greatest satisfaction." In other words, when one's sentiment or ambition becomes too great and is not fulfilled until after seemingly hopeless tribulation, that is taken as the greatest satisfaction. Once the cowherd boys in Vṛndāvana were vainly searching after Kṛṣṇa for a long time, and for that reason their faces became blackened, and their complexions appeared faded. Just then they could hear on the hill a faint vibration from Kṛṣṇa's flute. Immediately all of them became very much gladdened. This is an instance of satisfaction in the midst of disappointment.

Śrīla Rūpa Gosvāmī says that although he has no expert knowledge about the sounds and meanings and mellows of the symptoms of ecstatic love, he has tried to give some examples of different varieties of love of Kṛṣṇa. He further states that the thirty-three disturbing symptoms of ecstatic love, plus eight other symptoms, all taken together equal forty-one primary symptoms of ecstatic love. These symptoms create transformations of bodily activities as well as movements of the senses. All of them can be accepted as different feelings of the heart. Sometimes some of the feelings are quite natural. Sometimes some of the feelings are just temporary appearances. Those symptoms which are very natural always remain, both within and without the devotee.

As one can detect the color of dye a cloth was soaked in by looking at the cloth, so, simply by understanding the different signs of these symptomatic features, one can understand the actual position. In other words, attachment for Kṛṣṇa is one, but because there exist different kinds of devotees, such attachment is manifested in many varieties. As clothing tinged red appears red, so the temporary appearance of a certain type of feeling can be detected or observed by the specific ecstatic symptom. In fact, all the different humors and mellows of the devotees produce various specific feelings within the mind. And according to these differences, the symptoms of ecstatic love appear in different forms and degrees. If one's heart is highly elevated, grave and magnanimous, or if one's heart is rough and crude, different symptoms of ecstatic love will appear, influenced by the condition of the heart. Actually, people cannot generally understand such different qualities of mentality, but when one's heart is very soft or gentle, these symptoms become very easily visible, and one can understand them very clearly. The heart of one who is highly elevated and grave is compared to gold. If one's heart is very soft and gentle, his heart is compared to a cotton swab. When there is an ecstatic sensation within the mind, the golden heart or grave heart is not agitated, but the soft heart immediately becomes agitated.

To offer another example, a grave, magnanimous heart is compared to a great city, and a soft heart to an insignificant cottage. There may be many lights, or even great elephants in the big city, but no one will take particular notice of them. But when such lights or elephants are seen near a small cottage, everyone can distinctly point them out.

A hard heart is compared to a lightning bolt, to gold and to lac. The lightning bolt is very strong and never becomes soft. Similarly, the hearts of those who are engaged in severe austerities and penances do not become very easily softened. The golden heart becomes melted at high temperature, as in ecstatic love. And the lac heart is very easily melted in slight temperature.

A soft heart is compared to honey, to butter and to nectar. And the condition of the mind is compared to sunshine. As honey and butter become melted even in slight sunshine, softhearted persons become easily melted. Nectar, however, is by its nature always liquid. And the hearts of those who are in pure ecstatic love with Kṛṣṇa are by nature always liquefied, just like nectar.

A pure devotee of Kṛṣṇa is always specifically qualified with nectarean qualifications and sometimes with the qualifications of butter and honey. On the whole, the heart in any of the different conditions mentioned above can be melted under certain circumstances, just as a hard diamond is sometimes melted by a combination of certain chemicals. In the *Dāna-keli-kaumudī* it is stated, "When love develops in the heart of a devotee, he cannot check the transformation of his sentiments. His heart is just like the ocean at the rising of the moon, when the ebb tide cannot be checked: immediately there must be movement of high waves." Although in its natural state the ocean is always grave and unfathomable, when the moon rises, nothing can check the ocean's agitation. Similarly, those who are pure devotees cannot on any account check the movement of their feelings within.

32

Symptoms of Continuous Ecstasy

The continuous ecstasy of love can remain like a powerful king, subduing all temporary manifestations of love as well as any opposing elements of anger. It can be exhibited directly or indirectly, and thus ecstatic love can be described as direct or indirect. These symptoms of ecstatic love are possible only when one is fully situated in a transcendental position. Direct ecstatic love can be divided into two groups—namely, selfish and selfless.

When noncontradictory symptoms of ecstatic love are distinctly manifest, any contradictory symptoms create a sense of abomination. Contradictory ecstatic love is called selfish. That ecstatic love which can adjust all contradictory or noncontradictory symptoms is called direct selfless love. These selfless symptoms can again be divided into five groups: neutrality, servitude, fraternity, parenthood and conjugal love. Such ecstatic love assumes a particular mode in contact with different objects of love.

Neutrality

Neutrality can be further subdivided into general, transparent and peaceful. An attraction for Kṛṣṇa by the people in general or by children cannot take any specific or satisfactory position. It can be manifest sometimes in trembling of the body and changing of the color of the eyes (to red, white, etc.), although there is no symptom of any particular affection.

One old man was told by a young man, "Just see how this child—only three years old—is so jubilant! Simply by seeing Kṛṣṇa he is running so swiftly, making a tumultuous sound. Just see!" This is an instance of neutral ecstatic love in the heart of a child, without any specific subdivision.

Due to the different types of attraction for Kṛṣṇa, there are different varieties of devotees. Their symptoms are manifested transparently, just like jewels. It is said that a great devotee *brāhmaṇa* would sometimes address the Supreme Personality of Godhead as master and sometimes joke with the Lord, using different kinds of familiar words. Sometimes he would protect the Lord with a paternal affection, sometimes he would cry out to the Lord, addressing the Lord as his beloved, and sometimes he would meditate on the Lord as the Supersoul. This means that the *brāhmaṇa* expressed his ecstatic loving symptoms in different ways at different times. But in each instance, because of ecstatic love, the *brāhmaṇa* merged himself in the ocean of happiness and became situated in pure love. Thus he was a transparent medium, like a jewel that shows reality in varying colors according to its own nature.

When the great sage Nārada was glorifying the pastimes of the Lord with his *vīṇā,* the four Kumāras, headed by Sanaka, although merged in the impersonal conception of Brahman, were trembling all over. Another devotee once exclaimed, "Although I can achieve liberation simply by serving the devotees, my mind is still very much anxious to see the Supreme Personality of Godhead, whose bodily complexion is just like a dark cloud." When a devotee is so anxious to contact the Supreme Personality of Godhead, that can also be accepted as a symptom of neutral love.

Pure and Mixed Flavors

Generally, a devotee of Lord Kṛṣṇa may be placed into one of three groups. One group consists of those who are completely dependent on the merciful affection of the Supreme Personality of Godhead, another group consists of devotees who are dealing with Kṛṣṇa on friendly terms and the third group consists of those who are dealing with Kṛṣṇa as His superiors, with parental affection. These three classes of devotees gradually develop different relationships of transcendental mellow with the Personality of Godhead. When the attraction for Kṛṣṇa is based on only one particular humor, that humor is called *kevalā,* or the pure state. One in this pure state of devotional service gradually develops the desire to follow in the footsteps of an eternal associate of Kṛṣṇa, e.g., to follow in the footsteps of Rasāla, the personal attendant of Kṛṣṇa in Goloka Vṛndāvana, or to follow Kṛṣṇa's friends, like Śrīdāmā and Sudāmā, or to follow Nanda and Yaśodā, devotees in parenthood. Ecstatic love for Kṛṣṇa is never manifested directly with Kṛṣṇa Himself. The devotee has to follow in the footsteps of the eternal associates of Kṛṣṇa in Goloka Vṛndāvana.

When transcendental humors in relationship with Kṛṣṇa become mixed (e.g., when the relationships with Kṛṣṇa in friendship, servitorship and parental love become mixed together), the result is called mixed humor or flavor. Such mixed transcendental flavors are manifested by such devotees as Uddhava, Bhīma and Mukharā, the personal attendant of Mother Yaśodā. Although devotional humors are sometimes found in mixtures, a particular humor is always found to be a prominent and constant factor. That prominent humor is to be accepted as the devotee's main relationship with Kṛṣṇa. For example, Uddhava is in relationship with Kṛṣṇa as a friend, but in Uddhava's character a trace of servitude to Kṛṣṇa is also visible. Such friendship is called friendship in reverence. The friendship typified by Śrīdāmā and Sudāmā, however, is the standard of friendship without any tinge of reverence.

Subordinate Ecstatic Love

The devotees who always think of Kṛṣṇa as a superior are in subordinate ecstatic love. To such a devotee the concept of inferiority to the Lord is very prominent, and he rarely takes interest in any other kind of transcendental loving humor with the Lord.

In the *Mukunda-mālā-stotra,* compiled by King Kulaśekhara, one of the prayers says, "My dear Lord, You are the deliverer of living entities from the hellish condition of materialistic life, but that does not matter to me. Whether I am elevated to the heavenly platform or remain on this earthly planet or am dispatched to some hellish planet, that does not matter at all to me. My only prayer is that at the time of my death I may simply remember Your two beautiful feet, which are just like lotus flowers fructifying during the autumn season."

Friendship

As far as friendship is concerned, those high-grade devotees who are almost like Kṛṣṇa are considered to be great authorities in the modes of friendly relations with the Supreme Personality of Godhead. On that friendly platform there are different kinds of laughing and joking conversations. For example, once Kṛṣṇa was thinking, "Today, while I was engaged in tending the cows in the pasturing ground of Vṛndāvana, I went to collect some flowers in a beautiful garden. At that time My friends, the cowherd boys, were unhappy even to tolerate a two-minute separation from Me. And when they found Me, there was competition between us as to who would touch the other first with the flowers we had in hand."

One friend criticized Kṛṣṇa thus: "My dear Dāmodara, although You have been defeated by Śrīdāmā and have become sufficiently minimized in strength, by a false expression of strength You have somehow covered Your shameful condition of defeat."

Parenthood, or Superiority

When Mother Yaśodā heard that Kṛṣṇa's cows were being forcibly moved by the strong servants of Kaṁsa and that the tender cowherd boys were trying to protect their cows, she began to think, "How can I protect these poor boys from the invasion of Kaṁsa's servants?" This is an instance of a superior attitude in a devotee.

As soon as Mother Yaśodā found her son Kṛṣṇa returning from the pasturing ground, she immediately began to pat Him, touching her fingers to the cheeks of the Lord.

Conjugal Love

Above even the humor of love between Kṛṣṇa and His parents is the relationship of conjugal love. The Lord and the young *gopīs* exhibit this in different ways—glancing, moving the eyebrows, speaking very sweet words and exchanging smiles.

There is a statement in *Govinda-vilāsa* to this effect: "Śrīmatī Rādhārāṇī was looking for Kṛṣṇa very anxiously and almost disappointedly." When there is such an indirect expression of conjugal love, there is smiling, astonishment, enthusiasm, lamentation, anger, dread and sometimes ghastliness. These seven exchanges of conjugal love form another state of ecstatic love.

In a direct relationship of conjugal love, there is laughter, astonishment, chivalry, lamentation, anger and dread, but there is no ghastliness. These expressions are considered to be great reservoirs of pleasure. When these seven kinds of ecstatic loving exchanges are manifested, they attain the status of steadiness by which the taste of conjugal love expands.

33

Indirect Expressions of Ecstatic Love

Laughter

After He had stolen some yogurt from the pots of two *gopīs*, Kṛṣṇa told one of His *gopī* friends, "My dear beautiful friend, I can take an oath that I have not stolen even a drop of yogurt from your pot! But still your friend Rādhārāṇī is very shamelessly smelling the flavor of My mouth. Kindly forbid Her from this devious policy of putting Her face near Mine." When Kṛṣṇa was speaking like this, the friends of Rādhārāṇī could not check their laughter. This is an instance of laughter in ecstatic love.

Astonishment

Once Brahmā was watching all the cows and the cowherd boys dressed in yellow garments and decorated with valuable jewels. The boys were expanding their four arms and were being worshiped by many hundreds of other Brahmās. All the cowherd boys began to express their joyfulness for being with Kṛṣṇa, the Supreme Brahman. At that time, Brahmā showed his astonishment by exclaiming, "What am I seeing here?" This is an instance of astonishment in ecstatic love.

Chivalry

On the bank of the Yamunā, once there was the crackling sound of dry leaves, giggling from the cowherd boys and thundering from the sky. Śrīdāmā was tightening his belt to fight with Kṛṣṇa, the conqueror of the demon Agha. This is an instance of chivalry in ecstatic love.

Lamentation

In the Tenth Canto, Seventh Chapter, verse 25, of *Śrīmad-Bhāgavatam*, there is a description of Kṛṣṇa's being taken away by the whirlwind demon, Tṛṇāvarta. As Kṛṣṇa was being thus carried up into the sky, all the *gopīs* began to cry aloud. They approached Mother Yaśodā, stating that they could not find the son of Nanda. He had been taken away by a whirlwind. This is an instance of lamentation in ecstatic love.

When Kṛṣṇa was fighting with Kāliya, Mother Yaśodā exclaimed, "Kṛṣṇa is now entrapped within the hoods of the Kāliya snake, and yet I am not tattered to pieces! So I must admit how wonderful is the preserving power of this material body!" This is another instance of lamentation in ecstatic love.

Anger

When Jaṭilā, the mother of Abhimanyu, saw Kṛṣṇa wearing a necklace, she could understand that the jeweled ornament had been given to Him by Rādhārāṇī. She therefore became absorbed in anger and began to move her eyebrows, expressing her anger in ecstatic love.

Ghastliness

There is a statement by Yāmunācārya to this effect: "Since I have begun to enjoy these transcendental exchanges of love, which are always newer and newer, whenever I remember the pleasure of past sex life, my lips curl and I wish to spit on the idea." This is an instance of ecstatic love in ghastliness.

Dread

One old devotee said, "My dear Lord, when we are away from You we become so anxious to see You again, and there is great misery in our lives. But then when we do see You, there immediately comes the fear of separation. Under the circumstances, both when we see You and when we do not see You, we are subjected to different kinds of tribulation." This is an instance of a contradictory mixture of ecstatic love for Kṛṣṇa. Such ecstatic love is palatable, and expert critics have compared such ecstatic love to a mixture of curd, sugar candy and a little black pepper. The combined taste is very palatable.

34

The Nectar of Devotion

The particular type of ecstatic loving sentiment that develops within the heart of a particular devotee is considered to be *vibhāva*. And the resultant manifestations such as moving of the eyebrows, fear, astonishment and smiling, which have been explained hereinbefore, are called *anubhāva*. The different causes for developing *anubhāva* and *vibhāva* are called steady ecstasy, or *sañcāri-bhāva*.

Whenever there is a recitation of poetry or a dramatic play on the different pastimes of Kṛṣṇa, the audience develops different kinds of transcendental loving service for the Lord. They enjoy different types of *vibhava, anubhāva* and *sañcāri-bhāva*.

No one, while remaining on the material platform, should discuss these different descriptions of *bhāva* and *anubhāva* by quoting different statements of transcendental literatures. Such manifestations are displays of the transcendental pleasure potency of the Lord. One should simply try to understand that on the spiritual platform there are many varieties of reciprocal love. Such loving exchanges should never be considered to be material. In the *Mahābhārata, Bhīṣma-parva,* it is warned that things which are inconceivable should not be subjected to arguments. Actually, the transactions of the spiritual world are inconceivable to us in our present state of life. Great liberated souls like Rūpa Gosvāmī and others have tried to give us some hints of transcendental activities in the spiritual world, but on the whole these transactions will remain inconceivable to us at the present moment. Understanding the exchanges of transcendental loving service with Kṛṣṇa is possible only when one is actually in touch with the pleasure potency of the Supreme Lord.

In this connection Śrī Rūpa Gosvāmī gives an example of the clouds in the sky. The clouds in the sky arise from the ocean, and when the clouds become water again and fall to the ground, they glide back to the ocean.

Thus the pleasure potency of Kṛṣṇa is compared to the ocean. The pure devotee is the pleasure-possessing cloud, and when he is filled with transcendental loving service, then he can bestow his mercy as a downpour of rain—and the pleasure potency returns to the ocean of Kṛṣṇa.

Direct and Indirect Attraction for Kṛṣṇa

Transcendental pleasure derived from devotional service can be divided into two groups: direct devotional service and indirect devotional service. Direct devotional service is divided into five transcendental humors or flavors, and indirect devotional service is divided into seven transcendental humors. Direct devotional services are as follows: neutrality, servitude, fraternity, parenthood and conjugal love. Indirect devotional service is divided into laughter, compassion, anger, chivalry, dread, astonishment and ghastliness. Devotional service can therefore be divided into twelve types, each of which has a different color. The colors are white, multicolored, orange, red, light green, gray, yellow, off-whitish, smoky, pink, black and cloudy. The twelve different kinds of transcendental humors are controlled by different incarnations of God, such as Kapila, Mādhava, Upendra, Nṛsiṁha, Nanda-nandana, Balarāma, Kūrma, Kalki, Rāghava, Bhārgava, Varāha and Matsya.

Sustenance, manifestation, expansion, reflection and lamentation are the five visible symptoms in exchanges of ecstatic love. The test of devotional service can therefore be made in terms of these five symptoms. In the devotional service of neutrality there is sustenance, in chivalrous devotional service there is expansion, in compassionate devotional service there is reflection, in angry devotional service there is lamentation, and so on.

An apparently pitiable condition in devotional service may appear distressing to the inexperienced student, but the feelings of the devotee in this pitiable condition are considered to be ecstatic by expert devotees. For example, the subject matter of the *Rāmāyaṇa* is sometimes considered pitiable and distressing to the heart, but actually that is not the fact. The *Rāmāyaṇa* narrates how Lord Rāma was sent to the forest by His father just when He was going to be enthroned. After Lord Rāma's departure, Mahārāja Daśaratha, His father, died. In the forest His wife, Sītādevī, was kidnapped by Rāvaṇa, and there was a great war. When Sītādevī was finally delivered from the clutches of Rāvaṇa,

Rāvaṇa's whole family and kingdom, and Rāvaṇa himself, were vanquished. When Sītādevī came home she was tried by fire, and after some days she was again banished to the forest. All of these subjects in the *Rāmāyaṇa* seem very pitiable, and they may appear very distressing to the reciter, but actually they are not. Otherwise, why would Hanumān, the great devotee of Lord Rāmacandra, read daily about the activities of Lord Rāmacandra, as described in the *Rāmāyaṇa* itself? The fact is that in any of the above-mentioned twelve transcendental humors of devotional service, everything is transcendentally pleasing.

Śrīla Rūpa Gosvāmī mourns in this connection for persons who are in the fire of false renunciation, the dry speculative habit, and who neglect devotional service. Persons who are attached to the ritualistic ceremonies recommended in the *Vedas* and to the impersonal Brahman cannot relish the transcendental pleasure of devotional service. Śrī Rūpa Gosvāmī advises, therefore, that devotees who have already tasted the nectar of devotion be very careful to protect devotional service from such dry speculators, formal ritualistic elevationists and impersonal salvationists. Devotees should protect their valuable jewel of spiritual love from the clutches of thieves and burglars. In other words, a pure devotee should not describe devotional service and its different analytical aspects to dry speculators and false renouncers.

Those who are not devotees can never achieve the benefits of devotional service. For them the subject of devotional service is always very difficult to understand. Only persons who have dedicated their lives unto the lotus feet of the Supreme Personality of Godhead can relish the real nectar of devotion.

When one transcends the status of ecstatic love and thus becomes situated on the highest platform of pure goodness, one is understood to have cleansed the heart of all material contamination. In that pure stage of life, one can taste this nectar, and this tasting capacity is technically called *rasa,* or transcendental mood.

Thus ends the Bhaktivedanta summary study of the second division of Bhakti-rasāmṛta-sindhu, *in the matter of general devotional service.*

PART THREE

35

Neutral Love of God

Śrīla Rūpa Gosvāmī offers his respectful prayers to the eternal Supreme Personality of Godhead, who is always so beautiful and to whom the pure devotees are always engaged in loving transcendental service. This third division of *Bhakti-rasāmṛta-sindhu* describes the five primary kinds of devotional service—namely neutrality, servitude, fraternity, parenthood and conjugal love. These five items will be very elaborately explained here, and thus they have been figuratively described as the five waves on the western side of this ocean of the nectar of devotion.

When one is actually able to maintain the transcendental position, his stage is called neutrality in devotional service. Some great sages have attained this neutral position by practicing austerity, penance and meditation to control the senses. Such sages are generally called mystic *yogīs,* and in most cases they are inclined to appreciate the spiritual pleasure of the impersonal feature of the Absolute Truth. They are practically unaware of the transcendental pleasure derived from personal contact with the Supreme Godhead.

Actually the transcendental pleasure derived in association with the Supreme Person is far greater than the pleasure derived from impersonal Brahman realization, because of the direct meeting with the eternal form of the Lord. Impersonalists do not directly derive the transcendental pleasure of association with the Lord by hearing of His pastimes. As such, the impersonalists cannot derive any relishable transcendental pleasure from the topics of *Bhagavad-gītā,* in which the Lord is personally talking with Arjuna. The basic principle of their impersonal attitude does not allow them the transcendental pleasure which is relished by a devotee whose basic principle of understanding is the Supreme Person. The impersonalistic commentary on *Bhagavad-gītā* is therefore disastrous, because without understanding the transcendental pleasure of the

Gītā, the impersonalist wants to interpret it in his own way. If an impersonalist can, however, come in contact with a pure devotee, his transcendental position can be changed for greater elevation. Great sages are therefore recommended to worship the form of the Lord in order to achieve that highest transcendental pleasure.

Without worshiping the *arcā-vigraha,* the form or Deity of the Lord, one cannot understand such literature as *Bhagavad-gītā* and *Śrīmad-Bhāgavatam.* For those great sages situated in the position of transcendental neutrality, the beginning should be to take shelter of Lord Viṣṇu, the four-handed eternal form of the Supreme Personality of Godhead. The mystic *yogīs* are therefore advised to meditate on the form of Lord Viṣṇu, as recommended by Kapila Muni in the *sāṅkhya-yoga* system. Unfortunately, many mystic *yogīs* try to meditate on something void, and as stated in the *Gītā,* the result is that they simply undergo trouble and do not achieve any tangible result.

When some great saintly persons who had undergone penances and austerities saw the four-handed transcendental form of Viṣṇu, they remarked, "This four-handed form of the Lord, manifested in a bluish color, is the reservoir of all pleasure and the center of our living force. Actually, when we see this eternal form of Viṣṇu, we, along with many other *paramahaṁsas,* become immediately captivated by the beauty of the Lord." This appreciation of Lord Viṣṇu by saintly persons is an instance of situation in *śānta-rasa,* or the neutral stage of devotional service. In the beginning, those who are aspiring for salvation try to get out of the material entanglement by performing painful austerities and penances, and ultimately they come to the impersonal status of spiritual realization. At this *brahma-bhūta* stage of liberation from material entanglement, the symptoms, as explained in *Bhagavad-gītā,* are that one becomes joyous beyond any hankering or lamentation and gains a universal vision. When the devotee is situated in the *śānta-rasa,* or neutral stage of devotional service, he appreciates the Viṣṇu form of the Lord.

Actually, all Vedic culture is aiming at understanding Lord Viṣṇu. In the *Ṛg Veda* one *mantra* says that any advanced saintly person is always aspiring to be fixed in meditation upon the lotus feet of Viṣṇu.

In *Śrīmad-Bhāgavatam* it is said that the foolish do not know that Viṣṇu is the ultimate goal of life. According to the conclusion of all authoritative Vedic scriptures, when a person comes to the stage of appreciating Viṣṇu, he is at the beginning of devotional service. If one cultivates devotional service further and further, under proper guidance, other features of devotional service will gradually become manifest. At this stage of *śānta-rasa,* one can see Lord Viṣṇu, the Supreme Personality of Godhead, the deliverer of even the demons. The Lord is appreciated by such would-be devotees as the eternal transcendental form, the chief of all self-realized souls, the Supersoul and the Supreme Brahman. He is also appreciated as being completely peaceful, completely controlled and pure, merciful to the devotees and untouched by any material condition. This appreciation of Lord Viṣṇu in awe and veneration by the saintly is to be understood as the sign that they are situated in the *śānta-rasa,* or the neutral stage of devotional service.

This stage of *śānta-rasa* can be attained by the impersonalists only when they are in association with pure devotees. Otherwise it is not possible. After Brahman realization, when a liberated soul comes in contact with a pure devotee of Lord Kṛṣṇa and submissively accepts the teachings of Lord Kṛṣṇa without misinterpretation, he becomes situated in this neutral stage of devotional service. The best example of saintly persons situated in the *śānta-rasa* are Sanaka, Sanātana, Sananda and Sanat-kumāra, the Kumāra brothers. These four saintly persons (known as Catuḥ-sana) are sons of Lord Brahmā. After their birth, when they were ordered by their father to become householders and increase human society, they refused the order. They said that they had already decided not to become entangled with family life; they would rather live as saintly *brahmacārīs* for their own perfection. So these great saints have been living for millions of years now, but still they appear to be just like boys of four or five years. Their complexions are very fair, there is an effulgence in their bodies, and they always travel naked. These four saintly persons almost always remain together.

In one of the prayers of the Kumāra brothers, this declaration is made: "O Lord Mukunda [Kṛṣṇa, the giver of liberation], only so long as one does not happen to see Your eternal form of bliss and knowledge, appearing just like a newly-grown *tamāla* tree, with a bluish hue—only for so long can the impersonal feature of the Absolute Truth, known as Brahman, be very pleasing to a saintly person."

The qualifications of a saintly person are described in the *Bhakti-rasāmṛta-sindhu* as follows. A saintly person is one who understands fully that simply by discharging devotional service he can become confident of liberation. He is always situated in the regulative principles of devotional life and at the same time aspires to be liberated from material entanglement.

A saintly person thinks like this: "When shall I be able to live alone in the caves of the mountains? When shall I be dressed simply with undergarments? When shall I be satisfied by eating simply a little fruit and vegetables? When will it be possible for me to think always of the lotus feet of Mukuṇda, who is the source of the Brahman effulgence? When, in such a spiritual condition of life, shall I fully understand my days and nights to be insignificant moments in eternal time?"

The devotees and self-realized persons who are engaged in preaching the glories of the Lord always maintain an ecstatic love for the Lord within their hearts. Thus they are benefited by the rays of the ecstatic moon, and they are called saintly persons.

The impulse of a saintly person is to be engaged in the study of the *Vedas,* especially the Upaniṣadic portions, to live always in a place where there is no disturbance from the common people, to think always of the eternal form of Kṛṣṇa, to be ready to consider and understand the Absolute Truth, to be always prominent in exhibiting knowledge, to see the Supreme Lord in His universal form (*viśva-rūpa*), to associate always with learned devotees and to discuss the conclusion of the *Vedas* with similarly elevated persons. All of these qualifications of a saintly person serve to raise him to the status of *śānta-rasa.*

In the *Bhakti-rasāmṛta-sindhu* it is stated that all those who attended the pious meeting held by Lord Brahmā for the study of Vedic literature like the *Upaniṣads* became overwhelmed with ecstatic love for Kṛṣṇa, the chief of the Yadu dynasty. Actually, the result of studying the *Upaniṣads* is to understand the Supreme Personality of Godhead. Negation of material existence is only one of the subjects of the *Upaniṣads.* The next subject concerns becoming situated in the impersonal realization. And then, after penetrating through the impersonal Brahman, when one comes to the platform of associating with the Supreme Personality of Godhead, one reaches the ultimate goal in studying the *Upaniṣads.*

Those who are situated on the platform of *śānta-rasa* get their impetus for advancement in devotional service by smelling the *tulasī* offered at the lotus feet of the Lord, by hearing the sound of His conchshell, by seeing a sanctified place in some mountain or hill, by observing a forest like the ones in Vṛndāvana, by going to a place of pilgrimage, by visiting the course of the Ganges River, by being victorious over the dictations of bodily demands (i.e., eating, sleeping, mating and defending), by understanding the devastation of eternal time and by constantly associating with devotees engaged in Kṛṣṇa consciousness. All these different items are favorable in elevating saintly persons situated in *śānta-rasa* to the advanced stage of devotional service.

In the Third Canto, Fifteenth Chapter, verse 43, of the *Śrīmad-Bhāgavatam,* there is a statement concerning the four saintly persons known as Catuḥ-sana, headed by Sanaka-kumāra. They went to visit the Lord of Vaikuṇṭhaloka in the spiritual sky, and when they bowed down before the Lord, the aroma of the *tulasī,* mixed with saffron, entered their nostrils and immediately attracted their minds. Although these four saintly persons were always absorbed in the thought of impersonal Brahman, from association with the Lord and from smelling the *tulasī* leaves the hairs on their bodies immediately stood up. This shows that even a person who is situated in Brahman realization, if he is put into association with devotees in pure devotional service, will immediately become attracted to the personal feature of the Lord.

There are certain symptoms of great sages who are situated in *śānta-rasa* devotional service, and these symptoms are exhibited as follows. They concentrate their eyesight on the tip of the nose, and they behave just like an *avadhūta. Avadhūta* means a highly elevated mystic who does not care for any social, religious or Vedic conventions. Another symptom is that such persons are very careful to step forward when giving speeches. When they speak, they join together the forefinger and thumb. (This is called the *jñana-mudrā* position.) They are not against the atheists, nor are they particularly inclined to the devotees. Such persons give stress to liberation and detachment from the materialistic way of life. They are always neutral and have no affection for nor misidentification with anything material. They are always grave, but fully absorbed in thoughts of the Supreme Personality of Godhead. These uncommon features develop in devotees who are situated in *śānta-rasa.*

Regarding concentration of the eyesight on the tip of the nose, there is a statement in the *Bhakti-rasāmṛta-sindhu* by a devotee who observed this being performed by a *yogī.* He remarked, "This great sage is concentrating his eyesight on the tip of his nose, and from this it appears that he has already realized the eternal form of the Lord within himself."

Sometimes a devotee in *śānta-rasa* yawns, stretches his limbs, instructs on devotional service, offers respectful obeisances unto the form of the Lord, offers nice prayers to the Lord and has a desire to give direct service with his body. These are some of the common symptoms of the devotee who is situated in neutrality. One devotee, after observing the yawning of another devotee, addressed him thus: "My dear mystic, I think that within your heart there is some ecstatic devotional love which is causing you to yawn." It is sometimes found that a devotee in the *śānta-rasa* falls down on the ground, his hairs stand up on his body, and he trembles all over. In this way, different symptoms of ecstatic trance are exhibited automatically by such devotees.

In the *Bhakti-rasāmṛta-sindhu* it is said that when Lord Kṛṣṇa was blowing His conchshell, known as Pāñcajanya, many great sages who were living in the caves of the mountains immediately reacted, being awakened from their trance of meditation. They immediately saw that the hairs of their bodies were standing. Sometimes devotees in *śānta-rasa* become stunned, peaceful, jubilant, deliberate, reflective, anxious, dexterous and argumentative. These symptoms indicate continuous ecstasy, or established emotion.

Once a great realized sage was lamenting that the Supreme Lord Kṛṣṇa was living in Dvārakā but that he was unable to take advantage of seeing Him. After thinking this, the sage immediately became stunned. He was thinking that he was simply wasting his time. In other words, the sage lamented because the Supreme Personality of Godhead was personally present but he still could not take advantage of this because of his meditation.

When a mystic is transcendental to all kinds of mental concoctions and is situated in Brahman, his state is called trance, beyond the influence of the material conception of life. In that stage, when one hears about the transcendental pastimes of the Lord, there may be shivering in the body.

When a Brahman-realized devotee who has come to the stage of steady trance comes into contact with the eternal form of Kṛṣṇa, his transcendental pleasure increases millions of times. One great sage once inquired from another, "My dear friend, do you think that after I perfect the eightfold *yoga* performance I shall be able to see the eternal form of the Supreme Personality of Godhead?" This inquiry from the sage is an instance of inquisitiveness in a devotee situated in the neutral stage of devotional service.

When Lord Kṛṣṇa, along with His elder brother Balarāma and sister Subhadrā, came to Kurukṣetra in a chariot on the occasion of a solar eclipse, many mystic *yogīs* also came. When these mystic *yogīs* saw Lord Kṛṣṇa and Balarāma, they exclaimed that now that they had seen the excellent bodily effulgence of the Lord, they had almost forgotten the pleasure derived from impersonal Brahman realization. In this connection one of the mystics approached Kṛṣṇa and said, "My dear Lord, You are always full with transcendental bliss, excelling all other spiritual positions. And so, simply by seeing You from a distant place, I have come to the conclusion that there is no need of my being situated in the transcendental bliss of impersonal Brahman."

When a great mystic was once awakened from his meditative trance by hearing the vibration of Kṛṣṇa's Pāñcajanya conchshell, the mystic became overpowered—so much so, in fact, that he began to bash his head on the ground, and with eyes full of tears of ecstatic love, he violated all the rules and regulations of his *yoga* performances. Thus he at once neglected the process of Brahman realization.

Bilvamaṅgala Ṭhākura, in his book *Kṛṣṇa-karṇāmṛta,* says, "Let the impersonalists be engaged in the process of transcendental realization by worshiping the impersonal Brahman. Although I was also initiated into that path of Brahman realization, I have now become misled by a naughty boy—one who is very cunning, who is very much attached to the *gopīs* and who has made me His maidservant. So I have now forgotten the process of Brahman realization."

Bilvamaṅgala Ṭhākura was first spiritually initiated for impersonal realization of the Absolute Truth, but later on, by his association with Kṛṣṇa in Vṛndāvana, he became an experienced devotee. The same thing happened to Śukadeva Gosvāmī, who also reformed himself by the grace of the Lord and took to the path of devotional service, giving up the way of impersonal realization.

Śukadeva Gosvāmī and Bilvamaṅgala Ṭhākura, who gave up the impersonal conception of the Absolute Truth to take to devotional service, are the best examples of devotees situated in the neutral state. According to some authorities, this condition cannot be accepted as one of the transcendental humors, or *rasas,* but Śrīla Rūpa Gosvāmī says that even if one does not accept it as a transcendental humor, one must still accept it as the beginning position of devotional service. However, if one is not further raised to the platform of actual service to the Lord, he is not considered to be on the platform of transcendental mellow. In this connection, in the Eleventh Canto of *Śrīmad-Bhāgavatam,* Lord Kṛṣṇa personally instructs Uddhava like this: "The state of being established in My personal form is called *śānta-rasa,* and without being situated in this position, no one can advance to actual pure devotional service." In other words, no one can be situated in the personal feature of the Supreme Personality of Godhead without being situated at least in *śānta-rasa.*

36

Transcendental Affection (Servitude)

The transcendental mellow of affection has been accepted by authorities like Śrīdhara Svāmī as a perfectional stage of devotion. It is just above the humor of neutrality and is a requisite for the development of the serving humor. In literature such as *Nāma-kaumudī* this state of existence is accepted as continuous affection for or attraction to Kṛṣṇa. Authorities like Sudeva consider this stage of affection to be in the neutral stage, but in any case this affection is relished by the devotees in different transcendental tastes, and therefore the general name for this state is affection, or pure affection for Kṛṣṇa.

Devotees engaged in servitude are attached to Kṛṣṇa in the affection of reverence. Some of the inhabitants of Gokula (Vṛndāvana as exhibited on earth) are attached to Kṛṣṇa on this platform of affection in reverence. The inhabitants of Vṛndāvana used to say, "Kṛṣṇa is always manifest before us with a complexion like a blackish cloud. He holds His wonderful flute in His lotus hands. He is dressed in yellow silks and bedecked with a peacock feather on His head. When Kṛṣṇa walks near Govardhana Hill with these personal features, all the inhabitants of the heavenly planets, as well as the inhabitants of this earth, feel transcendental bliss and consider themselves the eternal servants of the Lord." Sometimes the devotee becomes filled with the same awe and reverence by seeing a picture of Viṣṇu, who is dressed like Kṛṣṇa and who has a similar complexion. The only difference is that Viṣṇu has four hands, in which He holds the conchshell, the disc, the club and the lotus flower. Lord Viṣṇu is always decorated with many valuable jewels, such as the *candrakānta* stone and the *sūryakānta* stone.

In the *Lalita-mādhava* by Rūpa Gosvāmī there is the following statement by Dāruka, one of the servants of Kṛṣṇa: "Certainly Lord Viṣṇu is very beautiful with His necklace of *kaustubha* jewels, His four hands holding conchshell, disc, club and lotus flower, and His dazzlingly beautiful jewelry. He is also very beautiful in His eternal position, riding upon the shoulder of Garuḍa. But now the same Lord Viṣṇu is present as the enemy of Kaṁsa, and by His personal feature I am completely forgetting the opulence of Vaikuṇṭha."

Another devotee once said, "This Supreme Personality of Godhead, from whose bodily pores come millions of universes, permanently rising, who is the ocean of mercy, who is the owner of inconceivable energies, who is always equipped with all perfections, who is the origin of all incarnations, who is the attraction for all liberated persons—this very Supreme Personality of Godhead is the supreme controller and the supremely worshipable. He is all-cognizant, fully determined and fully opulent. He is the emblem of forgiveness and the protector of surrendered souls. He is munificent, true to His promise, expert, all-auspicious, powerful and religious. He is a strict follower of the scripture, He is the friend of the devotees, and He is magnanimous, influential, grateful, reputable, respectable, full of all strength, and submissive to pure love. Surely He is the only shelter of devotees who are attracted to Him by the affection of servitorship."

The devotees of the Lord in servitude are divided into four classes: appointed servants (such as Lord Brahmā and Lord Śiva, who are appointed to control the material modes of passion and ignorance), devotees in servitude who are protected by the Lord, devotees who are always associates and devotees who are simply following in the footsteps of the Lord.

Appointed Servants

In a conversation between Jāmbavatī, one of Kṛṣṇa's wives, and Kālindī, her friend, Jāmbavatī inquired, "Who is this personality circumambulating our Kṛṣṇa?"

Kālindī replied, "She is Ambikā, the superintendent of all universal affairs."

Then Jāmbavatī inquired, "Who is this personality who is trembling at the sight of Kṛṣṇa?"

Kālindī replied, "He is Lord Śiva."

Then Jāmbavatī inquired, "Who is the person offering prayers?"

Kālindī replied, "He is Lord Brahmā."

Jāmbavatī then asked, "Who is that person who has fallen on the round and is offering respect to Kṛṣṇa?"

Kālindī replied, "He is Indra, the King of heaven."

Jāmbavatī next inquired, "Who is this person who has come with the emigods and is laughing with them?"

Kālindī replied, "He is my elder brother, Yamarāja, the superinten-ent of death."

This conversation offers a description of all the demigods, including amarāja, who are engaged in services appointed by the Lord. They re called *adhikṛta-devatā*, or demigods appointed to particular types f departmental service.

evotees Under the Protection and Shelter of the Lord

One resident of Vṛndāvana once told Lord Kṛṣṇa, "My dear Kṛṣṇa, pleasure of Vṛndāvana! Being afraid of this material existence, we ave taken shelter of You, for You can completely protect us! We are ell aware of Your greatness. As such, we have given up our desire for beration and have taken complete shelter under Your lotus feet. Since e have heard about Your ever-increasing transcendental love, we have oluntarily engaged ourselves in Your transcendental service." This state-ient is by a devotee who is under the protection and shelter of Lord ṛṣṇa.

Upon being chastised by Kṛṣṇa's constant kicking on his head, Kāliya, ie black snake of the Yamunā, came to his senses and admitted, "My ear Lord, I have been so offensive unto You, but still You are so kind iat You have marked my head with the impression of Your lotus feet." his is also an instance of one's taking shelter under the lotus feet of ṛṣṇa.

In the *Aparādha-bhañjana* a pure devotee expresses his feelings: "My ear Lord, I am ashamed to admit before You that I have carried out ie orders of my masters named lust, anger, avarice, illusion and envy. ometimes I have carried out their orders in a way most abominable. et in spite of my serving them so faithfully, they are not satisfied, or are they kind enough to give me relief from their service. They are ot even ashamed of taking service from me in that way. My dear ord, O head of the Yadu dynasty, now I have come to my senses, and I am taking shelter of Your lotus feet. Please engage me in Yo service." This is another instance of surrendering and taking shelter the lotus feet of Kṛṣṇa.

There are many instances in the various Vedic writings of perso who were aspiring after liberation by speculative knowledge but ga up this process in order to take complete shelter under the lotus fe of Kṛṣṇa. Examples of such persons are the *brāhmaṇas* headed Śaunaka in the forest of Naimiṣāraṇya.* Learned scholars accept the as devotees having complete wisdom. There is a statement in the *Har bhakti-sudhodaya* in which these great *brāhmaṇas* and sages, heade by Śaunaka Ṛṣi, told Sūta Gosvāmī, "My dear great soul, just see ho wonderful it is! Although as human beings we are contaminated wit so many taints of material existence, simply by our conversing wit you about the Supreme Personality of Godhead we are now graduall decrying our desire for liberation."

In *Padyāvalī* a devotee says, "Persons who are attached to specul tive knowledge for self-realization, who have decided that the suprer truth is beyond meditation and who have thus become situated in t mode of goodness—let them peacefully execute their engagement. for us, we are simply attached to the Supreme Personality of Godhea who is by nature so pleasing, who possesses a complexion like a blac ish cloud, who is dressed in yellow garments, and who has beautif lotuslike eyes. We wish only to meditate upon Him."

Those who are from the very beginning of their self-realization a tached to devotional service are called *sevā-niṣṭha. Sevā-niṣṭha* mea "simply attached to devotional service." The best examples of su devotees are Lord Śiva, King Indra, King Bahulāśva, King Ikṣvāk Śrutadeva and Puṇḍarīka. One devotee says, "My dear Lord, Yo transcendental qualities attract even the liberated souls and carry the to the assembly of devotees where Your glories are constantly chante Even great sages who are accustomed to living in solitary places a also attracted by the songs of Your glory. And, observing all Your tra scendental qualities, I have also become attracted and have decided dedicate my life to Your loving service."

---

*These are the *brāhmaṇas* to whom *Śrīmad-Bhāgavatam* was spoken by Sūta Gosvāmī, described in the author's *Śrīmad-Bhāgavatam,* First Canto, First Chapter.

Constant Associates

In the city of Dvārakā the following devotees are known as Kṛṣṇa's close associates: Uddhava, Dāruka, Sātyaki, Śrutadeva, Śatrujit, Nanda, Upananda and Bhadra. All of these personalities remain with the Lord as His secretaries, but still they are sometimes engaged in His personal service. Among the Kuru dynasty, Bhīṣma, Mahārāja Parīkṣit and Vidura are also known as close associates of Lord Kṛṣṇa. It is said, "All the associates of Lord Kṛṣṇa have lustrous bodily features, and their eyes are just like lotus flowers. They have sufficient power to defeat the strength of the demigods, and the specific feature of their persons is that they are always decorated with valuable ornaments."

When Kṛṣṇa was in the capital Indraprastha, someone addressed Him thus: "My dear Lord, Your personal associates, headed by Uddhava, are always awaiting Your order by standing at the entrance gate of Dvārakā. They are mostly looking on with tears in their eyes, and in the enthusiasm of their service they are not afraid even of the devastating fire generated by Lord Śiva. They are souls simply surrendered unto Your lotus feet."

Out of the many close associates of Lord Kṛṣṇa, Uddhava is considered the best. The following is a description of him: "His body is blackish like the color of the Yamunā River, and it is similarly as cool. He is always decorated with flower garlands first used by Lord Kṛṣṇa, and he is dressed with yellow silk clothing. His two arms are just like the bolts of a door, his eyes are just like lotus flowers, and he is the most important devotee among all the associates. Let us therefore offer our respectful obeisances unto Uddhava's lotus feet."

Uddhava has described the transcendental qualities of Śrī Kṛṣṇa as follows: "Lord Śrī Kṛṣṇa, who is our master and worshipable Deity, the controller of Lord Śiva and Lord Brahmā, and the controller of the whole universe as well, accepts the controlling orders of Ugrasena, His grandfather. He is the proprietor of millions of universes, but still He begged a little land from the ocean. And although He is just like an ocean of wisdom, He sometimes consults me. He is so great and magnanimous, yet He is engaged in His different activities just like an ordinary person."

Followers of the Lord

Those who are constantly engaged in the personal service of the Lord are called *anugas,* or followers. Examples of such followers are Sucandra Maṇḍana, Stamba and Sutamba. They are all inhabitants of the city o Dvārakā, and they are dressed and ornamented like the other associates The specific services entrusted to the *anugas* are varied. Maṇḍana alway bears the umbrella over the head of Lord Kṛṣṇa. Sucandra is engaged i fanning with the white *cāmara* bunch of hair, and Sutamba is engaged i supplying betel nuts. All of them are great devotees, and they are alway busy in the transcendental loving service of the Lord.

As there are *anugas* in Dvārakā, so there are many *anugas* i Vṛndāvana also. The names of the *anugas* in Vṛndāvana are as follows Raktaka, Patraka, Patrī, Madhukaṇṭha, Madhuvrata, Rasāla, Suvilāsa Premakanda, Marandaka, Ānanda, Candrahāsa, Payoda, Bakula Rasada and Śārada.

Descriptions of the bodily features of the *anugas* in Vṛndāvana ar given in the following statement: "Let us offer our respectful obei sances unto the constant associates of the son of Mahārāja Nanda They always stay in Vṛndāvana, and their bodies are decorated wit garlands of pearls and with bangles and bracelets of gold. Their color are like black bees and the golden moon, and they are dressed just t suit their particular special bodily features. Their specific duties ca be understood from a statement by Mother Yaśodā, who said, 'Bakula please cleanse the yellowish dress of Kṛṣṇa. Vārika, you just perfum the bathing water with *aguru* scent. And Rasāla, you just prepare th betel nuts. You can all see that Kṛṣṇa is approaching. There is dus overhead, and the cows can be seen very distinctly.'"

Among all the *anugas,* Raktaka is considered to be the chief. Th description of his bodily features is as follows: "He wears yellow cloth ing, and his bodily color is just like newly grown grass. He is ver expert in singing and is always engaged in the service of the son c Mahārāja Nanda. Let us all become the followers of Raktaka in o fering transcendental loving service to Kṛṣṇa!" An example of the a tachment felt by Raktaka toward Lord Kṛṣṇa can be understood fror his statement to Rasada: "Just hear me! Please place me so that I ma always be engaged in the service of Lord Kṛṣṇa, who has now becom famous as the lifter of the Govardhana Hill."

The devotees of Kṛṣṇa engaged in His personal service are always ver cautious, because they know that becoming personal servitors of Lor

Kṛṣṇa is not an ordinary thing. A person who offers respect even to the ants engaged in the service of the Lord becomes eternally happy, so what is there to say of one who offers Kṛṣṇa direct service? Raktaka once said within himself, "Not only is Kṛṣṇa my worshipable and servable Lord, but also the girlfriends of Kṛṣṇa, the *gopīs,* are equally worshipable and servable by me. And not only the *gopīs,* but anyone who is engaged in the service of the Lord is also worshipable and servable by me. I know that I must be very careful not to become overly proud that I am one of the servitors and devotees of the Lord." From this statement one can understand that the pure devotees, those who are actually engaged in the service of the Lord, are always very cautious and are never overly proud of their service.

This mentality of the direct servitor of Kṛṣṇa is called *dhūrya.* According to expert analytical studies of the direct associates of the Lord, Śrīla Rūpa Gosvāmī has divided these into three classes—namely *dhūrya, dhīra* and *vīra.* Raktaka is classified among the *dhūrya,* or those who are always attached to serving the most beloved *gopīs.*

One *dhīra* associate of Kṛṣṇa is the son of Satyabhāmā's nurse. Satyabhāmā is one of the queens of Lord Kṛṣṇa in Dvārakā, and when she was married to Kṛṣṇa, the son of her nurse was allowed to go with her because they had lived together from childhood as brother and sister. So this gentleman, the son of Satyabhāmā's nurse, used to live with Kṛṣṇa as His brother-in-law, and sometimes as brother-in-law he used to play jokes with Kṛṣṇa. He once addressed Kṛṣṇa in this way: "My dear Kṛṣṇa, I never tried to gain the favor of the goddess of fortune, who is married to You, but still I am so fortunate that I am considered one of the members of Your house, the brother of Satyabhāmā."

A *vīra* associate once expressed his pride, declaring, "Lord Baladeva may be a great enemy of Pralambāsura, but I have nothing to worry about from Him. And as far as Pradyumna is concerned, I have nothing to take from him, because he is simply a boy. Therefore I do not expect anything from anyone else. I simply expect the favorable glance of Kṛṣṇa upon me, and so I am not even afraid of Satyabhāmā, who is so dear to Kṛṣṇa."

In the Fourth Canto of *Śrīmad-Bhāgavatam,* Twentieth Chapter, verse 28, King Pṛthu addresses the Lord, saying, "My dear Lord, it may happen that the goddess of fortune becomes dissatisfied with my work, or I may even have some misunderstanding with her, but I will not mind this, because I have full confidence in You. You are always causelessly merciful to Your servants, and You consider even their menial service to be very much advanced. So I have confidence that You will accept my humble service, although it is not worthy of being recognized. My dear Lord, You are self-sufficient. You can do anything You like without the help of anyone else. So even if the goddess of fortune is not satisfied with me, I know that You will always accept my service anyway."

Devotees attached to the transcendental loving service of the Lord may be described either as surrendered souls, as souls advanced in devotional knowledge, or as souls completely engaged in transcendental loving service. Such devotees are called (respectively) neophyte, perfect and eternally perfect.

37

Impetuses for Kṛṣṇa's Service

The causeless mercy of Kṛṣṇa, the dust of His lotus feet, His *prasāda* and association with His devotees are some impetuses toward a devotee's engagement in transcendental loving service to the Lord.

Kṛṣṇa exhibited His causeless mercy when He was present at the departure of Grandfather Bhīṣma. During the Battle of Kurukṣetra, Bhīṣmadeva, the grandfather of Arjuna, was lying on a bed of arrows before departing from this mortal world. When Lord Kṛṣṇa, Mahārāja Yudhiṣṭhira and the other Pāṇḍavas approached Bhīṣmadeva, he was very grateful to Lord Kṛṣṇa, and he addressed the *brāhmaṇa* military commander Kṛpācārya thus: "My dear Kṛpācārya, just see the wonderful causeless mercy of Lord Kṛṣṇa! I am most unfortunate. I have no qualification. I was opposing Kṛṣṇa's most intimate friend, Arjuna—I even tried to *kill* him! I have so many disqualifications, and yet the Lord is still so kind that He has come to see me at the last point of my life. He is worshipable by all great sages, but still He is so merciful that He has come to see an abominable person like me."

Sometimes the vibration of Lord Kṛṣṇa's flute, His bugling, His smiling, His footmarks on the ground, the transcendental fragrance of His body and the appearance of a new cloud in the sky also become impetuses for ecstatic love of Him.

In the *Vidagdha-mādhava* there is the following statement: "When Kṛṣṇa was playing on His flute, Baladeva very anxiously declared, 'Just see how, after hearing the transcendental sound of Kṛṣṇa's flute, Indra, the King of heaven, is crying in his heavenly kingdom! And from his teardrops falling on the ground, Vṛndāvana appears to have become a celestial residence for the demigods.'"

Ecstatic love for Kṛṣṇa, which is known as *anubhāva,* is symptomized by the following signs: one becomes engaged exclusively in the service of the Lord, being attentive to carry out the orders of the Lord faithfully; one becomes undisturbed and nonenvious in full transcendental loving service to the Lord; and one makes friendship with the devotees of the Lord who are situated in faithful service to Him. All of these symptoms are called *anubhāva,* ecstatic love.

The first symptom of *anubhāva,* or engagement in a particular type of service, is exemplified by Dāruka, a servant of Kṛṣṇa who used to fan Kṛṣṇa with a *cāmara,* a bunch of hair. When he was engaged in such service, he was filled with ecstatic love, and the symptoms of ecstatic love became manifest in his body. But Dāruka was so serious about his service that he checked all of these manifestations of ecstatic love and considered them hindrances to his engagement. He did not care very much for these manifestations, although they automatically developed.

In *Śrīmad-Bhāgavatam,* Tenth Canto, Eighty-sixth Chapter, verse 38, there is a statement of how Śrutadeva, a *brāhmaṇa* from the country called Mithilā in northern India, became so overpowered with joy as soon as he saw Kṛṣṇa that immediately after bowing to the Lord's lotus feet he stood up and began to dance, raising his two arms above his head.

One of the devotees of Lord Kṛṣṇa once addressed Him in this manner: "My dear Lord, although You are not a professional dancer, by Your dancing You have so astonished us that we can understand that You are personally the master of all dancing. Certainly You must have learned this dancing art directly from the goddess of love." When a devotee dances in ecstatic love, there are manifestations of symptoms which are called *sāttvika. Sāttvika* means that they are from the transcendental platform. They are not symptoms of material emotion; they come from the soul proper.

In *Śrīmad-Bhāgavatam,* Tenth Canto, Eighty-fifth Chapter, verse 38, Śukadeva Gosvāmī tells Mahārāja Parīkṣit that after surrendering everything unto the lotus feet of Vāmanadeva, Bali Mahārāja immediately caught hold of the lotus feet of the Lord and pressed them to his heart. Being overwhelmed with joy, he manifested all the symptoms of ecstatic love, with tears in his eyes and a faltering voice.

In such expressions of ecstatic love there are many other subsidiary symptoms, such as jubilation, withering, silence, disappointment, moroseness, reverence, thoughtfulness, remembrance, doubtfulness, confidence, eagerness, indifference, restlessness, impudence, shyness, inertness, illusion, madness, ghastliness, contemplation, dreaming, disease and signs of death. When a devotee meets Kṛṣṇa, there are symptoms of jubilation, pride and perseverance, and when he is feeling great separation from Kṛṣṇa, the symptoms of ghastliness, disease and signs of death become prominent.

It is stated in the First Canto of *Śrīmad-Bhāgavatam,* Eleventh Chapter, verse 5, that when Lord Kṛṣṇa returned from the Battlefield of Kurukṣetra to His home at Dvārakā, all the residents of Dvārakā began to talk with Him, as a child talks lovingly to his father after the father's return from foreign countries. This is an example of jubilation.

When Bahulāśva, the King of Mithilā, saw Kṛṣṇa at his palace, he decided to offer his respects by bowing down before Him at least a hundred times, but he was so overcome by feelings of love that after bowing down only once, he forgot his position and could not rise again.

In the *Skanda Purāṇa* a devotee tells Lord Kṛṣṇa, "My dear Lord, as the sun evaporates all the water on the ground by its scorching heat, so my mental state has dried away the luster of my face and body, due to separation from You." This is an example of withering in ecstatic love.

An expression of disappointment was made by Indra, the King of heaven. When he saw the sun god, Indra told him, "My dear sun god, your sunshine is very glorious because it reaches unto the lotus feet of Lord Kṛṣṇa, the master of the Yadu dynasty. I have thousands of eyes, but they have proved to be useless because not even for a moment are they able to see the lotus feet of the Lord."

Reverential devotion for the Lord gradually increases and transforms itself into ecstatic love, then affection and then attachment. In the Tenth Canto of *Śrīmad-Bhāgavatam,* Thirty-eighth Chapter, verse 6, Akrūra says, "Because I am going to see Lord Kṛṣṇa today, all symptoms of inauspiciousness have already been killed. My life is now successful, because I shall be able to offer my respects unto the lotus feet of the Supreme Personality of Godhead!"

Another devotee in ecstatic reverential affection once said, "When will that glorious day in my life come when it will be possible for me to go to the bank of the Yamunā and see Lord Śrī Kṛṣṇa playing there as a cowherd boy?"

When there is no diminishing of this ecstatic love and when it is freed from all kinds of doubt, the devotee has reached the stage called steady love for Kṛṣṇa. In this stage, all expressions of unhappiness by the devotee are called *anubhāva,* or ecstatic loving symptoms.

The symptom of ecstatic affection with reverence felt by Bali Mahārāja was expressed as follows: "My dear Lord, You have simultaneously punished me and showed me Your causeless mercy. My conclusion is that when I have taken shelter of Your lotus feet I shall never be disturbed in any condition of life. Whether You give me the opportunity to enjoy all the yogic perfections or You put me into the most abominable condition of hellish life, I shall never be disturbed."

Kṛṣṇa Himself, after seeing Bali Mahārāja, told Uddhava, "My dear friend, how can I express the glorious characteristics of Bali Mahārāja, the son of Virocana? Although the King of the *suras* [demigods] was cursed by this son of Virocana, and although I cheated him in My incarnation as Vāmana, taking away his dominions throughout the universe, and although I still criticized him for not fulfilling his promise, I have just now seen him in his kingdom, and he feelingly expressed his *love* for Me."*

When such a feeling of love becomes intensified, it is called affection. In that affectional stage, one cannot bear separation from Kṛṣṇa even for a moment.

One devotee told Dāruka, the servant of Kṛṣṇa, "My dear Dāruka, when you become like wood because of your separation from Kṛṣṇa, it is not so wonderful. Whenever *any* devotee sees Kṛṣṇa, his eyes become filled with water, and in separation any devotee like you would become stunned, standing just like a wooden doll. That is not a very wonderful thing."

There is a statement about Uddhava's symptoms of love. When he saw Lord Kṛṣṇa his eyes filled with tears and created a river which flowed down toward the sea of Kṛṣṇa to offer tribute, as a wife offers tribute to

---

*Bali was a king of the demons who waged war against the demigods and nearly conquered the universe. When the demigods prayed for help, the Lord appeared as Vāmanadeva, a dwarf *brāhmaṇa,* and asked Bali for three paces of land. Bali agreed, and Vāmana covered all the worlds with His first two steps. Then He demanded to know where His third pace was to be. Bali offered his own head beneath the Lord's foot and thus became a *mahājana,* or great devotee.

her husband. When his body erupted with goose pimples, he appeared like the *kadamba* flower, and when he began to offer prayers, he appeared completely distinct from all other devotees.

When affection is symptomized by direct happiness and distress, it is called attraction. In such an attracted state of ecstatic love, one can face all kinds of disadvantages calmly. Even at the risk of death such a devotee is never bereft of the transcendental loving service of the Lord. A glorious example of this ecstatic love was exhibited by King Parīkṣit when he was at the point of death. Although he was bereft of his entire kingdom, which spread over all the world, and although he was accepting not even a drop of water in the seven days remaining to him, because he was engaged in hearing the transcendental pastimes of the Lord from Śukadeva Gosvāmī he was not in the least distressed. On the contrary, he was feeling direct transcendental ecstatic joy in association with Śukadeva Gosvāmī.

One devotee has confidently expressed this opinion: "If a drop of Lord Kṛṣṇa's mercy can be bestowed upon me, then I shall feel completely carefree, even in the midst of a fire or an ocean. But if I become bereft of His causeless mercy, then even if I became the King of Dvārakā, I would be simply an object for pinpricks."

Devotees such as Mahārāja Parīkṣit and Uddhava are all situated in ecstatic attraction on the basis of affection, and in that state of affection a feeling of friendship becomes manifest. When Uddhava was freed from all material contamination, he saw the Lord, and his throat became choked up, and he could not speak. By the movements of his eyebrows alone he was embracing the Lord. Such ecstatic love has been divided by great scholars into two groups—addition and subtraction. If a devotee is not directly associated with the Lord, it is called subtraction. In this state of love, one is constantly fixed with his mind at the lotus feet of the Lord. A devotee in this state becomes very eager to learn of the transcendental qualities of the Lord. The most important business of such a devotee is attaining the association of the Lord.

In the *Nṛsiṁha Purāṇa* there is a statement about King Ikṣvāku which illustrates this state of ecstatic love. Because of his great affection for Kṛṣṇa, King Ikṣvāku became greatly attached to the black cloud, the black deer, the deer's black eyes and the lotus flower, which is always compared to the eyes of the Lord. In the Tenth Canto, Thirty-eighth

Chapter, verse 10, of the *Bhāgavatam,* Akrūra thinks, "Since the Lord has now appeared to diminish the great burden of the world and is now visible to everyone's eyes in His personal transcendental body, when we see Him before us, is that not the ultimate perfection of our eyes?" In other words, Akrūra realized that the perfection of the eyes is fulfilled when one is able to see Lord Kṛṣṇa. Therefore, when Lord Kṛṣṇa was visible on the earth by direct appearance, everyone who saw Him surely attained perfection of sight.

In the *Kṛṣṇa-karṇāmṛta,* written by Bilvamaṅgala Ṭhākura, there is this expression of eagerness in ecstatic love: "How miserable it is, my dear Kṛṣṇa, O friend of the hopeless! O merciful Lord, how can I pass these thankless days without seeing You?" A similar sentiment was expressed by Uddhava when he wrote a letter to Kṛṣṇa and said, "My dear Supreme King of Vraja, You are the vision of nectar for the eyes, and without seeing Your lotus feet and the effulgence of Your body, my mind is always morose. I cannot perceive any peace under any circumstance. Besides that, I am feeling every moment's separation to be like the duration of many, many long years."

In the *Kṛṣṇa-karṇāmṛta* it is also said, "My dear Lord, You are the ocean of mercy. With my arms placed upon my head, I am bowing down before You with all humility and sincerity. I am praying unto You, my Lord. Would You be pleased just to sprinkle a little of the water of Your glance upon me? That will be a great satisfaction."

A devotee of Lord Kṛṣṇa said, "When even Śaśiśekhara [Lord Śiva] is unable to see You, what chance is there for me, who am lower than an ordinary worm? I have only committed misdeeds. I know that I am not at all fit to offer my prayers to You, but because You are known as Dīnabandhu, the friend of the fallen, I humbly pray that You will kindly purify me by the beams of Your transcendental glance. If I become thoroughly bathed by Your merciful glance, then I may be saved. Therefore, my Lord, I am requesting You to please bestow upon me Your merciful glance."

38

Indifference and Separation

The great devotee Uddhava once wrote a letter to Kṛṣṇa, "My dear Kṛṣṇa, I have just finished the study of all kinds of philosophical books and Vedic verses about the goal of life, and so now I have a little reputation for my studies. But still, in spite of my reputation, my knowledge is condemned, because although enjoying the effulgence of Vedic knowledge, I could not appreciate the effulgence emanating from the nails of Your toes. Therefore, the sooner my pride and Vedic knowledge are finished, the better it will be!" This is an example of indifference.

Another devotee very anxiously expressed himself thus: "My mind is very flickering, so I cannot concentrate it upon Your lotus feet. And seeing this inefficiency in myself I become ashamed, and the whole night I am unable to sleep because I am exasperated by my great inability."

In the *Kṛṣṇa-karṇāmṛta* Bilvamaṅgala Ṭhākura has explained his restlessness as follows: "My dear Lord, Your naughtiness in boyhood is the most wonderful thing in the three worlds. And You Yourself know what this naughtiness is. As such, You can very easily understand my flickering mind. This is known to You and me. Therefore, I am simply yearning to know how I can fix my mind on Your lotus feet."

Another devotee expressed his impudence by saying, "My dear Lord, without considering my lowly position, I must confess to You that my eyes are just like black wasps, desiring to hover at Your lotus feet."

In the Seventh Canto of *Śrīmad-Bhāgavatam,* Fourth Chapter, verse 37, the great sage Nārada informs Mahārāja Yudhiṣṭhira about Prahlāda Mahārāja, who was a devotee from the very beginning of his life. The proof of Prahlāda's natural devotion is that even when he was a small child he did not play with his playmates, but was always eager to preach the glories of the Lord. Instead of joining in their sportive acrobatic feats, he remained an inactive child because he was always in trance, meditating on Kṛṣṇa. As such, there was no possibility of his being touched by the external world.

The following statement is about a *brāhmaṇa* devotee: "This *brāhmaṇa* is very expert in all kinds of activities, but I do not know why he is looking up without moving his eyes. It appears that his body is fixed motionless just like a doll's. I can guess that in this condition he has been captivated by the transcendental beauty of that expert flute-player, Śrī Kṛṣṇa, and being attached to Him, he is simply staring at the black cloud, remembering the bodily hue of Śrī Kṛṣṇa." This is an example of how a devotee can become inert due to ecstatic love.

In *Śrīmad-Bhāgavatam,* Seventh Canto, Fourth Chapter, verse 40, Prahlāda Mahārāja says that even in his childhood, when he was loudly speaking the glories of the Lord, he used to dance just like a shameless madman. And sometimes, being fully absorbed in thought on the pastimes of the Lord, he used to imitate such pastimes. This is an instance of a devotee's being almost like a madman. Similarly, it is said that the great sage Nārada was so ecstatically in love with Kṛṣṇa that he would sometimes dance naked, and sometimes his whole body would become stunned. Sometimes he would laugh very loudly, sometimes he would cry very loudly, sometimes he would remain silent, and sometimes he would appear to be suffering from some disease, although he had no disease. This is another instance of becoming like a madman in the ecstasy of devotion.

In the *Hari-bhakti-sudhodaya* it is stated that when Prahlāda Mahārāja was thinking himself unfit to approach the Supreme Personality of Godhead, he immersed himself in great distress, in an ocean of unhappiness. As such, he used to shed tears and lie down on the floor as though unconscious.

The students of a great devotee once talked among themselves in this way: "My dear godbrothers, our spiritual master, after seeing the lotus feet of the Lord, has thrown himself into the fire of lamentation, and because of this fire the water of his life has almost dried away. Let us now pour the nectar of the holy name through his ears, and by our doing so the swan of his life may again show signs of life."

When Lord Kṛṣṇa went to the city of Śoṇitapura to fight with Bali's son Bāṇa and to cut off all his hands, Uddhava, being separated from

Kṛṣṇa and thinking of His fight, was almost completely stunned into unconsciousness.

When a devotee is fully in love with the Supreme Personality of Godhead, there may be the following symptoms due to his feelings of separation from the Lord: a feverish condition of the body, withering of the body, lack of sleep, nonattachment, inertness, appearing diseased, madness, unconsciousness and sometimes death.

As far as the feverish condition of the body is concerned, Uddhava once told Nārada, "My dear great sage, the lotus flower that is a friend of the sun may be a cause of distress for us, the fire in the ocean may cause us some burning sensation, and Indīvara, the friend of the moon, may distress us in various ways—we do not mind. But the most regrettable factor is that all of them remind us of Kṛṣṇa, and this is giving us too much distress!" This is an instance of the feverish condition which is due to being separated from Kṛṣṇa.

Some of the devotees who went to see Kṛṣṇa at Dvārakā and were detained at the door said, "My dear Kṛṣṇa, O friend of the Pāṇḍus, as the swan loves to dive into the water among the lily flowers and would die if taken from the water, so we wish only to be with You. Our limbs are shrinking and fading because You have been taken away from us."

The King of Bahula, although very comfortably situated in his palace, began to think the nights very long and distressing because of his separation from Kṛṣṇa.

King Yudhiṣṭhira once said, "Kṛṣṇa, the chariot driver of Arjuna, is the only relative of mine within the three worlds. Therefore, my mind is becoming maddened day and night with separation from His lotus feet, and I do not know how to situate myself or where I shall go to attain any steadiness of mind." This is another example of lack of sleep.

Some of the cowherd friends of Kṛṣṇa said, "Dear Kṛṣṇa, O enemy of the Mura demon, just think of Your personal servant Raktaka. Simply because he saw a peacock feather, he is now closing his eyes and is no longer attentive to pasturing the cows. Rather, he has left them in a faraway pasture and has not even bothered to use his stick to control them." This is an instance of mental imbalance due to separation from Kṛṣṇa.

When Lord Kṛṣṇa went to the capital of King Yudhiṣṭhira, Uddhava was so afflicted by the fire of separation from Śrī Kṛṣṇa that the perspiration from his inflamed body and the tears from his eyes poured from him, and in this way he became completely stunned.

When Śrī Kṛṣṇa left the city of Dvārakā to seek out the Syamantaka jewel and He was late returning home, Uddhava became so afflicted that the symptoms of disease became manifest in his body. Actually, due to his excessive ecstatic love for Kṛṣṇa, Uddhava became known in Dvārakā as crazy. To his great fortune, on that day Uddhava's reputation as a crazy fellow was firmly established. Uddhava's craziness was practically proved when he went to Raivataka Hill to minutely observe the congested black clouds. In his disturbed condition, he began to pray to these clouds, and he expressed his jubilation by bowing down before them.

Uddhava informed Kṛṣṇa, "My dear leader of the Yadu dynasty, Your servants in Vṛndāvana cannot sleep at night thinking of You, so now they are all lying down on the bank of the Yamunā almost paralyzed. And it appears that they are almost dead, because their breathing is very slow." This is an instance of becoming unconscious due to separation from Kṛṣṇa.

Kṛṣṇa was once informed, "You are the life and soul of all the inhabitants of Vṛndāvana. So because You have left Vṛndāvana, all of the servitors of Your lotus feet there are suffering. It is as if the lakes filled with lotus flowers have dried up from the scorching heat of separation from You." In the example given here, the inhabitants of Vṛndāvana are compared to lakes filled with lotus flowers, and because of the scorching heat of separation from Kṛṣṇa, the lakes—along with the lotus flowers of their lives—are being burned up. And the swans in the lakes, who are compared to the vitality of the inhabitants of Vṛndāvana, are no longer desiring to live there. In other words, because of the scorching heat, the swans are leaving the lakes. This metaphor is used to describe the condition of the devotees separated from Kṛṣṇa.

39

Ways of Meeting Kṛṣṇa

When Kṛṣṇa and His devotees meet, the meeting is technically called *yoga,* or linking up with the Lord. Such meetings between Kṛṣṇa and His devotees can be divided into three classes—namely perfection, satisfaction and steadiness.

When the devotee meets with Kṛṣṇa in great eagerness, that state of meeting is called perfection. In the *Kṛṣṇa-karṇāmṛta,* Bilvamaṅgala Ṭhākura describes how Kṛṣṇa meets His devotee—with peacock feather on His head, with *marakata* jewels on His chest and with His ever-enchanting smile, His restless eyes and His very delicate body.

In the Tenth Canto of *Śrīmad-Bhāgavatam,* Thirty-eighth Chapter, verse 34, Śukadeva Gosvāmī tells King Parīkṣit, "My dear King, as soon as Akrūra the chariot driver saw Lord Kṛṣṇa and His elder brother Balarāma in Vṛndāvana, he immediately got down from the chariot and, being greatly afflicted by affection for the transcendental Lord, fell down upon His lotus feet to offer respectful obeisances." These are some of the instances of perfectional meetings with Kṛṣṇa.

When a devotee meets Kṛṣṇa after long separation, the meeting is one of satisfaction. In the First Canto of *Śrīmad-Bhāgavatam,* Eleventh Chapter, verse 10, it is stated that when Lord Kṛṣṇa returned to His capital, Dvārakā, the inhabitants said, "Dear Lord, if You remain in foreign countries for so long, we shall certainly be bereft of seeing Your smiling face! Upon observing Your face, we, Your eternal servitors, become greatly satisfied. All the anxieties of our existence are immediately mitigated. If we cannot see You because You are long absent from Dvārakā, then it will be impossible for us to live anymore." This is an instance of satisfaction in meeting Kṛṣṇa after long separation.

Kṛṣṇa's personal servant, Dāruka, seeing Kṛṣṇa at the door of Dvārakā, forgot to offer Him respects with folded hands.

When a devotee is ultimately situated in association with Kṛṣṇa, his position is called steadiness in devotional service. This steady position in devotional service is explained in the book known as *Haṁsadūta.* It is described there how Akrūra, who was considered by the *gopīs* to be terror personified, would talk with Kṛṣṇa about the activities of the Kuru dynasty. A similar steady position was held by Uddhava, the disciple of Bṛhaspati. He would always massage the lotus feet of Kṛṣṇa while kneeling down on the ground before Him.

When a devotee is engaged in the service of the Lord, he is said to have reached the attainment of *yoga.* The English equivalent of the word *yoga* is "linking up." So actual linking up with Kṛṣṇa, the Supreme Personality of Godhead, begins when the devotee renders service unto Him. Devotees situated in the transcendental *rasa* of servitorship render their particular service whenever there is an opportunity. Sometimes they sit down in front of Kṛṣṇa to receive orders. Some persons are reluctant to accept this level of devotional service as actual *bhakti-yoga,* and in some of the *Purāṇas* also this servitorship in devotional service to Kṛṣṇa is not accepted as the actual *bhakti-yoga* system. But *Śrīmad-Bhāgavatam* has clearly indicated that the servitor relationship with Kṛṣṇa is the actual beginning of *yoga* realization.

In the Eleventh Canto of *Śrīmad-Bhāgavatam,* Third Chapter, verse 32, it is stated that when devotees are engaged in the discharge of *bhakti-yoga,* sometimes they cry from thinking of Kṛṣṇa, sometimes they laugh, sometimes they become jubilant, and sometimes they talk in very uncommon ways. Sometimes they dance, sometimes they sing, sometimes they are actually engaged in the service of the Lord, and sometimes they sit down silently as if absorbed in trance.

Similarly, in the Seventh Canto of *Śrīmad-Bhāgavatam,* Chapter Seven, verse 34, Prahlāda Mahārāja says to his friends, "My dear friends, as soon as pure devotees of Lord Kṛṣṇa hear of the transcendental pastimes of the Lord, who is the eternal reservoir of pastimes, or hear about His transcendental qualities, they become overpowered with jubilation. Ecstatic symptoms are manifested in their bodies. They shed tears, talk falteringly, glorify the Lord in a loud voice and chant and dance in ecstasy. These ecstasies are always there, but sometimes they overcome all limits, and the symptoms become manifest to all."

In the process of surrender unto the Supreme Personality of Godhead there are six items: to accept everything favorable for devotional service, to reject everything unfavorable for devotional service, to believe that Kṛṣṇa will always give protection, to identify oneself with Kṛṣṇa's devotees, always to feel inability without the help of Kṛṣṇa and always to think oneself inferior to Kṛṣṇa, even though one may have full capacity to perform something on his own. When one is substantially convinced that he is always protected by Kṛṣṇa in all circumstances, that feeling is called reverential devotion. Reverential devotion is executed in relation with the Supreme Personality of Godhead and with His other protected devotees.

When Kṛṣṇa was residing in Dvārakā, some of the elderly members of the Yadu family would occasionally put some important matter before Him. At such a time, Kṛṣṇa would carefully give attention to those matters. And if there were some humorous topics mentioned, Kṛṣṇa would immediately respond with a smiling face. Sometimes when Kṛṣṇa was executing His duties in the assembly known as Sudharmā, He would ask the elderly members for good advice. By such activities He is manifest as the supreme spiritual master, the supreme executive head, the superior intelligence and the supreme power, protector and maintainer.

40

Reverential Devotion of Sons and Other Subordinates

True reverential devotion is exhibited by persons who think themselves subordinate to Kṛṣṇa and by persons who think themselves sons of Kṛṣṇa. The best examples of this subordination are Sāraṇa, Gada and Subhadrā. They were all members of the Yadu dynasty, and they always used to think themselves protected by Kṛṣṇa. Similarly, Kṛṣṇa's sons, such as Pradyumna, Cārudeṣṇa and Sāmba, felt the same way. Kṛṣṇa had many sons in Dvārakā. He begot ten sons by each of His 16,108 queens, and all of these sons, headed by Pradyumna, Cārudeṣṇa and Sāmba, used to think themselves always protected by Kṛṣṇa. When Kṛṣṇa's sons dined with Him, they would sometimes open their mouths for Kṛṣṇa to feed them. Sometimes when Kṛṣṇa would pat one of His sons, the son would sit on Kṛṣṇa's lap, and while Kṛṣṇa was blessing the son's head by smelling it, the others would shed tears, thinking how many pious activities he must have performed in his previous life. Out of Kṛṣṇa's many sons, Pradyumna, a son of Kṛṣṇa's chief queen, Rukmiṇī, is considered the leader. Pradyumna's bodily features resemble Kṛṣṇa's exactly. Pure devotees of Kṛṣṇa glorify Pradyumna because he is so fortunate: like father, like son.

There is a description in the *Hari-vaṁśa* of Pradyumna's activities when he kidnapped Prabhāvatī. Pradyumna addressed Prabhāvatī at that time and said, "My dear Prabhāvatī, just look at the head of our family, Śrī Kṛṣṇa. He is Viṣṇu Himself, the supreme driver of Garuḍa, and He is our supreme master. Because we have become so proud and confident of His protecting us, we sometimes do not even care about fighting with Tripurāri [Lord Śiva]."

There are two kinds of devotees engaged in devotional service with awe and veneration—the Lord's subordinates and His sons. The servitors in the abode of Dvārakā always worship Kṛṣṇa as the most respectable and revered Personality of Godhead. They are captivated by Kṛṣṇa because of His superexcellent opulences. The members who always thought themselves protected by Kṛṣṇa could readily convert their conviction into practical demonstration, because it was sometimes found that the sons of Kṛṣṇa acted very unlawfully in various places but were nonetheless given full protection by Kṛṣṇa and Balarāma.

Even Balarāma, the elder brother of Kṛṣṇa, sometimes unknowingly offered respect to Him. Once when Kṛṣṇa came before Lord Balarāma, Kṛṣṇa was anxious to offer His respects to His elder brother, but at that time Balarāma's club was lowered down upon Kṛṣṇa's lotus feet. In other words, the club in Balarāma's hand offered its own respects to Kṛṣṇa. These feelings of subordination, as explained above, are sometimes manifested as *anubhāva.*

When demigods from the heavenly planets came to Śrī Kṛṣṇa, all of Kṛṣṇa's sons followed them, and Lord Brahmā sprinkled water from his *kamaṇḍalu* upon them. When the demigods came before Kṛṣṇa, the sons, instead of sitting on golden chairs, sat down on the floor, which was covered with deerskin.

Sometimes the behavior of Kṛṣṇa's sons appears similar to the behavior of His personal servants. For example, the sons used to offer their obeisances, they were silent, submissive and gentle, and they were always ready to carry out Kṛṣṇa's orders, even at the risk of life. When present before Kṛṣṇa, they bowed down on the ground. They were very silent and steady, and they used to restrain coughing and laughing before the Lord. Also, they never discussed Kṛṣṇa's pastimes in conjugal love. In other words, devotees who are engaged in reverential devotional service should not discuss the conjugal loving affairs of Kṛṣṇa. No one should claim his eternal relationship with Kṛṣṇa unless he is liberated. In the conditioned state of life, the devotees have to execute the prescribed duties as recommended in the codes of devotional service. When one is mature in devotional service and is a realized soul, he can know his own eternal relationship with Kṛṣṇa. One should not artificially try to establish some relationship. In the premature stage it is sometimes found that a lusty, conditioned person will artificially try to establish some relationship with Kṛṣṇa in conjugal love. The result of this is that one becomes *prākṛta-sahajiyā,* or one who takes everything very cheaply. Although such persons may be very anxious to establish a relationship with Kṛṣṇa in conjugal love, their conditioned life in the material world is still most abominable. A person who has actually established his relationship with Kṛṣṇa can no longer act on the material plane, and his personal character cannot be criticized.

When Cupid came on one occasion to visit Lord Kṛṣṇa, some devotee addressed him thus: "My dear Cupid, because you have been so fortunate as to have placed your eyesight on the lotus feet of Kṛṣṇa, the drops of perspiration on your body have become frozen, and they resemble *kaṇṭakī* fruits [a kind of small fruit found in thorny bushes]." These are signs of ecstasy and veneration for the Supreme Personality of Godhead. When the princes of the Yadu dynasty heard the vibration of Kṛṣṇa's Pāñcajanya conchshell, the hairs on their bodies immediately stood up in ecstatic jubilation. It seemed at that time that all the hairs on the bodies of the princes were dancing in ecstasy.

In addition to jubilation, there are sometimes symptoms of disappointment. Pradyumna once addressed Sāmba with these words: "My dear Sāmba, you are such a glorified personality! I have seen that once when you were playing on the ground, your body became covered with dust; yet our father, Lord Kṛṣṇa, still took you up on His lap. But I am so unfortunate that I could never get such love from our father!" This statement is an example of disappointment in love.

To regard Kṛṣṇa as one's superior is called reverential feeling, and when, in addition to this, a devotee feels that Kṛṣṇa is his protector, his transcendental love for Kṛṣṇa is increased, and his combined feelings are called reverential devotion. When this steady reverential devotion increases further, it is called love of Godhead in reverential devotion. Attraction and affection are two prominent symptoms of this stage. In this reverential devotional attitude, Pradyumna never talked to his father in a loud voice. In fact, he never so much as unlocked the lips of his mouth, nor did he ever show his face filled with tears. He would always glance only at the lotus feet of his father.

There is another example of steady and fixed love for Kṛṣṇa in the instance of Arjuna's informing Him of the death of Arjuna's son, Abhimanyu, who was also the nephew of Kṛṣṇa. Abhimanyu was the son of Subhadrā, Kṛṣṇa's younger sister. He was killed at the Battle of Kurukṣetra by the combined efforts of all the commanders in King Duryodhana's army—namely Karṇa, Aśvatthāmā, Jayadratha, Bhīṣma,

Kṛpācārya and Droṇācārya. In order to assure Kṛṣṇa that there was no change of love on Subhadrā's part, Arjuna informed Him, "Although Abhimanyu was killed almost in Your presence, Subhadrā's love for You is not agitated at all, nor has it even slightly changed its original color."

The affection that Kṛṣṇa has for His devotees was expressed by Him when He asked Pradyumna not to feel so bashful before Him. He addressed Pradyumna thus: "My dear boy, just give up your feeling of inferiority, and do not hang your neck. Just talk with Me in a clear voice, and do not shed tears. You may look straight at Me, and you may place your hands on My body without any hesitation. There is no need of exhibiting so much reverence before your father."

Pradyumna's attachment for Kṛṣṇa was always exhibited by his action. Whenever he was ordered by his father to execute something, he would immediately execute the order, taking the task as nectarean even though it may have been poison. Similarly, whenever he would find something to be disapproved of by his father, he would immediately reject it as poison, even though it may have been nectarean.

Pradyumna's attachment in anxiety for Kṛṣṇa was expressed when he said to his wife Rati, "The enemy, Śambara, is already killed. Now I am very anxious to see my father, who is my spiritual master and who always carries the conchshell known as Pāñcajanya." Pradyumna felt great separation from Kṛṣṇa when He was absent from Dvārakā at the Battlefield of Kurukṣetra. He said, "Since my father has left Dvārakā, I do not take much pleasure in practicing fighting, nor am I interested in any kind of sporting pastimes. And what need is there to speak of these things? I do not even wish to stay at Dvārakā in the absence of my father."

When Pradyumna came back home after killing Śambarāsura and saw his father, Kṛṣṇa, before him, he at once became so overjoyed that he himself could not understand his joy on that occasion. This is an instance of success in separation. A similar satisfaction was observed when Kṛṣṇa returned from the Battlefield of Kurukṣetra to His home at Dvārakā. All of His sons were so overjoyed that out of ecstasy they repeatedly made many mistakes. These mistakes were a sign of complete satisfaction.

Every day Pradyumna looked over Kṛṣṇa's lotus feet with tears in his eyes. These signs of reverential devotion on the part of Pradyumna may be described in the same way they have been described in the cases of other devotees.

41

Fraternal Devotion

When a devotee is permanently situated in devotional service, and by different symptoms of ecstasy he has developed and matured a fraternal mellow or flavor in relationship with the Personality of Godhead, his feeling is called fraternal love of Godhead.

The impetus for such fraternal love of God is God Himself. When one is liberated and discovers his eternal relationship with the Supreme Lord, the Lord Himself becomes the impetus for increasing fraternal love. The eternal associates of the Lord in Vṛndāvana have described this as follows: "The Lord, Hari, whose bodily hue is like the *indranīla* jewel, whose smiling is as beautiful as the *kunda* flower, whose silk dress is as yellow as golden autumn foliage, whose chest is beautified with garlands of flowers and who is always playing upon His flute—this enemy of the Agha demon is always attracting our hearts by wandering about Vṛndāvana."

There are similar statements of fraternal love expressed outside the jurisdiction of Vṛndāvana. When the sons of Pāṇḍu, headed by Mahārāja Yudhiṣṭhira, saw Kṛṣṇa in His four-handed form on the Battlefield of Kurukṣetra, holding His conchshell, disc, club and lotus flower, they completely forgot themselves and became merged in the ocean of nectarean happiness. This shows how the sons of Pāṇḍu—King Yudhiṣṭhira, Bhīma, Arjuna, Nakula and Sahadeva—were all caught up in fraternal love for Kṛṣṇa.

Sometimes Kṛṣṇa's different names, forms, paraphernalia and transcendental qualities provoke fraternal love. For instance, Kṛṣṇa's nice dress, His strongly built body, the all-auspicious symptoms on His body, His knowledge of different languages, His learned teachings in *Bhagavad-gītā,* His uncommon genius in all fields of endeavor, His exhibition of expert knowledge, His mercy, His chivalry, His behavior as a conjugal lover, His intelligence, His forgiveness, His attraction for all kinds of men, His opulence and His happiness—all provoke fraternal love.

The impetus to fraternal love upon seeing the associates of Kṛṣṇa in Vṛndāvana is also very natural, for their personal bodily features, their qualities and their dress are all equal to Kṛṣṇa's. These associates are always happy in their service to Kṛṣṇa, and they are generally known as *vayasyas,* or friends of the same age. The *vayasyas* are fully confident of protection by Kṛṣṇa. Devotees sometimes pray, "Let us offer our respectful obeisances unto the *vayasyas* of Kṛṣṇa, who are firmly convinced of Kṛṣṇa's friendship and protection and whose devotion to Kṛṣṇa is ever fixed. They are fearless, and on a level equal with Kṛṣṇa they discharge their transcendental loving devotional service." Such eternal *vayasyas* are also found beyond the jurisdiction of Vṛndāvana, in places such as Dvārakā and Hastināpura. Except for Vṛndāvana, all the places of Kṛṣṇa's pastimes are called *puras* (towns). Mathurā and Hastināpura, the capital of the Kurus, are both *puras.* Personalities like Arjuna, Bhīma, Draupadī and Śrīdāmā Brāhmaṇa are counted among Kṛṣṇa's fraternal devotees in the *puras.*

How the sons of Pāṇḍu, the Pāṇḍavas, enjoy Kṛṣṇa's association is described as follows: "When Śrī Kṛṣṇa arrived in Indraprastha, the capital of the Kurus, Mahārāja Yudhiṣṭhira immediately came out to smell the fragrance of Kṛṣṇa's head." It is the Vedic custom that a superior smells the heads of his subordinates when the subordinates offer respect to the superior by touching his feet. Similarly, Arjuna and Bhīma embraced Kṛṣṇa with great jubilation, and the two younger brothers, namely Nakula and Sahadeva, touched the lotus feet of Kṛṣṇa with tears in their eyes and offered their respects. In this way all the five Pāṇḍava brothers enjoyed the fraternal friendship of Kṛṣṇa in transcendental mellow. Of the five Pāṇḍavas, Arjuna is the most intimately connected with Kṛṣṇa. He has a nice bow called Gāṇḍīva in his hand. His thighs are compared to the trunks of elephants, and his eyes are always reddish. When Kṛṣṇa and Arjuna are together on a chariot, they become celestial beauties, pleasing to the eyes of everyone. It is said that once Arjuna was lying on his bed with his head upon Kṛṣṇa's lap and was talking and joking with Kṛṣṇa in great relaxation, enjoying Kṛṣṇa's company with smiling and great satisfaction.

As far as the *vayasyas* (friends) in Vṛndāvana are concerned, they become greatly distressed when they cannot see Kṛṣṇa even for a moment.

There is the following prayer by a devotee for the *vayasyas* in Vṛndāvana: "All glories to Kṛṣṇa's *vayasyas,* who are just like Kṛṣṇa in their age, qualities, pastimes, dress and beauty. They are accustomed to playing on their flutes made of palm leaves, and they all have buffalo-horn bugles ornamented like Kṛṣṇa's with jewels such as *indranīla* and with gold and coral. They are always jubilant like Kṛṣṇa. May these glorious companions of Kṛṣṇa always protect us!"

The *vayasyas* in Vṛndāvana are in such intimate friendship with Kṛṣṇa that sometimes they think themselves as good as Kṛṣṇa. Here is an instance of such friendly feeling: When Kṛṣṇa was holding up Govardhana Hill with His left hand, the *vayasyas* said, "Dear friend, You have been standing for the last seven days and nights without any rest. This is very troublesome for us, because we see that You have undertaken a severely laborious task. We think, therefore, that You need not continue to stand in that way holding the hill. You can just transfer it onto Sudāmā's hand. We are very much aggrieved to see You in this position. If you think that Sudāmā is not able to support Govardhana Hill, then at least You should change hands. Instead of supporting it with Your left hand, please transfer it to Your right hand, so that we can give Your left hand a massage." This is an instance of intimacy, showing how much the *vayasyas* considered themselves to be equal to Kṛṣṇa.

In *Śrīmad-Bhāgavatam,* Tenth Canto, Twelfth Chapter, verse 11, Śukadeva Gosvāmī tells King Parīkṣit, "My dear King, Kṛṣṇa is the Supreme Personality of Godhead to the learned transcendentalist, He is the supreme happiness for the impersonalist, He is the supreme worshipable Deity for the devotee, and He is just like an ordinary boy to one who is under the spell of *māyā.* And just imagine—these cowherd boys are now playing with the Supreme Person as though they were on an equal level! By this anyone can understand that these boys must have accumulated heaps of the results of pious activities to enable them to associate with the Supreme Personality of Godhead in such intimate friendship."

There is a description of Kṛṣṇa's feeling for His *vayasyas* in Vṛndāvana. He once said to Balarāma, "My dear brother, when My companions were being devoured by the Aghāsura, hot tears poured down from My eyes. And as they were washing My cheeks, My dear elder brother, for at least one moment I completely lost Myself."

Within Gokula, Kṛṣṇa's *vayasyas* are generally divided into four groups: (1) well-wisher friends, (2) friends, (3) confidential friends and (4) intimate friends. Kṛṣṇa's well-wisher friends are a little bit older than Kṛṣṇa, and they have some parental affection for Him. Because of their being older than Kṛṣṇa, they always try to protect Him from any harm. As such, they sometimes bear weapons so that they can chastise any mischievous persons who want to do harm to Kṛṣṇa. Counted among the well-wisher friends are Subhadra,* Maṇḍalībhadra, Bhadravardhana, Gobhaṭa, Yakṣa, Indrabhaṭa, Bhadrāṅga, Vīrabhadra, Mahāguṇa, Vijaya and Balabhadra. They are older than Kṛṣṇa and are always thinking of His welfare.

One of the elderly friends said, "My dear Maṇḍalībhadra, why are you wielding a shining sword as though you were running toward Ariṣṭāsura to kill him? My dear Baladeva, why are You unnecessarily bearing that heavy plow? My dear Vijaya, don't be unnecessarily agitated. My dear Bhadravardhana, there is no need to make these threatening motions. If you will all look more closely you will see that it is only a thundercloud upon Govardhana Hill; it is not the Ariṣṭāsura in the shape of a bull, as you have imagined." These older, well-wishing friends of Kṛṣṇa had imagined a large cloud to be the Ariṣṭāsura, appearing in the shape of a huge bull. In the midst of their excitement one of them ascertained that it was actually only a cloud on Govardhana Hill. He therefore informed the others not to take the trouble of worrying about Kṛṣṇa, because there was no present danger from Ariṣṭāsura.

Among the well-wisher friends, Maṇḍalībhadra and Balabhadra are the chiefs. Maṇḍalībhadra is described as follows. His complexion is yellowish, and his dress is very attractive. He always carries a stick of various colors. He wears a peacock feather on his head and always looks very beautiful. Maṇḍalībhadra's attitude is revealed in this statement: "My dear friends, our beloved Kṛṣṇa is now very tired from working with the cows in the pasturing grounds and from traveling all over the forests. I can see that He is very fatigued. Let me massage His head silently while He is taking rest in His house. And you, Subala—you just massage His thighs."

One devotee described the personal beauty of Baladeva as follows "Let me take shelter of the lotus feet of Balarāma, whose beauty is en-

*Not to be confused with Kṛṣṇa's sister, Subhadrā.

hanced by the earrings touching His cheeks. His face is decorated with *tilaka* made from *kastūrī* [musk], and His broad chest is decorated with a garland of *guñjā* [small conchshells]. His complexion is as white as an autumn cloud, He wears garments of blue color, and His voice is very grave. His arms are very long, touching His thighs, and He has shown His great strength by killing the Pralamba demon. Let me take shelter of this chivalrous Balarāma."*

Baladeva's affection for Kṛṣṇa is illustrated in this statement to Subala: "My dear friend, please inform Kṛṣṇa not to go to Kāliya's lake today. Today is His birthday, and so I wish to go along with Mother Yaśodā to bathe Him. Tell Him He should not leave the house today." This shows how Balarāma, Kṛṣṇa's elder brother, took care of Kṛṣṇa with parental love, within the scope of fraternal affection.

Friends who are younger than Kṛṣṇa, who are always attached to Him and who give Him all kinds of service are called ordinary friends, or, simply, friends. Such ordinary friends are called *sakhās,* and the names of some *sakhās* are Viśāla, Vṛṣabha, Ojasvī, Devaprastha, Varūthapa, Maranda, Kusumāpīḍa, Maṇibandha and Karandhama. All of these *sakhā* friends of Kṛṣṇa seek only to serve Him. Sometimes some of them would rise early in the morning and immediately go to Kṛṣṇa's place and wait at the door to see Kṛṣṇa and to accompany Him to the pasturing grounds. In the meantime, Kṛṣṇa would be dressed by Mother Yaśodā, and when she would see a boy standing at the door, she would call him, "Well, Viśāla, why are you standing there? Come here!" So with the permission of Mother Yaśodā, he would immediately enter the house. And while Mother Yaśodā was dressing Kṛṣṇa, he would try to help put on Kṛṣṇa's ankle bells, and Kṛṣṇa would jokingly strike him with His flute. Then Mother Yaśodā would call, "Kṛṣṇa, what is this? Why are You teasing Your friend?" And Kṛṣṇa would laugh, and the friend would also laugh. These are some of the activities of Kṛṣṇa's *sakhās.* Sometimes the *sakhās* would take care of the cows who were going hither and thither. They would tell Kṛṣṇa, "Your cows were going off here and there," and Kṛṣṇa would thank them.

Sometimes when Kṛṣṇa and His *sakhās* went to the pasturing ground, Kaṁsa would send a demon to kill Kṛṣṇa. Therefore, almost every day

*Balarāma and Baladeva are different names for the same expansion of Kṛṣṇa. He is Kṛṣṇa's elder brother.

there was a fight with some different kind of demon. After fighting with a demon, Kṛṣṇa would feel fatigued, the hairs on His head would be scattered, and the *sakhās* would immediately come and try to relieve Him in different ways. Some friends would say, "My dear Viśāla, please take this fan of lotus leaves and fan Kṛṣṇa so that He may feel some comfort. Varūthapa, you just brush the scattered hairs on Kṛṣṇa's head which have fallen upon His face. Vṛṣabha, don't talk unnecessarily! Immediately massage Kṛṣṇa's body. His arms have become tired from fighting and wrestling with that demon. Oh, just see how our friend Kṛṣṇa has become tired!" These are some examples of the treatment given to Kṛṣṇa by the *sakhās.*

One of the *sakhās,* known as Devaprastha, is described as follows. He is very strong, a ready scholar, and is very expert in playing ball. He wears a white dress, and he ties his hair into a bunch with a rope. Whenever there is a fight between Kṛṣṇa and the demons, Devaprastha is the first to help, and he fights just like an elephant.

One of the *gopīs* once said to her friend, "My dear beautiful friend, when Kṛṣṇa, the son of Mahārāja Nanda, was taking rest within the cave of a hill, He was keeping His head on the arms of Śrīdāmā, and He was putting His left hand on Dāmā's chest. Taking this opportunity, Devaprastha, out of his strong affection for Kṛṣṇa, immediately began to massage His legs." Such are the activities of Kṛṣṇa's friends out on the pasturing grounds.

The more confidential friends are called *priya-sakhās* and are almost Kṛṣṇa's age. Because of their very confidential friendship, their behavior is only on the basis of pure friendship. The behavior of other friends is on the ground of paternal love or servitude, but the basic principle of the confidential friends is simply friendship on an equal level. Some confidential friends are as follows: Śrīdāmā, Sudāmā, Dāmā, Vasudāmā, Kiṅkiṇi, Stoka-kṛṣṇa, Aṁśu, Bhadrasena, Vilāsī, Puṇḍarīka, Viṭaṅka and Kalaviṅka. By their various activities in different pastimes, all of these friends used to give transcendental pleasure to Kṛṣṇa.

The behavior of these confidential friends is described by a friend of Rādhārāṇī who told Rādhārāṇī, "My dear graceful Rādhārāṇī, Your intimate friend Kṛṣṇa is also served by His intimate boyfriends. Some of them cut jokes with Him in mild voices and please Him very much by this." For example, Kṛṣṇa had one *brāhmaṇa* friend whose name was Madhumaṅgala. This boy would joke by playing the part of a greedy *brāhmaṇa.* Whenever the friends ate, he would eat more than all others, especially *laḍḍus,* of which he was very fond. Then after eating more *laḍḍus* than anyone else, Madhumaṅgala would still not be satisfied, and he would say to Kṛṣṇa, "If You give me one more *laḍḍu,* then I shall be pleased to give You my blessings so that Your friend Rādhārāṇī will be very much pleased with You." The *brāhmaṇas* are supposed to give blessings to the *vaiśyas* (farming and merchant caste), and Kṛṣṇa presented Himself as the son of Mahārāja Nanda, a *vaiśya;* so the *brāhmaṇa* boy was right in giving blessings to Kṛṣṇa. Thus Kṛṣṇa was very pleased by His friend's blessings, and He would supply him with more and more *laḍḍus.*

Sometimes a confidential friend would come before Kṛṣṇa and embrace Him with great affection and love. Another friend would then come up from the rear and cover Kṛṣṇa's eyes with his hands. Kṛṣṇa would always feel very happy by such dealings with His confidential friends.

Out of all these confidential friends, Śrīdāmā is considered to be the chief. Śrīdāmā used to put on a yellow-colored dress. He would carry a buffalo horn, and his turban was of reddish, copper color. His bodily complexion was blackish, and around his neck there was a nice garland. He would always challenge Kṛṣṇa in joking friendship. Let us pray to Śrīdāmā to bestow his mercy upon us!

Sometimes Śrīdāmā used to address Kṛṣṇa, "Oh, You are so cruel that You left us alone on the bank of the Yamunā, and we were all mad from not seeing You there! Now it is our great fortune that we are able to see You here. If You want to pacify us, You must embrace each one of us with Your arms. But believe me, my dear friend, a moment's absence from You creates great havoc, not only for us but for the cows also. Everything becomes disarranged, and we become mad after You."

There are other friends who are still more confidential. They are called *priya-narmā,* or intimate friends. Counted among the *priya-narmā* friends are Subala, Arjuna, Gandharva, Vasanta and Ujjvala. There was talk among the friends of Rādhārāṇī, the *gopīs,* about these most intimate friends. One *gopī* addressed Rādhārāṇī thus: "My dear Kṛśāṅgī [delicate one], just see how Subala is whispering Your message into Kṛṣṇa's ear, how he is delivering the confidential letter of Śyāmādāsī silently into Kṛṣṇa's hand, how he is delivering the betel nuts prepared by Pālikā into Kṛṣṇa's mouth, and how he is decorating Kṛṣṇa with the garland prepared by Tārakā. Did you know, my dear friend, that all these most intimate friends of Kṛṣṇa are always engaged in His service in this way?" Out of the many intimate *priya-narmās,* Subala and Ujjvala are considered to be the most prominent.

Subala's body is described as follows. His complexion is just like molten gold. He is very, very dear to Kṛṣṇa. He always has a garland around his neck, and he wears yellow clothing. His eyes are just like lotus-flower petals, and he is so intelligent that by his talking and his moral instructions all the other friends take the highest pleasure. Let us all offer our respectful obeisances unto Kṛṣṇa's friend Subala!

The degree of intimacy shared by Kṛṣṇa and Subala can be understood by the fact that the talks between them were so confidential that no one else could understand what they were saying.

The description of Ujjvala, another intimate friend, is given as follows. Ujjvala always wears some garment of orange color, and the movements of his eyes are always very restless. He likes to decorate himself with all kinds of flowers, his bodily hue is almost like Kṛṣṇa's, and on his neck there is always a necklace of pearls. He is always very dear to Kṛṣṇa. Let us all worship Ujjvala, the most intimate friend of Kṛṣṇa!

About the confidential service of Ujjvala, this statement is to be found, addressed by Rādhārāṇī to one of Her friends: "My dear friend, it is impossible for Me to keep My prestige! I wanted to avoid talking to Kṛṣṇa anymore—but just see! There again is His friend Ujjvala, coming to Me with his canvassing work. His entreaties are so powerful that it is very difficult for a *gopī* to resist her love for Kṛṣṇa, even though she may be very bashful, devoted to her family duties and most faithful to her husband."

The following is a statement by Ujjvala, showing his jubilant nature: "My dear Kṛṣṇa, O killer of Aghāsura, You have extended Your loving affairs so much that You can be compared to the great ocean, which is without limitations. At the same time, the young girls of the world, who are all searching after the perfect lover, have become just like rivers running into this ocean. Under the circumstances, all these rivers of young girls may try to divert their courses to some other place, but at the end they must come unto You."

Among the groups of different friends of Kṛṣṇa, some are well known from various scriptures, and some are well known by popular tradition. There are three divisions among Kṛṣṇa's friends: some are eternally in friendship with Kṛṣṇa, some are elevated demigods, and some are perfected devotees. In all of these groups there are some who by nature are fixed in Kṛṣṇa's service and are always engaged in giving counsel; some of them are very fond of joking and naturally cause Kṛṣṇa to smile by their words; some of them are by nature very simple, and by their simplicity they please Lord Kṛṣṇa; some of them create wonderful situations by their activities, apparently against Kṛṣṇa; some of them are very talkative, always arguing with Kṛṣṇa and creating a debating atmosphere; and some of them are very gentle and give pleasure to Kṛṣṇa by their sweet words. All of these friends are very intimate with Kṛṣṇa, and they show expertise in their different activities, their aim always being to please Kṛṣṇa.

42

Fraternal Loving Affairs

ṛṣṇa's age, His beauty, His bugle, His flute, His conchshell and His leasing attitude all provoke love in friendship for Him. His excepional joking abilities, exhibited sometimes by His pretending to be a oyal prince, or even the Supreme Personality of Godhead, also give mpetus to devotees developing love for Kṛṣṇa in friendship.

Learned scholars have divided Kṛṣṇa's age into three periods: the age p through five years is called *kaumāra,* the age from the sixth through he tenth year is called *paugaṇḍa,* and the age from the eleventh through fteenth year is called *kaiśora.* While Kṛṣṇa is spending His days as a owherd boy, He is in the *kaumāra* and *paugaṇḍa* ages. In the *kaiśora* ge, when Kṛṣṇa appeared in Gokula, He acted as a cowherd boy, and hen, when He was sixteen, He went to Mathurā to kill Kaṁsa.

The *kaumāra* age is just suitable for reciprocating the love of a child ith Mother Yaśodā. In the Tenth Canto, Thirteenth Chapter, verse 1, of *Śrīmad-Bhāgavatam,* Śukadeva Gosvāmī tells King Parīkṣit, My dear King, although Lord Krsna is the supreme enjoyer and the eneficiary of all kinds of sacrificial ceremonies, He still used to eat ith His cowherd boyfriends. This is because at that time He accepted e pastimes of an ordinary boy, keeping His flute under His arm and is bugle on the right side in His belt, along with His cane. In His ft hand He would hold a lump of rice paste with yogurt, and in His ngers would be *pīlu,* the king of fruits. When He would thus sit among is friends, it would appear that He was the whorl of a lotus flower nd that the friends surrounding Him were petals. As they thus enjoyed king among themselves, the denizens of heaven would become struck ith wonder and would only stare at the scene."

Kṛṣṇa's *paugaṇḍa* age can be further divided into three periods—namely the beginning, middle and end. In the beginning of the *paugaṇḍa* age there is a very nice reddish luster on His lips, His abdomen is very thin, and on His neck are circles like those on a conchshell. Sometimes, some outside visitors would return to Vṛndāvana to see Kṛṣṇa and, upon seeing Him again, would exclaim, "My dear Mukunda, Your beauty is gradually increasing, just like the leaf on a banyan tree! My dear lotus-eyed one, Your neck is gradually manifesting circles like those of the conchshell. And in the shining moonlight Your teeth and cheeks are competing with the *padmarāga* jewels in their beautiful arrangement. I am sure that Your beautiful bodily development is now giving much pleasure to Your friends."

At this age Kṛṣṇa was garlanded with various kinds of flowers. He used to put on a silk dress, colored with various kinds of dye. Such beautiful decorations are considered cosmetics for Kṛṣṇa. Kṛṣṇa would wear this dress when He used to go into the forest to tend the cows. Sometimes He would wrestle there with His different friends, and sometimes they would dance all together in the forest. These are some of the specific activities of the *paugaṇḍa* age.

The cowherd friends of Kṛṣṇa were so happy in His company that they expressed their transcendental feelings within themselves thus: "Dear Kṛṣṇa, You are always busy tending the cows which are scattered all over beautiful Vṛndāvana. You have a beautiful garland, a small conchshell, a peacock feather on Your turban, yellow-colored silk cloth, decorations of *karṇikāra* flowers on Your ears and a *mallikā* flower garland on Your chest. Appearing so beautiful, when You pretend, just like an actor, to be fighting with us, You give us unlimited transcendental bliss."

When Kṛṣṇa is more grown up, in the middle age of *paugaṇḍa,* His nails become finely sharp, and His chubby cheeks become lustrous and round. On the two sides of His waist above His belt there are three distinct lines of folded skin, called *trivalī.*

The cowherd boyfriends of Kṛṣṇa felt very proud of their association with Him. At that time the tip of His nose defeated the beauty of sesame flowers, the luster of His cheeks defeated the glow of pearls, and the two sides of His body were exquisitely beautiful. In this age Kṛṣṇa wore a silk dress that glittered like lightning, His head was decorated with a silk turban covered with gold lace, and in His hand He carried a stick about fifty-six inches long.* Seeing this exquisitely beautiful dress of Kṛṣṇa, one devotee addressed his friend in this manner: "My dear friend, just look at Kṛṣṇa! See how He is carrying in His hand a stick which is bound up and down with golden rings, how His turban with golden lace is showing such a beautiful luster, and how His dress is giving His friends the highest transcendental pleasure!"

At the end of Kṛṣṇa's *paugaṇḍa* age, Kṛṣṇa's hair sometimes hangs down to His hips, and sometimes it becomes scattered. In this age His two shoulders become higher and broader, and His face is always decorated with marks of *tilaka*. When His beautiful hair scatters over His shoulders, it appears to be a goddess of fortune embracing Him, and this embracing is highly relished by His friends. Subala once addressed Him in this way: "My dear Keśava, Your round turban, the lotus flower in Your hand, the vertical marks of *tilaka* on Your forehead, Your *kuṅkuma*-scented musk and all of Your beautiful bodily features are defeating me today, although I am usually stronger than You or any of our friends. Since this is so, I do not know how these features of Your body can fail to defeat the pride of all the young girls of Vṛndāvana. When I am so defeated by this beauty, what chance is there for those who are naturally very simple and flexible?"

At this age Kṛṣṇa took pleasure in whispering into the ears of His friends, and the subject of His talks was the beauty of the *gopīs,* who were just tarrying before them. Subala once addressed Kṛṣṇa thus: "My dear Kṛṣṇa, You are very cunning. You can understand the thoughts of others; therefore I am whispering within Your ear that all of these five *gopīs,* who are most beautiful, have been attracted by Your dress. And I believe that Cupid has entrusted them with the responsibility of conquering You." In other words, the beauty of the *gopīs* was capable of conquering Kṛṣṇa, although Kṛṣṇa is the conqueror of all universes.

The symptoms of the *kaiśora* age have already been described, and it is at this age that devotees generally most appreciate Kṛṣṇa. Kṛṣṇa with Rādhārāṇī is worshiped as Kiśora-kiśorī. Kṛṣṇa does not increase

*The specific pastimes in this period took place in the forest known as Bhāṇḍīravana. This Bhāṇḍīravana, along with the eleven other *vanas,* or forests, is still existing in the Vṛndāvana area, and devotees who circumambulate the whole area of Vṛndāvana can know the beauty of these forests even today.

His age beyond this form of *kaiśora,* and it is confirmed in the *Brahma-saṁhitā* that although He is the oldest personality and has innumerable different forms, His original form is always youthful. In the pictures of Kṛṣṇa on the Battlefield of Kurukṣetra we can see that He is youthful, although at that time He was old enough to have sons, grandsons and great-grandsons. The cowherd boyfriends of Kṛṣṇa once said, "Dear Kṛṣṇa, You need not decorate Your body with so many ornaments. Your transcendental features are themselves so beautiful that You do not require any ornamentation." At this age, whenever Kṛṣṇa begins to vibrate His flute early in the morning, all of His friends immediately get up from bed just to join Him in going to the pasturing grounds. One of the friends once said, "My dear cowherd friends, the sound of Kṛṣṇa's flute from above Govardhana Hill is telling us that we need not go to search Him out on the bank of the Yamunā."

Pārvatī, the wife of Lord Śiva, told her husband, "My dear Pañcamukha [five-faced], just look at the Pāṇḍavas! After hearing the sound of Kṛṣṇa's conchshell, known as Pāñcajanya, they have regained their strength and are just like lions."

At this age, Kṛṣṇa once dressed Himself up exactly like Rādhārāṇī, just to create fun among His friends. He put on golden earrings, and because He was blackish, He smeared the pulp of *kuṅkuma* all over His body in order to become as fair as She. By seeing this dress, Kṛṣṇa's friend Subala became very astonished.

Kṛṣṇa played with His intimate friends sometimes by fighting or wrestling with their arms, sometimes by playing ball and sometimes by playing chess. Sometimes they carried one another on their shoulders, and sometimes they exhibited their expertness at whirling logs. And the cowherd friends used to please Kṛṣṇa by sitting together with Him on couches or on swings, by lying together on their beds, by joking together and by swimming in the pool. All these activities are called *anubhāva.* Whenever all the friends would assemble in the company of Kṛṣṇa, they would immediately engage in all these functions, especially in dancing together. Regarding their wrestling, one friend once asked Kṛṣṇa, "My dear friend, O killer of the Agha demon, You are very proudly wandering among Your friends trying to exhibit Your arms as very strong. Is it that You are envious of me? I know that You cannot defeat me in wrestling, and I also know that You were sitting idly for a long time because You were hopeless of defeating me."

All the friends were very daring and would risk any difficulty, because they were confident that Kṛṣṇa would help them to be victorious in all adventures. They used to sit together and advise one another what to do, sometimes inducing one another to be engaged in welfare work. Sometimes they would offer betel nuts to one another, decorate one another's faces with *tilaka* or smear pulp of *candana* on one another's bodies. Sometimes, for the sake of amusement, they used to decorate their faces in strange ways. Another business of the friends was that each of them wanted to defeat Kṛṣṇa. Sometimes they used to snatch His clothing or snatch away the flowers from His hands. Sometimes one would try to induce another to decorate his body for him, and failing this, they were always ready to fight, challenging one another to combat in wrestling. These were some of the general activities of Kṛṣṇa and His friends.

Another important pastime of the friends of Kṛṣṇa was that they served as messengers to and from the *gopīs;* they introduced the *gopīs* to Kṛṣṇa and canvassed for Kṛṣṇa. When the *gopīs* were in disagreement with Kṛṣṇa, these friends would support Kṛṣṇa's side in His presence—but when Kṛṣṇa was not present, they would support the side of the *gopīs.* In this way, sometimes supporting one side, sometimes the other, they would talk very privately, with much whispering in the ears, although none of the business was very serious.

The servants of Kṛṣṇa were sometimes engaged in collecting flowers, decorating His body with valuable ornaments and trinkets, dancing before Him, singing, helping Him herd the cows, massaging His body, preparing flower garlands and sometimes fanning His body. These were some of the primary duties of the servants of Kṛṣṇa. The friends and servants of Kṛṣṇa were combined together in serving Him, and all of their activities are known as *anubhāva.*

When Kṛṣṇa came out from the Yamunā after chastising the Kāliya-nāga, Śrīdāmā wanted to embrace Him first, but he could not raise his arms because of his great feeling of respect.

When Kṛṣṇa used to play on His flute, the vibration appeared just like the roaring of clouds in the sky during the constellation of Svātī. According to Vedic astronomical calculation, if there is rain during the constellation of the Svātī star, any rain falling on the sea will produce pearls, and rain falling on a serpent will produce jewels. Similarly, when Kṛṣṇa's flute roared like a thundercloud under the Svātī constellation, the resulting perspiration on Śrīdāmā's body appeared to be just like pearls.

When Kṛṣṇa and Subala were embracing one another, Śrīmatī Rādhārāṇī became a little envious, and hiding Her hot temperament She said, "My dear Subala, you are very fortunate because even in the presence of superiors you and Kṛṣṇa have no hesitation in putting your arms on each other's shoulders. I think it must be admitted that in your previous lives you have succeeded in many kinds of austerities." The idea is that although Rādhārāṇī was accustomed to putting Her arms on Kṛṣṇa's shoulders, it was not possible for Her to do such a thing in the presence of Her superiors, whereas Subala could do so freely. Rādhārāṇī therefore praised his good fortune.

When Kṛṣṇa entered the lake of Kāliya, His intimate friends became so perturbed that their bodily colors faded, and they all produced horrible gurgling sounds. At that time all of them fell down on the ground as if unconscious. Similarly, when there was a forest fire, all of Kṛṣṇa's friends neglected their own protection and surrounded Kṛṣṇa on all sides to protect Him from the flames. This behavior of the friends toward Kṛṣṇa is described by thoughtful poets as *vyabhicārī*. In *vyabhicārī* ecstatic love for Kṛṣṇa there is sometimes madness, dexterity, fear, laziness, jubilation, pride, dizziness, meditation, disease, forgetfulness and humbleness. These are some of the common symptoms in the stage of *vyabhicārī* ecstatic love for Kṛṣṇa.

When there are dealings between Kṛṣṇa and His friends which are completely devoid of any feelings of respect and they all treat one another on an equal level, such ecstatic love in friendship is called *sthāyī*. When one is situated in this confidential friendly relationship with Kṛṣṇa, one shows symptoms of love such as attraction, affection, affinity and attachment. An example of *sthāyī* was exhibited when Arjuna* told Akrūra, "My dear son of Gāndinī, please ask Kṛṣṇa when I shall be able to embrace Him in my arms."

*This Arjuna, living in Vṛndāvana, is different from the friend of the same name to whom the *Bhagavad-gītā* was spoken.

When there is full knowledge of Kṛṣṇa's superiority and yet in dealsings with Him on friendly terms respectfulness is completely absent, that stage is called affection. There is one brilliant example of this affection. When the demigods, headed by Lord Śiva, were offering respectful prayers to Kṛṣṇa, describing the glorious opulences of the Lord, Arjuna* stood before Him with his hand on His shoulders and brushed the dust from His peacock feather.

When the Pāṇḍavas were banished by Duryodhana and forced to live incognito in the forest, no one could trace out where they were staying. At that time, the great sage Nārada met Lord Kṛṣṇa and said, "My dear Mukunda, although You are the Supreme Personality of Godhead, the all-powerful person, by making friendship with You the Pāṇḍavas have become bereft of their legitimate right to the kingdom of the world—and, moreover, they are now living in the forest incognito. Sometimes they must work as ordinary laborers in someone else's house. These symptoms appear to be very inauspicious materially, but the beauty is that the Pāṇḍavas have not lost their faith in You or their love for You, in spite of all these tribulations. In fact, they are always thinking of You and chanting Your name in ecstatic friendship."

Another example of acute affection for Kṛṣṇa is given in the Tenth Canto, Fifteenth Chapter, verse 18, of *Śrīmad-Bhāgavatam*. In the pasturing ground Kṛṣṇa felt a little tired and wanted to take rest, so He lay down on the ground. At that time, many cowherd boys assembled there and with great affection began to sing suitable songs so that Kṛṣṇa would rest very nicely.

There is a nice example of the friendship between Kṛṣṇa and Arjuna on the Battlefield of Kurukṣetra. When the fighting was going on, Aśvatthāmā, the son of Droṇācārya, unceremoniously attacked Kṛṣṇa, although according to the prevailing rules of chivalry one's chariot driver should never be attacked by the enemy. Aśvatthāmā behaved heinously in so many ways that he did not hesitate to attack Kṛṣṇa's body, although Kṛṣṇa was acting only as charioteer for Arjuna. When Arjuna saw that Aśvatthāmā was releasing various kinds of arrows to hurt Kṛṣṇa, he immediately stood in front of Kṛṣṇa to intercept all of them. At that time, although Arjuna was being harmed by those arrows, he felt an ecstatic love for Kṛṣṇa, and the arrows appeared to him like showers of flowers.

There is another instance of ecstatic love for Kṛṣṇa in friendship.

Once when a cowherd boy named Vṛṣabha was collecting flowers from the forest to prepare a garland to be offered to Kṛṣṇa, the sun reached its zenith, and although the sunshine was scorching hot, Vṛṣabha felt it to be like the moonshine. That is the way of rendering transcendental loving service to the Lord; when devotees are put into great difficulties—even like the Pāṇḍavas, as described above—they feel all their miserable conditions to be great facilities for serving the Lord.

Another instance of Arjuna's friendship with Kṛṣṇa was described by Nārada, who reminded Kṛṣṇa, "When Arjuna was learning the art of shooting arrows, he could not see You for so many days. But when You arrived there, he stopped all His activities and immediately embraced You." This means that even though Arjuna was engaged in learning about the military art, he had not forgotten Kṛṣṇa for a moment, and as soon as there was an opportunity to see Kṛṣṇa, Arjuna immediately embraced Him.

One servant of Kṛṣṇa named Patrī once addressed Him like this: "My dear Lord, You protected the cowherd boys from the hunger of the Aghāsura demon, and You protected them from the poisonous effects of the Kāliya snake. And You also saved them from the fierce forest fire. But I am suffering from Your separation, which is more severe than the hunger of Aghāsura, the poison of Lake Kāliya and the burning of the forest fire. So why should You not protect me from the pangs of separation?" Another friend once told Kṛṣṇa, "My dear enemy of Kaṁsa, since You have left us, the heat of separation has become extraordinary. And this heat is felt more severely when we understand that in Bhāṇḍīravana You are being refreshed by the waves of the cooling river known as Bhānu-tanayā [Rādhārāṇī]." The purport is that when Kṛṣṇa was engaged with Rādhārāṇī, the cowherd boys headed by Subala were feeling great separation, and that was unbearable for them.

Another friend addressed Kṛṣṇa thus: "My dear Kṛṣṇa, O killer of Aghāsura, when You left Vṛndāvana to kill King Kaṁsa in Mathurā, all the cowherd boys became bereft of their four *bhūtas* [the elements earth, water, fire and space]. And the fifth *bhūta,* the air, was flowing very rapidly within their nostrils." When Kṛṣṇa went to Mathurā to kill King Kaṁsa, all the cowherd boys became so afflicted by the separation that they almost died. When a person is dead it is said that he has given up the five elements, known as *bhūtas,* as the body again mixes with the five elements from which it was prepared. In this case, although the four elements earth, water, fire and ether were already gone, the remaining element, air, was still very prominent and was blowing through their nostrils furiously. In other words, after Kṛṣṇa left Vṛndāvana, the cowherd boys were always anxious about what would happen in His fight with King Kaṁsa.

Another friend once informed Kṛṣṇa, "When one of Your friends was feeling much separation from You, there were tears covering his lotus eyes, and so the black drones of sleep became discouraged from entering his eyes and left that place." When there is a lotus flower, the black drones fly into it to collect honey. The eyes of Kṛṣṇa's friend are compared to the lotus flower, and because they were full of tears the black drones of sleep could not collect honey from his lotus eyes and therefore left the place. In other words, because he was too much afflicted, his eyes were full of tears, and he could not sleep. This is an example of staying up at night because of separation from Kṛṣṇa.

An example of helplessness is described in the following statement: "Due to Kṛṣṇa's departure from Vṛndāvana to Mathurā, Kṛṣṇa's dearest cowherd boys felt as mentally light as possible. They were like fragments of cotton, lighter than the air, and were all floating in the air without any shelter." In other words, the minds of the cowherd boys became almost vacant on account of Kṛṣṇa's separation. An example of impatience was also shown by the cowherd boys when Kṛṣṇa went to Mathurā. Out of the sorrow of separation, all these boys forgot to take care of their cowherding and tried to forget all the melodious songs they used to sing in the pasturing ground. At last they had no desire to live anymore, being separated from Kṛṣṇa.

An example of stillness was described by a friend of Kṛṣṇa's who informed Him in Mathurā that all the cowherd boys had become just like leafless trees on the tops of hills. They appeared almost naked, being skinny and frail, and did not carry any fruits or flowers. He informed Kṛṣṇa that all the cowherd boys residing in Vṛndāvana were as still as the trees at the tops of hills. Sometimes they felt diseased from their separation from Kṛṣṇa, and being so greatly disappointed, they were aimlessly wandering on the banks of the Yamunā.

There is also an example of madness caused by separation from Kṛṣṇa. When Kṛṣṇa was absent from Vṛndāvana, all the cowherd boys became bewildered, and having given up all kinds of activities, they appeared to be mad and forgot all their regular business. They were sometimes lying down on the ground, sometimes rolling in the dust, sometimes laughing and sometimes running very swiftly. All of these symptoms gave them the appearance of madmen. One friend of Kṛṣṇa's criticized Him by saying, "My dear Lord, You have become the King of Mathurā after killing Kaṁsa, and that is very good news for us. But at Vṛndāvana all the residents have become blind from their continuous crying over Your absence. They are full only of anxieties and are not cheered at all by Your becoming the King of Mathurā."

Sometimes there were also signs of death caused by separation from Kṛṣṇa. Once Kṛṣṇa was told, "My dear enemy of Kaṁsa, because of their separation from You, the cowherd boys are suffering too much, and they are now lying down in the valleys, breathing only slightly. In order to sympathize with the boys' regrettable condition, even the forest friends, the deer, are shedding tears."

In the *Mathurā-khaṇḍa* chapter of the *Skanda Purāṇa,* there is a description of Kṛṣṇa and Balarāma, surrounded by all the cowherd boys, always engaged in taking care of the cows and calves. When Kṛṣṇa was met by Arjuna at a potter's shop in the city of Drupada-nagara, because of the similarity of their bodily features they made intimate friendship. This is an instance of friendship caused by the attraction of similar bodies.

In the Tenth Canto of *Śrīmad-Bhāgavatam,* Seventy-first Chapter, verse 27, it is stated that when Kṛṣṇa arrived in the city of Indraprastha, Bhīma was so overwhelmed with joy that with tears in his eyes and a smiling face he immediately embraced his maternal cousin. Following him were his young brothers Nakula and Sahadeva, along with Arjuna, and they all became so overwhelmed at seeing Kṛṣṇa that with full satisfaction they embraced the Lord, who is known as Acyuta (the infallible). There is a similar statement about the cowherd boys of Vṛndāvana. When Kṛṣṇa was on the Battlefield of Kurukṣetra, all the cowherd boys came to see Him, wearing jeweled earrings in their ears. Becoming so greatly overjoyed, they extended their arms and embraced Kṛṣṇa as their old friend. These are instances of full satisfaction in friendship with Kṛṣṇa.

In the Tenth Canto, Twelfth Chapter, verse 12, of *Śrīmad-Bhāgavatam,* it is stated that even after undergoing severe penances and austerities and performing the yogic principles, the great mystic *yogīs* can hardly become eligible to achieve the dust of the lotus feet of Kṛṣṇa, but the same Personality of Godhead, Kṛṣṇa, is easily available to the vision of the residents of Vṛndāvana. This means there is no comparison to the great fortune of these devotees. The friendly relationship of the cowherd boys with Kṛṣṇa is a particular type of spiritual ecstasy almost similar to the ecstasy of conjugal love. This ecstasy of loving affairs between the cowherd boys and Kṛṣṇa is very difficult to explain. Great expert devotees like Rūpa Gosvāmī express their astonishment at the inconceivable feelings which are in Kṛṣṇa and His cowherd boyfriends.

This particular type of ecstatic love shared between Kṛṣṇa and His confidential friends further develops into parental love, and on from there it may develop into conjugal love, the most exalted humor, or mellow, of ecstatic love between Lord Kṛṣṇa and His devotees.

43

Parenthood

When ecstatic love develops into the relationship of parenthood and becomes steadily established, the relationship is called *vātsalya-rasa*. The exhibition of this *vātsalya-rasa* standard of devotional service can be found in the dealings of Kṛṣṇa with His devotees who represent themselves as superior personalities like father, mother and teacher.

Learned scholars have described the impetuses for parental love for Kṛṣṇa, existing in the elderly personalities who are in relation with Him, as follows: "The Supreme Personality of Godhead, whose bodily complexion is just like a bluish, new-grown lotus flower, whose body is very delicate and whose lotus eyes are surrounded by scattered hair as black as bees, was walking on the streets of Vṛndāvana when Mother Yaśodā, the beloved wife of Nanda Mahārāja, saw Him. Immediately the milk began to flow from her breasts, soaking her body." Some specific provocations for parental love of Kṛṣṇa are listed as His blackish bodily hue, which is very attractive and pleasing to see, His all-auspicious bodily features, His mildness, His sweet words, His simplicity, His shyness, His humility, His constant readiness to offer respect to the elderly and His charity. All of these qualities are considered ecstatic provocations for parental love.

In *Śrīmad-Bhāgavatam,* Tenth Canto, Eighth Chapter, verse 45, it is stated by Śukadeva Gosvāmī that Mother Yaśodā accepted Lord Kṛṣṇa as her son, although He is accepted in the *Vedas* as the King of heaven, in the *Upaniṣads* as the impersonal Brahman, in philosophy as the supreme male, by the *yogīs* as the Supersoul and by the devotees as the Supreme Personality of Godhead. Once Mother Yaśodā addressed one of her friends in this way: "Nanda Mahārāja (the leader of the cowherd men) and I worshiped Lord Viṣṇu, and as a result of this worship Kṛṣṇa has been saved from the clutches of Pūtanā and other demons. The twin *arjuna* trees were, of course, broken due to a strong wind, and although Kṛṣṇa appeared to have lifted Govardhana Hill along with Balarāma, I think that Nanda Mahārāja actually held the mountain. Otherwise how could it have been possible for a little boy to lift such a great hill?" This is another example of ecstasy in parental love. This kind of parental love is generated in a devotee out of his conviction, in love, that he himself is superior to Kṛṣṇa and that without being taken care of by such a devotee Kṛṣṇa could not possibly live. One devotee therefore prayed to the parents of Lord Kṛṣṇa as follows: "Let me take shelter of the elderly parental devotees of Lord Kṛṣṇa. They are always anxious to serve Kṛṣṇa and to maintain Him, and they are always so kind to Him. Let us offer our respectful obeisances unto them for being so kind to the Supreme Personality of Godhead, who is the parent of the whole universe!"

There is a similar prayer by a *brāhmaṇa* who says, "Let others worship the *Vedas* and the *Upaniṣads,* and let others worship the *Mahābhārata* if they are afraid of material existence and want to become liberated from that condition. But as far as I am concerned, I wish only to worship Mahārāja Nanda, because the supreme absolute Personality of Godhead, Kṛṣṇa, is crawling in his courtyard as his own child."

Following is a list of respectful personalities who enjoy parental affection toward Kṛṣṇa: (1) Mother Yaśodā, the Queen of Vraja, (2) Mahārāja Nanda, the King of Vraja, (3) Mother Rohiṇī, the mother of Balarāma, (4) all the elderly *gopīs* whose sons were taken away by Lord Brahmā, (5) Devakī, the wife of Vasudeva, (6) the other fifteen wives of Vasudeva, (7) Kuntī, the mother of Arjuna, (8) Vasudeva, the real father of Kṛṣṇa and (9) Sāndīpani Muni, Kṛṣṇa's teacher. All these are considered respectable elderly personalities with parental love for Kṛṣṇa. This list is in order of superior importance, and thus we can see that Mother Yaśodā and Mahārāja Nanda are considered to be the supermost of all elderly personalities.

In *Śrīmad-Bhāgavatam,* Tenth Canto, Ninth Chapter, verse 3, Śukadeva Gosvāmī gives Mahārāja Parīkṣit a description of the form and beauty of Mother Yaśodā. He says, "My dear King, the wide hips of Mother Yaśodā were surrounded by silk and linen clothes, and her breasts were flowing with milk because of her affection. When she was churning butter and tightly holding the rope, the bangles on her hands and the earrings on her ears were moving, and from the nice decoration in her hair the flowers were slackening and falling down. Due to her excessive labor, there were drops of perspiration on her face."

There is another description of Mother Yaśodā in a devotee's prayer: "Let me be given protection by Mother Yaśodā, whose curly hairs are bound with thread, whose hair is very brightly beautified by the vermilion placed in the part, and whose bodily frame derides all her ornaments. Her eyes are always engaged in seeing the face of Kṛṣṇa, and thus they are always filled with tears. Her complexion, which resembles the bluish lotus flower, is enhanced in beauty by her dressing herself with many colorful garments. Let her merciful glance fall on all of us so that we may be protected from the clutches of *māyā* and smoothly progress in our devotional service!"

There is the following description of Mother Yaśodā's affection for Kṛṣṇa. After rising early in the morning, Mother Yaśodā first of all offered her breast milk to Kṛṣṇa, and then she began to chant various *mantras* for His protection. Then she would decorate His forehead very nicely and tie protective talismans on His arms. By all of these activities, it is definitely understood that she is the emblem of all maternal affection for Kṛṣṇa.

The description of Nanda Mahārāja's bodily features is as follows. The hairs on his head are generally black, but some of them are gray. His garments are of greenish color, like the new-grown leaves of a banyan tree. His belly is fatty, his complexion is exactly like the full moon, and he has a beautiful mustache. When Kṛṣṇa was a baby, one day He was walking in the courtyard, capturing the finger of His father, and because He could not walk steadily He appeared to be almost falling down. While Nanda Mahārāja was giving protection to his transcendental son in this way, all of a sudden there were drops of tears in his eyes, and he became overwhelmed with joy. Let us all offer our respectful obeisances unto the lotus feet of King Nanda!

Childhood age, childish dress, movements by the child, sweet words spoken by the child, nice smiling and various forms of childish play are considered provocations for increasing parental love for Kṛṣṇa. The childhood ages of Kṛṣṇa are divided into three periods: the beginning of the *kaumāra* age, the middle of the *kaumāra* age and the end of the *kaumāra* age. During the beginning and middle of the *kaumāra* age, Kṛṣṇa's thighs are fatty, and the inner parts of His eyes are whitish.

There are signs of teeth coming out, and He is very mild and gentle. He is described as follows: "When Kṛṣṇa had only three or four teeth coming out of His gums, His thighs were fatty, His body was very, very short, and He began to enhance the parental love of Nanda Mahārāja and Mother Yaśodā with the activities of His childish body. He was sometimes stepping with His legs again and again, sometimes crying, sometimes smiling, sometimes sucking His thumb and sometimes lying down flat. These are some of the different activities of the child Kṛṣṇa. When Kṛṣṇa was lying down flat, sometimes sucking the toes of His feet, sometimes throwing His legs upward, sometimes crying and sometimes smiling, Mother Yaśodā, seeing her son in such pastimes, did not show any sign of restricting Him, but rather began to watch her child with eagerness, enjoying these childhood pastimes." In the beginning of Kṛṣṇa's *kaumāra* age, the nails of tigers were set in a golden necklace about His neck. There was protective *tilaka* on His forehead, black mascara around His eyes and silk thread around His waist. These are the descriptions of Kṛṣṇa's dress at the beginning of the *kaumāra* age.

When Nanda Mahārāja saw the beauty of child Kṛṣṇa, with tiger nails on His chest, a complexion like the new-grown *tamāla* tree, beautifully decorated *tilaka* made with cow's urine, arm decorations of nice silk thread, and silk clothes tied around His waist—when Nanda Mahārāja saw his child like this, he never became satiated by the child's beauty.

In the middle *kaumāra* age, the upper portion of Kṛṣṇa's hair falls around His eyes. Sometimes He is covered with cloth around the lower part of His body, and sometimes He is completely naked. Sometimes He tries to walk, taking step by step, and sometimes He talks very sweetly, in broken language. These are some of the symptoms of His middle *kaumāra* age. He is thus described when Mother Yaśodā once saw Him in His middle *kaumāra* age: His scattered hairs were touching His eyebrows, and His eyes were restless, but He could not express His feelings with proper words; still, when He was talking, His talk was so nice and sweet to hear. When Mother Yaśodā looked at His little ears and saw Him naked, trying to run very quickly with His little legs, she was merged into the ocean of nectar. Kṛṣṇa's ornaments at this age are a pearl hanging from the septum of His nose, butter on His lotuslike palms, and some small bells hanging from His waist. It is stated that when Mother Yaśodā saw that the child was moving, ringing the bells on His waist, smiling at her with a pearl between His nostrils and with butter on His hands, she became wonderfully pleased to see her little child in that fashion.

While Kṛṣṇa was in the middle of His *kaumāra* age, His waist became thinner, His chest became broader, and His head was decorated with curly hair hanging down and resembling the wings of a crow. These wonderful features of Kṛṣṇa's body never failed to astonish Mother Yaśodā. At the end of His *kaumāra* age, Kṛṣṇa carried a small stick in His hand, His clothing was a little longer, and He had a knot around His waist, resembling the hood of a snake. In that dress He used to take care of the calves near the house, and sometimes He played with cowherd boys of about the same age. He had a slender flute and a buffalo-horn bugle, and sometimes He played on a flute made from the leaves of trees. These are some of the symptoms of the end of Kṛṣṇa's *kaumāra* age.

When Kṛṣṇa was a little grown up and was taking care of the small calves, He would often go near the forest. And when He was a little bit late returning home, Nanda Mahārāja would immediately get up on the *candra-śālikā* (a small shed built on the roof for getting a bird's-eye view all around), and he would watch for Him. Worrying about the late arrival of his little son, Nanda Mahārāja would remain on the *candra-śālikā* until he could indicate to his wife that Kṛṣṇa, surrounded by His little cowherd friends, was coming back with the calves. Nanda Mahārāja would point out the peacock feather on his child's head and would inform his beloved wife how the child was pleasing his eyes.

Mother Yaśodā would then address Nanda Mahārāja, "See my dear son, whose eyes are white, who has a turban on His head, a wrapper on His body and leg bells which tinkle very sweetly on His feet. He is coming near, along with His *surabhi* calves, and just see how He is wandering upon the sacred land of Vṛndāvana!"

Similarly, Mahārāja Nanda would address his wife, "My dear Yaśodā, just look at your offspring, Kṛṣṇa! See His blackish bodily luster, His eyes tinged with red color, His broad chest and His nice golden necklace! How wonderful He looks, and how He is increasing my transcendental bliss more and more!"

When Kṛṣṇa, the beloved son of Nanda Mahārāja, steps into His *kaiśora* age, although He becomes more beautiful, His parents still consider Him to be in the *paugaṇḍa* age—even though He is between the ages of ten and fifteen. When Kṛṣṇa is in His *pauganda* age, some of His servants also accept Him as being in the *kaiśora* age. When Kṛṣṇa performs His childish pastimes, His general practice is to break the milk and yogurt pots, throw the yogurt in the courtyard and steal the cream from the milk. Sometimes He breaks the churning rod, and sometimes He throws butter on the fire. In this way, He increases the transcendental pleasure of His mother, Yaśodā.

In this connection Mother Yaśodā once told Mukharā, her maidservant, "Just look at Kṛṣṇa looking stealthily toward all sides and slowly stepping forward from the bushes. It appears that He is coming just to steal the butter. Don't expose yourself or He may understand that we are looking toward Him. I want to enjoy the sight of His eyebrows moving in this cunning way, and I want to see His fearful eyes and beautiful face."

In enjoying Kṛṣṇa's attitude of stealing butter very stealthily, Mother Yaśodā experienced the ecstasy of maternal love by smelling His head, sometimes patting His body with her hand, sometimes offering blessings, sometimes ordering Him, sometimes gazing at Him, sometimes maintaining Him and sometimes giving Him good instructions not to become a thief. Such activities are in maternal ecstatic love. An important point to be observed in this connection is that the childish propensity of stealing is there even in the Supreme Personality of Godhead, and therefore this propensity is not artificial. However, in the spiritual relationship there is no inebriety to this stealing propensity, as there is in the material world.

In *Śrīmad-Bhāgavatam,* Tenth Canto, Thirteenth Chapter, verse 33, Śukadeva Gosvāmī tells King Parīkṣit, "My dear King, as soon as the elderly *gopīs* saw their sons coming, there was an inexpressible sign of parental love, and all of them became absorbed in affection. At first they were planning to chastise their sons for stealing butter, but as soon as the sons came before their eyes, they lost all of their angry attitudes and became overwhelmed with affection. They began to embrace their sons and smell their heads. While doing this, they became almost mad after their children." In their childhood pastimes, all these cowherd boys joined with Kṛṣṇa in stealing butter. But rather than become angry, Mother Yaśodā became wet from the milk flowing out of her breasts. Out of her affection for Kṛṣṇa, she began to smell His head repeatedly.

The general activities of all the mothers of the cowherd boys were to kiss them, to embrace them, to call them by their names and sometimes to chastise them mildly for their stealing habits. These manifestations of parental love are called *sāttvika* ecstasy, wherein manifestations of eight kinds of ecstatic symptoms are visible in full. In *Śrīmad-Bhāgavatam,* Tenth Canto, Thirteenth Chapter, verse 22, Śukadeva Gosvāmī tells King Parīkṣit, "All the mothers of the cowherd boys were illusioned by the covering influence of the *yogamāyā* potency of the Personality of Godhead, and as soon as they heard the flute-playing of their boys, they immediately stood up and mentally embraced their sons, who had been created by the direct internal potency of Kṛṣṇa. Accepting them as their born sons, they lifted them into their arms and began to embrace them, resting the children's bodies upon their own. The emotions created by this incident were sweeter than nectar turned into a palatable intoxicant, and the milk flowing out of their breasts was immediately drunk up by the children."

In the *Lalita-mādhava,* compiled by Rūpa Gosvāmī, Kṛṣṇa is addressed as follows: "My dear Kṛṣṇa, when You are engaged in herding the animals, the dust caused by the hooves of the calves and cows covers Your nice face and artistic *tilaka,* and You appear very dusty. But when You return home, the milk flowing out of the breasts of Your mother washes Your face of its dust covering, and You appear to be purified by this milk, just as when the Deity is washed during the performance of the *abhiṣeka* ceremony." It is the custom in the temples of Deities that if there have been some impure activities, the Deity has to be washed with milk. Kṛṣṇa is the Supreme Personality of Godhead, and He was washed by the milk from the breast of Mother Yaśodā, which purified Him from the dust covering.

Sometimes there are examples of Mother Yaśodā's becoming stunned in ecstasy. This was exhibited when she saw her son lifting Govardhana Hill. When Kṛṣṇa was standing, raising the hill, Mother Yaśodā hesitated to embrace Him and became stunned. The dangerous position that Kṛṣṇa had accepted by lifting the hill brought tears to her eyes. With her eyes filled with tears she could not see Kṛṣṇa anymore, and because her throat was choked up by anxiety she could not even instruct Kṛṣṇa as to what He should do in that position. This is a symptom of becoming stunned in ecstatic love.

Mother Yaśodā sometimes enjoyed transcendental ecstasy in happiness when her child was saved from a dangerous situation, such as being attacked by Pūtanā or some other demon. In *Śrīmad-Bhāgavatam,* Tenth Canto, Seventeenth Chapter, verse 19, Śukadeva Gosvāmī says that Mother Yaśodā felt very, very fortunate when she got back her lost child. She immediately placed Him on her lap and began to embrace Him again and again. While she was thus embracing her son repeatedly, torrents of tears fell from her eyes, and she was unable to express her transcendental joy. It is stated in the *Vidagdha-mādhava* of Śrīla Rūpa Gosvāmī, "My dear Kṛṣṇa, the touch of Your mother is so pleasing and cooling that it surpasses the cooling capacity of the pulp of sandalwood and of bright moonshine mixed with the pulp of *uśīra* root." (*Uśīra* is a kind of root which when soaked with water has a very, very cooling effect. It is especially used in the scorching heat of the sun.)

The parental love of Mother Yaśodā for Kṛṣṇa steadily increases, and her love and ecstasy are sometimes described as intense affection and sometimes as overwhelming attachment. An example of attachment for Kṛṣṇa with overwhelming affection is given in *Śrīmad-Bhāgavatam*, Tenth Canto, Sixth Chapter, verse 43, where Śukadeva Gosvāmī addresses Mahārāja Parīkṣit in this way: "My dear King, when magnanimous Nanda Mahārāja returned from Mathurā, he began to smell the head of his son, and he was merged in the ecstasy of parental love." A similar statement is there in connection with Mother Yaśodā when she was too anxious to hear the sound of Kṛṣṇa's flute, expecting Him back from the pasturing ground. Because she thought that it was getting very late, her anxiety to hear the sound of Kṛṣṇa's flute became doubled, and milk began to flow from her breast. In that condition she was sometimes going within the house, sometimes coming out of the house. She was constantly looking to see if Govinda was coming back along the road. When many very great sages were offering prayers to Lord Kṛṣṇa, glorifying His activities, the Queen of Gokula, Mother Yaśodā, entered the Battlefield of Kurukṣetra, wetting the lower part of her sari with the milk flowing from her breast. This entrance of Mother Yaśodā at Kurukṣetra was not during the Battle of Kurukṣetra. At another time Kṛṣṇa went to Kurukṣetra from His paternal home (Dvārakā) during a solar eclipse, and at that time the residents of Vṛndāvana also went to see Him there.

When Kṛṣṇa arrived at Kurukṣetra on pilgrimage, all the people assembled there began to say that Kṛṣṇa, the son of Devakī, had arrived. At that time, Devakī, just like an affectionate mother, began to pat Kṛṣṇa's face. And again when people cried that Kṛṣṇa, the son of Vasudeva, had come, both King Nanda and Mother Yaśodā became overwhelmed with affection and expressed their great pleasure.

When Mother Yaśodā, the Queen of Gokula, was going to see her son Kṛṣṇa at Kurukṣetra, one of her friends addressed her thus: "My dear Queen, the milk flowing out of your breast-mountain has already whitened the river Ganges, and the tears from your eyes, mixed with black mascara, have already blackened the color of the Yamunā. And as you are standing just between the two rivers, I think that there is no need for your anxiety to see your son's face. Your parental affection has already been exhibited to Him by these two rivers!"

The same friend of Mother Yaśodā addressed Kṛṣṇa as follows: "My dear Mukunda, if Mother Yaśodā, the Queen of Gokula, is forced to stand on fire but is allowed to see Your lotus face, then this fire will appear to her like the Himalaya Mountains: full of ice. In the same way, if she is allowed to stay in the ocean of nectar but is not allowed to see the lotus face of Your Grace, then even this ocean of nectar will appear to her like an ocean of arsenic poison." Let the anxiety of Mother Yaśodā of Vraja, always expecting to see the lotus face of Kṛṣṇa, be glorified all over the universe!

A similar statement was given by Kuntīdevī to Akrūra: "My dear brother Akrūra, my nephew Mukunda is long absent from us. Will you kindly tell Him that His Aunt Kuntī is sitting among the enemy and would like to know when she will be able to see His lotus face again?"

In *Śrīmad-Bhāgavatam,* Tenth Canto, Forty-sixth Chapter, verse 28, there is this statement: "When Uddhava was present at Vṛndāvana and was narrating the activities of Kṛṣṇa in Dvārakā, Mother Yaśodā, while hearing this narration, began to pour milk from her breasts and shed tears from her eyes." Another incident demonstrating Yaśodā's extreme love for Kṛṣṇa occurred when Kṛṣṇa went to Mathurā, the kingdom of Kaṁsa. In separation from Kṛṣṇa, Mother Yaśodā was looking at Kṛṣṇa's makeup utensils, and she fell down on the ground almost unconscious, with a great sound. When she was rolling over on the ground, there were many scratches on her body, and in that piteous condition she began to cry, "O my dear son! My dear son!" And she slapped her breasts with her two hands. This activity of Mother Yaśodā is explained by expert devotees as ecstatic love in separation. Sometimes there are many other symptoms, such as great anxiety, lamentation, frustration, being stunned, humility, restlessness, madness and illusion.

As far as Mother Yaśodā's anxieties are concerned, when Kṛṣṇa was out of the house in the pasturing ground, a devotee once told her, "Yaśodā, I think your movements have been slackened, and I see that you are full of anxieties. Your two eyes appear to be without any movement, and I feel in your breathing a kind of warmth, which is bringing your breast milk to the boiling point. All these conditions prove that out of separation from your son you have a severe headache." These are some of the symptoms of Mother Yaśodā's anxiety for Kṛṣṇa.

When Akrūra was present in Vṛndāvana and was narrating the activities of Kṛṣṇa in Dvārakā, Mother Yaśodā was informed that Kṛṣṇa had married so many queens and was very busy there in His householder affairs. Hearing this, Mother Yaśodā lamented how unfortunate she was that she could not get her son married just after He passed His *kaiśora* age and that she therefore could not receive both her son and daughter-in-law at her home. She exclaimed, "My dear Akrūra, you are simply throwing thunderbolts on my head!" These are signs of lamentation on the part of Mother Yaśodā in separation from Kṛṣṇa.

Similarly, Mother Yaśodā felt frustration when she thought, "Although I have millions of cows, the milk of these cows could not satisfy Kṛṣṇa. Therefore let a curse be on this milk! And I also am condemned, because although I am so opulent in material prosperity, I am now unable to smell the head of my child and feed Him with my breast milk as I used to do when He was here in Vṛndāvana." This is a sign of frustration on the part of Mother Yaśodā in separation from Kṛṣṇa.

One friend of Kṛṣṇa's addressed Him thus: "My dear lotus-eyed one, when You were living in Gokula You were always bearing a stick in Your hand. That stick is now lying idle in the house of Mother Yaśodā, and whenever she sees it she becomes motionless just like the stick." This is a sign of becoming stunned in separation from Kṛṣṇa. In separation from Kṛṣṇa, Mother Yaśodā became so humble that she prayed to the creator of the universe, Lord Brahmā, with tears in her eyes, "My dear creator, won't you kindly bring my dear son Kṛṣṇa back to me so that I can see Him at least for a moment?" Sometimes, in restlessness like a madwoman, Mother Yaśodā used to accuse Nanda Mahārāja, "What are you doing in the palace? You shameless man! Why do people call you the King of Vraja? It is very astonishing that while being separated from your dear son Kṛṣṇa, you are still living within Vṛndāvana as a hardhearted father!"

Someone informed Kṛṣṇa about the madness of Mother Yaśodā in the following words: "In madness Mother Yaśodā has addressed the *kadamba* trees and inquired from them, 'Where is my son?' Similarly, she has addressed the birds and the drones and inquired from them whether Kṛṣṇa has passed before them, and she has inquired if they can say anything about You. In this way, Mother Yaśodā in illusion was asking everybody about You, and she has been wandering all over Vṛndāvana." This is madness in separation from Kṛṣṇa.

When Nanda Mahārāja was accused by Mother Yaśodā of being "hardhearted," he replied, "My dear Yaśodā, why are you becoming so agitated? Kindly look more carefully. Just see, your son Kṛṣṇa is standing before you! Don't become a madwoman like this. Please keep my home peaceful." And Kṛṣṇa was informed by some friend that His father Nanda was also in illusion in this way, in separation from Him.

When all the wives of Vasudeva were present in the arena of Kaṁsa, they saw the most pleasing bodily features of Kṛṣṇa, and immediately, out of parental affection, milk began to flow from their breasts, and the lower parts of their saris became wet. This symptom of ecstatic love is an example of the result of fulfillment of desire.

In the First Canto of *Śrīmad-Bhāgavatam,* Eleventh Chapter, verse 29, it is stated, "When Kṛṣṇa entered Dvārakā after finishing the Battle of Kurukṣetra, He first of all saw His mother and all His different stepmothers and offered His respectful obeisances unto their feet. The mothers immediately took Kṛṣṇa upon their laps, and because of their parental affection, there was milk flowing out of their breasts. So their breast milk, mixed with the water of tears, became the first offering to Kṛṣṇa." This is one of the examples of being satisfied after a great separation.

There is a similar statement in the *Lalita-mādhava:* "How wonderful it is that Yaśodā, the wife of King Nanda, out of her parental affection for Kṛṣṇa, mixed her tears and the milk from her breasts and thus bathed her dear son Kṛṣṇa." In *Vidagdha-mādhava,* a devotee addresses Lord Kṛṣṇa as follows: "My dear Mukunda, just after seeing Your face, which was full with the scent of the lotus flower, Mother Yaśodā, being attracted by the moonlight of Your face, became so overjoyed in her affection that immediately from the nipples of her waterpotlike breasts, milk began to flow." She was thus constantly engaged in supplying milk to Kṛṣṇa after wetting the covering cloth over the jug.

These are some of the signs of parental love for Kṛṣṇa by His mother, His father and elderly persons. Symptoms of ecstatic love in parental affection are expressed when Kṛṣṇa is accepted as the son. These constant transcendental emotions for Kṛṣṇa are called steady ecstasy in parental love.

Śrīla Rūpa Gosvāmī states herein that according to some learned scholars, the three kinds of transcendental mellow so far described—namely servitude, fraternity and parental affection—are sometimes mixed. For example, the fraternal feelings of Balarāma are mixed with servitude and parental affection. Similarly, King Yudhiṣṭhira's attraction for Kṛṣṇa is also mixed with parental affection and servitude. Similarly, the transcendental mellow of Ugrasena, Kṛṣṇa's grandfather, is mixed with servitude and parental affection. The affection of all the elderly *gopīs* in Vṛndāvana is a mixture of parental love, servitude and fraternity. The affection of the sons of Mādrī—Nakula and Sahadeva—as well as the affection of the sage Nārada, is a mixture of friendship and servitude. The affection of Lord Śiva, Garuḍa and Uddhava is a mixture of servitude and fraternity.

44

Devotional Service in Conjugal Love

A pure devotee's attraction to Kṛṣṇa in conjugal love is called devotional service in conjugal love. Although such conjugal feelings are not at all material, there is some similarity between this spiritual love and material activities. Therefore, persons who are interested only in material activities are unable to understand this spiritual conjugal love, and these devotional reciprocations appear very mysterious to them. Rūpa Gosvāmī therefore describes conjugal love very briefly.

The impetuses of conjugal love are Kṛṣṇa and His very dear consorts, such as Rādhārāṇī and Her immediate associates. Lord Kṛṣṇa has no rival; no one is equal to Him, and no one is greater than Him. His beauty is also without any rival, and because He excels all others in the pastimes of conjugal love, He is the original object of all conjugal love.

In the *Gīta-govinda*, by Jayadeva Gosvāmī, one *gopī* tells her friend, "Kṛṣṇa is the reservoir of all pleasure within this universe. His body is as soft as the lotus flower. And His free behavior with the *gopīs*, which appears exactly like a young boy's attraction to a young girl, is a subject matter of transcendental conjugal love." A pure devotee follows in the footsteps of the *gopīs* and worships the *gopīs* as follows: "Let me offer my respectful obeisances to all the young cowherd girls, whose bodily features are so attractive. Simply by their beautiful attractive features they are worshiping the Supreme Personality of Godhead, Kṛṣṇa." Out of all the young *gopīs*, Śrīmatī Rādhārāṇī is the most prominent.

The beauty of Śrīmatī Rādhārāṇī is described as follows: "Her eyes defeat the attractive features of the eyes of the *cakorī* bird. When one sees the face of Rādhārāṇī, he immediately hates the beauty of the moon. Her bodily complexion defeats the beauty of gold. Thus, let us all look upon the transcendental beauty of Śrīmatī Rādhārāṇī." Kṛṣṇa's attraction for Rādhārāṇī is described by Kṛṣṇa Himself thus: "When I create some joking phrases in order to enjoy the beauty of Rādhārāṇī, Rādhārāṇī hears these joking words with great attention; but by Her bodily features and counterwords She neglects Me. And I even possess unlimited pleasure by Her neglect of Me, for She becomes so beautiful that She increases My pleasure one hundred times." A similar statement can be found in *Gīta-govinda,* wherein it is said that when the enemy of Kaṁsa, Śrī Kṛṣṇa, embraces Śrīmatī Rādhārāṇī, He immediately becomes entangled in a loving condition and gives up the company of all other *gopīs.*

In the *Padyāvalī* of Rūpa Gosvāmī it is stated that when the *gopīs* hear the sound of Kṛṣṇa's flute, they immediately forget all rebukes offered by the elderly members of their families. They forget their defamation and the harsh behavior of their husbands. Their only thought is to go out in search of Kṛṣṇa. When the *gopīs* meet Kṛṣṇa, the display of their exchanging glances as well as their joking and laughing behavior is called *anubhāva,* or subecstasy in conjugal love.

In the *Lalita-mādhava,* Rūpa Gosvāmī explains that the movements of Kṛṣṇa's eyebrows are just like the Yamunā and that the smiling of Rādhārāṇī is just like the moonshine. When the Yamunā and the moonshine come in contact on the bank of the river, the water tastes just like nectar, and drinking it gives great satisfaction. It is as cooling as piles of snow. Similarly, in the *Padyāvalī,* one constant companion of Rādhārāṇī says, "My dear moon-faced Rādhārāṇī, Your whole body appears very content, yet there are signs of tears in Your eyes. Your speech is faltering, and Your chest is also heaving. By all these signs I can understand that You must have heard the blowing of Kṛṣṇa's flute, and as a result of this, Your heart is now melting."

In the same *Padyāvalī* there is the following description, which is taken as a sign of frustration in conjugal love. Śrīmatī Rādhārāṇī said, "Dear Mr. Cupid, please do not excite Me by throwing your arrows at My body. Dear Mr. Air, please do not arouse Me with the fragrance of flowers. I am now bereft of Kṛṣṇa's loving attitude, and so, under the circumstances, what is the use of My sustaining this useless body? There is no need for such a body by any living entity." This is a sign of frustration in ecstatic love for Kṛṣṇa.

Similarly, in *Dāna-keli-kaumudī,* Śrīmatī Rādhārāṇī, pointing to

Kṛṣṇa, says, "This clever boy of the forest has the beauty of a bluish lotus flower, and He can attract all the young girls of the universe. Now, after giving Me a taste of His transcendental body, He has enthused Me, and it is more than I can tolerate. I am now feeling like a female elephant who has been enthused by a male elephant!" This is an instance of jubilation in ecstatic love with Kṛṣṇa.

The steady ecstasy of conjugal love is the original cause of bodily enjoyment. In the *Padyāvalī* this original cause of union is described when Rādhārāṇī tells one of Her constant companions, "My dear friend, who is this boy whose eyelids, dancing constantly, have increased the beauty of His face and attracted My desire for conjugal love? His ears are decorated with buds of *aśoka* flowers, and He has dressed Himself in yellow robes. By the sound of His flute, this boy has already made Me impatient."

The conjugal love of Rādhā-Kṛṣṇa is never disturbed by any personal consideration. The undisturbed nature of the conjugal love between Rādhā and Kṛṣṇa is described thus: "Just a little distance away from Kṛṣṇa was Mother Yaśodā, and Kṛsna was surrounded by all of His friends. In front of His eyes was Candrāvalī, and, at the same time, on a chunk of stone in front of the entrance to Vraja stood the demon known as Vṛṣāsura. But even in such circumstances, when Kṛṣṇa saw Rādhārāṇī standing just behind a bush of many creepers, immediately His beautiful eyebrows moved just like lightning toward Her."

Another instance is described as follows: "On one side of the courtyard the dead body of Śaṅkhāsura was lying, surrounded by many jackals. On another side were many learned *brāhmaṇas* who were all self-controlled. They were offering nice prayers, which were as soothing as the cool breeze in summer. In front of Kṛṣṇa, Lord Baladeva was standing, causing a cooling effect. But even amid all these different circumstances of soothing and disturbing effects, the lotus flower of ecstatic conjugal love that Kṛṣṇa felt for Rādhārāṇī could not wither." This love of Kṛṣṇa for Rādhārāṇī is often compared to a blooming lotus; the only difference is that Kṛṣṇa's love remains ever-increasingly beautiful.

Conjugal love is divided into two portions: *vipralambha,* or conjugal love in separation, and *sambhoga,* or conjugal love in direct contact. *Vipralambha,* separation, has three subdivisions, known as (1) *pūrvarāga,* or preliminary attraction, (2) *māna,* or seeming anger, and (3) *pravāsa,* or separation by distance.

When the lover and the beloved have a distinct feeling of not meeting each other, that stage is called *pūrva-rāga,* or preliminary attraction. In *Padyāvalī* Rādhārāṇī told Her companion, "My dear friend, I was just going to the bank of the Yamunā, and all of a sudden a very nice boy whose complexion is like a dark blue cloud became visible in front of My eyes. He glanced over Me in a way that I cannot describe. But since this has occurred, I am sorry that I can no longer engage My mind in the duties of My household affairs." This is an instance of preliminary attraction for Kṛṣṇa. In *Śrīmad-Bhāgavatam,* Tenth Canto, Fifty-third Chapter, verse 2, Kṛṣṇa told the messenger *brāhmaṇa* who came from Rukmiṇī, "My dear *brāhmaṇa,* just like Rukmiṇī I cannot sleep at night, and My mind is always fixed on her. I know that her brother Rukmī is against Me and that due to his persuasion My marriage with her has been cancelled." This is another instance of preliminary attraction.

As far as *māna,* or anger, is concerned, there is the following incident described in *Gīta-govinda:* "When Śrīmatī Rādhārāṇī saw Kṛṣṇa enjoying Himself in the company of several other *gopīs,* She became a little jealous because Her special prestige was being dimmed. Therefore, She immediately left the scene and took shelter in a nice flower bush where the black drones were humming. Then, hiding Herself behind the creepers, She began to express Her sorrow to one of Her consorts." This is an instance of a seeming disagreement.

An example of *pravāsa,* or being out of contact because of living in a distant place, is given in the *Padyāvalī* as follows: "Since the auspicious day when Kṛṣṇa left for Mathurā, Śrīmatī Rādhārāṇī has been pressing Her head on one of Her hands and constantly shedding tears. Her face is always wet now, and therefore there is no chance of Her sleeping even for a moment." When the face becomes wet, the sleeping tendency is immediately removed. So when Rādhārāṇī was always weeping for Kṛṣṇa because of His separation, there was no chance of Her getting any sleep for Herself. In the *Prahlāda-saṁhitā* Uddhava says, "The Supreme Personality of Godhead, Govinda, painstricken due to being pierced by the arrows of Cupid, is always thinking of you [the *gopīs*], and He is not even accepting His regular lunch. Nor is He getting any proper rest."

When the lover and beloved come together and enjoy one another by direct contact, this stage is called *sambhoga.* There is a statement in *Padyāvalī* as follows: "Kṛṣṇa embraced Śrīmatī Rādhārāṇī in such an expert manner that He appeared to be celebrating the dancing ceremony of the peacocks."

Śrī Rūpa Gosvāmī thus ends the western section of his *Ocean of the Nectar of Devotion.* He offers his respectful obeisances to the Supreme Personality of Godhead, who appeared as Gopāla, the eternal form of the Lord.

Thus ends the Bhaktivedanta summary study of the third division of Bhakti-rasāmṛta-sindhu *in the matter of the five primary relationships with Kṛṣṇa.*

PART FOUR

45

Laughing Ecstasy

n the fourth division of *Bhakti-rasāmṛta-sindhu,* Śrīla Rūpa Gosvāmī has lescribed seven kinds of indirect ecstasies of devotional service, known as aughing, astonishment, chivalry, compassion, anger, dread and ghastliiess. In this portion, Śrīla Rūpa Gosvāmī further describes these ecstasies f devotional feelings, some being compatible and others incompatible vith one another. When one kind of ecstatic devotional service overlaps vith another in a conflicting way, this state of affairs is called *rasābhāsa,* r a perverted presentation of mellows.

Expert learned scholars say that laughing is generally found among oungsters or in the combination of old persons and young children. This cstatic loving laughing is sometimes also found in persons who are very rave by nature. Once an old mendicant approached the door of Mother 'aśodā's house, and Kṛṣṇa told Yaśodā, "My dear mother, I don't wish to o near this skinny villain. If I go there, he might put Me within his begging ag and take Me away from you!" In this way, the wonderful child, Kṛṣṇa, egan to look at His mother, while the mendicant, who was standing in ie door, tried to hide his smiling face, although he could not do so. He nmediately expressed his smiling. In this instance, Kṛṣṇa Himself is the bject of laughing affairs.

Once one of Kṛṣṇa's friends informed Him, "My dear Kṛṣṇa, if You will pen Your mouth, then I shall give You one nice sugar candy mixed with ogurt." Kṛṣṇa immediately opened His mouth, but instead of giving Him igar candy with yogurt, the friend dropped a flower in His mouth. After isting this flower, Kṛṣṇa turned His mouth in a disfigured way, and upon eing this all His friends standing there began to laugh very loudly.

Once a palmist came to the house of Nanda Mahārāja, and Nanda Iahārāja asked him, "My dear sage, will you kindly check the hand of my child, Kṛṣṇa? Tell me how many years He will live and whether He will become the master of thousands of cows." Upon hearing this, the palmist began to smile, and Nanda Mahārāja asked him, "My dear sir, why are you laughing, and why are you covering your face?"

In such a laughing ecstasy of love, Kṛṣṇa or matters pertaining to Kṛṣṇa are the cause of the laughter. In such laughing devotional service, there are symptoms of jubilation, laziness, concealed feelings and similar other seemingly disturbing elements.

According to Śrīla Rūpa Gosvāmī's calculation, laughter in ecstatic love can be broken down into six divisions. These divisions, according to different degrees of smiling, are called in the Sanskrit language *smita, hasita, vihasita, avahasita, apahasita* and *atihasita*. These six classes of smiling can be classified as major and minor. The major division includes *smita, hasita* and *vihasita* smiling, and the minor division includes *avahasita, apahasita* and *atihasita* smiling.

When one is smiling but his teeth are not visible, one can distinctly mark a definite change in the eyes and in the cheeks. This is called *smita* smiling. Once when Kṛṣṇa was stealing yogurt, Jaratī, the headmistress of the house, could detect His activities, and she was therefore coming very hurriedly to catch Him. At that time, Kṛṣṇa became very much afraid of Jaratī and went to His elder brother, Baladeva. He said, "My dear brother, I have stolen yogurt! Just see—Jaratī is coming hurriedly to catch Me!" When Kṛṣṇa was thus seeking the shelter of Baladeva because He was being chased by Jaratī, all the great sages in the heavenly planets began to smile. This smiling is called *smita* smiling.

Smiling in which the teeth are slightly visible is called *hasita* smiling. One day Abhimanyu, the so-called husband of Rādhārāṇī, was returning home, and at that time he could not see that Kṛṣṇa was there in his house. Kṛṣṇa immediately changed His dress to look exactly like Abhimanyu and approached Abhimanyu's mother, Jaṭilā, addressing her thus: "My dear mother, I am your real son Abhimanyu, but just see—Kṛṣṇa, dressed up like me, is coming before you!" Jaṭilā, the mother of Abhimanyu, immediately believed that Kṛṣṇa was her own son and thus became very angry at her real son who was coming home. She began to drive away her real son, who was crying, "Mother! Mother! What are you doing?" Seeing this incident, all the girlfriends of Rādhārāṇī, who were present there began to smile, and a portion of their teeth was visible. This is an instance of *hasita* smiling.

When the teeth are distinctly visible in a smile, that is called *vihasita*. One day when Kṛṣṇa was engaged in stealing butter and yogurt in the house of Jaṭilā, He assured His friends, "My dear friends, I know that this old lady is now sleeping very profoundly, because she is breathing very deeply. Let us silently steal butter and yogurt without making any disturbance." But the old lady, Jaṭilā, was not sleeping; so she could not contain her smiling, and her teeth immediately became distinctly visible. This is an instance of *vihasita* smiling.

In a state of smiling when the nose becomes puffed and the eyes squint, the smiling is called *avahasita*. Once, early in the morning when Kṛṣṇa returned home after performing His *rāsa* dance, Mother Yaśodā looked upon Kṛṣṇa's face and addressed Him thus: "My dear son, why do Your eyes look like they have been smeared with some oxides? Have You dressed Yourself with the blue garments of Baladeva?" When Mother Yaśodā was addressing Kṛṣṇa in that way, a girlfriend who was nearby began to smile with a puffed nose and squinting eyes. This is an instance of *avahasita* smiling. The *gopī* knew that Kṛṣṇa had been enjoying the *rāsa* dance and that Mother Yaśodā could not detect her son's activities or understand how He had become covered with the *gopīs'* makeup. Her smiling was in the *avahasita* feature.

When tears from the eyes are added to the smiling and the shoulders are shaking, the smile is called *apahasita*. When child Kṛṣṇa was dancing in response to the singing of the old maidservant Jaratī, Nārada was astonished. The Supreme Personality of Godhead, who controls all the movements of great demigods like Brahmā, was now dancing to the indications of an old maidservant. Seeing this fun, Nārada also began to dance, and his shoulders trembled, and his eyes moved. Due to his smiling, his teeth also became visible, and on account of the glaring effulgence from his teeth, the clouds in the skies turned silver.

When a smiling person claps his hands and leaps in the air, the smiling expression changes into *atihasita*, or overwhelming laughter. An example of *atihasita* was manifested in the following incident. Kṛṣṇa once addressed Jaratī thus: "My dear good woman, the skin of your face is now slackened, and so your face exactly resembles a monkey's. As such, the

King of the monkeys, Balīmukha, has selected you as his worthy wife." While Kṛṣṇa was teasing Jaratī in this way, she replied that she was certainly aware of the fact that the King of the monkeys was trying to marry her, but she had already taken shelter of Kṛṣṇa, the killer of many powerful demons, and therefore she had already decided to marry Kṛṣṇa instead of the King of the monkeys. On hearing this sarcastic reply by the talkative Jaratī, all the cowherd girls present there began to laugh very loudly and clap their hands. This laughter, accompanied by the clapping of hands, is called *atihasita.*

Sometimes there are indirect sarcastic remarks which also create *atihasita* circumstances. An example of one such remark is a statement which was made by one of the cowherd girls to Kuṭilā, the daughter of Jaṭilā and sister of Abhimanyu, the so-called husband of Rādhārāṇī. Indirectly Kuṭilā was insulted by the following statement: "My dear Kuṭilā, daughter of Jaṭilā, your breasts are as long as string beans—simply dry and long. Your nose is so gorgeous that it defies the beauty of the noses of frogs. And your eyes are more beautiful than the eyes of dogs. Your lips defy the flaming cinders of fire, and your abdomen is as beautiful as a big drum. Therefore, my dear beautiful Kuṭilā, you are the most beautiful of all the cowherd girls of Vṛndāvana, and because of your extraordinary beauty, I think you must be beyond the attraction of the sweet blowing of Kṛṣṇa's flute!"

46

Astonishment and Chivalry

Astonishment

The ecstasy of astonishment in devotional service is perceived in two ways: directly, by the experience of one's own eyes, and indirectly, by hearing from others.

When Nārada came to see the activities of the Lord at Dvārakā and he saw that Kṛṣṇa was present within every palace in the same body and was engaged in different activities, he was struck with wonder. This is one of the examples of astonishment in devotional service by direct perception. One of the friends of Mother Yaśodā said, "Yaśodā, just see the fun! On the one hand, there is your child, who is always captivated by sucking the milk from your breast, and on the other hand there is the great Govardhana Hill, which can obstruct the passing of the clouds. But still, just see how wonderful it is that this great Govardhana Hill is resting on the finger of your child's left hand, just as though it were a toy. Is this not very mysterious?" This statement is another example of astonishment in devotional service by direct perception.

An instance of astonishment in devotional service by indirect perception occurred when Mahārāja Parīkṣit heard from Śukadeva Gosvāmī about Kṛṣṇa's killing Narakāsura, who had been fighting Kṛṣṇa with eleven *akṣauhiṇī* divisions of soldiers. Each division of *akṣauhiṇī* soldiers contained several thousand elephants, several thousand horses and chariots and several hundreds of thousands of infantry soldiers. Narakāsura possessed eleven such divisions, and all of them were throwing arrows toward Kṛṣṇa, but Kṛṣṇa killed them all, simply by throwing three arrows from His side. When Mahārāja Parīkṣit heard of this wonderful victory, he immediately rubbed the tears from his eyes and became overwhelmed with joy. This instance is an example of astonishment in devotional service by indirect perception through aural reception.

There is another example of indirect astonishment. Trying to test Kṛṣṇa to see if He were truly the Supreme Personality of Godhead, Lord Brahmā stole all the cowherd boys and cows from Him. But after a few seconds, he saw that Kṛṣṇa was still present with all the cows, calves and cowherd boys, exactly in the same way as before. When Lord Brahmā described this incident to his associates on the Satyaloka planet, they all became astonished. Brahmā told them that after taking away all the boys, he saw Kṛṣṇa again playing with the same boys in the same fashion. Their bodily complexion was blackish, almost like Kṛṣṇa's, and they all had four arms. The same calves and cows were still present there, in the same original fashion. Even while describing this incident, Brahmā became almost overwhelmed. "And the most astonishing thing," he added, "was that many other Brahmās from many different universes had also come there to worship Kṛṣṇa and His associates."

Similarly, when there was a forest fire in the Bhāṇḍīravana, Kṛṣṇa instructed His friends to close their eyes tightly, and they all did this. Then when Kṛṣṇa had extinguished the fire, the cowherd boys opened their eyes and saw that they had been relieved from the danger and that their cows and calves were all safe. They began to perceive the wonder of the situation simply by guessing how Kṛṣṇa had saved them. This is another instance of indirect perception causing astonishment in devotional service.

The activities of a person, even if they are not very extraordinary, create an impression of wonder in the heart and mind of the person's friends. But even very wonderful activities performed by a person who is not one's friend will not create any impression. It is because of love that one's wonderful activities create an impression in the mind.

Chivalry

When on account of love and devotional service for the Lord there is special valorous enthusiasm, the resultant activities are called chivalrous. These chivalrous activities can be manifested in the acts of mock-fighting, giving charity, showing mercy and executing religious principles. By performing chivalrous activities in fighting, one is called *yuddha-vīra*. By charitable activities one is called *dāna-vīra*. By showing extraordinary mercy one is called *dayā-vīra*. And when one is munificent in executing religious rites, he is called *dharma-vīra*. In all such different chivalrous activities, Kṛṣṇa is the object.

When a friend wants to satisfy Kṛṣṇa by performing some chivalrous activities, the friend becomes the challenger, and Kṛṣṇa Himself becomes the opponent; or else Kṛṣṇa may give audience to the fighting, and by His desire another friend becomes the opponent. A friend once challenged Kṛṣṇa thus: "My dear Mādhava, You are very restless because You think that no one can defeat You. But if You do not flee from here, then I shall show You how I can defeat You. And my friends will be very satisfied to see this!"

Kṛṣṇa and Śrīdāmā were very intimate friends, yet Śrīdāmā, out of anger with Kṛṣṇa, challenged Him. When both of them began to fight, all the friends on the bank of the Yamunā enjoyed the wonderful fighting of the two friends. They prepared some arrows for mock-fighting, and Kṛṣṇa began to throw his arrows at Śrīdāmā. Śrīdāmā began to block these arrows by whirling his pole, and by Śrīdāmā's chivalrous activities, Kṛṣṇa became very satisfied. Such mock-fighting generally takes place among chivalrous persons and creates wonderful excitement for all viewers.

There is a statement in the *Hari-vaṁśa* that sometimes Arjuna and Kṛṣṇa fought in the presence of Kuntī, and Arjuna would be defeated by Kṛṣṇa.

In such chivalrous fighting between friends, there is sometimes bragging, complacence, pride, power, taking to weapons, challenging and standing as an opponent. All of these symptoms become impetuses to chivalrous devotional service.

One friend challenged Kṛṣṇa thus: "My dear friend Dāmodara, You are an expert only in eating. You have defeated Subala only because he is weak and You adopted cheating means. Don't advertise Yourself to be a great fighter by such action. You have advertised Yourself as a serpent, and I am the peacock who will now defeat You." The peacock is the ablest enemy of the serpent.

In such fighting between friends, when the self-advertisement becomes personal, learned scholars say that it is subecstasy. When there is a roaring challenge, certain kinds of movement for fighting, enthusiasm, no weapons, and assurance given to frightened witnesses—all these chivalrous activities are called subecstasy.

One friend addressed Kṛṣṇa in this manner: "My dear Madhusūdana, You know my strength, yet You are encouraging Bhadrasena, and not me, to challenge mighty Baladeva. By this action You are simply insulting me, because my arms are as strong as the bolts of the gate!"

A devotee once said, "My dear Lord Kṛṣṇa, may Your challenger Śudāmā become glorious for his chivalrous activities, such as vibrating like a thundercloud and roaring like a lion. May all glories go to Śudāmā's chivalrous activities!" Chivalrous activities in the matter of fighting, charity, mercy and execution of religious rituals are called constitutional, whereas expressions of pride, emotion, endurance, kindness, determination, jubilation, enthusiasm, jealousy and remembrance are called unconstitutional. When Stoka-kṛṣṇa, one of the many friends of Kṛṣṇa, was fighting with Him, his father chastised him for fighting with Kṛṣṇa, who was the life and soul of all residents of Vṛndāvana. Upon hearing these chastisements, Stoka-kṛṣṇa stopped his fighting. But Kṛṣṇa continued to challenge him, and thus, in order to meet the challenge, Stoka-kṛṣṇa took his pole and began to display his dexterity by whirling it.

Once Śrīdāmā challenged Bhadrasena and said to him, "My dear friend, you needn't be afraid of me yet. I shall first of all defeat our brother Balarāma, then I shall beat Kṛṣṇa, and then I shall come to you." Bhadrasena therefore left the party of Balarāma and joined Kṛṣṇa, and he agitated his friends as much as the Mandara Hill had agitated the whole ocean. By his roaring sounds he deafened all his friends, and he inspired Kṛṣṇa with his chivalrous activities.

Once Kṛṣṇa challenged all His friends and said, "My dear friends, just see—I am jumping with great chivalrous prowess. Please do not flee away." Upon hearing these challenging words, a friend named Varūthapa counterchallenged the Lord and struggled against Him.

One of the friends once remarked, "Sudāmā is trying his best to see Dāmodara defeated, and I think that if our powerful Subala joins him, they will be a very beautiful combination, like a valuable jewel bedecked with gold."

In these chivalrous activities, only Kṛṣṇa's friends can be the opponents. Kṛṣṇa's enemies can never actually be His opponents. Therefore, this challenging by Kṛṣṇa's friends is called devotional service in chivalrous activities.

Dāna-vīra, or chivalry in giving charity, may be divided into two parts: munificence and renunciation. A person who can sacrifice everything for the satisfaction of Kṛṣṇa is called munificent. When a person desires to make a sacrifice because of seeing Kṛṣṇa, Kṛṣṇa is called the impetus of the munificent activity. When Kṛṣṇa appeared as the son of Nanda Mahārāja, in clear consciousness Nanda Mahārāja desired all auspiciousness for his son and thus began to give valuable cows in charity to all the *brāhmaṇas.* The *brāhmaṇas* were so satisfied by this charitable action that they were obliged to say that the charity of Nanda Mahārāja had excelled the charity of such past kings as Mahārāja Pṛthu and Nṛga.

When a person knows the glories of the Lord completely and is prepared to sacrifice everything for the Lord, he is called *sampradānaka,* or one who gives everything in charity for the sake of Kṛṣṇa.

When Mahārāja Yudhiṣṭhira went with Kṛṣṇa into the arena of the Rājasūya sacrifice, in his imagination he began to anoint the body of Kṛṣṇa with pulp of sandalwood, he decorated Kṛṣṇa with a garland hanging down to His knees, he gave Kṛṣṇa garments all embroidered with gold, he gave Kṛṣṇa ornaments all bedecked with valuable jewels, and he gave Kṛṣṇa many fully decorated elephants, chariots and horses. He further wished to give Kṛṣṇa in charity his kingdom, his family and his personal self also. After so desiring, when there was nothing actually to give in charity, Mahārāja Yudhiṣṭhira became very perturbed and anxious.

Similarly, Mahārāja Bali once told his priest, Śukrācārya, "My dear sage, you are fully expert in knowledge of the *Vedas,* and as such you worship the Supreme Personality of Godhead, Viṣṇu, by Vedic rituals. As far as this dwarf *brāhmaṇa* [the incarnation Vāmanadeva] is concerned, if He is Lord Viṣṇu, a simple *brāhmaṇa* or even my enemy, I have decided to give to Him in charity all the land He has asked for." Mahārāja Bali was so fortunate that the Lord extended before him His hand, which was reddish from touching the breast of the goddess of fortune, who is always smeared with red *kuṅkuma* powder. In other words, although the Personality of Godhead is so great that the goddess of fortune is always under His command for enjoyment, He still extended His hands to take charity from Mahārāja Bali.

A person who wants to give everything in charity to Kṛṣṇa but does not want anything in return is considered the real renouncer. Thus, a devotee will refuse to accept any kind of liberation, even if it is offered by the Lord. Real love of Kṛṣṇa becomes manifested when Kṛṣṇa becomes the recipient of charity and the devotee becomes the giver.

In the *Hari-bhakti-sudhodaya* there is another example, forwarded by Mahārāja Dhruva. He says there, "My dear Lord, I have practiced austerities and penances because I was desiring to receive something from You, but in exchange You have allowed me to see You, who are never visible even to the great sages and saintly persons. I had been searching out some pieces of broken glass, but instead I have found the most valuable jewel. I am therefore fully satisfied, my Lord. I do not wish to ask anything more from Your Lordship."

A similar statement is to be found in the Third Canto of *Śrīmad-Bhāgavatam,* Fifteenth Chapter, verse 48. The four sages headed by Sanaka Muni addressed the Lord as follows: "Dear Supreme Personality of Godhead, Your reputation is very attractive and free from all material contamination. Therefore You are worthy of being glorified and are actually the reservoir of all places of pilgrimage. Auspicious persons who are fortunate enough to be engaged in glorifying Your attributes and who actually know what Your transcendental position is do not even care to accept liberation offered by You. Because they are so transcendentally enriched, they do not care to accept even the post of Indra, the heavenly King. They know that the post of the King of heaven is also fearful, whereas for those who are engaged in glorifying Your transcendental qualities there is only joyfulness and freedom from all danger. As such, why should persons with this knowledge be attracted by a post in the heavenly kingdom?"

One devotee has described his feelings about the charity exhibited by King Mayūradhvaja: "I am faltering even to speak about the activities of Mahārāja Mayūradhvaja, to whom I offer my respectful obeisances." Mayūradhvaja was very intelligent, and he could understand why Kṛṣṇa came to him once, in the garb of a *brāhmaṇa.* Kṛṣṇa demanded from him half of his body, to be sawed off by his wife and son, and King Mayūradhvaja agreed to this proposal. On account of his intense feeling of devotional service, King Mayūradhvaja was always thinking of Kṛṣṇa, and when he understood that Kṛṣṇa had come in the garb of a *brāhmaṇa,* he did not hesitate to part with half of his body. This sacrifice of Mahārāja Mayūradhvaja for Kṛṣṇa's sake is unique in the world, and we should offer our all-respectful obeisances to him. He had full knowledge of the Supreme Personality of Godhead in the garb of a *brāhmaṇa,* and he is known as the perfect *dāna-vīra,* or renouncer.

Any person who is always ready to satisfy Kṛṣṇa and who is always dexterous in executing devotional service is called *dharma-vīra,* or chivalrous in executing religious rituals. Only advanced devotees performing religious ritualistic performances can come to this stage of *dharma-vīra. Dharma-vīras* are produced after going through the authoritative scriptures, following moral principles, being faithful and tolerant and controlling the senses. Persons who execute religious rituals for the satisfaction of Kṛṣṇa are steady in devotional service, whereas persons who execute religious rituals without intending to please Kṛṣṇa are only called pious.

The best example of a *dharma-vīra* is Mahārāja Yudhiṣṭhira. A devotee once told Kṛṣṇa, "My dear Kṛṣṇa, O killer of all demons, Mahārāja Yudhiṣṭhira, the eldest son of Mahārāja Pāṇḍu, has performed all kinds of sacrifices just to please You. He has always invited the heavenly King, Indra, to take part in the *yajñas* [sacrifices]. Because King Indra was thus absent so often from Śacīdevī, she had to pass much of her time pining over Indra's absence, with her cheeks upon her hands."

The performance of different *yajñas* for the demigods is considered to be worship of the limbs of the Supreme Lord. The demigods are considered to be different parts of the universal body of the Lord, and therefore the ultimate purpose in worshiping them is to please the Lord by partially worshiping His different limbs. Mahārāja Yudhiṣṭhira had no such material desire; he executed all sacrifices under the direction of Kṛṣṇa, and not to take any personal advantage from them. He desired only to please Kṛṣṇa and was therefore called the best of the devotees. He was always merged in the ocean of loving service.

47

Compassion and Anger

Compassion

When the ecstasy of devotional service produces some kind of lamentation in connection with Kṛṣṇa, it is called devotional service in compassion. The impetuses for this devotional service are Kṛṣṇa's transcendental qualities, form and activities. In this ecstasy of devotional service there are sometimes symptoms like regret, heavy breathing, crying, falling on the ground and beating upon one's chest. Sometimes symptoms like laziness, frustration, defamation, humility, anxiety, moroseness, eagerness, restlessness, madness, death, forgetfulness, disease and illusion are also visible. When in the heart of a devotee there is expectation of some mishap to Kṛṣṇa it is called devotional service in bereavement. Such bereavement is another symptom of this devotional service in compassion.

In *Śrīmad-Bhāgavatam,* Tenth Canto, Sixteenth Chapter, verse 10, there is the following description. When Kṛṣṇa was chastising the Kāliya-nāga in the Yamunā, the big snake wrapped his coils all over Kṛṣṇa's body, and upon seeing Kṛṣṇa in this situation, all His dear cowherd friends became greatly disturbed. Out of bereavement, distress and fear, they became bewildered and began to fall on the ground. Because the cowherd boys were under the illusion that Kṛṣṇa could be in some mishap, their symptoms are not at all astonishing; they had dedicated their friendship, their possessions, their desires and their very selves to Kṛṣṇa.

When Kṛṣṇa entered the Yamunā River, which had become very poisonous from the presence of Kāliya, Mother Yaśodā feared all kinds of mishaps, and she was breathing hotly. Tears from her eyes were soaking her clothes, and she was almost collapsing.

Similarly, when the Śaṅkhāsura demon was attacking Kṛṣṇa's queens one after another, Lord Baladeva became more and more bluish.

In the *Haṁsadūta,* the following incident is described. The *gopīs* requested Haṁsadūta to search after the marks of Kṛṣṇa's lotus feet and to accept them as Lord Brahmā had accepted them on his helmet after he had stolen all Kṛṣṇa's cowherd boys. Regretting his challenge to Kṛṣṇa, Lord Brahmā had bowed down before the Lord, and his helmet became marked with the footprints of Kṛṣṇa. The *gopīs* reminded Haṁsadūta that sometimes even the great sage Nārada becomes very ecstatic by seeing these footprints, and sometimes great liberated sages also aspire to see them. "You should therefore seek very enthusiastically to find the footprints of Kṛṣṇa," they urged. This is another instance of devotional service in compassion.

There is an instance when Sahadeva, the younger brother of Nakula, became greatly gladdened at seeing the effulgent glowing of Kṛṣṇa's footprints. He began to cry and call out, "Mother Mādrī! Where are you now? Father Pāṇḍu! Where are you now? I am very sorry that you are not here to see these footprints of Kṛṣṇa!" This is another instance of devotional service in compassion.

In devotional service without strong attraction to the Lord, there may sometimes be smiling and other symptoms, but never the stress or lamentation that are symptoms of devotional service in compassion. The basic principle of this compassion is always ecstatic love. The apprehension of some mishap to Kṛṣṇa or to His beloved queens, as exhibited by Baladeva and Yudhiṣṭhira, has been explained above. This apprehension is due not exactly to their ignorance of the inconceivable potencies of Kṛṣṇa but to their intense love for Him. This kind of apprehension of some mishap to Kṛṣṇa first of all becomes manifested as an object of lamentation, but gradually it develops into such compassionate loving ecstasy that it turns to another channel and gives transcendental pleasure.

Anger

In ecstatic loving service to Kṛṣṇa in anger, Kṛṣṇa is always the object. In *Vidagdha-mādhava,* Second Act, verse 37, Lalitā-gopī expressed her anger, which was caused by Kṛṣṇa, when she addressed Śrīmatī Rādhārāṇī thus: "My dear friend, my inner desires have been polluted. Therefore I shall go to the place of Yamarāja. But I am sorry to see that Kṛṣṇa has still not given up His smiling over cheating You. I do not know how You could repose all Your loving propensities upon this lusty young boy from the neighborhood of the cowherds."

After seeing Kṛṣṇa, Jaratī sometimes said, "O You thief of young girls' properties! I can distinctly see the covering garment of my daughter-in-law on Your person." Then she cried very loudly, addressing all the residents of Vṛndāvana to inform them that this son of King Nanda was setting fire to the household life of her daughter-in-law.

Similar ecstatic love for Kṛṣṇa in anger was expressed by Rohiṇī-devī when she heard the roaring sound of the two falling *arjuna* trees to which Kṛṣṇa had been tied. The whole neighborhood proceeded immediately toward the place where the accident had taken place, and Rohiṇī-devī took the opportunity to rebuke Mother Yaśodā as follows: "You may be very expert in giving lessons to your son by binding Him with rope, but don't you look to see if your son is in a dangerous spot? The trees are falling on the ground, and He is simply loitering there!" This expression of Rohiṇī-devī's anger toward Yaśodā is an example of ecstatic love in anger caused by Kṛṣṇa.

Once, while Kṛṣṇa was in the pasturing ground with His cowherd boys, His friends requested Him to go to the Tālavana forest, where Gardabhāsura, a disturbing demon in the shape of an ass, resided. The friends of Kṛṣṇa wanted to eat the fruit from the forest trees, but they could not go because of fear of the demon. Thus they requested Kṛṣṇa to go there and kill Gardabhāsura. After Kṛṣṇa did this, they all returned home, and their report of the day's activity perturbed Mother Yaśodā because Kṛṣṇa had been sent alone into such danger in the Tālavana forest. Thus she looked upon the boys with anger.

There is another instance of anger on the part of a friend of Rādhārāṇī's. When Rādhārāṇī was dissatisfied with the behavior of Kṛṣṇa and had stopped talking with Him, Kṛṣṇa was very sorry for Rādharāṇī's great dissatisfaction, and in order to beg forgiveness, He fell down at Her lotus feet. But even after this, Rādhārāṇī was not satisfied, and She did not talk with Kṛṣṇa. At that time, one of Her friends chastised Her in the following words: "My dear friend, You are allowing Yourself to be churned by the rod of dissatisfaction, so what can I say unto You? The only advice I can give You is that You had better leave this scene immediately, because Your misbehavior is giving me too much pain. I cannot bear to see Your behavior, because even though Kṛṣṇa's peacock feather has touched Your feet, You still appear to be red-faced."

The above attitudes of dissatisfaction and anger in devotional service are called *īrṣyu.*

When Akrūra was leaving Vṛndāvana, some of the elderly *gopīs* rebuked him as follows: "O son of Gāndinī, your cruelty is defaming the dynasty of King Yadu. You are taking Kṛṣṇa away, keeping us in such a pitiable condition without Him. Now, even before you have left, the life air of all the *gopīs* has practically disappeared."

When Kṛṣṇa was insulted by Śiśupāla in the assembly of the Rājasūya *yajña* convened by Mahārāja Yudhiṣṭhira, there was a great turmoil among the Pāṇḍavas and Kurus, involving grandfather Bhīṣma. At that time Nakula said with great anger, "Kṛṣṇa is the Supreme Personality of Godhead, and the nails of His toes are beautified by the light emanating from the jeweled helmets of the authorities of the *Vedas.* If He is derided by anyone, I declare herewith as a Pāṇḍava that I will kick his helmet with my left foot and I will strike him with my arrows, which are as good as *yama-daṇḍa,* the scepter of Yamarāja!" This is an instance of ecstatic love for Kṛṣṇa in anger.

In such a transcendental angry mood sometimes sarcastic remarks, unfavorable glances and insulting words are exhibited. Sometimes there are other symptoms, like rubbing of the two hands, clacking of the teeth, clamping of the lips, moving of the eyebrows, scratching of the arms, lowering of the head, rapid breathing, uttering of strong words, nodding of the head, yellowishness at the corners of the eyes, and trembling lips. Sometimes the eyes turn red, and sometimes they fade. And there are sometimes chastisement and silence. All these symptoms of anger may be divided into two parts: constitutional and unconstitutional, or permanent and temporary symptoms. Sometimes great emotion, bewilderment, pride, frustration, illusion, impotence, jealousy, dexterity, negligence and signs of hard labor are also manifest as unconstitutional symptoms.

In all these humors of ecstatic love, the feeling of anger is accepted as the steady factor.

When Jarāsandha angrily attacked the city of Mathurā, he looked at Kṛṣṇa with sarcastic glances. At that time Baladeva took up His plow weapon and gazed upon Jarāsandha with colored eyes.

There is a statement in the *Vidagdha-mādhava* wherein Śrīmatī

Rādhārāṇī, in an angry mood, addressed Paurṇamāsī after she had accused Rādhārāṇī of going to Kṛṣṇa. "My dear mother," Rādhā declared, "what can I say to you? Kṛṣṇa is so cruel that He often attacks Me on the street, and if I want to cry out very loudly, this boy with a peacock feather on His head immediately covers My face so that I cannot cry. And if I want to go away from the scene because I am afraid of Him, He will immediately spread His arms to block My path. If I piteously fall down at His feet, then this enemy of the Madhu demon, in an angry mood, bites My face! Mother, just try to understand My situation, and don't be unnecessarily angry with Me. Instead, please tell Me how I can save Myself from these terrible attacks of Kṛṣṇa!"

Sometimes among contemporary personalities there are signs of ecstasy in anger because of love for Kṛṣṇa. An example of such anger was exhibited in a quarrel between Jaṭilā and Mukharā. Jaṭilā was the mother-in-law of Rādhārāṇī, and Mukharā was Her grandmother. Both of them were talking about Kṛṣṇa's unnecessary harassment of Rādhārāṇī when She was walking on the street. Jaṭilā said, "You cruel-faced Mukharā! By hearing your words my heart feels like it is burning in a fire!" And Mukharā replied, "You sinful Jaṭilā, by hearing your words, there is aching in my head! You cannot give any evidence that Kṛṣṇa has attacked Rādhārāṇī, the daughter of my daughter Kīrtidā."

Once, when Rādhārāṇī was taking off the necklace given to Her by Kṛṣṇa, Jaṭilā, her mother-in-law, told a friend, "My dear friend, just see the beautiful necklace that Kṛṣṇa has presented to Rādhārāṇī. She is now holding it, but still She wants to tell us that She has no connection with Kṛṣṇa. This girl's activities have disgraced our whole family!"

Natural jealousy of Kṛṣṇa by persons like Śiśupāla cannot be accepted as ecstatic love in anger with Kṛṣṇa.

48

Dread and Ghastliness

Dread

In ecstatic love for Kṛṣṇa in dread, there are two causes of fear: either Kṛṣṇa Himself or some dreadful situation for Kṛṣṇa. When a devotee feels himself to be an offender at Kṛṣṇa's lotus feet, Kṛṣṇa Himself becomes the object of dreadful ecstatic love. And when, out of ecstatic love, friends and well-wishers of Kṛṣṇa apprehend some danger for Him, that situation becomes the object of their dread.

When Ṛkṣarāja was in front of Kṛṣṇa fighting and suddenly realized that Kṛṣṇa is the Supreme Personality of Godhead, Kṛṣṇa addressed him thus: "My dear Ṛkṣarāja, why is your face so dry? Please do not feel threatened by Me. There is no need for your heart to tremble like this. Please calm yourself down. I have no anger toward you. You may, however, become as angry as you like with Me—to expand your service in fighting with Me and to increase My sporting attitude." In this dreadful situation in ecstatic love for Kṛṣṇa, Kṛṣṇa Himself is the object of dread.

There is another instance of a dreadful situation with Kṛṣṇa as the object as follows. After being sufficiently chastised by child Kṛṣṇa in the Yamunā River, the Kāliya snake began to address the Lord, "O killer of the Mura demon, I have acquired many mystic powers by my austerity and penances, but before You I am nothing; I am most insignificant. Therefore, please be kind upon a poor soul like me, and don't be angry with me. I did not know Your actual position, and out of ignorance I have committed such horrible offenses. Please save me. I am a most unfortunate, foolish creature. Please be merciful to me." This is another instance of the ecstasy of dread in devotional service.

When the Keśī demon was causing disturbances in Vṛndāvana by assuming a large horse's body that was so big that he could jump over the trees, Mother Yaśodā told her husband, Nanda Mahārāja, "Our child is very restless, so we had better keep Him locked up within the house. I have been very worried about the recent disturbances of the Keśī demon, who has been assuming the form of a giant horse." When it was learned that the demon was entering Gokula in an angry mood, Mother Yaśodā became so anxious to protect her child that her face dried up and there were tears in her eyes. These are some of the signs of the ecstasy of dread in devotional service, caused by seeing and hearing something that is dangerous to Kṛṣṇa.

After the Pūtanā witch had been killed, some friends of Mother Yaśodā inquired from her about the incident. Mother Yaśodā at once requested her friends, "Please stop! Please stop! Don't bring up the incident of Pūtanā. I become distressed just by remembering this incident. The Pūtanā witch came to devour my son, and she deceived me into letting her take the child on her lap. After that, she died and made a tumultuous sound with her gigantic body."

In the ecstasy of devotional service in dread, the unconstitutional symptoms are drying up of the mouth, exuberance, glancing behind oneself, concealing oneself, bewilderment, searching after the endangered lovable object and crying very loudly. Some other unconstitutional symptoms are illusion, forgetfulness and expectation of danger. In all such circumstances the ecstatic dread is the steady or constant factor. Such dread is caused either by offenses committed or by dreadful circumstances. Offenses may be committed in varieties of ways, and the dread is felt by the person who has committed the offense. When dread is caused by a fearful object, this fearful object is generally a person who is fearsome in his features, nature and influence. An example of an object which caused ecstatic dread is the Pūtanā witch. Dread may be caused by mischievous demoniac characters, such as King Kaṁsa, and it may be caused by great powerful demigods, such as Indra or Śaṅkara.

Demons like Kaṁsa feared Kṛṣṇa, but their feelings cannot be described as ecstatic dread in devotional service.

Ghastliness

It is understood from authoritative sources that an attachment for Kṛṣṇa because of feelings of disgust sometimes presents a ghastly ecstasy in devotional service. The person experiencing such ecstatic love for Kṛṣṇa is almost always in the neutral stage of devotional service, or *śānta-rasa.* A description of ecstatic love caused by ghastliness is found in the following statement: "This person was formerly interested solely in the matter of lust and sense gratification, and he had perfected the greatest skill in exploiting women to fulfill his lusty desires. But now how wonderful it is that this same man is chanting the names of Kṛṣṇa with tears in his eyes, and as soon as he sees the face of a woman, he immediately becomes disgusted. From the indication of his face, I would think that now he hates sex life."

In this mellow of devotional service in ghastliness, the subecstatic symptoms are spitting upon the consideration of one's past life, contorting the face, covering the nose and washing the hands. There is also trembling of the body, forcible twisting of the body, and perspiration. Other symptoms which may be present are shame, exhaustion, madness, illusion, frustration, humility, self-pity, restlessness, eagerness and stunning of the body.

When a devotee, lamenting for his past abominable activities, shows special symptoms on his body, his feeling is called ecstasy in devotional service in ghastliness. This is caused by the awakening of his Kṛṣṇa consciousness.

In this connection there is the following statement: "How can a person take pleasure in the enjoyment of sex life in this body, which is a bag of skin and bones, filled with blood and covered by skin and flesh, and which produces mucus and evil smells?" This perception is possible only for one who is awakened to Kṛṣṇa consciousness and who has become fully cognizant of the abominable nature of this material body.

A fortunate child in the womb of his mother prayed to Kṛṣṇa as follows: "O enemy of Kaṁsa, I am suffering so much because of this material body. Now I am trapped within a mess of blood, urine and liquid stool, within the womb of my mother. Because I am living in such a condition, I am suffering great pangs. Therefore, O divine ocean of mercy, please be kind to me. I have no ability to engage in Your loving devotional service, but please save me!" There is a similar statement by a person fallen in a hellish condition of life. He addressed the Supreme Lord thus: "My dear Lord, Yamarāja has placed me in a situation which is full of filthy and obnoxious smells. There are so many insects and worms, surrounded by the stools left by different kinds of diseased persons. And after seeing this horrible scene, my eyes have become sore, and I am becoming nearly blind. I therefore pray, O my Lord, O deliverer from the hellish conditions of life. I have fallen into this hell, but I shall try to remember Your holy name always, and in this way I shall try to keep my body and soul together." This is another instance of ecstatic love for Kṛṣṇa in an abominable situation.

It is to be understood that any person who is constantly engaged in chanting the holy names of the Lord—Hare Kṛṣṇa, Hare Kṛṣṇa, Kṛṣṇa Kṛṣṇa, Hare Hare/ Hare Rāma, Hare Rāma, Rāma Rāma, Hare Hare—has attained a transcendental affection for Kṛṣṇa, and as such, in any condition of life, he remains satisfied simply by remembering the Lord's name in full affection and ecstatic love.

In conclusion, it may be stated that ecstatic love for Kṛṣṇa in ghastliness appears during the development of dormant neutrality into developed affection.

49

Mixing of Rasas

As already described, there are twelve different kinds of *rasas,* or ecstatic relationships which are shared with Kṛṣṇa. Five of these *rasas* are direct, and they are listed as neutrality, servitude, fraternal love, parental love and conjugal love. Seven of the *rasas* are indirect, and they are listed as humor, astonishment, chivalry, compassion, anger, dread and ghastliness. The five direct *rasas* are eternally manifested in the Vaikuṇṭha world, the spiritual kingdom, whereas the seven indirect *rasas* are eternally manifesting and unmanifesting in Gokula Vṛndāvana, where Kṛṣṇa displays His transcendental pastimes in the material world.

Very often, in addition to one's regular *rasa,* there is found the presence of some other *rasa,* and the mixture of these loving humors is sometimes compatible, or palatable, and sometimes incompatible, or unpalatable. The following is a scientific analysis of the compatibility and incompatibility of the mixtures of these various *rasas,* or loving moods.

When in the *rasa* of neutral love (*śānta-rasa*) there are found traces of ghastliness or astonishment, the result is compatible. When with this neutral love there are manifestations of conjugal love, chivalry, anger or dread, the result is incompatible.

When in the ecstasy of a serving humor there are manifestations of dread, neutral love or chivalry (such as *dharma-vīra* and *dāna-vīra*), the result is compatible. The ecstasy of devotional service in chivalry (*yuddha-vīra*) and anger are directly produced by Kṛṣṇa Himself.

With the ecstasy of fraternal love a mixture of conjugal love, laughter or chivalry is highly compatible. With the same fraternal love, a mixture of dread or parental love is most incompatible.

Although there are gulfs of differences between them, with the ecstasy of parental affection a mixture of laughter, compassion or dread is compatible.

With the ecstasy of parental love a mixture of conjugal love, chivalry or anger is incompatible.

With the ecstasy of devotion in conjugal love a mixture of laughter or fraternity is compatible.

According to certain expert opinions, in the ecstasy of conjugal love the feelings of chivalry known as *yuddha-vīra* and *dharma-vīra* are the only compatible additions. According to this view, except for these two humors, all other manifestations are taken as incompatible with conjugal love.

With the ecstasy of devotional laughter a mixture of dread, conjugal love or parental love is compatible, whereas a mixture of compassion or ghastliness is incompatible.

With the ecstasy of devotion in astonishment a mixture of chivalry or neutral love is compatible, whereas a mixture of anger or dread is always incompatible.

With the ecstasy of devotional chivalry a mixture of astonishment, laughter or servitude is compatible, whereas a mixture of dread or conjugal love is incompatible. According to some expert opinions, the ecstasy of neutral love is always compatible with devotional service in chivalry.

With the ecstasy of compassion in devotional service a mixture of anger or parental love is compatible, whereas a mixture of laughter, conjugal love or astonishment is always incompatible.

With the ecstasy of anger in devotional service a mixture of compassion or chivalry is compatible, whereas a mixture of laughter, conjugal union or dread is completely incompatible.

With the ecstasy of dread in devotional service a mixture of ghastliness or compassion is compatible.

With the ecstasy of chivalry in devotional service a mixture of conjugal union, laughter or anger is always incompatible.

In the ecstasy of ghastliness in devotional service, feelings of neutral love, laughter or servitude are compatible, whereas feelings of conjugal union and fraternity are incompatible.

The above analysis is a sample of the study of *rasābhāsa,* or incompatible mixing of *rasas.* This transcendental science of *rasābhāsa* can thoroughly explain the humors in ecstatic love which are compatible and incompatible with one another. When Lord Caitanya Mahāprabhu was residing in Jagannātha Purī, many poets and devotees used to come to Him and offer their different kinds of poetry, but the regulation was that Lord Caitanya's secretary, Svarūpa Dāmodara, first examined all of these writings scrutinizingly, and if he would find that there were no incompatibilities in the *rasas,* or transcendental mellows, he would then allow the poet to approach Lord Caitanya and recite his poetry.

The topic of incompatibility is a very important one, and those who are pure devotees always expect to find perfect compatibility in descriptions of the different relationships with the Personality of Godhead. The study of compatibility and incompatibility sometimes becomes very involved, and a hint of why this is so is given as follows. When a friend meets another friend, the mellow produced out of that meeting is generally taken as very palatable. But actually with such meetings between two friends, there are so many feelings involved that it is difficult to ascertain when these feelings are actually becoming compatible and when they are becoming incompatible.

Expert literary scholars have analyzed the *rasas* which are compatible with one another by contrasting the various *rasas* in a particular mixture under the names *whole* and *part.* According to this method, the prominent feeling is called the whole, and the subordinate feeling is called the part.

The following statement elucidates the subject of part and whole: "All living entities are just like sparks from the supreme fire, and as such, I do not know if I, a tiny spark, shall be able to engage myself in the transcendental loving service of this supreme fire, Lord Kṛṣṇa." In this statement, the feelings of neutral love are taken as the whole, whereas the desire to serve the Lord is taken as the part. Actually, in the Brahman effulgence there is no chance for reciprocation of loving ecstasy between the Lord and the devotee.

There is another quotation, from a devotee who laments as follows: "Alas, I am still trying to relish different pleasurable states from this body, which is simply some skin covering mucus, semen and blood. In this state of consciousness I am so condemned that I cannot relish the transcendental ecstasy of remembering the Supreme Personality of Godhead." In this statement there are two ecstatic loving humors, namely neutrality and ghastliness. Neutrality is taken here as the whole, whereas the ecstasy of ghastliness is the part.

There is a similar statement by a devotee as follows: "I shall now begin my service of fanning the Supreme Personality of Godhead, Śrī Kṛṣṇa, who is seated on a golden throne. He is the supreme Parabrahman in His eternal transcendental form with a cloudy blackish complexion. Now I shall give up my affection for my material body, which is nothing but a bunch of flesh and blood." Herein also there is a combination of servitude and ghastliness, where the ecstasy of servitude is taken as the whole and the ecstasy of ghastliness is taken as the part.

There is another statement as follows: "When shall I be freed from the mode of ignorance? And being thus purified, when shall I attain the stage of serving Kṛṣṇa eternally? Only then shall I be able to worship Him, always observing His lotus eyes and beautiful face." In this statement the whole is the ecstasy of neutrality, and the part is servitorship.

There is another statement as follows: "Please look at this devotee of the Lord who is dancing just from remembering the lotus feet of Kṛṣṇa. Simply by observing his dance you will lose all interest in even the most beautiful women!" In this statement the whole is in neutrality, and the part is in ghastliness.

One devotee boldly said, "My dear Lord, now I am turning my face from any thought of association with young girls. As far as Brahman realization is concerned, I have lost all interest, because I am completely absorbed in thinking about You. And being absorbed so blissfully, I have lost all other desires, even the desire for mystic powers. Now my mind is attracted only to worshiping Your lotus feet." In this statement, the whole is the ecstasy of neutrality, and the part is chivalry.

In another statement, Subala is addressed thus: "My dear Subala, the damsels of Vṛndāvana who had the opportunity of enjoying Kṛṣṇa's kissing must be the foremost of all the fortunate women in the world." In this example, the ecstasy of fraternal devotional service is the whole, and the ecstasy of conjugal love is the part.

The following statement was made by Kṛṣṇa to the *gopīs:* "My dear enchanted, don't gaze at Me with longing eyes like this. Be satisfied and return to your homes in Vṛndāvana. There is no necessity of your presence here." While Kṛṣṇa was joking in this way with the damsels of Vraja, who with great hope had come to enjoy the *rāsa* dance with Him, Subala was also on the scene, and he began to look at Kṛṣṇa with wide and laughing eyes. Subala's feeling contained a mixture of fraternity and laughter in devotional service. Fraternity is considered here to be the whole, and the laughter is considered the part.

The following example contains a mixture of ecstatic fraternity and laughter, taken respectively as the whole and part. When Kṛṣṇa saw that Subala, in the dress of Rādhārāṇī, was silently hiding under the shade of a beautiful *aśoka* tree on the bank of the Yamunā, He immediately arose from His seat in surprise. Upon seeing Kṛṣṇa, Subala tried to hide his laughter by covering his cheeks.

There is also an example of a mixture of parental love and compassion in devotional service. When Mother Yaśodā was thinking that her son was walking in the forest without any umbrella or shoes, she became greatly perturbed to think of how much difficulty Kṛṣṇa must have been feeling. In this example the whole is the parental love, and the part is compassion.

There is the following example of a mixture of parental love and laughter. A friend of Mother Yaśodā told her, "My dear Yaśodā, your son has very cunningly stolen a lump of butter from my home. And to make me blame my own son for His mischief, He has smeared some of the butter on my son's face while he was sleeping!" Upon hearing this, Mother Yaśodā shook her curved eyebrows. She could only look at her friend with a smiling face. May Mother Yaśodā bless everyone with this smiling attitude. In this example the whole is the parental love, and the part is the laughter.

There is an example of a mixture of several humors with devotional service as follows. When Kṛṣṇa was holding up Govardhana Hill with His left hand, His hair became scattered all over His shoulders, and He appeared to be perspiring. When Mother Yaśodā saw this scene, she began to tremble. Then, as she stared at the scene with broadened eyes, she saw Kṛṣṇa begin to exhibit varieties of facial caricatures. Mother Yaśodā then became very happy and began to smile. Then again, when she thought that Kṛṣṇa was holding up the hill for such an extremely long time, her clothes became soaked with perspiration. May Mother Yaśodā Vrajeśvarī protect the whole universe by her infinite mercy! In this example, the whole is parental love, and the parts are dread, wonder, laughter, compassion, etc.

There is an example of a mixture of conjugal love and fraternal affection when Śrīmatī Rādhārāṇī said, "My dear friends, just see how Kṛṣṇa is resting His hand on the shoulder of Subala, who is dressed up just like a young girl! I think He must be sending some message to Me through Subala." The purport is that the superiors of Rādhārāṇī do not like Kṛṣṇa or His cowherd friends to associate with Her; therefore these friends sometimes clothe themselves in female dress so they can give Rādhārāṇī a message from Kṛṣṇa. In this example the whole is conjugal love, and the part is fraternity.

The following is an example of a mixture of conjugal love and laughter in devotional service. Kṛṣṇa, in the dress of a young girl, told Rādhārāṇī, "Oh, You hardhearted girl! Don't You know that I am Your sister? Why are You unable to recognize Me? Be merciful upon Me and please capture My shoulders and embrace Me with love!" While Kṛṣṇa was dressed up exactly like Rādhārāṇī, He was speaking these nice words, and Śrīmatī Rādhārāṇī could understand His purpose. But because She was in front of many of Her superiors, She simply smiled and did not say anything. In this instance, the ecstasy of conjugal love is taken as the whole, and the ecstasy of laughter is taken as the part.

The following illustrates a mixture of several feelings. When one of the consort friends of Candrāvalī saw that Kṛṣṇa was preparing to fight with the Vṛṣāsura demon, she began to think, "How wonderful Kṛṣṇa is! His mind is captivated by the eyebrows of Candrāvalī in a smiling spirit, His snakelike arms are on the shoulder of His friend, and at the same time He is roaring like a lion to encourage Vṛṣāsura to fight with Him!" This is an example of conjugal love, fraternity and chivalry. The conjugal love is taken here as the whole, and the fraternity and chivalry are taken as the parts.

When Kubjā caught hold of Kṛṣṇa's yellow garment because she was feeling almost lusty with sex urge, Kṛṣṇa simply bowed down His head with His cheeks glowing in front of the many people who were standing there and laughing. This is an example of a mixture of ecstatic conjugal love and laughter. The laughter is taken as the whole, and the conjugal love is taken as the part.

Viśāla, a cowherd boy who was attempting to fight with Bhadrasena, was addressed by another cowherd boy as follows: "Why are you attempting to show your chivalrous spirit before me? Before this, you even attempted to fight with Śrīdāmā, but you must know that Śrīdāmā does not even care to fight with hundreds of Balarāmas. So why are you acting so enthusiastically when you actually have no importance at all?" This is an example of a mixture of devotional fraternity and chivalry. The chivalry is taken as the whole, and the fraternity is taken as the part.

Śiśupāla was habituated to calling Kṛṣṇa ill names, and by his insults he irritated the sons of Pāṇḍu more than he irritated Kṛṣṇa. The Pāṇḍavas therefore equipped themselves with all kinds of weapons to kill Śiśupāla. Their feelings were a mixture of ecstatic anger and fraternity, the anger being taken as the whole and fraternity as the part.

Once Kṛṣṇa was watching Śrīdāmā very expertly using his stick to fight with Balarāma, who was an expert club fighter and who had even killed the Pralambāsura demon with His club. When Kṛṣṇa saw Balarāma finally defeated by Śrīdāmā, who was using only a small stick, Kṛṣṇa became filled with pleasure and began to look upon Śrīdāmā with great wonder. In this instance there is a mixture of astonishment, fraternity and chivalry in devotional service. The fraternity and chivalry are considered the parts, and the astonishment is considered the whole.

Expert analysts of these various kinds of mellows instruct us that when different mellows overlap one another, the mellow which is the whole, or the prominent humor, is called the permanent ecstasy. It is confirmed in the *Viṣṇu-dharmottara* that when there are many mellows of devotional ecstasy mixed together, the prominent one, or the whole, is called the steady ecstasy of devotional service. Although the subordinate mellow may be manifested for a certain time, at length it will become merged into the prominent whole. Thus it is called an unconstitutional ecstasy of devotional service.

There is a good analogy in this connection, showing the relationship between the part and whole. Lord Vāmanadeva is actually the Supreme Personality of Godhead, but He appeared to have been "born" as one of the brothers of Indra. Although Vāmanadeva is sometimes taken as a less important demigod, He is actually the maintainer of Indra, the King of the demigods. Thus, although sometimes Vāmanadeva is considered to be a subordinate demigod, His actual position is that of the supreme whole, the source of the entire demigod system. In the same way, a *rasa* which is actually prominent may sometimes appear to be manifested in a subordinate way, although its actual position is as the main or prominent loving feeling of a devotee.

When an unconstitutional ecstasy of devotional service is manifested prominently at a certain time, it is still accepted as the part. If it is not very prominently manifested, it appears only slightly and merges quickly back into the whole. At such times of slight appearance, no consideration is given to it; when one is eating some palatable dishes, if one also eats a small blade of grass he will not taste it, nor will he care to distinguish what its taste is like.

50

Further Analysis of Mixed Rasas

As already described, if certain kinds of mellows become mixed and there is a joining of opposite mellows, then the situation is called incompatible. When one is eating sweet rice and something salty or sour is mixed in, the mixture is not very tasteful, and it is called incompatible.

An exemplary instance of incompatibility is a statement by an impersonalist who was lamenting aloud, "I have been attached simply to the impersonal Brahman feature, and I have passed my days uselessly in practicing trance. I have not given any proper attention to Śrī Kṛṣṇa, who is the source of the impersonal Brahman and who is the reservoir of all transcendental pleasures." In this statement there are traces of neutrality and conjugal love, and the resulting humor is incompatible.

Sometimes it is found in places like Vṛndāvana that a person with a slight devotional attitude of neutral love for Kṛṣṇa may immediately and artificially try to attain to the platform of conjugal love. But because of the incompatibility of neutrality and conjugal love, the person is found to fall from the standard of devotional service.

Incompatibility was expressed by a great devotee on the platform of neutrality when he sarcastically prayed, "I am very anxious to see Kṛṣṇa, the Supreme Personality of Godhead, who is many millions of times more affectionate than the Pitās [forefathers] in the Pitṛloka and who is always worshiped by the great demigods and sages. I am a little surprised, however, that although Kṛṣṇa is the husband of the goddess of fortune, His body is often marked with the nail pricks of ordinary society girls!" Here is an example of incompatibility due to a mixture of neutrality and high conjugal love.

There is the following statement by a *gopī:* "My dear Kṛṣṇa, the first thing You should do is just embrace me with Your strong arms. Then, my dear friend, I shall first smell Your head, and then I shall enjoy with You." This is an example of incompatibility in which conjugal love is the whole and servitorship is the part.

One devotee said, "My dear Kṛṣṇa, how can I address You as my son when You are addressed by the great Vedāntists as the Absolute Truth and by the Vaiṣṇavas who follow the principles of *Nārada-pañcarātra* as the Supreme Personality of Godhead? You are the same Supreme Person, so how shall my tongue be so extraordinarily bold as to address You as an ordinary son?" In this statement there is a mixture of neutrality and parental love, and the result is incompatible.

Another devotee said, "My dear friend, my youthful beauty is as temporary as lightning in the sky, and therefore my possessing attractive bodily features is unimportant. I have never met Kṛṣṇa, so I request you to please arrange for my meeting Him immediately." In this statement there is the incompatibility of a neutral mellow mixed with conjugal love.

A lusty woman in Kailāsa once told Kṛṣṇa, "My dear Kṛṣṇa, may You have a long life!" Then, after saying this, she embraced Kṛṣṇa. This is an example of incompatibility resulting from a mixture of parental love and conjugal love.

The purpose of the above analysis is to show that in the mixture of various mellows, or reciprocations of ecstatic love between Kṛṣṇa and the devotees, if the result is not pure there will be incompatibility. According to the opinion of stalwart devotees like Rūpa Gosvāmī, as soon as there are contradictory feelings, the result is incompatible.

Once an ordinary female devotee addressed Kṛṣṇa, "My dear boy, I know that my body is just a composition of flesh and blood and can never be enjoyable to You. But still, I have been so attracted by Your beauty that I wish that You accept me as Your conjugal lover." In this statement there is incompatibility caused by a mixture of ghastliness and conjugal love in devotional service.

Śrīla Rūpa Gosvāmī warns devotees to not commit such incompatibilities in their writings or in their dealings. The presence of such contradictory feelings is called *rasābhāsa*. When there is *rasābhāsa* in any book of Kṛṣṇa consciousness, no learned scholar or devotee will accept it.

In the *Vidagdha-mādhava,* Second Act, verse 17, Paurṇamāsī tells Nāndīmukhī, "Just see how wonderful it is! Great sages meditate upon

Kṛṣṇa after being relieved from all material transactions, and with great difficulty they try to situate Kṛṣṇa in their hearts. And opposed to this, this young girl is trying to withdraw her mind from Kṛṣṇa so that she can apply it in the material activities of sense gratification. What a regrettable thing it is that this girl is trying to drive away from her heart the same Kṛṣṇa who is sought after by great sages through severe austerities and perseverance!" Although in this statement there are contradictory mellows of ecstatic devotion, the result is not incompatible, because the conjugal love is so elevated that it is defeating all other varieties of mellows. Śrīla Jīva Gosvāmī comments in this connection that such a loving state of mind is not possible for all. It is possible only in the case of the *gopīs* of Vṛndāvana.

There are many other instances of contradictory mellows where there is no perverted experience of *rasābhāsa*. Once some minor demigod of the heavenly planets remarked, "Kṛṣṇa, whose joking words were once the source of so much laughter for the residents of Vraja, has now been attacked by the serpent king, Kāliya, and He has become the object of everyone's overwhelming lamentation!" In this instance there is a mixture of laughter and compassion, but there is no incompatibility, because by both of these *rasas* the loving affection for Kṛṣṇa is increased.

Śrīmatī Rādhārāṇī was once told that although She had stopped all activities, She was still the supreme source of inspiration for all kinds of devotional service. The statement says, "My dear Rādhārāṇī, in separation from Kṛṣṇa You are now as still as the most beautiful tree, whose gracefulness is not blocked by any covering of leaves. Your tranquil mood makes You appear to be completely merged in Brahman realization!" In this example there is a mixture of conjugal love and neutral love, but the conjugal love has surpassed everything. Actually, Brahman realization is only a stunted existence. There is the following statement by Kṛṣṇa Himself: "Śrīmatī Rādhārāṇī has become peace personified for Me. Because of Her, I now go without sleep. I stare constantly without blinking My eyes, and I am always in a meditative mood. Because of Her I have even made My home in the cave of a mountain!" This is an example of conjugal love mixed with neutral love, but there is no incompatibility.

The following is a conversation consisting of questions put before Rambhā, a celebrated beautiful woman, and her corresponding answers.

Rambhā was asked, "My dear Rambhā, who are you?" She answered, "I am peace personified." Question: "Then why are you in the sky?" Answer: "I am in the sky to experience the Supreme Absolute Truth." Question: "Then why are you staring?" Answer: "Just to look into the supreme beauty of the Absolute Truth." Question: "Then why do you appear to be disturbed in mind?" Answer: "Because Cupid is acting." In the above example also there is no perverted representation of mellows, because on the whole the ecstasy of conjugal love has exceeded the neutral position of devotional service.

In the Tenth Canto of *Śrīmad-Bhāgavatam,* Sixtieth Chapter, verse 45, Rukmiṇī-devī said, "My dear husband, a woman who has no taste for the transcendental pleasure available from Your personal contact must be inclined to accept as her husband somebody who is externally a combination of mustache, beard, body hairs, fingernails and some head hair. And within him there are muscles, bones, blood, intestinal worms, stools, mucus, bile and similar things. Actually, such a husband is only a dead body, but due to not being attracted to Your transcendental form, a woman will have to accept this combination of stools and urine for her husband." This statement, which lists the ingredients of a material body, is not a perverted mellow in transcendental realization, because it shows correct discrimination between matter and spirit.

In the *Vidagdha-mādhava,* Second Act, verse 31, Kṛṣṇa tells His friend, "My dear friend, what a wonderful thing it is that since I have seen the beautiful lotus eyes of Śrīmatī Rādhārāṇī, I have developed a tendency to spit on the moon and the lotus flower!" This is an example of conjugal love mixed with ghastliness, but there is no incompatibility.

The following is a statement which describes different mellows of devotional service: "Although Kṛṣṇa was invincible to any enemy, the cowherd boys of Vṛndāvana became almost blackish with astonishment upon seeing His wonderful royal garments and His fighting feats on the Battlefield of Kurukṣetra." In this statement, although there is a mixture of chivalrous activities and dread in devotional service, there is no perverted reflection of mellows.

One resident of Mathurā requested her father to bolt the doors and then go with her to the school of Sāndīpani Muni to find Kṛṣṇa. She complained that Kṛṣṇa had completely stolen her mind. In this incident there is a mixture of conjugal love and parental love, but there is no incompatibility.

A *brahmānandī* (impersonalist) expressed his desire as follows: "When shall I be able to see that supreme absolute Personality of Godhead who is eternal bliss and knowledge and whose chest has become smeared with red *kuṅkuma* powder by touching the breast of Rukmiṇī?" Here there is a mixture of conjugal love and neutrality. Although this is a contradiction of mellows, there is no incompatibility, because even a *brahmānandī* will become attracted to Kṛṣṇa.

Nanda Mahārāja told his wife, "My dear Yaśodā, although your son, Kṛṣṇa, is as delicate and soft as the *mallikā* flower, He has gone to kill the Keśī demon, who is as strong as a mountain. Therefore I have become a little disturbed. But never mind, all auspiciousness to my son! I shall raise this hand, which is as strong as a pillar, and I shall kill the Keśī demon, just to give freedom from all anxieties to the inhabitants of Vraja-maṇḍala!" In this statement there are two kinds of mellows: chivalry and dread. Both of them, however, improve the position of parental love, and therefore there is no incompatibility.

In the *Lalita-mādhava* of Śrīla Rūpa Gosvāmī it is stated, "After Kṛṣṇa's arrival in Kaṁsa's arena, Kaṁsa's priest looked at Kṛṣṇa with a detestful expression. The entire arena was filled with dread on the part of Kaṁsa and his priest and restless expressions of pleasure on the cheeks of Kṛṣṇa's friends. Frustration was felt by His envious rivals. The great sages meditated. Hot tears were in the eyes of Devakī and other motherly ladies, and hairs stood on the bodies of the expert warriors. There was astonishment in the hearts of demigods such as Indra. The servants danced, and the restless eyes of all the young girls glanced about." In this statement there is a description of a combination of different mellows, but there is no incompatibility.

A similar statement, which is free from incompatibility, is in the *Lalita-mādhava*, wherein the author blesses all the readers of the book in the following manner: "Although the Supreme Personality of Godhead is able to lift a mountain with a finger of His left hand, He is always humble and meek. He is always very kind to His loving devotees. He has frustrated Indra's attempt at vengeance by refusing him the sacrifice of Indra-yajña. He is the cause of all pleasure to all young girls. May He be ever compassionate upon you all!"

51

Perverted Expression of Mellows

Rasābhāsa, or incompatible mixtures of mellows, may be classified as *uparasa* (false expression), *anurasa* (imitation) and *aparasa* (perverted or misrepresented mellows).

There is the following statement by an impersonalist who had just seen Kṛṣṇa: "When a person has passed completely from all contamination of material existence, he relishes a transcendental bliss of being established in trance. But as soon as I saw You, the original Personality of Godhead, I experienced the same bliss." This perverted reflection of mellows is called *śānta-uparasa,* or a perverted reflection of mixed impersonalism and personalism.

There is another statement as follows: "Wherever I am glancing I simply see Your personality. Therefore I know that You are the uncontaminated Brahman effulgence, the supreme cause of all causes. I think that there is nothing but You in this cosmic manifestation." This is another example of *uparasa*, or a perverted reflection of impersonalism and personalism.

When Madhumaṅgala, an intimate friend of Kṛṣṇa, was dancing before Kṛṣṇa in a joking manner, no one was paying attention to him, and he jokingly said, "My dear Lord, please be merciful upon me. I am praying for Your mercy." This is an example of *uparasa* in fraternal affection and neutrality.

Kaṁsa once addressed his sister Devakī as follows: "My dear sister, having seen your dear son Kṛṣṇa, I think that He is so strong that He can kill even wrestlers as strong as the mountains. So I will have no more anxieties about Him, even if He is engaged in a terrible fight." This is an instance of *uparasa* in a perverted reflection of parental love.

In the *Lalita-mādhava,* Śrīla Rūpa Gosvāmī says, "The wives of the *yājñika brāhmaṇas* were all young girls, and they were attracted to Kṛṣṇa in the same way as the *gopīs* of Vṛndāvana. Out of their attraction, they distributed food to Kṛṣṇa." Here the two devotional mellows are conjugal love and parental love, and the result is called *uparasa* in conjugal love.

One of the friends of Śrīmatī Rādhārāṇī told Her, "My dear friend Gāndharvikā [Rādhārāṇī], You were the most chaste girl in our village, but now You have divided Yourself and are partially chaste and partially unchaste. It is all due to Cupid's influence upon You after You saw Kṛṣṇa and heard the sound of His flute." This is another example of *uparasa* caused by divided interests in conjugal love.

According to some expert learned scholars, the feelings between lover and beloved create perverted reflections of mellows in many ways.

"The *gopīs* have become purified by Kṛṣṇa's glance, and as such, Cupid's influence is distinctly visible on their bodies." Although in the material sense the glancing of a boy at a girl is a kind of pollution, when Kṛṣṇa threw His transcendental glance at the *gopīs,* they became purified. In other words, because Kṛṣṇa is the Absolute Truth, any action by Him is transcendentally pure.

After Kṛṣṇa chastised the Kāliya-nāga in the Yamunā River by dancing on his heads, the Kāliya-nāga's wives addressed Kṛṣṇa, "Dear cowherd boy, we are all only young wives of the Kāliya-nāga, so why do You agitate our minds by sounding Your flute?" Kāliya's wives were flattering Kṛṣṇa so that He would spare their husband. Therefore this is an example of *uparasa,* or false expression.

One devotee said, "My dear Govinda, here is a nice flowery bush in Kailāsa. I am a young girl, and You are a young poetic boy. After this, what more can I say? You just consider." This is an example of *uparasa,* caused by impudence in conjugal love.

When Nārada Muni was passing through Vṛndāvana, he came to the Bhāṇḍīravana forest and saw in one of the trees the famous parrot couple that always accompanies Lord Kṛṣṇa. The couple was imitating some discussion they had heard upon the *Vedānta* philosophy, and thus were seemingly arguing upon various philosophical points. Upon seeing this, Nārada Muni was struck with wonder, and he began to stare without moving his eyelids. This is an example of *anurasa,* or imitation.

When Kṛṣṇa was fleeing from the battlefield, from a distant place Jarāsandha was watching Him with restless eyes and was feeling very proud. Being thus puffed up with his conquest, he was repeatedly laughing. This is an example of *aparasa*.

Everything in connection with Kṛṣṇa is called ecstatic devotional love, although it may be exhibited in different ways: sometimes in right order and sometimes as a perverted reflection. According to the opinion of all expert devotees, anything that will arouse ecstatic love for Kṛṣṇa is to be taken as an impetus for transcendental mellow.

Thus ends the Bhaktivedanta summary study of Śrī Bhakti-rasāmṛta-sindhu *by Śrīla Rūpa Gosvāmī.*

Concluding Words

Śrīla Rūpa Gosvāmī concludes by saying that *Bhakti-rasāmṛta-sindhu* is very difficult for ordinary men to understand, yet he hopes that Lord Kṛṣṇa, the eternal Supreme Personality of Godhead, will be pleased with his presentation of this book.

By rough calculation it is estimated that Śrīla Rūpa Gosvāmī finished *Śrī Bhakti-rasāmṛta-sindhu* in Gokula Vṛndāvana in the year 1552. While physically present, Śrīla Rūpa Gosvāmī was living in different parts of Vṛndāvana, and his headquarters were in the temple of Rādhā-Dāmodara in the present city of Vṛndāvana. The place of Rūpa Gosvāmī's *bhajana,* execution of devotional service, is commemorated still. There are two different tomblike structures in the Rādhā-Dāmodara temple; one structure is called his place of *bhajana,* and in the other his body is entombed. Behind this very tomb I have my place of *bhajana,* but since 1965 I have been away. The place, however, is being taken care of by my disciples. By Kṛṣṇa's will, I am now residing at the Los Angeles temple of the International Society for Krishna Consciousness. This purport is finished today, the 30th of June, 1969.

APPENDIXES

The Author

His Divine Grace A. C. Bhaktivedanta Swami Prabhupāda appeared in this world in 1896 in Calcutta, India. He first met his spiritual master, Śrīla Bhaktisiddhānta Sarasvatī Gosvāmī, in Calcutta in 1922. Bhaktisiddhānta Sarasvatī, a prominent religious scholar and the founder of sixty-four Gauḍīya Maṭhas (Vedic institutes), liked this educated young man and convinced him to dedicate his life to teaching Vedic knowledge. Śrīla Prabhupāda became his student and, in 1933, his formally initiated disciple.

At their first meeting, in 1922, Śrīla Bhaktisiddhānta Sarasvatī requested Śrīla Prabhupāda to broadcast Vedic knowledge in English. In the years that followed, Śrīla Prabhupāda wrote a commentary on the *Bhagavad-gītā,* assisted the Gauḍīya Maṭha in its work, and, in 1944, started *Back to Godhead,* an English fortnightly magazine. Singlehandedly, Śrīla Prabhupāda edited it, typed the manuscripts, checked the galley proofs, and even distributed the individual copies. The magazine is now being continued by his followers.

In 1950 Śrīla Prabhupāda retired from married life, adopting the *vānaprastha* (retired) order to devote more time to his studies and writing. He traveled to the holy city of Vṛndāvana, where he lived in humble circumstances in the historic temple of Rādhā-Dāmodara. There he engaged for several years in deep study and writing. He accepted the renounced order of life (*sannyāsa*) in 1959. At Rādhā-Dāmodara, Śrīla Prabhupāda began work on his life's masterpiece: a multivolume commentated translation of the eighteen-thousand-verse *Śrīmad-Bhāgavatam* (*Bhāgavata Purāṇa*). He also wrote *Easy Journey to Other Planets*.

After publishing three volumes of the *Śrīmad-Bhāgavatam,* Śrīla Prabhupāda came to the United States, in September 1965, to fulfill the mission of his spiritual master. Subsequently, His Divine Grace wrote more than fifty volumes of authoritative commentated translations and summary studies of the philosophical and religious classics of India.

When he first arrived by freighter in New York City, Śrīla Prabhupāda was practically penniless. Only after almost a year of great difficulty did he establish the International Society for Krishna Consciousness, in July of 1966. Before he passed away on November 14, 1977, he had guided the Society and seen it grow to a worldwide confederation of more than one hundred *āśramas,* schools, temples, institutes, and farm communities.

In 1972 His Divine Grace introduced the Vedic system of primary and secondary education in the West by founding the *gurukula* school in Dallas, Texas. Since then his disciples have established similar schools throughout the United States and the rest of the world.

Śrīla Prabhupāda also inspired the construction of several large international cultural centers in India. At Śrīdhāma Māyāpur, in West Bengal, devotees are building a spiritual city centered on a magnificent temple—an ambitious project for which construction will extend over many years to come. In Vṛndāvana are the Kṛṣṇa-Balarāma Temple and International Guesthouse, *gurukula* school, and Śrīla Prabhupāda Memorial and Museum. There are also major temples and cultural centers in Mumbai, New Delhi, Ahmedabad, Siliguri, and Ujjain. Other centers are planned in many important locations on the Indian subcontinent.

Śrīla Prabhupāda's most significant contribution, however, is his books. Highly respected by scholars for their authority, depth, and clarity, they are used as textbooks in numerous college courses. His writings have been translated into over fifty languages. The Bhaktivedanta Book Trust, established in 1972 to publish the works of His Divine Grace, has thus become the world's largest publisher of books in the field of Indian religion and philosophy.

In just twelve years, despite his advanced age, Śrīla Prabhupāda circled the globe fourteen times on lecture tours that took him to six continents. In spite of such a vigorous schedule, Śrīla Prabhupāda continued to write prolifically. His writings constitute a veritable library of Vedic philosophy, religion, literature, and culture.

"Waves" of The Nectar of Devotion

Like the watery ocean, the *Bhakti-rasāmṛta-sindhu* is originally divided into four sections—eastern, southern, western and northern. Within each of these sections, there are various subsections, which are called "waves." The table below shows how the chapters of *The Nectar of Devotion* correspond to these original divisions of the *Bhakti-rasāmṛta-sindhu*.

References

The text of *The Nectar of Devotion* is confirmed by standard Vedic authorities. The following authentic scriptures are cited:

Ādi Purāṇa, 102, 104, 107

Agastya-saṁhitā, 52

Agni Purāṇa, 87, 153

Aparādha-bhañjana, 295–96

Bhagavad-gītā, 17, 51–52, 90, 113, 121, 169, 192

Bhaviṣya Purāṇa, 76, 87, 104

Brahmāṇḍa Purāṇa, 76, 121–22

Brahma Purāṇa, 62

Brahma-saṁhitā, 188, 198

Brahma-yāmala, 60–61

Bṛhad-vāmana Purāṇa, 191

Agastya saṁhitā, 52

Caitanya-caritāmṛta, 14

Dāna-keli-kaumudī, 234, 270, 354–55

Garuḍa Purāṇa, 89, 259

Gīta-govinda, 189, 353, 356

Govinda-vilāsa, 274

Haṁsadūta, 247, 374

GLOSSARY

A

Ācārya—one who teaches by example; a bona fide spiritual master.
Ārati—the standard worship ceremony of offering lamps and other items to the Lord in His Deity form.
Arcana—Deity worship as a part of the practice of devotional service.

B

Bhagavad-gītā—the discourse between the Supreme Lord, Kṛṣṇa, and His devotee Arjuna, expounding devotional service as both the principal means and the ultimate end of spiritual perfection.
Brahmā—the first created living being and secondary creator of the material universe.
Brahman—the Supreme Absolute Truth, especially the impersonal aspect of the Absolute.
Brāhmaṇa—one wise in the *Vedas* who can guide society; the first Vedic social order.
Brahmānanda—the pleasure of realizing Brahman.
Brahmāstra—a nuclear weapon produced by Vedic chants.

C

Candana—sandalwood, or a cosmetic paste made with sandalwood.
Caraṇāmṛta—remnants of the water that has bathed the feet of the Deity of the Lord.

D

Dāsya—the devotional attitude of servitorship; one of the five major *rasas*.
Demigods—living beings who are specially empowered by the Supreme Lord to act as controllers in universal affairs.
Dvārakā—the site of Lord Kṛṣṇa's city pastimes as an opulent prince.

E

Ekādaśī—a special day for increased remembrance of Kṛṣṇa that comes on the eleventh day after both the full and new moon. Abstinence from grains and beans is prescribed.

G

Gauḍīya Vaiṣṇava sampradāya—the school of Vaiṣṇavism following in the line of Lord Śrī Caitanya Mahāprabhu.

Goloka Vṛndāvana—the topmost planet in the spiritual universe; the personal abode of Lord Kṛṣṇa in His original, two-armed form.

Gopī-candana—sacred earth from Vṛndāvana, used by devotees in making auspicious markings on the body.

Gopīs—Kṛṣṇa's cowherd girlfriends in Vṛndāvana, His most confidential servitors.

I

Indra—the chief of the administrative demigods and king of the heavenly planets.

Indranīla jewel—sapphire.

K

Kaiśora—the period of Kṛṣṇa's age beginning from His eleventh year and continuing up to His fifteenth.

Kamaṇḍalu—a *sannyāsī's* waterpot; a symbol of Lord Brahmā.

Kaumāra—the period of Kṛṣṇa's age from babyhood up to five years.

Kīrtana—chanting of the names and glories of the Supreme Lord, one of the nine major processes of devotional service.

Kṣatriya—a warrior or administrator; the second Vedic social order.

Kuṅkuma—cosmetic vermilion powder.

M

Madana-mohana—Lord Kṛṣṇa, who is the enchanter even of Cupid.

Mantra—a Vedic chant; a sound vibration that can deliver the mind from illusion.

Marakata jewel—emerald.

Māyā—the illusory energy of the Supreme Lord; also, the state of forgetfulness of one's relationship with Kṛṣṇa.

Mukti—liberation from the cycle of repeated birth and death.

N

Nṛsiṁha—the incarnation of the Supreme Lord Viṣṇu as half-man, half-lion. He appeared in order to deliver His devotee Prahlāda and kill the demon Hiraṇyakaśipu.

P

Padmarāga jewel—ruby.

Pāṇḍus—the Pāṇḍavas, the five sons of King Pāṇḍu.

Pauganda—the period of Kṛṣṇa's age from His sixth year to His tenth.

Piṇḍa—a special offering of food to departed ancestors.

Prākṛta-sahajiyā—a pseudo-Vaiṣṇava who takes cheaply the idea of conjugal love of God.

Prasāda—"the Lord's mercy"; food that has become spiritualized by first being offered to the Lord.

Purāṇas—the historical supplements to the *Vedas,* which include accounts of the various incarnations of the Supreme Lord and detailed instructions on the practices of devotional service.

R

Rasa—the transcendental "taste" of a particular spiritual relationship with the Supreme Lord.

Rasābhāsa—inappropriate mixing of conflicting *rasas.*

Ratha-yātrā—the annual festival in which the Supreme Lord in His Deity form as Lord Jagannātha, along with His brother Baladeva and sister Subhadrā, come out of the temple to ride on large chariots.

S

Sādhaka—one who is striving toward perfection in spiritual life.

Sādhana-bhakti—devotional service in the preliminary stage of regulated practice.

Samutkaṇṭhā—extreme eagerness.

Saṅkīrtana—congregational chanting of the holy names of God, the recommended method of spiritual realization in the current age.

Sannyāsī—one in the renounced order of life; the fourth order of Vedic spiritual life.

Śānta—the neutral attitude of devotees who are in appreciation of the greatness of God but are not actively engaged in His service; one of the five major *rasas.*

Śāstras—revealed scriptures; the *Vedas,* along with their supplements and commentaries.

Siddhis—mystic powers achievable by practice of *yoga.*

Śrīmad-Bhāgavatam—the "spotless *Purāṇa,*" which deals exclusively with the subject of pure devotional service to the Supreme Lord. It was spoken five thousand years ago by Śukadeva Gosvāmī to Parīkṣit Mahārāja and then retold by Sūta Gosvāmī to the assembly of sages at Naimiṣāraṇya. It contains eighteen thousand verses in twelve cantos.

Śūdras—laborers; the lowest of the four occupational orders of Vedic society.

T

Tilaka—auspicious clay markings on the body of the devotee.

U

Upaniṣads—philosophical treatises included within the *Vedas* meant for bringing the student closer to understanding the personal nature of the Absolute Truth.

V

Vaikuṇṭha—the kingdom of God, which is "free from all anxiety."

Vaiṣṇavas—devotees of Lord Viṣṇu, Kṛṣṇa.

Vaiśyas—farmers and merchants; the third of the four occupational orders of Vedic society.

Vātsalya—the devotional attitude of parenthood; one of the five major *rasas*.

Vedānta—the "conclusion of the *Vedas*"; Śrīla Vyāsadeva's compilation of *sūtras* summarizing the nature of the Absolute Truth.

Vedas—the original revealed scriptures, first spoken by the Supreme Lord Himself.

Vraja—*See:* Vṛndāvana

Vṛndāvana—Kṛṣṇa's personal abode, where He fully manifests His quality of sweetness; a village in North India, where Kṛṣṇa performed His most intimate pastimes during His appearance on this planet.

Y

Yamarāja—the demigod in charge of death and the punishment of sinful living entities.

Sanskrit Pronunciation Guide

The system of transliteration used in this book conforms to a system that scholars have accepted to indicate the pronunciation of each sound in the Sanskrit language.

The short vowel **a** is pronounced like the **u** in b**u**t, long **ā** like the **a** in f**a**r. Short **i** is pronounced as in p**i**n, long **ī** as in p**i**que, short **u** as in p**u**ll, and long **ū** as in r**u**le. The vowel **ṛ** is pronounced like the **ri** in **ri**m, **e** like the **ey** in th**ey**, **o** like the **o** in g**o**, **ai** like the **ai** in **ai**sle, and **au** like the **ow** in h**ow**. The *anusvāra* (**ṁ**) is pronounced like the **n** in the French word *bon*, and *visarga* (**ḥ**) is pronounced as a final **h** sound. At the end of a couplet, **aḥ** is pronounced **aha**, and **iḥ** is pronounced **ihi**.

The guttural consonants—**k, kh, g, gh,** and **ṅ**—are pronounced from the throat in much the same manner as in English. **K** is pronounced as in **k**ite, **kh** as in Ec**kh**art, **g** as in **g**ive, **gh** as in di**g h**ard, and **ṅ** as in si**ng**.

The palatal consonants—**c, ch, j, jh,** and **ñ**—are pronounced with the tongue touching the firm ridge behind the teeth. **C** is pronounced as in **ch**air, **ch** as in staun**ch-h**eart, **j** as in **j**oy, **jh** as in he**dgeh**og, and **ñ** as in ca**ny**on.

The cerebral consonants—**ṭ, ṭh, ḍ, ḍh,** and **ṇ**—are pronounced with the tip of the tongue turned up and drawn back against the dome of the palate. **Ṭ** is pronounced as in **t**ub, **ṭh** as in ligh**t-h**eart, **ḍ** as in **d**ove, **ḍh** as in re**d-h**ot, and **ṇ** as in **n**ut. The dental consonants—**t, th, d, dh,** and **n**—are pronounced in the same manner as the cerebrals, but with the forepart of the tongue against the teeth.

The labial consonants—**p, ph, b, bh,** and **m**—are pronounced with the lips. **P** is pronounced as in **p**ine, **ph** as in u**ph**ill, **b** as in **b**ird, **bh** as in ru**b-h**ard, and **m** as in **m**other.

The semivowels—**y, r, l,** and **v**—are pronounced as in **y**es, **r**un, **l**ight, and **v**ine respectively. The sibilants—**ś, ṣ,** and **s**—are pronounced, respectively, as in the German word *s*prechen and the English words **sh**ine and **s**un. The letter **h** is pronounced as in **h**ome.

General Index

A

Abhimanyu, husband of Rādhārāṇī, 362
Abhimanyu, son of Arjuna, 317–18
Abhiṣeka (bathing ceremony), 347
Aborigines, 20
Absolute Truth
  compared to sun & sunshine, 120–21
  features of, three given, 120
  impersonal feature of
    appreciated by sages, 285
    attraction to Kṛṣṇa surpasses, 291
    Kṛṣṇa beyond, 186
    See also: Brahman
  independent & sentient, 183
  Kṛṣṇa as end of, 186
  spiritual distinction in, 120–21
Acāryas (saintly teachers)
  author's respects to, *xix*
  in Caitanya's line, 66
  compared to sharks, *xix–xx*
  decrying, atheism as, 61
  devotion to Kṛṣṇa learned from, *xxi*
  fix disciple's mind on Kṛṣṇa, 21
  following in footsteps of, *xx*, 53, 60–61, 118
  hearing from, about Lord, 90
  temple construction by, 66
  See also: Spiritual master
Activity (Activities)
  all kinds of, for Lord, 99
  basis of, pleasure as, *xiii*
  bondage by improper, 20–21
  devotion to Kṛṣṇa as, *xxi*
  glorifying Lord as ultimate, 80
  goal of, as Lord's satisfaction, 25, 27
  of Kṛṣṇa. *See:* Kṛṣṇa, activities of, pastimes of
  material
    birth & death from, 50
    Deity worship counteracts, 109, 110
    devotional service vs., *xxii*, 49–52
    giving up, via Kṛṣṇa consciousness, 90
    as madness, 20–21
    See also: Karma; Sense gratification
  mellow (loving mood) required for, 152
  negative & positive, *xxi*
Activity (*continued*)
  pious. *See:* Pious activities
  reaction of past, 91
  sinful. *See:* Sinful activities
  welfare. *See:* Welfare activity
  worship of Kṛṣṇa via, 26–27
  See also: Karma; Work
Ādi Purāṇa quoted
  on chanting Kṛṣṇa's name, 107
  on devotee, 104
  on devotee of devotee, 102
Affection for Kṛṣṇa, stage of
  attraction based on, 305
  as basis of serving humor, 293
  before further manifestations, 146
  in chanting Lord's names, 382
  development from reverence stage, 303, 304
  in equal friendship, 335
  examples of, 293–94, 303, 304, 305
  neutral love develops to, 382
  in reverential devotion, 293, 317–18
  spontaneous, example of, 144
  status of, 293
  as symptom of *sthāyī* love, 334
  See also: Kṛṣṇa, love for; Servitude
Agastya-saṁhitā
  cited on purifying nostrils, 85
  quoted on devotees free from rules, 52
Aghāsura, 321
Agni Purāṇa quoted
  on *vibhava*, 153
  on worshiping Deity, 87
Agnostics, 31
Aguru scent in Kṛṣṇa's bath, 298
Ahaṅgrahopāsanā realization, 141
Ajāmila, 6
Ākalpa decoration of Kṛṣṇa, 214
Ākarṣiṇī flute of Kṛṣṇa, 215, 216
Akbar, Emperor, 66
Akrūra
  attained perfection by prayers, 117
  doubtful about stealing, 240
  ecstatic at Kṛṣṇa's footprints, 216–17, 219
  ecstatic seeing Kṛṣṇa, 254–55, 311
  faltering of voice in, 227
  gopīs considered him cruel, 312, 376

Conditioned souls
absorbed in matter but must be free, 67
artificially attempt to love Kṛṣṇa, 316–17
birth & death result for, 50
cause own suffering & bondage, 20-21
curing madness of, 21
delivered by Ganges, 78
delivered by Lord only, 78
desire sense gratification, 50, 95
eternally conditioned, 205
gradually elevated by *varṇa* & *āśrama*, 95
revived by Hare Kṛṣṇa, 89
should confess sins, 81
sinful reactions affect all, 91
suffer from sins, 4
See also: Human beings; Living entities; Soul
Confidence
of devotee in Kṛṣṇa, 96, 97, 299–300, 305
as ecstatic symptom, 302–3
Confusion, ecstatic symptom of, 228–29, 247
Conjugal love for Kṛṣṇa
in adolescent age of Kṛṣṇa, 213
anger (*māna*) in, 355, 356
artificially trying for, 316-17
attained by sages, 128–29
attained by sons of fire-gods, 129
based not on body's sex, 128, 129
as cause of bodily enjoyment, 355
compatible mixtures of, 383, 384, 393–95
defeating other mellows, 392–93, 393–94
Deity worship invokes, 128
development of, steps in, 128
as direct *rasa,* 280, 383
discussing it restricted, 316–17
division of, as direct & indirect, 127–28
division of, as wife or lover, 129
divisions & subdivisions of, 355
examples of, 354–57, 387–88, 392–95
expressions of direct & indirect, 274–75
features of (picking quarrel, etc.), 213
by following *gopīs* or queens, 127, 128
frustration in, 354
of *gopīs,* examples of, 354
as group of symptoms of selfless love, 271
as husband-wife or lover-beloved, 129
impetuses to, 353
impossible from conditioned stage, 316–17
impudence in, 398
incompatible mixing of, no examples of, 392–95
incompatible mixtures of, 383, 384, 391–92, 397–98
Kṛṣṇa leader in, 213
Kṛṣṇa object of, 353
Conjugal love for Kṛṣṇa (*continued*)
māna (anger) in, 355, 356
materialists can't understand, 353
as "part" (subordinate) humor, 386, 388
perverted reflections of mellows in, 397–98
pravāsa (distant separation) in, 356
pūrva-rāga (preliminary attraction) in, 355, 356
as queen at Dvārakā, 127, 129
of Rādhārāṇī, 354-57
regulative principles precede, 128
in *sambhoga* (meeting), 355, 356–57
in separation, 355–56
similarity to material activities, 353
in *vipralambha* (separation), 355–56
as "whole" (prominent) humor, 387–88
See also: Gopīs; Kṛṣṇa, attraction to, love for; Rādhārāṇī
Conjunction of ecstatic symptoms, 266, 267
Consciousness, revival of true, 89
See also: Kṛṣṇa consciousness
Consideration, 263
Contamination(s)
at death in family, 69
See also: Modes of material nature; Sinful activities
Contemplation, ecstatic symptom of, 302–3
Continuous ecstatic symptoms, 264, 271
Contradictory ecstatic symptoms, 271
Controllers, two kinds of, 183
Conviction
of first-class devotee, 97
See also: Determination; Faith; Hope; Knowledge
Cosmic manifestation. *See:* Material world; Universe
Cottage of Rādhā & Kṛṣṇa, 247
Cowardice, 263–64
Cowherd boys. *See:* Friends of Kṛṣṇa
Cowherd girls. *See: Gopīs*
Cowherd men
Afraid of Govardhana Hill's shaking, 177
appealed to Kṛṣṇa in fire, 242
attached to Kṛṣṇa, 206
as eternally perfect devotees, 205–6
See also: *Vaiśyas*
Cowherd women. *See: Gopīs; Gopīs* (elderly *gopīs*)
Cows
attracted by Kṛṣṇa, 193
as charity, 173, 369
inert via hearing flute, 248
Kaṁsa's servants attacked, 274
Kṛṣṇa's expansions as, 153

D

G

I

Jewels (*continued*)
Syamantaka, 170, 240
on Viṣṇu, 293–94
Jhārikhaṇḍa Forest, 9
Jhulana-yātrā, 87
Jīva Gosvāmī, 147
Jñāna, 49
See also: Knowledge; Philosophy, speculative
Jñāna-karmādi, xxiv
Jñānī (wise man), 31–32
See also: Brāhmaṇas; Philosophers, speculative; Sages
Joking
of *gopīs* & Kṛṣṇa as *anubhāva,* 354
of Kṛṣṇa as gardening maid, 224
of Kṛṣṇa with young friend, 323
of Madhumaṅgala with Kṛṣṇa, 325
See also: Chivalry; Humor; Laughing ecstasy
Joyfulness
actually achieved in Kṛṣṇa, 186
as *brahma-bhūta* stage, 286
first principle of, as no anxieties, 186
of Pradyumna upon seeing Kṛṣṇa, 318
via regulative devotional service, 204
as symptom of spiritual life, 152
See also: Bliss; Ecstasy, devotional; Happiness; Jubilation; Pleasure
Jubilation, ecstatic symptom of
bodily color change by, 227
examples of, 302–3, 317, 355
in meeting Kṛṣṇa, 303
in reverential devotion, 317
as subsidiary ecstatic symptom, 302–3
as symptom of *vyabhicārī* love, 334
tears due to, 228
See also: Bliss; Ecstasy, devotional; Happiness; Joyfulness; Pleasure
Justice for thieves, 163

K

Kadamba tree(s), 111, 266
Kailāsa women address Kṛṣṇa, 392, 398
Kalaviṅka, 324
Kālayavana, 197
Kali, 25
Kālī, 25n, 72
Kālindī, 294–95
Kāliya
asks Kṛṣṇa's mercy, 379
atmosphere at time of fight with, 242
bit Kṛṣṇa, 255
Kāliya (*continued*)
coils around Kṛṣṇa, 373
discusses own acts, 379
Garuḍa angered by, 255–56
head marked by Kṛṣṇa, 295
Kṛṣṇa favored (vs. Brahmā), 183
Kṛṣṇa ordered, to leave, 161
Kṛṣṇa pacified, 161
Kṛṣṇa's punishment benefited, 172
mystic powers of, 379
poisoned river, 161
regrets fighting Kṛṣṇa, 379
took shelter of Kṛṣṇa, 295
wives of, flattered Kṛṣṇa, 398
wives of, miscarried via Kṛṣṇa's voice, 255
wives of, prayer to Kṛṣṇa by, 172
Kali-yuga (modern age), 26, 51, 90
See also: Society, human
Kalki incarnation, 189
Kāma-prāyā of Kubjā, 124
Kāmāvasāyitā mystic power, 12
Kaṁsa
aggregation of ecstatic symptoms in, 268
arena of, Kṛṣṇa as seen in, 395
attracted to Kṛṣṇa in fear, 120
calls Kṛṣṇa "crude," 265
changed color seeing Kṛṣṇa, 227
debates mentally about Kṛṣṇa, 268
demon-sending by, 323–24
denies Kṛṣṇa is God, 265–66
destination of, vs. *gopīs,* 120–21
discusses Kṛṣṇa's strength, 297
dread evidenced by, 395
friend went insane, 244
laments Keśī's death, 265–66
not in devotional service, *xxiii,* 120
priest of, Kṛṣṇa seen by, 395
prophecy to, 120
servants moved Kṛṣṇa's cows, 274
wrestlers of, 159
Kaṁsa (bell metal), analogy of transforming, 48
Kapiladeva, Lord, 3, 33–34, 133
Karabhājana Muni, 50, 52
Karandhama, 323
Kāraṇodakaśāyī Viṣṇu (Mahā-Viṣṇu), 186, 198
Karma (fruitive activities)
binds one to birth & death, 50
devotional service superior to, 38–39, 49–50
devotion to Kṛṣṇa free of, *xxi, xxiv*
freedom from. *See:* Liberation; Purification
insufficient to clear heart, 7
offering results of, to Kṛṣṇa, 95–96
as one of three paths, 49

Kṛṣṇa
associates of (*continued*)
qualities of Kṛṣṇa in, 206
surpass demigods, 297
transcendental status of, 206
in Vṛndāvana, 205–6, 298
Yadus as, 205, 206
See also: Anugas; Devotees; Friends of Kṛṣṇa
associating with
by chanting His name, 107
classes of, three described, 311
desired in ecstatic love, 305
desired in individual mode, 82
desired in neutral love, 272
as goal of *Upaniṣads,* 288
as pleasure beyond impersonalist's, 285–86
assures Ṛkṣarāja, 379
astonished at Śrīdāmā's fighting, 389
astonished boys by fighting, 394
ate Draupadī's morsel, 184
atheists curbed by, 181
atheists tricked by, as Buddha, 61–62
in atoms, 187, 188
attachment to
in anger, 265
by associating with pure devotees, 133, 140
caused by disgust, 380–82
confidentially kept by Kṛṣṇa, 139
desire for Mathurā due to, 264
development of, from reverence, 303
diminished by desire for salvation, 141
examples of, 37–38, 264–65, 318, 348
extinguished by offenses, 141
as freedom from danger, 23
in His pastimes, 138–39
in hopelessness, 265–66
imitative, 139–40
impossible for nondevotees, 139
manifests in many ways, 269
to one form of Lord only, 46
overwhelming in His parents, 348
perfected in pure heart, 131
in places Kṛṣṇa lived, 139, 140
proved in acts of Pradyumna, 318
in pure devotees only, 139
in *rāgānuga* (spontaneous) devotion, 21–22
rebirth as alternative to, 23
"shadow" attachment, 140
vs. speculative knowledge, 296
surpasses everything, 37–38
as symptom of *sthāyī* love, 334
by visiting holy places, 140

Kṛṣṇa
attachment to (*continued*)
without spiritual master, 140
See also: Affection for Kṛṣṇa, stage of; Kṛṣṇa, attraction to, love for
attacked by Aśvatthāmā, 335
attacked by Bakāsura, 247
attacked by elephants, 242–43
attacked Rādhā on street, 377
attacked Rādhā at Yamunā, 267
attaining form like, 62
attraction to
by all, *xix,* 193
via association with devotees, 29
based on affection, 119, 305
based on one humor (*rasa*), 272
via bodily similarity, 338
in candidate for devotional service, compared to magnet's attraction, 181
compared to that of boys & girls, 81
in conjugal love. *See:* Conjugal love
contaminations purified in, 119
in Cupid, 16
defined, 305
destinations for different kinds of, 120–21
detachment inspired by, 109, 110
via devotee's or Lord's grace, 134
in devotees surpasses all, 33–34
devotees vary in types of, 272
to different forms of Kṛṣṇa, 46
disadvantages faced calmly in, 305
in eagerness to meet Him, 138
to everyone's eyes (*rucira*), 158–59
examples of, *xix,* 120, 128–29, 134, 158–59, 181, 185, 192–93, 211, 212–13, 221, 289, 291, 296, 305, 338
favorable & unfavorable, 120
via flute-playing of Kṛṣṇa, 193
in footsteps of associate of Kṛṣṇa, 27
in *gopīs, xix,* 120, 181, 211, 212–13
as great fortune, 29
highest, to Kṛṣṇa (in Vṛndāvana), 45
highest to Kṛṣṇa's youth, 159–60
to His lotus feet, 34
to His pastimes, 138–39
to His speech, 161–62
in hopelessness, 265–66
in impersonalists, 186, 395
in *kevalā* (pure) state, 272
in Kṛṣṇa to His reflection, 193
in liberated souls, 45, 190–91, 296
liberation via, 221
liberation inferior to, 33–34

L

M

Mankind. *See:* Human beings; Society, human
Mānsiṅgh, Mahārāja, 66
Mantras
chanting of, loud & soft, 80
for reviving conditioned souls, 89
water collected by, 93
See also: Chanting; Hare Kṛṣṇa *mantra;* Sound
Maranda, 323
Marandaka, 298
Mārkaṇḍeya Ṛṣi, 41, 204
Marriage, kidnapping in, 258
"Masters" lust, anger, etc., 295–96
Material existence, 91, 189–90
See also: Materialism; Material world
Materialism
advancement in, as doom, 12–13
alternating status in, *xiii*
blocks devotional service, 32, 33, 47
causes bondage & suffering, 20–21
compared to madness, 20–21
compared to snakebite, 84, 89
competition in, 32–33
Deity worship counteracts, 109, 110
demigod worship as, 64
giving up, by Kṛṣṇa consciousness, 90
motivation for, *xiii*
oneness with God as, 32–33
temporary only, *xiii,* 12
See also: Attachment, material; Bodily concept; Desire, material; False ego; Greed; Materialists; Sense gratification
Materialists
addicted to bad habits, 9, 10
attracted by material comforts, 12
confused & frustrated, *xvi*
God as death for, *xiii*
lack good qualities, 9–10
meditation of, 10
modern unhappy, *xvi*
as nondevotee types, 64
rebirth risk for, 23
See also: Atheists; Conditioned souls; Demons; *Karmīs;* Nondevotees; Philosophers, speculative; Scientists, material
Material nature. *See:* Nature, material
Material scientists, 11, 12, 193–94
Material world
competition in, 32–33
controlled by Kṛṣṇa's order, 183
defeat in, 189–90
as external energy of Lord, *xxii*
giving up, by Kṛṣṇa consciousness, 90
Material world (*continued*)
happiness not in, 59
love as lust in, 143
miseries of, five described, 189–90
reactions part of, 91
service universal in, *xiii*
spiritualizing it, 26–27
See also: Māyā; Modes of material nature; Nature, material; Universe
Mathurā
beauty of, transcendental, 111
death of devotees at, 248
desires fulfilled by, 102, 108
devotee ecstatic hearing of, 217, 264
devotee regrets not seeing, 264, 268
devotion attained in, 103, 108–9
equals all pilgrimage sites, 102
invokes transcendental feelings, 111, 139, 217
Kṛṣṇa perfect in, 195
liberation in, 76
living in, 56–57, 103, 108–9, 139
nondevotees appreciate, 111
surpasses Vaikuṇṭha, 108
transcendental status of, 111
visiting, 76, 102, 108, 111, 139
weaver of, 239
See also: Vṛndāvana
Māyā
compared to snakebite, 89
defeat of all by, 189–90
kṣatriyas protect people from, 25
as madness, 20–21
See also: Bodily concept; False ego; Ignorance; Illusion; Material world; Nature, material
Māyāvāda philosophy, 129–30
See also: Impersonalism; Monism; Oneness with God
Māyāvādīs. *See:* Impersonalist philosophers; Philosophers, speculative
Mayūradhvaja Mahārāja, 370–71
Mayūradhvaja, Vaiṣṇavas of, 48
Meat-eating, 62
Meditation
always on form of Viṣṇu, 23, 92, 286
brahmajyoti attained by, 122
breathing exercise for, 93
common formerly, 93
concentrating on tip of nose, 289
defined, 23, 92
on Deity form, 56, 93–94
on devotees (Vaiṣṇavas), 64
devotees don't practice, 10

Misery (*continued*)
See also: Pain; Suffering
Mithilā, King of. *See:* Bahulāśva
Mitra (sun globe), demons attained, 190
Mixed humor, or *rasa*. *See: Rasas,* mixed
Modern age. *See:* Kali-yuga
Modes of material nature
devotee's sleep beyond, 258–59
Kṛṣṇa & devotee beyond, 183–84
See also: Goodness; Ignorance; *Māyā*
Mokṣa. *See:* Liberation
Money (Wealth)
becoming devotee via needing, 30, 31–32
for building temples, 66, 78
for ceremonies for Lord, 103
exemplary distribution of, *xii*
as gift to Deity, 85
spiritual master carried away by, 116
of spiritual world, 173
used by unqualified men, 66
See also: Materialism; Opulence
Monism, 141
See also: Impersonalism; Kṛṣṇa, merging with; Māyāvāda philosophy; Oneness with God; Philosophy, speculative
Monists, 130, 141, 171
See also: Impersonalist philosophers; Philosophers, speculative
Monkey, Jaratī compared to, 363–64
Monkeys, King of, 166, 363–64
Moon spots, devotee's faults compared to, 142
Morality (Moral principles)
death for thieves, 163
inferior to devotional service, 50
of Kṛṣṇa, 163
as part of learning, 162
See also: Religiosity
Moroseness, 302–3, 373
Mṛti defined, 190
Mucukunda, 164, 236
Muhammadans, associated with by Rūpa, Sanātana & Haridāsa, *xi*
Mukharā, 273, 346, 377
Mukunda-mālā-stotra quoted on remembering Lord's lotus feet, 273
Muralī flute of Kṛṣṇa, 215
Mūrti of Kṛṣṇa, 109, 110
See also: Deity form
Mystic perfections
by chanting *mahā-mantra,* 107
devotees don't desire, 38, 40, 41
in Kṛṣṇa fully, 187
as materialistic perfections, 11–12
Mystics. *See: Yogīs*

N

Nāgapatnīs (wives of Kāliya), 255, 398
Naimiṣāraṇya, sages of, 31, 296
Nakula, 319, 320, 338, 352, 376
Nalakūvara, 42–43
Nanda (of Dvārakā), 297
Nanda Mahārāja (Kṛṣṇa's father)
accused by Yaśodā, 350–51
asks palmist about Kṛṣṇa, 361–62
blissful seeing Kṛṣṇa, 345
bodily features of, 343
calms Yaśodā, 253, 351
charity given by, 369
climbed shed to see Kṛṣṇa, 345
considering oneself as, 130, 206
cows of, one million, 254
declares Kṛṣṇa present, 351
description of, 343
discusses drowning with Kṛṣṇa, 233
discusses getting Kṛṣṇa back, 253
discusses his satisfaction, 254
discusses killing Keśī, 395
discusses Kṛṣṇa & elephant, 235
discusses Kṛṣṇa's appearance, 345
enjoyed Kṛṣṇa's childhood, 344, 345
as ever-liberated devotee, 205–6
following in footsteps of, 125–26, 129–30
foremost in parental love, 342
goddess of fortune with, 254
"hardhearted," 350–51
in illusion in separation from Kṛṣṇa, 351
Kṛṣṇa "child" of, 342
Kṛṣṇa's sweet words to, 161–62
at Kurukṣetra with Kṛṣṇa, 348–49
laments Kṛṣṇa & elephant, 235
love for Kṛṣṇa of, 125
munificent, 369
palmist questioned by, 361–62
satisfied by position, 254
smelled Kṛṣṇa's head on return, 348
thinking oneself to be, 130, 206
walking with Kṛṣṇa, 343
watched for Kṛṣṇa's return, 345
worshiped as Kṛṣṇa's father, 342
Nārada Muni
astonished by Kṛṣṇa at Dvārakā, 365
astonished by parrots, 398
chanting by, loudly, 220
chanting by, purifying effect of, 180

O

Q

R

GENERAL INDEX

Reincarnation. *See:* Transmigration of the soul
Relationships
  mundane, counteracted by Deity worship, 109, 110
  should be with Kṛṣṇa, 32
  with Kṛṣṇa. *See:* Kṛṣṇa, relationship with
Religion. *See:* Devotional service; Kṛṣṇa consciousness; Surrender
Religiosity, 112, 173, 371
  See also: Faith; Morality; Purification; Sacrifices; *Varṇāśrama;* Worship
Remembering Kṛṣṇa. *See:* Kṛṣṇa, remembering Kṛṣṇa
Renouncers. See: *Sannyāsīs*
Renunciation
  of all not offered to Krsna, 114
  alternating enjoyment &, *xiii*
  of bad habits by devotee, 9–10
  by Bharata Mahārāja, 37–38, 136
  by Bilvamaṅgala Ṭhākura, 111
  blocks devotion if false, 281
  of body & all in surrender, 97–98
  defined, 114, 136, 369
  Deity worship inspires, 109, 110
  despite allurements, 136
  by devotee, 9–10, 38, 39, 40, 41, 98, 114, 136
  devotional candidate lacking, 29
  as devotional principle, 53
  in devotional service not essential, 113
  of duty (mundane) for devotional service, 49–52
  enjoyment alternated with, *xiii*
  false, 114–15, 281
  by impersonalists, 114–15
  by Prahlāda, 307–8
  via Kṛṣṇa consciousness, 90, 114–15
  for *Śrīmad-Bhāgavatam* study, 110
  via superior engagement, 90
  See also: Detachment
"Reservation" in ecstatic love, 136
Respect
  to *brāhmaṇas*, cows, devotees & sacred trees, 63–64
  concealment caused by, 251
  to Deity, 69
  to demigods, 67, 70
  of devotee for all, 67
  for scripture, 71
  See also: Obeisances
Restlessness, ecstatic symptom of, 264, 302–3, 307, 349–51, 373, 381
Reverential devotion (for Kṛṣṇa)
  affection developed beyond, 303, 304
Reverential devotion (*continued*)
  affection in, 293, 304, 305, 317–18
  attraction in, 305, 317
  based on reverential feeling, 317
  confidence in Kṛṣṇa's protection in, 313, 317
  defined, 313, 317
  development of, 317
  ecstatic symptoms of, 317
  examples of, 293, 304, 315–18
  friendship in, 273
  increased to love of Godhead, 317
  for Kṛṣṇa in Vṛndāvana, 293
  Kṛṣṇa not discussed in, 316
  Kṛṣṇa seen as protector in, 313, 315, 316, 317
  Kṛṣṇa seen as superior in, 317
  in sons & subordinates, 315
  as subsidiary symptom, 302–3
  in Vṛndāvana inhabitants, 293
Rich men to build temples, 78
Risk-taking for Kṛṣṇa, 56
Ritual(s), Vedic
  block Kṛṣṇa consciousness, 281
  vs. bowing to Deity, 75
  Buddha stopped, 174
  in chivalrous devotion, 366–67, 371
  devotees beyond, 49, 52
  devotional service superior to, 49
  as devotional service to Kṛṣṇa, 95–96
  devotion not attained via, 14
  dog-eaters made fit for, 5–6
  Hare Kṛṣṇa not, 72
  for householder devotees, 95
  insufficient to clear heart, 7
  as *karma, xxiv*, 49
  material enjoyment via, 14
  of *piṇḍa* offering to forefathers, 51
  for purification (*prāyaścitta*), 19, 52
  unfavorable to Kṛṣṇa consciousness, *xxiv*, 289
  varṇa & *āśrama* involve, 112
  See also: Festive occasions; Sacrifices; Worship
Ṛkṣarāja (Jāmbavān), 166, 379
Rohiṇī(devī), 342, 375
Rolling on ground in ecstasy, 219
Rope, ego compared to, 7–8
Ṛṣabhadeva, quoted on fruitive workers, 50
Rucira, Kṛṣṇa as, 158–59
Rukmī, 356
Rukmiṇī
  asked Kṛṣṇa to kidnap Her, 253–54, 257–58
  concealed anger (jealousy) of, 250
  considered Kṛṣṇa's glories, 253–54
  discusses women unattracted to Kṛṣṇa, 394
  impudent in letter to Kṛṣṇa, 258

U

W

Y

The International Society for Krishna Consciousness

CENTERS AROUND THE WORLD

Founder-Acarya: His Divine Grace A. C. Bhaktivedanta Swami Prabhupada

CANADA

Calgary, Alberta — 313 Fourth St. N.E., T2E 3S3/ Tel. (403) 265-3302/ Fax: (403) 547-0795/ vamanstones@shaw.ca

Edmonton, Alberta — 9353 35th Ave. NW, T6E 5R5/ Tel. (780) 439-9999/ edmonton@harekrishnatemple.com

Montreal, Quebec — 1626 Pie IX Boulevard, H1V 2C5/ Tel. & fax: (514) 521-1301/ iskconmontreal@gmail.com

◆ **Ottawa, Ontario** — 212 Somerset St. E., K1N 6V4/ Tel. (613) 565-6544/ Fax: (613) 565-2575/ radha_damodara@yahoo.com

Regina, Saskatchewan — 1279 Retallack St., S4T 2H8/ Tel. (306) 525-1640

◆ **Toronto, Ontario** — 243 Avenue Rd., M5R 2J6/ Tel. (416) 922-5415/ Fax: (416) 922-1021/ toronto@pamho.net

◆ **Vancouver, B.C.** — 5462 S.E. Marine Dr., Burnaby V5J 3G8/ Tel. (604) 433-9728/ Fax: (604) 648-8715; Govinda's Bookstore & Cafe: (604) 433-7100 or (888) 433-8722/ akrura@krishna.com

RURAL COMMUNITY

Ashcroft, B.C. — Saranagati Dhama (mail: P.O. Box 99, V0K 1A0)/ saranagativillage@hotmail.com

U.S.A.

Atlanta, Georgia — 1287 South Ponce de Leon Ave., N.E., 30306/ Tel. & fax: (404) 377-8680/ info@atlantaharekrishnas.com

Austin, Texas — 10700 Jonwood Way, 78753/ Tel. (512) 835-2121/ Fax: (512) 835-8479/ sda@backtohome.com

Baltimore, Maryland — 200 Bloomsbury Ave., Catonsville, 21228/ Tel. (410) 719-1776/ Fax: (410) 799-0642/ info@baltimorekrishna.com

Berkeley, California — 2334 Stuart Street, 94705/ Tel. (510) 649-8619/ Fax: (510) 665-9366

Boise, Idaho — 1615 Martha St., 83706/ Tel. (208) 344-4274/ boise_temple@yahoo.com

Boston, Massachusetts — 72 Commonwealth Ave., 02116/ Tel. (617) 247-8611/ darukrishna@iskconboston.org

◆ **Chicago, Illinois** — 1716 W. Lunt Ave., 60626/ Tel. (773) 973-0900/ Fax: (773) 973-0526/ chicagoiskcon@yahoo.com

Columbus, Ohio — 379 W. Eighth Ave., 43201/ Tel. (614) 421-1661/ Fax: (614) 294-0545/ rmanjari@sbcglobal.net

◆ **Dallas, Texas** — 5430 Gurley Ave., 75223/ Tel. (214) 827-6330/ Fax: (214) 823-7264/ txkrishnas@aol.com; restaurant: vegetariantaste@aol.com

◆ **Denver, Colorado** — 1400 Cherry St., 80220/ Tel. (303) 333-5461/ Fax: (303) 321-9052/ info@krishnadenver.com

Detroit, Michigan — 383 Lenox Ave., 48215/ Tel. (313) 824-6000/ gaurangi108@hotmail.com

Gainesville, Florida — 214 N.W. 14th St., 32603/ Tel. (352) 336-4183/ Fax: (352) 379-2927/ kalakantha.acbsp@pamho.net

Hartford, Connecticut — 1683 Main St., E. Hartford, 06108/ Tel. & fax: (860) 289-7252/ pyari@sbcglobal.net

◆ **Honolulu, Hawaii** — 51 Coelho Way, 96817/ Tel. (808) 595-3947/ rama108@bigfoot.com

Houston, Texas — 1320 W. 34th St., 77018/ Tel. (713) 686-4482/ Fax: (713) 956-9968/ management@iskconhouston.org

Kansas City, Missouri — Rupanuga Vedic College (Men's Seminary), 5201 The Paseo, 64110/ Tel. (800) 340-5286/ Fax: (816) 361-0509/ rvc@rvc.edu

Laguna Beach, California — 285 Legion St., 92651/ Tel. (949) 494-7029/ info@lagunatemple.com

◆ **Los Angeles, California** — 3764 Watseka Ave., 90034/ Tel. (310) 836-2676/ Fax: (310) 839- 2715/ membership@harekrishnala.com

◆ **Miami, Florida** — 3220 Virginia St., 33133/ Tel. (305) 442-7218/ Fax: (305) 444-7145

New Orleans, Louisiana — 2936 Esplanade Ave., 70119/ Tel. (504) 304-0032 (office) or (504) 638-3244 (temple)/ iskcon.new.orleans@pamho.net

New York, New York — 305 Schermerhorn St., Brooklyn, 11217/ Tel. (718) 855-6714/ Fax: (718) 875-6127/ ramabhadra@aol.com

New York, New York — 26 Second Avenue, 10003/ Tel. (212) 253-6182/ krsna.nyc@gmail.com

Philadelphia, Pennsylvania — 41 West Allens Lane, 19119/ Tel. (215) 247-4600/ Fax: (215) 247-8702/ savecows@aol.com

Philadelphia, Pennsylvania — 1408 South St., 19146/ Tel. (215) 985-9303/ savecows@aol.com

Phoenix, Arizona — 100 S. Weber Dr., Chandler, 85226/ Tel. (480) 705-4900/ Fax: (480) 705- 4901/ svgd108@yahoo.com

Portland, Oregon — 3766 SE Division, 97202/ Tel. (503) 236-6734; info@iskconportland.com

◆ **St. Louis, Missouri** — 3926 Lindell Blvd., 63108/ Tel. (314) 535-8085 or 534-1708/ Fax: (314) 535-0672/ iskcon.stl@pamho.net

◆ **San Diego, California** — 1030 Grand Ave., Pacific Beach, 92109/ Tel. (310) 895-0104/ Fax: (858) 483-0941/ krishna.sandiego@gmail.com

San Jose, California — 951 S. Bascom Ave., 95128/ Tel. (408) 293-4959/ jrawson77@yahoo.com

Seattle, Washington — 1420 228th Ave. S.E., Sammamish, 98075/ Tel. (425) 391-3293/ Fax: (425) 868-8928/ info@iskconseattle.com

◆ **Spanish Fork, Utah** — Krishna Temple Project & KHQN Radio, 8628 S. State Road, 84660/ Tel. (801) 798-3559/ Fax: (810) 798-9121/ carudas@earthlink.net

Tallahassee, Florida — 1323 Nylic St., 32304/ Tel. & fax: (850) 224-3803/ darudas@hotmail.com

Towaco, New Jersey — 100 Jacksonville Rd. (mail: P.O. Box 109), 07082/ Tel. & fax: (973) 299-0970/ samikrsi@yahoo.com

◆ **Tucson, Arizona** — 711 E. Blacklidge Dr., 85719/ Tel. (520) 792-0630/ Fax: (520) 791-0906/ tucphx@cs.com

Washington, D.C. — 10310 Oaklyn Dr., Potomac, Maryland 20854/ Tel. (301) 299-2100/ Fax: (301) 299-5025/ ad@pamho.net

RURAL COMMUNITIES

Alachua, Florida (New Raman Reti) — 17306 N.W. 112th Blvd., 32615 (mail: P.O. Box 819, 32616)/ Tel. (386) 462-2017/ Fax: (386) 462-2641/ alachuatemple@alltel.net

Carriere, Mississippi (New Talavan) — 31492 Anner Road, 39426/ Tel. (601) 749-9460 or 799-1354/ Fax: (601) 799-2924/ talavan@hughes.net

Gurabo, Puerto Rico (New Govardhana Hill) — Carr. 181, Km. 16.3, Bo. Santa Rita, Gurabo (mail: HC-01, Box 8440, Gurabo, PR 00778)/ Tel. & fax: (787) 737-4265/ iskcon_pr@yahoo.com

Hillsborough, North Carolina (New Goloka) — 1032 Dimmocks Mill Rd., 27278/ Tel. (919) 732-6492/ bkgoswami@earthlink.net

◆ **Moundsville, West Virginia (New Vrindaban)** — R.D. No. 1, Box 319, Hare Krishna Ridge, 26041/ Tel. (304) 843-1600; Guest House, (304) 845-5905/ Fax: (304) 854-0023/ mail@newvrindaban.com

Mulberry, Tennessee (Murari-sevaka) — 532 Murari Lane, 37359 (mail: P.O. Box 108, Lynchburg, TN 37352)/ Tel. (931) 632-0632/ Fax: (931) 759-6888/ murari_sevaka@yahoo.com

Port Royal, Pennsylvania (Gita Nagari) — R.D. No. 1, Box 839, 17082/ Tel. (717) 527-4101/ kaulinidasi@hotmail.com

Sandy Ridge, North Carolina (Prabhupada Village) — 1264 Prabhupada Rd., 27046/ Tel. (336) 593-9888

ADDITIONAL RESTAURANTS

Gurabo, Puerto Rico — Goura's, Calle Andrés Arúz 200, Plaza Nazario, 00778/ Tel. (787) 712-0000

Hato Rey, Puerto Rico — Tamal Krishna's Veggie Garden, 131 Eleanor Roosevelt, 00918/ Tel. (787) 754-6959/ Fax: (787) 756-7769/ tkveggiegarden@aol.com

Philadelphia, Pennsylvania — Govinda's, 1408 South. St., 19146/ Tel. (215) 985-9303/ Fax: (215) 966-1242

Seattle, Washington — My Sweet Lord, 5521 University Way, 98105/ Tel. (425) 643-4664

UNITED KINGDOM AND IRELAND

Belfast, Northern Ireland — Brooklands, 140 Upper Dunmurray Lane, BT17 OHE/ Tel. +44 (028) 9062 0530

Birmingham, England — 84 Stanmore Rd., Edgbaston B16 9TB/ Tel. +44 (0121) 420 4999/ nitaicharan@fsmail.net

Cardiff, Wales — The Soul Centre, 116 Cowbridge Rd., Canton/ Tel. +44 (02920) 390391/ the.soul.centre@pamho.net

Coventry, England — Kingfield Rd., Coventry (mail: 19 Gloucester St., Coventry CV1 3BZ)/ Tel. +44 (024) 7655 2822 or 5420/ kov@krishnaofvrindavan.com

Leicester, England — 21 Thoresby St., North Evington, LE5 4GU/ Tel. +44 (0116) 276 2587/ pradyumna.jas@pamho.net

Lesmahagow, Scotland — Karuna Bhavan, Bankhouse Rd., Lesmahagow, Lanarkshire, ML11 0ES/ Tel. +44 (01555) 894790/ Fax: +44 (01555) 894526/ karunabhavan@aol.com

◆ **London, England (city)** — 10 Soho St., W1D 3DL/ Tel. +44 (020) 7437-3662; residential /pujaris, 7439-3606; shop, 7287-0269; Govinda's Restaurant, 7437-4928/ Fax: +44 (020) 7439-1127/ london@pamho.net

◆ **London, England (country)** — Bhaktivedanta Manor, Dharam Marg, Hilfield Lane, Watford, Herts, WD25 8EZ/ Tel. +44 (01923) 857244/ Fax: +44 (01923) 852896/ bhaktivedanta.manor@pamho.net; (for accommodations:) bmguesthouse@gmail.com

London, England (south) — 42 Enmore Road, South Norwood, SE25 5NG/ Tel. +44 (020) 8656 4296

London, England (Kings Cross) — 102 Caledonain Rd., Kings Cross, Islington, N1 9DN/ Tel. +44 (020) 7168 5732/ foodforalluk@aol.com

Manchester, England — 20 Mayfield Rd., Whalley Range, M16 8FT/ Tel. +44 (0161) 226-4416

Newcastle-upon-Tyne, England — 304 Westgate Rd., NE4 6AR/ Tel. +44 (0191) 272 1911/ newcastle@iskcon.org.uk

◆ **Swansea, Wales** — 8 Craddock St., SA1 3EN/ Tel. +44 (01792) 468469/ iskcon.swansea@pamho.net; restaurant: govindas.swansea@pamho.net

RURAL COMMUNITIES

Upper Lough Erne, Northern Ireland — Govindadwipa Dhama, Inisrath Island, Derrylin, Co. Fermanagh, BT92 9GN/ Tel. +44 (028) 6772 1512/ manu.sdg@pamho.net

London, England — (contact Bhaktivedanta Manor)

ADDITIONAL RESTAURANTS

Dublin, Ireland — Govinda's, 4 Aungier St., Dublin 2/ Tel. +353 (01) 475 0309/ Fax: (01) 478 6204/ info@govindas.ie

Dublin, Ireland — Govinda's, 83 Middle Abbey St., Dublin 1/ Tel. +353 (01) 661 5095/ info@govindas.ie

Dublin, Ireland — Govinda's, 18 Merrion Row, Dublin 2/ Tel. +353 (01) 661 5095/ praghosa.sdg@pamho.net

AUSTRALASIA

AUSTRALIA

Adelaide — 25 Le Hunte St. (mail: P.O. Box 114, Kilburn, SA 5084)/ Tel. & fax: +61 (08) 8359-5120/ iskconsa@tpg.com.au

Brisbane — 95 Bank Rd., Graceville (mail: P.O. Box 83, Indooroopilly), QLD 4068/ Tel. +61 (07) 3379-5455/ Fax: +61 (07) 3379-5880/ brisbane@pamho.net

Canberra — 44 Limestone Ave., Ainslie, ACT 2602 (mail: P.O. Box 1411, Canberra, ACT 2601)/ Tel. & fax: +61 (02) 6262-6208/ iskcon@harekrishnacanberra.com

Melbourne — 197 Danks St. (mail: P.O. Box 125), Albert Park , VIC 3206/ Tel. +61 (03) 9699-5122/ Fax: +61 (03) 9690-4093/ melbourne@pamho.net

Perth — 144 Railway Parade (corner of The Strand) [mail: P.O. Box 102], Bayswater, WA 6053/ Tel. +61 (08) 9370-1552/ Fax: +61 (08) 9272-6636/ perth@pamho.net

Sydney — 180 Falcon St., North Sydney, NSW 2060 (mail: P.O. Box 459, Cammeray, NSW 2062)/Tel. +61 (02) 9959-4558/ Fax: +61 (02) 9957-1893/ iskcon_sydney@yahoo.com.au

◆ **Sydney** — Govinda's Yoga and Meditation Centre, 112 Darlinghurst Rd., Darlinghurst NSW 2010 (mail: P.O. Box 174, Kings Cross 1340)/ Tel. +61 (02) 9380-5162/ Fax: +61 (02) 9360-1736/ sita@govindas.com.au

RURAL COMMUNITIES

Bambra, VIC (New Nandagram) — 50 Seaches Outlet, off 1265 Winchelsea Deans Marsh Rd., Bambra VIC 3241/ Tel. +61 (03) 5288-7383

Cessnock, NSW (New Gokula) — Lewis Lane (off Mount View Rd., Millfield, near Cessnock [mail: P.O. Box 399, Cessnock, NSW 2325])/ Tel. +61 (02) 4998-1800/ Fax: +61 (02) 9957-1893

Murwillumbah, NSW (New Govardhana) — Tyalgum Rd., Eungella (mail: P.O. Box 687), NSW 2484/ Tel. +61 (02) 6672-6579/ Fax: +61 (02) 6672-5498/ ajita@in.com.au

RESTAURANTS

Brisbane — Govinda's, 99 Elizabeth St., 1st floor, QLD 4000/ Tel. +61 (07) 3210-0255/ brisbane@iskcon.org.au

Brisbane — Krishna's Cafe, 1st Floor, 82 Venture St., West End, QLD 4000/ brisbane@pamho.net

Cairns — Gaura Nitai's, 55 Spence St., Cairns, QLD/ Tel. +61 (07) 4031-2255 or (0425) 725 901/ Fax: +61 (07) 4031 2256

Maroochydore — Govinda's Vegetarian Cafe, 2/7 First Avenue, QLD 4558/ Tel. +61 (07) 5451-0299

Melbourne — Crossways, 1st Floor, 123 Swanston St., VIC 3000/ Tel. +61 (03) 9650-2939

Melbourne — Gopal's, 139 Swanston St., VIC 3000/ Tel. +61 (03) 9650-1578

Newcastle — 110 King Street, NSW 2300/ Tel. +61 (02) 4929-6900/ info@govindascafe.com.au

Perth — Hare Krishna Food for Life, NSW 2300/ Tel. +61 (02) 4929-6900/ info@govindascafe.com.au

Sydney — Govinda's, 112 Darlinghurst Rd., Darlinghurst NSW 2010 (mail: P.O. Box 174, Kings Cross 1340)/ Tel. +61 (02) 9380-5162/ Fax: +61 (02) 9360-1736/ sita@govindas.com.au

NEW ZEALAND AND FIJI

Auckland, NZ — The Loft, 1st Floor, 103 Beach Rd./ Tel. +64 (09) 379-7301

Christchurch, NZ — 83 Bealey Ave. (mail: P.O. Box 25-190)/ Tel. +64 (03) 366-5174/ Fax: +64 (03) 366-1965/ iskconchch@clear.net.nz

Hamilton, NZ — 188 Maui St., RD 8, Te Rapa/ Tel. +64 (07) 850-5108/ rmaster@wave.co.nz

Labasa, Fiji — Delailabasa (mail: P.O. Box 133)/ Tel. +679 812912

Lautoka, Fiji — 5 Tavewa Ave. (mail: P.O. Box 125)/ Tel. +679 6664112/ regprakash@excite.com

Nausori, Fiji — Hare Krishna Cultural Centre, 2nd Floor, Shop & Save Building, 11 Gulam Nadi St., Nausori Town (mail: P.O. Box 2183, Govt. Bldgs., Suva)/ Tel. +679 9969748 or 3475097/ Fax : +679 3477436/ vdas@frca.org.fj

Rakiraki, Fiji — Rewasa (mail: P.O. Box 204)/ Tel. +679 694243

Sigatoka, Fiji — Queens Rd., Olosara. (mail: P.O. Box 1020)/ Tel. +679 6520866/ drgsmarna@connect.com.fj

Suva, Fiji — 166 Brewster St. (mail: P.O. Box 4299, Samabula)/ Tel. +679 3318441/ Fax: +679 3319097/ iskconsuva@connect.com.fj

Wellington, NZ — 105 Newlands Rd., Newlands/ Tel. +64 (04) 478-4108/ iskcon.wellington@paradise.net.nz

Wellington, NZ — Gaura Yoga Centre, 1st Floor, 175 Vivian St. (mail: P.O. Box 6271, Marion Square)/Tel. +64 (04) 801-5500

RURAL COMMUNITY

Auckland, NZ (New Varshan) — Hwy. 28, Riverhead, next to Huapai Golf Course (mail: R.D. 2, Kumeu)/ Tel. +64 (09) 412-8075/ Fax: +64 (09) 412-7130

RESTAURANT

Auckland, NZ — Hare Krishna Food for Life, 268 Karangahape Rd./ Tel. +64 (09) 300-7585

INDIA (partial list)*

Ahmedabad, Gujarat — Satellite Rd., Gandhinagar Highway Crossing, 380 054/ Tel. (079) 686-1945, -1645, or -2350/ jasomatinandan.acbsp@pamho.net

Allahabad, UP — Hare Krishna Dham, 161 Kashi Raj Nagar, Baluaghat 211 003/ Tel. (0532) 415294

Amritsar, Punjab — Chowk Moni Bazar, Laxmansar, 143 001/ Tel. (0183) 2540177

Aravade, Maharashtra — Hare Krishna Gram, Tal. Tagaon, Dist. Sangli/ Tel. (02346) 255-766/ iskcon.aravade@pamho.net

Bangalore, Karnataka — ISKCON Sri Jagannath Mandir, No.5 Sripuram, 1st cross, Sheshadripuram, Bangalore 560 020/ Tel. (080) 3536867 or 2262024 or 3530102

Baroda, Gujarat — Hare Krishna Land, Gotri Rd., 390 021/ Tel. (0265) 2310630 or 2331012/ iskcon.baroda@pamho.net

◆ **Bhubaneswar, Orissa** — N.H. No. 5, IRC Village, 751 015/ Tel. (0674) 2553517, 2553475, or 2554283

Chandigarh, Punjab — Hare Krishna Dham, Sector 36-B, 160 036/ Tel. (0172) 601590 or 603232/ iskcon.chandigarh@pamho.net

Chennai (Madras), TN — Hare Krishna Land, Bhaktivedanta Swami Road, Off ECR Road, Injam- bakkam, Chennai 600 041/ Tel. (044) 5019303 or 5019147/ iskconchennai@eth.net

◆ **Coimbatore, TN** — Jagannath Mandir, Hare Krishna Land, Aerodrome P.O., Opp. CIT, 641 014/ Tel. (0422) 2626509 or 2626508/ info@iskcon-coimbatore.org

Dwarka, Gujarat — Bharatiya Bhavan, Devi Bhavan Rd., 361 335/ Tel. (02892) 34606/ Fax: (02892) 34319

Guwahati, Assam — Ulubari Chariali, South Sarania, 781 007/ Tel. (0361) 2525963/ iskcon.guwahati@pamho.net

Haridwar, Uttaranchal — Prabhupada Ashram, G. House, Nai Basti, Mahadev Nagar, Bhimgoda/ Tel. (01334) 260818

Hyderabad, AP — Hare Krishna Land, Nampally Station Rd., 500 001/ Tel. (040) 24744969 or 24607089/ iskcon.hyderabad@pamho.net

Imphal, Manipur — Hare Krishna Land, Airport Rd., 795 001/ Tel. (0385) 2455245 or 2455247 or 2455693/ manimandir@sancharnet.in

Indore, MP — ISKCON, Nipania, Indore/ Tel. 9300474043/ mahaman.acbsp@pamho.net

Jaipur, Rajasthan — ISKCON Road, Opp. Vijay Path, Mansarovar, Jaipur 302 020 (mail: ISKCON, 84/230, Sant Namdev Marg, Opp. K.V. No. 5, Mansarovar, Jaipur 302 020)/ Tel. (0414) 2782765 or 2781860/ jaipur@pamho.net

Jammu, J&K — Srila Prabhupada Ashram, c/o Shankar Charitable Trust, Shakti Nagar, Near AG Office/ Tel. (01991) 233047

Kolkata (Calcutta), WB — 3C Albert Rd., 700 017 (behind Minto Park, opp. Birla High School)/ Tel. (033) 3028-9258 or -9280/ iskcon.calcutta@pamho.net

◆ **Kurukshetra, Haryana** — 369 Gudri Muhalla, Main Bazaar, 132 118/ Tel. (01744) 234806

Lucknow, UP — 1 Ashok Nagar, Guru Govind Singh Marg, 226 018/ Tel. (0522) 223556 or 271551

◆ **Mayapur, WB** — ISKCON, Shree Mayapur Chandrodaya Mandir, Shree Mayapur Dham, Dist. Nadia, 741 313/ Tel. (03472) 245239, 245240, or 245233/ Fax: (03472) 245238/ mayapur.chandrodaya@pamho.net

◆ **Mumbai (Bombay), Maharashtra** — Hare Krishna Land, Juhu 400 049/ Tel. (022) 26206860/ Fax: (022) 26205214/ info@iskconmumbai.com; guest.house.bombay@pamho.net

◆ **Mumbai, Maharashtra** — 7 K. M. Munshi Marg, Chowpatty 400 007 / Tel. (022) 23665500/ Fax: (022) 23665555/ info@radhagopinath.com

Mumbai, Maharashtra — Shristhi Complex, Mira Rd. (E), opposite Royal College, Dist. Thane, 401 107/ Tel. (022) 28454667 or 28454672/ Fax: (022) 28454981/ jagjivan.gkg@pamho.net

Mysore, Karnataka — #31, 18th Cross, Jayanagar, 570 014/ Tel. (0821) 2500582 or 6567333/ mysore.iskcon@gmail.com

Nellore, AP — ISKCON City, Hare Krishna Rd., 524 004/ Tel. (0861) 2314577 or (092155) 36589/ sukadevaswami@gmail.com

◆ **New Delhi, UP** — Hare Krishna Hill, Sant Nagar Main Road, East of Kailash, 110 065/ Tel. (011) 2623-5133, 4, 5, 6, 7/ Fax: (011) 2621-5421/ delhi@pamho.net; (Guesthouse) neel.sunder@pamho.net

◆ **New Delhi, UP** — 41/77, Punjabi Bagh (West), 110 026/ Tel. (011) 25222851 or 25227478 Noida, UP — A-5, Sector 33, opp. NTPC office, Noida 201 301/ Tel. (0120) 2506211/ iskcon.punjabi.bagh@pamho.net

Patna, Bihar — Arya Kumar Rd., Rajendra Nagar, 800 016/ Tel. (0612) 687637 or 685081/ Fax: (0612) 687635/ krishna.kripa.jps@pamho.net

Pune, Maharashtra — 4 Tarapoor Rd., Camp, 411 001/ Tel. (020) 26332328 or 26361855/ iyfpune@vsnl.com

Puri, Orissa — Bhakti Kuti, Swargadwar, 752 001/ Tel. (06752) 231440

Secunderabad, AP — 27 St. John's Rd., 500 026/ Tel. (040) 780-5232/ Fax: (040) 814021

Silchar, Assam — Ambikapatti, Silchar, Dist. Cachar, 788 004/ Tel. (03842) 34615

Sri Rangam, TN — 103 Amma Mandapam Rd., Sri Rangam, Trichy 620 006/ Tel. (0431) 2433945/ iskcon_srirangam@yahoo.com.in

Surat, Gujarat — Rander Rd., Jahangirpura, 395 005/ Tel. (0261) 765891, 765516, or 773386/ surat@pamho.net

◆ **Thiruvananthapuram (Trivandrum), Kerala** — Hospital Rd., Thycaud, 695 014/ Tel. (0471) 2328197/ jsdasa@yahoo.co.in

◆ **Tirupati, AP** — K.T. Rd., Vinayaka Nagar, 517 507/ Tel. (0877) 2230114 or 2230009/ revati.raman.jps@pamho.net (guesthouse: guesthouse.tirupati@pamho.net)

Udhampur, J&K — Srila Prabhupada Ashram, Srila Prabhupada Marg, Srila Prabhupada Nagar 182 101/ Tel. (01992) 270298/ info@iskconudhampur.com

Ujjain, MP — Hare Krishna Land, Bharatpuri, 456 010/ Tel. (0734) 2535000 or 3205000/ Fax: (0734) 2536000/ iskcon.ujjain@pamhho.net

Varanasi, UP — ISKCON, B 27/80 Durgakund Rd., Near Durgakund Police Station, Varanasi 221 010/ Tel. (0542) 246422 or 222617

◆ **Vrindavan, UP** — Krishna-Balaram Mandir, Bhaktivedanta Swami Marg, Raman Reti, Mathura Dist., 281 124/ Tel. & Fax: (0565) 2540728/ iskcon.vrindavan@pamho.net; (Guesthouse:) Tel. (0565) 2540022; ramamani@sancharnet.in

ADDITIONAL RESTAURANT

Kolkata, WB — Govinda's, ISKCON House, 22 Gurusaday Rd., 700 019/ Tel. (033) 24756922, 24749009

EUROPE (partial list)*

Amsterdam — Van Hilligaertstraat 17, 1072 JX/ Tel. +31 (020) 675-1404 or -1694/ Fax: +31 (020) 675-1405/ amsterdam@pamho.net

Bergamo, Italy — Villaggio Hare Krishna (da Medolago strada per Terno d'Isola), 24040 Chignolo d'Isola (BG)/ Tel. +39 (035) 4940706

Budapest — Lehel Street 15–17, 1039 Budapest/ Tel. +36 (01) 391-0435/ Fax: (01) 397-5219/ nai@pamho.net

Copenhagen — Skjulhoj Alle 44, 2720 Vanlose, Copenhagen/ Tel. +45 4828 6446/ Fax: +45 4828 7331/ iskcon.denmark@pamho.net

Grödinge, Sweden — Radha-Krishna Temple, Korsnäs Gård, 14792 Grödinge, Tel.+46 (08) 53029800/ Fax: +46 (08) 53025062 / bmd@pamho.net

Helsinki — Ruoholahdenkatu 24 D (III krs) 00180/ Tel. +358 (9) 694-9879 or -9837

◆ **Lisbon** — Rua Dona Estefânia, 91 R/C 1000 Lisboa/ Tel. & fax: +351(01) 314-0314 or 352-0038

Madrid — Espíritu Santo 19, 28004 Madrid/ Tel. +34 91 521-3096
Paris — 35 Rue Docteur Jean Vaquier, 93160 Noisy le Grand/ Tel. & fax: +33 (01) 4303-0951/ param.gati.swami@pamho.net
Prague — Jilova 290, Prague 5 - Zlicin 155 21/ Tel. +42 (02) 5795-0391/ info@harekrsna.cz
◆ **Radhadesh, Belgium** — Chateau de Petite Somme, 6940 Septon-Durbuy/ Tel. +32 (086) 322926 (restaurant: 321421)/ Fax: +32 (086) 322929/ radhadesh@pamho.net
◆ **Rome** — Govinda Centro Hare Krsna, via di Santa Maria del Pianto 16, 00186/ Tel. +39 (06) 68891540/ govinda.roma@harekrsna.it
◆ **Stockholm** — Fridhemsgatan 22, 11240/ Tel. +46 (08) 654-9002/ Fax: +46 (08) 650-881; Restaurant: Tel. & fax: +46 (08) 654-9004/ lokanatha@hotmail.com
Zürich — Bergstrasse 54, 8030/ Tel. +41 (01) 262-3388/ Fax: +41 (01) 262-3114/ kgs@pamho.net

RURAL COMMUNITIES

France (La Nouvelle Mayapura) — Domaine d'Oublaisse, 36360, Lucay le Mâle/ Tel. +33 (02) 5440-2395/ Fax: +33 (02) 5440-2823/ oublaise@free.fr
Germany (Simhachalam) — Zielberg 20, 94118 Jandelsbrunn/ Tel. +49 (08583) 316/ info@simhachalam.de
Hungary (New Vraja-dhama) — Krisna-völgy, 8699 Somogyvamos, Fö u, 38/ Tel. & fax: +36 (085) 540-002 or 340-185/ Info@krisnavolgy.hu
Italy (Villa Vrindavan) — Via Scopeti 108, 50026 San Casciano in Val di Pesa (FL)/ Tel. +39 (055) 820054/ Fax: +39 (055) 828470/ isvaripriya@libero.it
Spain (New Vraja Mandala) — (Santa Clara) Brihuega, Guadalajara/ Tel. +34 949 280436

ADDITIONAL RESTAURANTS

Barcelona — Restaurante Govinda, Plaza de la Villa de Madrid 4–5, 08002/ Tel. +34 (93) 318-7729
Copenhagen — Govinda's, Nørre Farimagsgade 82, DK-1364 Kbh K/ Tel. +45 3333 7444
Milan — Govinda's, Via Valpetrosa 5, 20123/ Tel. +39 (02) 862417
Oslo — Krishna's Cuisine, Kirkeveien 59B, 0364/ Tel. +47 (02) 260-6250
Zürich — Govinda Veda-Kultur, Preyergrasse 16, 8001/ Tel. & fax: +41 (01) 251-8859/ info@govinda-shop.ch

COMMONWEALTH OF INDEPENDENT STATES (partial list)*

Kiev — 16, Zorany per., 04078/ Tel. +380 (044) 433-8312, or 434-7028 or -5533
Moscow — 8/3, Khoroshevskoye sh. (mail: P.O. Box 69), 125284/ Tel. +7 (095) 255-6711/ Tel. & fax: +7 (095) 945-3317

ASIA (partial list)*

Bangkok, Thailand — Soi3, Tanon Itsarapap, Toonburi/ Tel. +66 (02) 9445346 or (081) 4455401 or (009) 7010023/ swami.bvv.narasimha@pamho.net
Dhaka, Bangladesh — 5 Chandra Mohon Basak St., Banagram,1203/ Tel. +880 (02) 236249/ Fax: (02) 837287/ iskcon_bangladesh@yahoo.com
Hong Kong — 6/F Oceanview Court, 27 Chatham Road South (mail: P.O. Box 98919)/ Tel. +852 (2) 739-6818/ Fax: +852 (2) 724-2186/ Iskcon.hong.kong@pamho.net
Jakarta, Indonesia — Yayasan Radha-Govinda, P.O. Box 2694, Jakarta Pusat 10001/ Tel. +62 (021) 489-9646/ matsyads@bogor.wasantara.net.id
Katmandu, Nepal — Budhanilkantha (mail: GPO Box 3520)/ Tel. +977 (01) 373790 or 373786/ Fax: +977 (01) 372976 (Attn: ISKCON)/ iskcon@wlink.com.np
Kuala Lumpur, Malaysia — Lot 9901, Jalan Awan Jawa, Taman Yarl, 58200 Kuala Lumpur/ Tel. +60 (3) 7980-7355/ Fax: +60 (3) 7987-9901/ president@iskconkl.com
Manila, Philippines — Radha-Madhava Center, #9105 Banuyo St., San Antonio village, Makati City/ Tel. +63 (02) 8963357; Tel. & fax: +63 (02) 8901947/ iskconmanila@yahoo.com
Myitkyina, Myanmar — ISKCON Sri Jagannath Temple, Bogyoke Street, Shansu Taung, Myitkyina, Kachin State/ mahanadi@mptmail.net.mm
Tai Pei City, Taiwan — Ting Zhou Rd. Section 3, No. 192, 4F, Tai Pei City 100/ Tel. +886 (02) 2365-8641/ dayal.nitai.tkg@pamho.net
Tokyo, Japan — Subaru 1F, 4-19-6 Kamitakada, Nakano-ku, Tokyo 164-0002/ Tel. +81 (03) 5343- 9147 or (090) 6544-9284/ Fax: +81 (03) 5343-3812/ damodara@krishna.jp

LATIN AMERICA (partial list)*

Buenos Aires, Argentina — Centro Bhaktivedanta, Andonaegui 2054, Villa Urquiza, CP 1431/ Tel. +54 (01) 523-4232/ Fax: +54 (01) 523-8085/ iskcon-ba@gopalnet.com
Caracas, Venezuela — Av. Los Proceres (con Calle Marquez del Toro), San Bernardino/ Tel. +58 (212) 550-1818
Guayaquil, Ecuador — 6 de Marzo 226 and V. M. Rendon/ Tel. +593 (04) 308412 or 309420/ Fax: +564 302108/ gurumani@gu.pro.ec
◆ **Lima, Peru** — Schell 634 Miraflores/ Tel. +51 (014) 444-2871
Mexico City, Mexico — Tiburcio Montiel 45, Colonia San Miguel, Chapultepec D.F., 11850/ Tel. +52 (55) 5273-1953/ Fax: +52 (55) 52725944
Rio de Janeiro, Brazil — Rua Vilhena de Morais, 309, Barra da Tijuca, 22793-140/ Tel. +55 (021) 2491-1887/ sergio.carvalho@pobox.com
San Salvador, El Salvador — Calle Chiltiupan #39, Ciudad Merliot, Nueva San Salvador (mail: A.P. 1506)/ Tel. +503 2278-7613/ Fax: +503 2229-1472/ tulasikrishnadas@yahoo.com
São Paulo, Brazil — Rua do Paraiso, 694, 04103-000/ Tel. +55 (011) 326-0975/ communicacaomandir@grupos.com.br
West Coast Demerara, Guyana — Sri Gaura Nitai Ashirvad Mandir, Lot "B," Nauville Flanders (Crane Old Road), West Coast Demerara/ Tel. +592 254 0494/ iskcon.guyana@yahoo.com

AFRICA (partial list)*

Accra, Ghana — Samsam Rd., Off Accra-Nsawam Hwy., Medie, Accra North (mail: P.O. Box 11686)/ Tel. & fax +233 (021) 229988/ srivas_bts@yahoo.co.in
Cape Town, South Africa — 17 St. Andrews Rd., Rondebosch 7700/ Tel. +27 (021) 6861179/ Fax: +27 (021) 686-8233/ cape.town@pamho.net
◆ **Durban, South Africa** — 50 Bhaktivedanta Swami Circle, Unit 5 (mail: P.O. Box 56003), Chatsworth, 4030/ Tel. +27 (031) 403-3328/ Fax: +27 (031) 403-4429/ iskcon.durban@pamho.net
Johannesburg, South Africa — 7971 Capricorn Ave. (entrance on Nirvana Drive East), Ext. 9, Lenasia (mail: P.O. Box 926, Lenasia 1820)/ Tel. +27 (011) 854-1975 or 7969/ iskconjh@iafrica.com
Lagos, Nigeria — 12, Gani Williams Close, off Osolo Way, Ajao Estate, International Airport Rd. (mail: P.O. Box 8793, Marina)/ Tel. +234 (01) 7744926 or 7928906/ bdds.bts@pamho.net
Mombasa, Kenya — Hare Krishna House, Sauti Ya Kenya and Kisumu Rds. (mail: P.O. Box 82224, Mombasa)/ Tel. +254 (011) 312248
Nairobi, Kenya — Muhuroni Close, off West Nagara Rd. (mail: P.O. Box 28946)/ Tel. +254 (203) 744365/ Fax: +254 (203) 740957/ iskcon_nairobi@yahoo.com
◆ **Phoenix, Mauritius** — Hare Krishna Land, Pont Fer (mail: P.O. Box 108, Quartre Bornes)/ Tel. +230 696-5804/ Fax: +230 696-8576/ iskcon.hkl@intnet.mu
Port Harcourt, Nigeria — Umuebule 11, 2nd tarred road, Etche (mail: P.O. Box 4429, Trans Amadi)/ Tel. +234 08033215096/ canakyaus@yahoo.com
Pretoria, South Africa — 1189 Church St., Hatfield, 0083 (mail: P.O. Box 14077, Hatfield, 0028)/ Tel. & fax: +27 (12) 342-6216/ iskconpt@global.co.za

RURAL COMMUNITY

Mauritius (ISKCON Vedic Farm) — Hare Krishna Rd., Vrindaban/ Tel. +230 418-3185 or 418-3955/ Fax: +230 418-6470v

---

To save space, we've skipped the codes for North America (1) and India (91). ◆ Temples with restaurants or dining
*The full list is always available at Krishna.com, where it also includes Krishna conscious gatherings.

Far from a Center?
Call us at 1-800-927-4152

Or contact us on the Internet

http://www.krishna.com

E-mail: bbt.usa@krishna.com